ONCE A GOD

A Family Historical Novel by

Allen E. Goldenthal

(Sixth Book of the Kahana Chronicles)

Copyright© 2018 By Allen Goldenthal
First published in USA
By Val D'Or Publishing,
1st Edition
ISBN 978-0-9942559-6-9

Val d'Or

VAL D'OR Publishing

ISBN: 978-0-9942559-6-9

LETTER FROM THE AUTHOR

To all the loyal readers of the Kahana Chronicles series of books, you are already aware of the role that the Kahana family has played in historical events over the last couple of millennia. Like the other stories written in the series, this book has similar origins, in that historical records have been passed down through the family both via oral tradition and written documentation. But these are not the only sources that have been used in the telling of this particular story. Of course the Tanach, or more commonly called the Old Testament, has been and always will serve as the primary source material for any retelling of the Exodus story and subsequently the conquest of Canaan, but what most readers of that particular religious episode don't appreciate, are the myriad of clues that are scattered throughout its pages that provide us not only with the religious significance behind the story, but also clear indication of the historical events and environment that were taking place simultaneously, so that to the knowledgeable reader they will understand that the Exodus was neither legend nor myth but an actual historical record of the 14th Century BCE. Combined with other source material written by Artabanus (3rd Century BCE), Manetho (3rd Century BCE), Lucius Cornelius Alexander Polyhistor (1st Century BCE), and Flavius Josephus (1st Century ACE) there is a wealth of information that provides us with a well-defined portrait of the historical Moses. Furthermore, many of the oral tradition stories that were passed down through the Jewish people, and occasionally recorded by rabbinical scholars were gathered into a comprehensive resource comprising thousands of pages by Louis Ginzberg, first published in 1913. Modern archaeology of the Middle East and volcanologists also provide us with a fascinating portrait of both political and geographical upheaval taking place between 1450 BCE and 1300 BCE. An upheaval of such tremendous magnitude that the exodus of thousands of slaves from Egypt was not only possible, but also endowed them with the ability to carve out a new nation amongst existing kingdoms with relative ease in a region of unprecedented turmoil.

Amongst all the books and reference material that were gleaned for information that contribute to the historical accuracy of this book, none was any more prominent than the **Book of the Yasher**. It is important to all those that consider the Old Testament as being the only acceptable recording of the early history of the Hebrew nation, that this is an inaccuracy perpetrated repeatedly by religious editors and redactors over the centuries within rabbinical spheres and the early Christian Church. Not only did they have the audacity to feel they had the right to determine which books would be canonized and which were to be rejected but in a continuum from the time of Ezra onwards, they considered themselves to be divinely inspired to alter and edit the actual texts. The **Book of the Yasher** is referenced twice in the Tanach, not as a companion text but as a resource text from which both the Books of Joshua and Samuel have drawn their material. Therefore it was a very ancient text which predated most of the other books in the Old Testament. The current dilemma is that there are now in existence several books with the title, **Book of the Yasher**. Some are easy to identify as later Greek period frauds. Some are Latin period frauds and one is even an 18th century English fraud but nevertheless, there are a select few versions that appear to contain segments from an original single source text, ending well before the establishment of David's Kingdom and therefore concerned only with the early events of the Children of Israel. Using a particular version, the **Sefer ha Yasher** written in Hebrew and published in 1613, it is possible to paint a very intriguing picture of the Exodus that correlates to actual historical events recorded in both Egypt and Canaan during the 14th Century BCE.

Many will raise the point that Egyptian historians never recorded the events of the plagues nor the exodus of the Hebrew slaves, an accurate statement, but to which I simply have to respond by saying, "Would the Egyptians have bothered mentioning the escape of approximately 15,000 slaves, especially if their leader was a known renegade prince from the Great House of Egypt, exactly how Moses is described within the Torah?" So the answer is, 'Of course not.' Like every other prince or Pharaoh that ran afoul of the gods of Egypt, their names were obliterated from history, literally chiselled out of the stone in which they had been engraved. And taking into consideration that the later dynasties wanted nothing more than to eliminate anything to do with the heretical 18th Dynasty that preceded their rise, it should be no surprise that as far as the Ramesids of the 19th Dynasty were concerned, it was not only their role but political purpose to expunge these 18th Dynasty heretics from the Book of Life. What cannot be erased though were the catastrophic events occurring during this epoch, as these phenomena of nature leave behind a geological and archaeological trail of evidence

These indisputable events of a scientifically proven timeframe, which extended from the early 15th to late 13th century BCE brought about the sudden collapse of the great Bronze Age civilizations of the Aegean and Near East, thus providing the perfect environment for the Exodus to be staged. The destruction of the palace at Knossos dated circa 1420-1380 B.C.E. by Sir Arthur Evan, has withstood close scrutiny and numerous counter arguments. Furthermore, if we examine the events just prior to 1300 BCE, then we witness that all the great civilizations had begun to unravel simultaneously with evidence of their cities being burned, and their once extensive trade empires becoming virtually non-existent. History records groups of people migrating in tremendous numbers from one place to another without any known justification during this time period. It should be stated that the Aegean raiders that sailed to the near east only to become known as the Philistines as recorded in Judges are to be considered no more or less a displaced people than were Moses and his followers wandering in the desert. Once this legacy of catastrophe ended, the world seemingly awakened from under this spectre of terror, and metamorphosed into a brave, new world of the magnificent Late Bronze Age, where two new peoples eventually arose, one of which we know of as the classical Greeks and the other being the biblical Israelites. Two peoples that suddenly appeared, that would come into direct contact and would ultimately define Western civilization as we know it today.

Regardless of what may have been erased from historical records, or even the aforementioned identification of catastrophic events, the most significant piece of evidence that could never be erased or buried through natural disaster is a mother's love for her son. So even when the Pharaoh of Egypt attempts to expunge the royal archives of any trace of his rebellious offspring, destroying every statuette, carving or personal belonging to this potential royal challenger, the one thing that he could never eliminate was the determination of a Queen to preserve at least one sacred memory, one last memento of her firstborn child. And so, the mummified pet of a banished Crown Prince, a cat that he cradled and called Ta-Miu (Lady Cat) becomes our best clue to the emergence of a disgraced prince, once considered a god, metamorphisizing into the man we all know as Moses.

Dr. Allen Goldenthal

The above coin known as a lepton is in the author's private collection. Dated between 103 to 76 BCE, it was issued by the Hasmonean King Alexander Jannai. It is unique for several reasons. Most coins issued at the time only used the Syrio-Phoenician script, which is evident on the reverse of this coin. The Tiberian or formal script as clearly seen in the above picture was reserved for the scribes writing or copying holy scripture. Therefore, the use on this coin was the King making a determined effort to declare himself to be sanctioned by God, an issue hotly contested at the time by the Pharisees, who not only argued against his right to rule but also incited the people to have the role of serving as High Priest stripped from Alexander Jannai. Essentially what is written served as the modern day equivalent on British coins of Dei Gratia or 'by the grace of God'. The four letters seen on the coin are the most controversial component of all. Whereas most modern theologists have accepted the Hebrew name of God being יהוה (pronounced as Yahweh) this inscription shows the actual name as אוהי, the H being a throaty sound, the vuv being a 'V-W' transition sound, and the aleph at the end of the word indicting a hard sounding 'o' or 'u' as the preceding vowel. Therefore God will be referred to as Yahvu in this book. As a footnote, it does explain when literally translated the mystery of God's own response to Moses of 'I AM THAT WHICH I AM' by declaring His name to be, 'HE THAT WILL'. Unlike other gods of the age, Yahvu is and always will be everlasting.

PROLOGUE:

The winds howled and roared, practically shrieking as they squeezed through narrow rock crevices, passing swiftly and forcibly between the prominent granite projections. It was growing late and the sun was beginning to hide behind the time-worn summit, casting a pale ghostly hue through the evening mist, only to be beaten back by the crackling flames that engulfed the brittle twigs used to trigger the straw-laced fire. Close at hand stood a stack of small branches, cut into even bundles, ensuring the campfire could be maintained for days, perhaps even a week, if necessary. Huddled beneath the overhanging shadow of the cave sat two hunched figures, quickly losing their corporeal outlines as the early fog of twilight settled around them. On a precipice about two hundred feet below another fire burned just as brightly, this one surrounded by ten men wrapped in woollen blankets to ward off the approaching cold. They talked and laughed, sharing tales to pass the time as they waited upon the two men perched high above them.

"So this is how I am supposed to die? Alone, shivering, and by the hand of my own son!" Slumped in the hollow between two weathered rocks at the mouth of the cave, the grey-bearded octogenarian lamented his current situation. The winds groaned with increasing intensity in response to his grief and the air began to taste like bitter tears, as if snow might be falling that night.

Rising from his haunches and then hovering over the elderly man, the younger man chose to speak. He was easily half the age of the first but the physical resemblance was unmistakable. "Father, you know that is not what this is all about." Placing a comforting hand upon his father's shoulder, he tried to reassure his elder that he was mistaken, but something in the son's sorrowful tone said otherwise.

"No! Then how do you describe dragging me up the side of a mountain and abandoning me to the elements, the rain and the cold?" As soon as the old man finished speaking he began to cough uncontrollably, his body shaking violently with each outburst.

Kneeling down beside his father, the son held him tightly until the coughing subsided. "You have everything you need here. You have this cave for shelter, enough food for the week should you last that long. Blankets to keep you warm. And don't exaggerate, the Levite guard carried you gently up the mountain; so no one dragged you."

"Carried, dragged, what's the difference? You're leaving me here to die if not from exposure, then by starvation after several days." Once again the old man began a fit of coughing but this time small droplets of dark blood spurted from his lips.

Still holding his father tightly, the son tried hard not to cry as tears welled in his eyes. "You know yourself that it won't be that long. You're already at death's door father. It is essential that you meet your final resting place in an undisclosed location. You understood that, you agreed to this, and now you are trying to make the rest of us feel guilty for your own decision."

The old man raised his fist angrily, shaking it in no particular direction. "This was not my decision; it was his! This is all his doing. Everything has been his decision. Always has been and now even he has my own son doing his bidding." The coughing became so severe that it forced him to double over in agony.

"Father, please, you are only causing yourself pain. Please calm down." He patted his father across his back hoping to help clear the blood rising from the lungs. "It is essential that we do this. We cannot let the people think of you as anything more than a man. You live, you die, and only the memory of you should survive. If we were to let the people enshrine you then you would become greater than just being a man. God wants no man to rise above his own humanity. No more pyramids to false gods! It was agreed by everyone."

Regaining his breath, the old man coughed out each word individually. "You mean your great leader and teacher wants no man to challenge his position as lawgiver. No one must ever challenge his legacy."

"That is not true! When his time nears, he has ordered us to with him as we have done with you. And I will see that it is so. No man must ever challenge the supremacy of God." There was the hint of doubt in his voice as if his father had made him realize that their lawgiver may have to be reminded of the oath they all swore.

Drawing a deep breath into his lungs his father was able to raise himself back into a sitting position. "Yet all the time I have known him he has ever played the role of a god. It was how he was born; it was how he was raised; it was how he was trained and in the end it is how you will all think of him." This time his voice was firm and unhampered by the coughing as if the importance of the words had overridden his infirmity.

The son made no argument. The leader was greater than any man that had ever existed but any power he displayed clearly came from God and no other. "I agree father, that there is a greatness about him that no man will ever be his equal. We cannot wipe the memories from sixty thousand people. They saw what they saw and believe in him without waiver. But it is my duty to see that no man ever makes claim of being more than a man. As High Priest, I will see that the people are taught that God is unique in the universe and only the Almighty is worthy of our worship."

Shaking his head, the father considered his son's response naïve at best. "And when he finds your message is not to his liking, will you end up dead like your brothers? Is that what it will take to open your eyes finally?" The thought of his dead sons, Nadab and Abihu, brought about an even more severe spasm of coughing, as small clots of blood landed between his feet.

"My brothers died because they offended God! The Lord struck them down as they did offense at His altar," the son defended the lawgiver against his father's accusation.

"Now I am ready to die," his father responded. "It is the punishment I deserved a long time ago. You all have been told this fable and to my eternal shame I have let the lie prevail. I am guilty of letting the murder of my sons go unavenged for the sake of keeping our squabbling factions united. What kind of father willingly sacrifices his own sons?" This time it was the father succumbing to tears.

"What lie?" his son insisted on being told, surprised by his father's confession.

"So many lies," the father cried as the tears became a long painful wail.

"Tell me father. For the sake of our people you must tell me." Hands upon both shoulders he gently shook the old man in order to force an answer.

The tears fell into the palms of his hands in a river of sorrow. "So many years. Now you want to listen and insist on bearing the curse of knowing the truth, my son. It is a burden that will pass through all our generations if I tell you. That will be our curse to bear forever."

"Then so be it father. If the Lord wants our family to bear a curse across time then He will see that it's so. But I must know the truth in order to guide our people properly."

"The people, the people! Always the people! Now you even sound like him!"

"I must know the truth father!"

"So be it my son. Make yourself comfortable; you will be on this mountain top a while. Probably until the day I actually die. You better send word to your guards below and make them aware that they will not be returning home this night. There is so much to tell. So much to confess for we have all lied. We are all sinners. God forgive me!"

Egypt (Kemet) in the time of Moses

CHAPTER ONE

"Something a little different this time."

"That's what you said the last time, Doc", Pearce protested with his usual petulance.

It was a refrain I had grown used to during all his previous visits. "Well, every time is different, so this time is no different than the last time in that it is different. Okay?" Pearce can be so frustrating at times.

"That makes absolutely no sense at all," he dismissed my argument with a rolling of his eyes. I hate when he does that.

"You know, I put out that series of articles entitled **The Book of Eleazar** on my blog. Now lots of people read it but the fact is that they still couldn't pull together the threads of what I was talking about. It was about what they're actually experiencing currently, over these past couple of years. Seriously, the world has gone completely down the drain and the writing is already on the wall for everyone. So how is it that you can tell people what is clearly apparent, and they can't see it for themselves?" I released a long sigh of frustration.

Pearce continued to shake his head. "Sorry Doc, I don't get the connection. What's that got to do with your historical novels? And what's that got to do with me being here now? If you wanted to discuss geopolitics then it wasn't necessary for me to fly all the way over here to China again. You could have sent me a series of tweets, everyone else does." Pearce laughed at the obvious reference he made to the President of the United States.

"Don't you see? That no matter what the truth might be, even if you exposed it to today's populace, it wouldn't make a difference. I tried. I failed. They don't want to learn anything. They don't even try to connect the dots. They don't want to see their reflection in the mirror because they don't want to view the truth. Answer me this! Why do you think I even write these books?"

"Because you always wanted to tell your family history, I guess, right Doc? Correct the mistakes of history, something like that. And in so doing, you get all those voices out of your head. That's what you told me a long time ago. I'm pretty sure that's what you said."

"Sure," I responded. "Those were my personal reasons for telling the stories but they weren't all there was behind my reasons. Do you even remember when I told you many, many years ago about how I found out that I was Kahana?"

"Vaguely," came his response. I could tell from the vacant stare glazed behind his eyeballs that he couldn't recollect much, if any of that particular conversation.

"Well what do you remember?" I pushed him harder to recall our conversation some eighteen years ago.

"Voice in the night," he sputtered, "calling your name, you go down into some hidden city and find a book with empty pages, etc. etc. etc."

"And…"

"And what?" he was clueless as to the significance of the little bit he was able to recall and describe.

"I had no sense of who I was at that time. My mother told me nothing about my father's family and she didn't think being the descendant of an ancient line of priests was of any significance. So I was oblivious to it all, living a normal life, with normal values and seeking what every fourteen year old wants in life. Which in most cases is a sixteen year old girl and a lot of cold showers. Then one night I get this calling and my life would never be the same. It wasn't so much about filling the blank pages of the book as much as it was that I was the book and the Lord decided that night he was going to cram my head full of a hundred lifetimes of memories until my brain felt like it was going to explode. That was the night I became cursed, forced to fulfil some destiny that I never asked for. And nothing was ever the same after that!"

"I thought you would have been delighted to have been given that gift," Pearce remarked, failing to comprehend the unbearable burden that was placed upon me.

"Well I guess you thought wrong," I snarled back at him. "When I first told you about GLEEM, I mentioned there had to be a trigger to release all the memories that all of us have stored within our genetic makeup. Well, His calling on me that night was my trigger. Following that event, my life just became weirder and weirder because there was no one I could even try to explain what was going on in my head. I was isolated, alone, stripped of my individuality and constantly seeing and hearing things which I couldn't even fathom where they were coming from. You try being a normal fourteen year old kid after that."

Pearce shifted in his chair trying to find a comfortable position. "I guess I always thought you were happy to have this connection with your past. Everyone is always searching for their roots and here it was handed to you all at once."

"Trust me Pearce, it's definitely a curse. I guess I won the family lottery this generation and received this wonderful prize that has changed my life forever. Just so you don't get confused, that's sarcasm on my part."

"Sort of figured Doc. You weren't smiling when you said it."

"Seems those of us that are selected are supposed to change the world by having this knowledge. But as I've related to you thus far, our success rate hasn't been too great. Zutra, Bustenai, Natronai, Yaakov Kahana, they all failed. Find the common theme in my stories and you will see that time after time we fail. So why should anyone expect that my turn up to bat would be any different? I certainly don't know."

Pointing his finger at me as if it was a stiletto, Pearce tried to push a point. "That's not true, Doc. Your books have made a big difference."

"Now you're the one that's crazy John. They've changed absolutely nothing. The world is still spinning out of control. No one wants to learn anything from past history. In fact, they deny past events, rewriting history until they have a version that supports their own personal beliefs and fantasies. Truth, honesty, integrity, those are values that no longer have any meaning in our world. News outlets spewing false news every day, government cover-ups, kids worshiping anti-heroes, it's all gone upside down as far as I'm concerned. You can't tell the good guys from the bad guys any longer. If somehow my books and revelations were supposed to change that, then you can only make one conclusion and that is that they failed. End of story!"

"So you're saying that when someone in your family has GLEEM unleashed then you're expected to do something with it." Pearce was finally appreciating what I've been telling him.

"Exactly. This curse is about forcing us to try and change the world before it drives us mad. And if God thinks one man can change the world, then He's crazy!"

"But it's happened before," Pearce interjected.

I knew exactly whom he meant. "Yeah, so look where a Jesus and a Mohammed got us to. At one another's throats more than ever now. Not that either was of the family Kahana. Those with this curse are expected to achieve the opposite. But that's never going to happen in this world as far as I'm concerned. My problem is, that my realizing this doesn't give me a get-out-of-jail free card to escape this curse. I'm stuck in this never ending nightmare."

"So how you supposed to break the curse?" Pearce was beginning to see my point of view more clearly.

"I can only presume that the curse ends when one of the Kahana actually does change the world in the way that God intended.

Pearce scratched the greying mop of hair that still looked like he'd never seen a comb in his life; exactly the same as the first day we met decades ago. "So how do you know when that happens?"

"That's the catch my friend. All our religious beliefs, even the political pontiffs speak of the utopia that mankind will achieve. Heaven on Earth, peace in our time, equality of all, freedom from disease, yada, yada, yada. Not going to happen!"

"Maybe someday it will Doc."

"You taking drugs on me now, John? Never going to happen. Read my lips! God's perfect world can only exist if inhabited by perfect creatures. Mankind is far from perfect. Humanity is so flawed that even when there's an opportunity to better itself it rejects that chance and accuses those offering the opportunity of having ulterior motives. Nobody wants to be equal. They all want to be better than their neighbour because that is human nature. And believe me, nothing is ever going to change that; not even God."

Pearce looked shocked right down to his Catholic roots. "How can you think that Doc? Not like you to admit defeat so easily." He shook his head in denial of my postulate.

"Be serious John. Do you know anyone that actually believes things are getting better in this world? If there is, then they must be delusional or taking drugs."

Still shaking his head, Pearce responded. "Pretty grim outlook. There are those of us that still believe things will get better."

"Look at your own words John. You talk about some of you, a few of you, perhaps even a cohort of you but you will never be able to say all of us. Trust me, in order for this world to be saved it would take all of us and that simply isn't going to happen. Not in this universe!"

"So does this mean you're giving up writing your family histories," he inquired as he squinted his eyes and screwed up his face trying to scrutinize my intentions for having him fly all the way to China for this visit.

"Don't be ridiculous Pearce. I still have to drain the swamp so to speak and release these stories from my memories. The more I can get on to paper the less my burden feels like it's trying to burst out of my skull."

"So where you going to take the readers this time?"

"It's a funny thing but it seems that the older I get, the further back into time the memories are extending." I winked at him to suggest this was going to go way back in time.

"Sort of like reverse Alzheimer's," Pearce made an attempt at humour, a characteristic that has never been one of his strong points. When he saw that I wasn't laughing he decided to push forward with the conversation. "So how far back did you go this time?"

"The beginning," I retorted.

"The beginning of time!" Pearce gasped in disbelief.

I sat up straight in my chair and threw him a menacing glance. "Don't be ridiculous, John! Beginning of time," I guffawed. "What was I, an amoeba? Like I'd have any memories of that! I think the older you get John, the more you are losing it! Beginning of time…." I was still laughing at that inane thought. "No, the beginning of my people," I restated. "What other beginning could I have been referring to? Sometimes I wonder about you Pearce."

"Oh, and like we don't all wonder about you Doc. You and your GLEEM, not like your brain is exactly wired like the rest of us.

"Just remember that GLEEM is now an accepted and established scientific principle and you've been writing about it for two decades now. You've been a man ahead of his time," I shot back at him. "Now scientists are even trying to identify exactly where in our DNA strands the memories are being encoded and stored. And don't forget that I warned you when we first met that if they ever figure that out, then none of us will be safe any longer. Everyone's memories will become available to the highest bidder and no guarantee that what goes to the grave will stay in the grave. The Matrix will no longer be a movie, it will be our nightmare!"

"Have to admit I've been thinking about that ever since I watched a few recent Sci-Fi movies where they were transferring memories. Seeing more and more of those movies produced now. It is getting scary to think about what might happen."

"I can only suggest John that you get real scared. And that someone in your Newspaper aligned office actually wakes up the public to the research going on and prevents it from happening. Had an old colleague tell me a joke but it was more serious than a joke. Went like this. Today we carry around our smartphones and ask them everything that has to do with our life. Tomorrow we will have our smartphones inserted directly into our brains so we communicate back and forth freely in a symbiotic life. But somewhere in the future they'll find a way to insert us into our smartphones and we've become irrelevant."

"Thank God we won't be here Doc when that day comes."

"That day is coming sooner than you think John. I'd be scared now. But before that happens I'll take advantage of my own genetically linked enzyme enhanced memories and let you in on a secret that should change history as we know it if only people wake up to what is happening."

"Thought you gave up on that happening, Doc?"

"Let's face it John, all my books have rewritten history as it is taught to us but they've hardly made a dent into the accepted chronicles of historical dogma that are passed down to us through our academic institutions. Part of keeping these succeeding generations dumb and dumber. Don't let them think, don't let them have an independent nuance, just give them the tools to sit in an office or factory performing the same task over and over again for thirty or forty years without resistance and without question. If they start acting up, throw them a bone to chew on, so they can run around in circles believing they are changing the world through protests, even violence but when the dust settles, and they've exhausted their little bit of independent exuberance, the reality is that nothing has changed. They then put on their white collar or blue collar suits and go off on their shuttle buses to the workplace and behave exactly as their parents did, and their children will because those that control the strings of this world, the one's that feed you the history of their choosing, know exactly how to keep the masses under their thumb."

"You've really been drinking the negative juju today Doc? Isn't there anything positive you can say about today's world?"

"Yeah, sure. The sun will come up tomorrow."

"Wow, that's it? Pretty negative Doc."

"Just telling it like it is."

"And no other possibilities," Pearce pressed for an alternative.

"There is one chance but it's pretty remote," I answered, now that Pearce had me thinking about it.

"And…are you going to tell me?"

"It's an old legend that may have some basis but probability is pretty low," I cautioned him. "So, I wouldn't raise your expectations too high my friend. You see, there's this line at the end of the Old Testament that reads, 'there will never be another man like Moses.' Which taken at face value means that there could never be another saviour like Moses either, so without a messiah of that calibre, the world would be doomed. But then my family apparently possessed this alternative legend that stated one day a man will be born, not the equal of Moses, but superior to him."

"I don't get it," Pearce looked confused. "How can there be anyone greater than Moses?"

"Well just think about it. We know Moses was this prophet or holy man, so the first quality is that of a religious leader. Then, he was also a teacher, bringing the history, law and social governance to the people. Next, he had the ability to cause lesions, sickness and also reverse or cure them, so he was a healer. A builder, architect, designer makes him an artist. But most important he was a warrior, a commander who trained an army of escaped slaves into a powerful force that conquered a land from established kingdoms. So we need someone to be born that will incorporate all these qualities."

"That's a lot to find in one person," Pearce realized the futility of the legend.

"Certainly is when you don't really know Moses at all."

"What are you talking about?" Pearce challenged my last comment. "We all know about Moses. Everyone's seen the movies."

I shrugged my shoulders and rolled my hands into a combined fist. "What do you really know about Moses? Where did he come from? What was his childhood like? What did he believe in? Truth is, you know nothing."

"And if we know nothing, then there's no hope then as far as you're concerned that anyone could be superior," Pearce lamented.

"I'm telling you that you know nothing! I'm not saying that I don't know anything."

"So that is why you asked me here," John finally figured out where I was heading with this conversation.

"Perhaps if I fill in the details then finally the world can appreciate the kind of man they must be looking for."

Pearce appeared subdued by my argument. "So you know about his life?"

"Of course I do," I grinned. "So stop asking useless questions, sit down, shut up and let me tell you how this all began."

CHAPTER TWO

"Life at Onu was calm and peaceful and usually without incident," Aaron described the routine of the old temple city to his son. "We had everything we needed, and all we had to do was keep the fires burning for Atum-Ra. It was an idyllic existence, we studied, we prayed and we kept all the secrets of the universe safe from one generation to the next. As a priesthood, we were hereditary, passing from one generation to the next, even before the Kemtu came. We were the 'Lebu' and as such, we were the first men to inhabit the delta and learn the secrets of paradise."

Eleazar scratched his head. "So what are you saying father? That we are not one of the twelve tribes of Israel? Is that what you are suggesting? How am I to reconcile the fact that my father, the High Priest of Israel was actually a priest of some foreign and strange god?"

The old priest shook his head, surprised by his son's lack of understanding. "What I am saying is that our entire tribal history is a fabrication. My original name was Ahrown. It is Mitzri meaning 'He who serves many gods'. My father thought it was appropriate at the time of my birth but even I had to be reborn during our sojourn in order to become who I am today. Why do you think we spent so many years in the desert, waiting for the older generation that knew the truth to die off? Success depended on the younger generation that knew only a life in exile with no past to obscure their faith, in order to take to heart the stories we would spin for them so that they could be unified by a singular identity, a common history, a feeling of brotherhood."

"But we are one people now," the son insisted defiantly.

"Yes!" the old man sputtered in reply. "Because we have made it so. You want to know the truth, then sit and listen and don't ask so many questions. Look at our tribes. Some are dark skinned, some are fair. Some appear no different than the Mitzri while others look identical to the Hyksos. Some are black like the Kush or as pale as we Lebu. There are those that are hawk-faced like the Kenites and Midianites, or round featured like the Pelishu. Look and you will see the truth of our origins. We are all that desired freedom from the Thebans. We are the Lebu, the Shasu, the Apiru, the Khabru, the Kepuru and the Nabu, and so many others. We are a confederacy of peoples from all over the lands and yet we are far more. We are God's people, and our history began the day a lone barge sailed down the Nile towards the delta. Now let me tell my story in case I die before it can be finished!"

Eleazar remained quiet, huddled around the warmth of the crackling fire as his father began the story of their origins, shivering occasionally from the icy touch of the cold breeze upon that isolated mountain top.

1375 BCE

Night quickly fell over the red mud-bricked city of Memphis. The moon rose and glistened across the dark shimmering waters of the Nile, which wound like a coiled black serpent all the way towards the Delta. Silently, the barge slipped through the waters towards Onu, laying to the north-east. One man stood at the stern, another at the bow, each carrying their long poles but the current was swift and they merely held their staffs above the waterline, letting the river carry them along their journey. Clusters of reeds attempted to slow the skiff's progress but the current would not permit the long grassy stems to impede it for long. At the centre of the boat sat several hooded figures, cloaked in black, their faces hidden from the lanterns of any other barges that might pass their way. Bullfrogs croaked, the hippopotami could be heard splashing in their deadly wake as they dived below the surface, while crocodiles swam alongside momentarily, measuring the bundled reed boat against their scaled bodies to determine their chances of capsizing the flimsy vessel. A quick prod of the pole between the eyes and these beasts soon disappeared beneath the waterline, searching for easier prey.

The barge continued its travels, silently, swiftly until it edged along the eastern bank with its dense thickets of papyrus reeds. In the distance the shadowy outlines of mudbrick homes and warehouses passed row after row until the river widened at the head of the delta into a series of rivulets breaking to the north, each with its own destination. Using their barge poles the river-men steered the skiff onto the correct watery path, the one that flowed past the Temples of the Sun. Eventually they angled the vessel towards the shore, the prow became entrenched in the thick, dark mud that the delta was famous for. Mud that would bring life to the crops each spring; mud that would build their cities and their monuments. This was the land where life began, a paradise brought about through this wondrous mud. As soon as they steadied the barge, the hooded passengers disembarked and moved directly towards the Temple of Atum-Ra. Their sandaled feet landed upon the wharf with a thud, immediately indicating that these were men of rank as compared to the barefooted barge workers that were busy tying their reed-bundled skiff to the docking poles. They entered the temple complex, marching their way along the narrow cobblestone lane. The armed priestly outer guard, upon hearing the unfamiliar footsteps aroused from the induced drowsiness of standing the long hours of sentry duty, suddenly jumped in front of the approaching strangers, his long-shafted scythe readied for action. He yelled out his challenge but the words quickly died on his lips as soon as he saw the royal cartouche borne on the hand of the man at the centre of the group, its beetle shaped stone glowing red in the flickering torchlight.

"Forgive me my Prince," the guard blurted, as he bowed apologetically praying for forgiveness at the same time because he had just threatened a member of the *savov* or royal family. "We had no word of your coming," he tried to explain his actions.

"Of course not," the Prince responded in a voice still high pitched enough to suggest he was only in the waxing of his teenage years. "No one was made aware of my coming. Now go fetch your *Hem-netjer-tepi* and the other wab-priests and let them know of my arrival."

"But I must stand guard, your Highness. I am not permitted to abandon my post," the priestly guard attempted weakly to avoid the request being made by the young prince.

"Sleeping at your post, abandoning your post, what's the difference," the prince jested to the laughter of his companions. "Let me assure you that these men with me are well suited to guard the entry to your Temple in your absence. Now go ahead and do my bidding."

Rising from his kneeling position on the hard stones, the guard was up and running as fast as he could into the complex in order to find his *Okai Wutinpow* or High Priest, known as the *Hem-netjer-tepi*. The prince and his companions listened with amusement as the excited shouts from a myriad voices bellowed and wailed with an unexpected panic as news spread within the Temple of their announced *savov* visitor. In the passing of minutes, an entourage of priests, hastily garbed and still desperately trying to pull their robes up and around their shoulders, ran towards the gates of the Temple. Clearly they were confused and startled by the surprise visit, fearful that there was something they had done wrong in the eyes of Pharaoh and now the *Neb* of the Two Lands had sent his firstborn son to mete out their punishment. Once they had all assembled before the group of strangers they quickly took to their knees, bowing in silent reverence.

"Your Majesty, we are greatly honoured by your presence this night", the *Okai Wutinpow* spoke, daring not to raise his head to gaze into the eyes of the young royal until he had been given permission to rise.

"Your Majesty is my father," the prince responded. "Your Highness will do. I am not one that needs such formalities." A point quickly dismissed by the *Okai Wutinpow* who knew all too well what happened to anyone that selectively forgot such formalities in the past. "You must be Nebwenenhef," the prince continued. "I was aware that you are now *Okai Wutinpow* of Atum-Ra. I presume it is quite a change from the Temple of Hathor. You may all rise now."

The dozen or so priests rose, the older ones having difficulty and requiring help from their colleagues to do so. "Yes, it has been a big change since serving the goddess, your Highness." Fumbling for words, the *Okai Wutinpow* suddenly fell silent, his nervousness spreading like an affliction to the rest of his entourage as they feared what might come next.

"Relax everyone," the prince commanded. "I guess you are all wondering why I am here." They all nodded in confirmation. "I have come to serve in your Temple. It is my time to consecrate myself to the gods and here is where I will stay for the next few years."

"But your Highness," Nebwenenhef interjected, "this is most unusual for you to arrive concealed by the darkness of the night, without even a word from your father. Furthermore, it was my understanding that you had been dedicated to the temple of Set-Ptah in Memphis."

"Plans change *Okai Wutinpow*. Plus my father is not aware that I have come here. You will need to conduct the apprentice ceremony as soon as possible before he discovers my true intentions."

"But your Highness," Nebwenenhef began sputtering, "this will greatly upset the great *Neb* of the Two Lands. Pharaoh Amenhotep will have my head for this betrayal of his edict." Nebwenenhef began to wring his hands subconsciously, terrified of what would happen once the Pharaoh found out about his son's disobedience.

"Leave your worries to my mother, the Queen will take care of everything. After all, it was her initial intention that I do my seminary training here. Therefore *Okai Wutinpow*, have no worries, you will not lose your head. My mother will have everything under control in a few days. Anyway, it my understanding that you have given your position here at Onu as a reward from my father for your faithful and diligent service at Karnak. I doubt he'd want to cause any embarrassment that would suggest his decision was in error. After all, these political appointments are filled with ramification if other's think they were unwarranted. So, you just do as I say, prepare my inception and make my room ready."

"Shall I send word to the Great *Neb* of the Two Lands that I will tend to your training personally, your Highness?"

"You most certainly will not," the Prince commanded. "You will not send word, until such time that my mother informs my father of my whereabouts, nor will you be the one responsible for my education. Who is that pale skinned priest over there?" The Prince pointed to one of the priests huddled amongst the rest to his left.

"That is the former High Priest Amun-Ramuse, your Highness." Nebwenenhef indicated by pointing at the fiftyish looking priest with red-tinged ringlets of beaded beard.

"No, not him. The one next to him." The Prince referred to the man that dressed and looked like a younger version of the former high priest.

Nebwenenhef looked surprised as he stepped back and waved his hand as if to say no-no. That is Ahrown, his son. He is too young to be your teacher your Highness. He is not yet fully adept in the degrees of the Temple."

"Is he not *Wab-tepi*?"

"Yes, but he is too young to be a mentor your Highness." Nebwenenhef was desperate to keep the two apart. The strain was evident in the taut lines of his face and the wavering of his voice.

"If he is *Wab-tepi* then he has access to all your libraries and all your teachings. I prefer to be around younger men with fresher ideas, if you understand my meaning. Have him come over here."

The *Okai Wutinpow* dug his right heel into the ground. "Your Highness, I must object. Forgive my impertinence but this has become a situation too tenuous for me to overlook. It is one thing to disobey your father and assure me that your mother will reason with him but for you to request that your education in our Temple be provided by a priest of the lower degrees is beyond even what your father will tolerate. I must insist that you be apprenticed to me, so that at least there is justification for your training here."

"But Nebwenenhef, you were only transferred here six moons ago. All your knowledge was gained in the studies of Hathor at Karnak. And when it came to replace you, was not it your choice to have your son take your position as *Okai Wutinpow* even though he had only attained the lower degrees?"

"This is different your Highness. I personally trained my son to be the next *Okai Wutinpow* as the position is hereditary."

"As it was here before my father changed the rules of inheritance and placed you as *Okai Wutinpow* of Onu. Ahrown!" the Prince shouted. "Who is your father? Show me."

The young priest was surprised to hear his name called out but upon the prince's request he grabbed the sleeve of his father, Amun-Ramuse.

"Ah, I see," the Prince sighed. "The former *Okai Wutinpow* of Onu, whom like you would have trained his son to take his place in what once was a hereditary position. I would think Ahrown is more than qualified to handle my formal education. The same way your son would have taught me had I gone to learn the ways of Hathor in Karnak. Would you not think so Nebwenenhef?"

Nebwenenhef knew that he had been caught in the web laid out by the young prince. Not even able to grow a beard yet and the boy had already bested him. Their relationship would be a difficult one to navigate, the priest thought, should this prince ever become Pharaoh. He had gained all the cunning wiles of his mother, Queen Tiye, and it was well known that she only believed in the elder gods. So why was the Prince actually here, he wondered. Clearly, he already had a specific plan and was already knowledgeable regarding the former High Priest Amun-Ramuse. Whatever his intentions, he knew that he better clearly report every event, no matter how trivial to Pharaoh, the *Neb* of the Two Lands.

Not waiting any longer for the *Okai Wutinpow* to enact his last instruction, the Prince called out to Ahrown, once more. "Ahrown son of Amun-Ramuse, come forward and meet your Prince."

The young priest stepped forward, knelt and bowed humbly before the prince, touching his forehead to the ground. Unlike the Kemtu race, his skin was pale, even paler than that of his father. His beard was neatly trimmed and he wore beads only in the braids of his right sidelocks. His garment was a simple white cotton robe, a hemp cord tied comfortably about his waist. He was still a young man under twenty but he was wise in the ways of Kemet and knew that this summons by the Prince meant an opportunity to his advantage. He waited in silence, knowing that he could not speak until the Prince had spoken to him first.

"I have journeyed from Memphis, *Wab-tepi* Ahrown. I have decided that I wish to be Sem-priest in your Temple of Atum-Ra. What is your opinion of my decision?" The Prince extended his right hand to help raise the young priest to his feet. Though the Prince was a couple of years younger, he was almost the same height as Ahrown, forcing the priest to turn his head slightly to the side so that he did not stare directly into the eyes of a royal.

Clearing his throat, Ahrown began his response. "I believe that whatever the Prince of the Two Lands chooses and decides, that it is the whispering of the gods that have led him to make the wisest of decisions."

The Prince laughed. "I did not ask you for your opinion of what the gods think, priest, but I want to know what you think of my decision. Now please favour me with an answer."

Nebwenenhef tried to hide the little smirk that attempted to surface on his lips. This would be the first of his reports to the Pharaoh, of how the young priest Ahrown failed to dissuade the Prince from coming, but instead would encourage him to abandon his responsibilities as first born son, the intended Sem-priest of Set, and defy his father's wishes. The response provided by Ahrown was even better than he had anticipated.

"Your Highness, you could not have made a wiser choice. Our Temple in Onu is the repository of knowledge since the beginning of the world. We were here when the land of Kemet was created, when the elder gods ruled the universe. Their secrets are our secrets. No other Temple in the land can claim to be our equal in knowledge and sanctity."

Nebwenenhef could barely conceal the sneer on his lips. Such pomposity, such arrogance, to claim superiority over all the other Temples. Yes, once upon a time, a very long time ago, the Temple of Atum-Ra was the focal point of the *tunkeh* or supreme belief in Ra, but those days had vanished into antiquity. Everyone knew that Seth-Ptah held supremacy in the lands but Amon reigned supreme. And is not the God-Mother Isis nothing more than a simple household god of the people now? Yes, such arrogance would displease Pharaoh tremendously.

"Exactly my reasons for being here," the Prince confirmed. "You and I will have much to talk about. Moreover, you have much to teach me. I need to learn it all."

"I'm afraid no man could ever master all of the knowledge held within the Temple, your Highness. It is too vast, the same way that no man could ever drink the oceans dry."

"Are you implying the Prince is a mere man," Nebwenenhef quickly interjected and chastised Ahrown. "He is the son of a god!" he exclaimed. "Forgive his impudence, as well as his insult, your Highness. Now you see why it is best that you leave your education to me. There will be no forgetting your rightful place within our Temple. These younger priests know nothing of the incarnation of the gods into human form and how that enabled Hequet to enhance the *ka* of the *savov* family."

Holding up his hand, the young prince silenced the *Okai Wutinpow*. "I know the story well," the Prince reminded him. "But even if my spirit was the length of the Nile, it still could not contain all the knowledge of our universe. Not even Thoth possessed that capability and he is the wisest of all the gods. Ahrown was correct in reminding me that even I have my limitations but it still will not stop my thirst for the knowledge I seek."

"Of course your Highness," Nebwenenhef apologized. "I merely wanted to ensure that none of the priests within my order doubt that your possess capabilities far beyond us mere mortals."

"I have no doubt that your priest is aware of that fact. After all, am I not named Thutmoses, the same as the god Thoth, whom all men acknowledge as the paragon of wisdom and learning? He merely has to say my name and he is reminded of it each time. Go ahead Ahrown, say my name and show your *Okai Wutinpow* that you have not forgotten who I am." The young priest hesitated, afraid to address the prince with such informality. "Go ahead, Ahrown, I insist!"

"Your Highness, I could not be so forward and discourteous as to do so," Ahrown remarked.

"Discourteous?" Thutmoses laughed, only to be joined in laughter by his guards that stood by him. "Do you think I was given a name so that it would never be used? How else would anyone ever draw my attention from my swarm of children that inhabit the palace if they never called out my name? Shout out Your Highness and ten heads would turn. If my guards can call me by my name then certainly my teacher can do so as well."

"Yes your Highness," Ahrown reluctantly agreed.

"I didn't quite hear you properly," the Prince taunted him.

"Yes, Thutmoses," Ahrown responded the second time.

"See, that wasn't so difficult. No lightning hurtling through the sky to strike you down. No sudden appearance of Anubis to guide you to the underworld. That is my name and I am pleased to hear it."

"Then shall we all now refer to you as Thutmoses, your Highness?" the *Okai Wutinpow* questioned.

"Of course not," Thutmoses responded matter-of-factly. "He is my teacher, so he has be given that privilege. You will continue to refer to me as your Highness."

"Of course, your Highness." Nebwenenhef, bowed and slightly withdrew.

"Now show me to my quarters," the Prince instructed. "We will have a busy day tomorrow and I want an early start. My guard, Othni, will stay with me, I will send the others back to Memphis. Ensure that Othni has quarters adjacent to mine. And when you finish writing your letter to my father tonight, High Priest, make certain that you acknowledge how pleased I am with your assistance on making all my arrangements. Best to let him know that I am happy with the kindness you have extended. Once he gets over his anger of my disobedience, he will want to be reassured that no one took it upon themselves to try to undermine my decision. I'm certain you understand his concern for my welfare and wellbeing." The young Prince smiled as he nodded to Nebwenenhef and then moved forward to take Ahrown by the upper right arm, as they proceeded into the Temple.

CHAPTER THREE

"And that is how we first met,"

"Who father?"

"Your uncle of course. Your great leader. Did you not wonder how we chanced upon each other?"

"But the stories say that he came looking for you in Goshen after he returned from his exile in the desert."

"Did I not tell you that everything has been twisted and altered? Of course he came looking for me because he had entrusted me to remain behind and prepare the people for his return. I was there waiting for him as soon as he crossed the frontier from Midian. But more about that later."

"But this would mean he's not your actual brother."

"Of course he's my brother. All of us that served within the Temple are brothers. We are all bonded together. All serving the same spiritual pathway of the Temple rituals. No longer do we have mother or father when we enter the priesthood, only the brotherhood of our bonding in our faith. We are more than a brother in flesh and blood could ever be."

"And the fact that they say that Amram was father to your both. That was a lie?"

"We belonged to the Temple of Atum-Ra. That made us sons of Atum-Ra. We were Atum-Ra-Meses, by our official temple titles. Furthermore, his father was Pharaoh Amenhotep Hequweset Nimmureya Ra Merimose, beloved son of Amun-Ra. My own father's names was Amun-Ramuse. So as you can see, it is true, in that Amram was both his father and mine. You just never questioned the origin of the name. No one does. And as we had calculated, no one ever will."

"And the entire story of his birth, and how he was carried down the river and found by the Princess, that's all a fabrication as well?"

"Some parts yes, some parts no."

"So which parts are actually true?"

Aaron held up his hand to signal for a moment's respite while he coughed. "You have to understand Eleazar, that the differences amongst all our people could only be overcome by unifying them through a common origin. We are so many tribes, sharing a common fate, but that is not going to make us one people unless we also become brothers and sisters in faith. For a generation we moved from one settlement to the next in the wilderness, from a well to an oasis and back again, until such time that the older generation had gone to the grave. With them, they took the truth of our origins into their coffins. The new generation had been raised on the stories we nursed them upon from the day they were born. They suckled upon the very teats that nursed the twelve sons of the Patriarch Jacob. Each of them that was neither Kenite nor Midianite, became affiliated with one of those twelve tribes and in so doing the fabric of our existence was woven into the cloth of destiny."

"So none of our earlier sojourn into Mitzrayim was true, is that what you are saying?"

"In that particular story, all of its true. Your uncle would not let go of that part of his personal heritage. It was actually what made him into the man he became. It was his justification for doing all that he did."

"I don't understand."

"Then stop asking so many questions and let me explain."

1374 BCE

"We have been at this a long time Ahrown," Thutmoses laid down the pile of papyrus sheets, their edges beginning to fray and crumble with the passing of decades.

"You said you wanted to understand how the universe is governed by the law of discs, well this explains it to you."

"This actually explains very little. It only pulls together a series of random events that don't have any obvious connections."

"That is because you can't see the image of the universe that lays before your eyes."

"Then paint me a picture because thus far I only see the chaos."

Smiling, the young priest congratulated his student on his first discovery. "Good, because chaos is the background to all that is. Chaos is Ptah and Ptah is everything. Now we lay on top of that background everything that springs from chaos."

"And that is supposed to help?" the prince mocked his tutor.

"Imagine a universe that is nothing more than a gigantic disc floating in chaos."

"Okay, I see a disc. Now what?"

"Picture this disc turning continuously and on the outer edge of this disc, all of the cosmos moving along the edge, completing circle after endless circle."

"And then?"

"Pick a point, any point along that circumference of the disc. That is our starting point. That is our world as it began, providing our particular viewpoint of creation."

"But there are numerous other points before and after the point I selected."

"Yes, and each of those is the beginning of time as viewed by whomever selects that point. Other worlds, other existences, but we build our framework based on where along the edge we select our initial point. But no matter where that is, the cosmos continues to roll along the edge of the disc, so really there is no beginning and there is no end. It will continually repeat."

"My head is beginning to hurt."

Ahrown chose to ignore Thutmoses' comment. "Now imagine the point which you selected is made up of other discs that are perpendicular to the point on the main disc. Like smaller rings spinning on the edge of this central larger ring. Those discs are the heavens that we can see and the time period that you exist within. The sun crossing the heavens days after day as it traverses the edge of this smaller disc. The constellations, changing from season to season as they also move around the outside of this small disc."

"This is all beginning to look very complicated."

"We're not finished yet. There are more than these two levels to our universe. Now perpendicular to these smaller discs are even smaller discs, completely surrounding each point. These are your life and the lives of everyone you know that moves in and out of your life. From birth to death they navigate the circumference of this third disc in the series. But even smaller discs extend perpendicular to these ones. They are the actual daily events of your life, the routines, and the achievements, all that transpires during every day your soul awakens. Our entire existence, our world, our universe and our cosmos are nothing more than wheels within wheels. Four in total, from the largest central disc of chaos down to the smallest ones that fill your day."

"So you're suggesting everything is interrelated and inseparable."

"Yes, but the impact is only in one direction. From the largest to the smallest. You cannot expect what you do in the smallest disc of your daily life will change the cosmos, but the converse is most definitely true."

"But if I place the role of the gods at this second level of discs, having impact only on the heavens and the world as I see it, then what governs that first disc, because it influences everything."

"Now you see it! Something greater than the gods. A being of infinite power that had the ability to create the cosmos from absolutely nothing because there is no disc that precedes that one, only the chaos. That is the Creator, the *Potohikap*, that we called Ptah, everything and everyone else is a lesser being and since the power through the cosmos moves in only one direction, from the great disc down through the smaller ones, then he must be infinite in his *wasur*, unchallenged and unfathomable."

"So you're saying Seth-Ptah is the great god at the centre of the universe and therefore I should have been doing my studies at that temple like my father wanted." Thutmoses threw Ahrown a look of disapproval.

"There is no Seth-Ptah," Ahrown spat out in response. "But don't tell anyone I said that!" Ahrown quickly glanced around to make certain that he had not been overheard. "When we Lebu first came to this land there was only Ptah. Originally this was the temple of Ptah-Atum, the Creator of the Universe, the sun his symbol of the central disc, and he was the great bull that carried the disc between his horns because the vastness of the cosmos was nothing more than a plaything that he carried about. But when the Kemtu came, they had their pantheon of gods, and they saw chaos as destruction and therefore Ptah, the *potohikap* of all things became divided into two, the one who made all things, Min, and the destroyer god, Seth. But they are not the same and Min and Seth are but puppets controlled by Ptah's hand."

And this unfathomable being that you called Ptah, central to the cosmos, is what your father tried to explain to my mother years ago as being identical to her father's tribal god, Eloah. But a tribal god seems so small and insignificant to what you've just explained. How could they possibly even be the same being?"

"Possibly, through some doorway into the universe, your ancestors gained a glimpse of this being at the centre of the cosmos. I don't know how and I don't know why, but they were able to bypass all these series of smaller discs that govern our universe and were able to peer directly into the core of creation. And this creator being chose also for some unfathomable reason to speak directly to your ancestors."

"And you know all of this because…"

"As I told you, we Lebu exist in our knowledge on the edge of the third disc, weaving in and out of the lives of all that exist, whereas you and the rest of mankind are focused on the smaller discs of your own everyday lives. Therefore our understanding of how all existence intersects is at a higher level of consciousness. For over a millennia we have been recording and describing how the discs revolve, while civilizations rise and disappear, rising like mountains and then blowing away like dust in the wind. We were here when the great pyramids were built, when Khafre carved his face onto the great Sphinx, and we understand that even the creation of these great monuments were based around the points of the second disc, influencing the Pharaoh's decisions concerning the fourth disc. All of this knowledge is concealed within these walls and if a man lives long enough, he might be able to coherently assimilate it but by that time he will already be passing into the grave."

"So why come to my mother? What could she possibly offer you that would help in your understanding of this knowledge?" Thutmoses held out his open palms as if to suggest that seeking his family's aid was futile in achieving any further insight.

"When it became clear that your grandfather and his ancestors had in some way developed a connection to the central pathway that ran from the centre of the cosmos down into our own world, it was thought by both my grandfather and my father that somehow your family was the key to unlocking all the mysteries that still remained.

After all, did not Pharaoh Amenhotep-Aakheperure name your grandfather as the *Hemneter* of Min, the first time a commoner has ever been deemed to be in commune with the gods? If we could discover how they did it then perhaps we too could gain a glimpse into the cosmos and be able to navigate our future by removing chance, just as they did. With the passing of your grandfather a few years ago, may the gods bless his name, that hope disappeared, and you're right in that it became clear to us that your mother did not harbour the same abilities as her father, but then there was you. And maybe, just maybe it is an ability only carried by the male line. That is why my father was so insistent that you mother ensure that when it came time for you to become a Sem-priest that you were sent here."

"But that's also the reason why my father replaced your father with Nebwenenhef. He felt your father was meddling in affairs that were none of his concern, attempting to restore the old gods, and now your family has been stripped of your hereditary position as high priests. Whatever you thought you could achieve had become your own undoing!"

"Do you really think over a millennia of knowledge and understanding can be stripped away so easily upon the command of Pharaoh? We are the Lebu! From across the sea we landed upon these shores, in a savage land and we gave them the gift of knowledge and created the great empire of Kemet. All that is and all you claim is because of our coming to this land. The people may deride us for our pale skin and our red tinted hair, but the fact still remains that it was we that unlocked the secrets of the universe and not the people of this land. And when they thirsted for knowledge, they came to us and drank from our fountain."

"How can I possibly forget? You are constantly reminding me," the prince chided him.

"And I always will. Your family may be able to communicate directly with the Creator but you have no comprehension of the how or the why. My family does, and for that reason we must share all that we know in order to unlock the mysteries of the universe. So I ask you once again, can you now see the image of the cosmos, the universal plan of all that exists?"

"Yes, I see these wheels within wheels. And if all events move around the circumference of these wheels, then there must be a repetition to all events that occur within our world. A cycle of events that once learned would permit me to predict the likelihood of events to reoccur. That's what I see and I want to understand and master this third disc. You say the Lebu were able to do so, then I too will understand this timetable of our heavens, if one exists."

"Of course it exists!" Ahrown reassured him. "Just as the tides have their known cycle, and the Nile has its cycle of inundation, so too is there a cycle for every event that takes place in our world."

"And you can show me where all this is recorded?"

"Of course. What kind of Wab-tepi would I be if I didn't know what manuscripts are archived within our own library. But there are others. Other papyri that record events of the great sea and the lands beyond. These are stored to the north in the archives of Temple of Isis."

"I want to see all these records. I want to know them all."

"And exactly why does the son of Pharaoh seek such knowledge of events that may be a lifetime or two away? I don't understand why you wish to burden yourself with such knowledge."

Thutmoses smiled menacingly at his tutor. "Just because I provided you with familiarity to speak freely with me Ahrown, doesn't mean that you get to challenge everything that I ask for."

"Of course not, my Prince, but I merely questioned why place such a heavy burden upon your shoulders when there is so much else to be learned right here." The words rolled off Ahrown's tongue bitter sweet and Thutmoses knew he was being mocked but their friendship had grown to such an extent that the Prince accepted the occasional snippet of modest sarcasm.

"Because you are aware of my grandfather's special relationship with this Creator as you've explained, then I will let you in on a secret. Repeat it to anyone else and it will be the last secret you ever reveal." The prince's smile suddenly became malevolent. Even friendship had its limits. "Before he died, my grandfather told me that I would be the greatest leader this world had ever witnessed but for this to take place, I must first learn to master the laws of nature. I'm not certain exactly what he meant but once I have gained this mastery, then his god is likely to ensure that everything will unfold for me as intended.

"So you believe the great *Etaty* Yuyu was telling you to understand the wheel that governs all the natural events of our world."

"I believe it, my mother believes it, and don't forget that my grandfather rose from *nehseyt* to being the second most powerful man in the kingdom because he had knowledge of the seven year cycle of the Nile's inundation. He knew the famine was coming and he saved our people from starvation. Why should I have any doubt in his predictions?"

"Certainly he was able to interpret Pharaoh Amenhotep-Aakheperure's dreams but that is significantly different from controlling the laws of nature, my Prince. When Thutmoses-Menkheperure became Pharaoh, he relied less and less on your grandfather."

"Yet, he still kept my grandfather as his advisor and for ten years his reign was peaceful and great alliances were made with the Mitanni."

"How much of this reliance was based on your grandfather's abilities versus the fact that he was married to Thutmoses' sister Tuya one cannot say. Perhaps it was the affinity for his sibling that made him amenable to Yuyu's constant displays of showmanship."

"Then I will let you in on another secret, Ahrown. My grandfather had no ability to interpret the *raswet* on his own. He relied solely on the Creator to tell him exactly what to say in each circumstance. The pomp and ceremony he performed to draw the attention of everyone else was merely a show. A distraction to conceal the source of his inspiration. Otherwise how could he explain the interpretations unless he convinced them that he was gifted with the ability to prophesize from the *raswet*? Other than you and your people, who would actually believe that a man could talk directly with a god? In that respect, my grandfather Yusef, your beloved Yuyu was a thespian, but believe me when I tell you that his predictions came from the centre of the cosmos itself. That is why Yuyu asked my mother to ensure I be mastered by the Lebu when I came of age, with the encouragement of your grandfather as well, of course. Whereas my grandfather was reliant solely upon hearing the *tunkeh* voice of the universe, he wanted me to know how to make prophecies come true even if that voice was silent towards me. He had no knowledge of whether I would inherit his gift or not, as you have already pointed out. But he knew with knowledge I would be able to deal with the situation if I did not hear this all-powerful voice. That is why you and I have been brought together. Together we will master this world and lead our people to greatness. Kemet will be the reigning empire of this world. I swear it upon my grandfather's tomb!"

"So all this great quest for the ancient secrets is merely a game of politics to you," Ahrown rebuffed his Prince. "You intend to use the knowledge for conquest and gain, whereas you grandfather used it for the benefit and safe-guarding of the people."

"I intend to use the knowledge to unite the world, something my father will never be able to do. Pharaoh lacks the military bearing of his grandfather, nor the acuity to assess potential alliances like his father. Not all the great constructs throughout the Empire bearing his name will compensate for those deficiencies. He may go down in history as Kemet's greatest builder but without unification of the people, how long do you think our empire will last?"

"Not all civilizations are built on the bodies of the dead through conquest Thutmoses."

Thutmoses nodded his head, affirming Ahrown's comment. "I agree with you *Wab-tepi*. So show me how we can do it without bloodshed and I will forever be in your debt. Do you not think that it was the Creator's intent that you and I should become teacher and student? You have knowledge and wisdom and I have force of will and the birth right of power. Here is your chance to change the world if you so desire. Grasp the opportunity that I present and we will do great things together."

"What is it you wish me to say, my Prince?"

"Say yes and make certain you make the arrangements necessary to visit the Temple of Isis. I hear the high-priestess there is a real bitch."

CHAPTER FOUR

"And now you know the truth of our finding our purpose in this world, my son. Not through chance but instead through the manipulations of one dead dream interpreter. Though admittedly, Yuyu was a master at it. Even from his tomb and the afterlife beyond he was still controlling our destinies. "

Eleazar was perplexed by the revelation. "Forgive me father but how can you tell the people one story about our great patriarch Yusef, when you know the truth of his actual history is very different?"

"How indeed! You are inferring that a deception has taken place, but I assure you there was no deception. What we told the people is the truth. Everything that Yusef did and achieved as Yuyu is the truth. Did he not rise from an imprisoned slave to the rank of Vizier, the second most powerful man in all of Mitzrayim? Did he not become Pharaoh's right hand? Was he not named a prophet of God, the King's Lieutenant and *Herey* of the Horse and Superintendent of Cattle? What other man ever achieved all that? I will tell you; no one! For over a decade he guided Amenhotep-Aakheperure through the great catastrophes that had befallen our neighbours across the sea. The sun failed to nurture the crops, the rivers did not flow their usual paths. Did he not save the people form seven years of famine? Did he not guide Amenhotep to pick his son Thutmoses-Menkheperure to become Pharaoh, a son from a lesser wife so that the alliances could be made with the Mitanni through marriage? Did he not become the most important and influential of the tribes, having two counts amongst the twelve through his lines of Manasseh and Ephraim? Did he not accumulate great wealth and lands in Akhmim, earning him the highest honours of burial within a tomb amongst the Valley of the Kings? Where is the deception, Eleazar, for I see none?"

"Then whose bones did we carry through the desert then, for I know for a fact that the tomb of Yuyu was never opened? Never did they summon his bones from the south of Thebes. Is that not a deception?"

"Does it really matter, my son? Whether the bones of a king or of a servant, it is the spirit of Yusef that we brought with us, uniting the tribes and placing the tribes of Yusef in their position of superiority. It is not the bones that mattered but the significance of their influence and in that respect what we did proved very effective."

"How can you claim this father? A double share to the tribes of Joseph, the right for lands and tithes throughout all the tribal lands for Levi and you see no wrong in what you have done?"

Aaron grew angry with his son's failure to appreciate the obvious. "Why shouldn't we claim a greater share amongst the tribes? Did the others challenge the might of Pharaoh? Did the Nabu bring the voice of the Almighty to the people? Did the Kenites bring the plagues down upon Mitzrayim and thus earn our freedom. Did the Shasu climb the mountain to hear the voice of our God? Did the Apiru part the waters of the sea to let us pass to our land of milk and honey? For years your uncle and I planned and devised the means to our freedom and those of our people and that is why our two tribes have greater claim from amongst the others. That is the reward for all that we achieved, for all that we have sacrificed. That is our reward from Yahvu!"

"So now you fully support Moses and all that he's done, whereas earlier you condemned him for the lies and his misdeeds. As soon as you gain from it then you are his ardent supporter. You cannot have it both ways father!"

"Of what we achieved in those early days, I bear nothing but love for my brother. We shaped a world together and did it with the blessing of the Creator. But what he has become I cannot condone. He seeks that which we swore neither of us would crave; the recognition deserving of a god. He seeks to have his name engraved on our hearts and mind for an eternity and no man should ever be given that much reverence. We must learn that when we have traversed the full circumference of that small disc that represents our lives, that our time is over. We are nothing more than memories that will fade as new discs arise to replace ours. That is the intention of the Creator of the universe and no man, no matter what his claim, has the right to challenge the laws of the cosmos."

"Yet your posterity and his shall always have the lion's share of our nation. Is that not so father?"

"Yes, that is so!" the anger slurred Aaron's words. "So what of it. The Lebu were here from the dawn of time. Now we who call ourselves Levi carry the words of the Creator with us throughout our lands and generations. The reward to our tribe ensures that we will never fail or falter in our duties. But as for those whom are the descendants of Yusef, you must ensure my son that they will forget that my brother was actually one of theirs and they must learn only to dwell on the achievements of Yusef their patriarch and how he saved all of us from extinction during the famine. For that reason, his descendants were awarded a double share. Give credit to my brother and I'm afraid one day his family will try to assert themselves as lords and kings above us all."

Eleazar laughed cynically. "So you are asking me to preserve our legacy and let that of Moses' wither and disappear. How hypocritical of you father. Who truly wants to ensure their memory is preserved like a god?"

"It is the way it must be Eleazar. To preserve his legacy will always create the desire amongst our people to return to Mitzrayim to claim their Pharaoh's birth-right.

We must forget that Moses was rightful Pharaoh. We must forget that he was chieftain of the tribe of Yusef. We must forget that our ancestry has blood ties to the land from which departed and thereby our desire to ever return must be extinguished. Only by forgetting our past can we secure our future!"

"And what makes us so special that our family claims must be preserved for an eternity?"

"Because we serve God and only by our being strong can we ensure others adhere to the laws and beliefs through our preservation of the truth of God's ways. Let others usurp our position and they will change our beliefs as surely as the Kemtu changed the truths given to them by the Lebu."

"Are you forgetting that Moses has sons? Will Gershom and Eliezer be tempted to so easily forget their birth right? Will they abandon any desire to rule like their father? How am I to ensure that never happens?"

"You will do whatever is necessary, my son. In this matter you will have the full support of Joshua. He is just as eager to see that Moses' offspring do not set themselves over the people as kings."

"Easier said than done, father."

"Not for a man like Joshua. He will do what needs to be done. It was why we appointed him as Moses' successor long ago. To ensure that what I feared would never happen.

"Should I now wonder why his children by Tharbis, born during our wanderings, never made it past infancy?"

Aaron coughed and spat a wad of phlegm into the fire, listening to it crackle as soon as it hit the flames. "Who are we to question the will of the Creator, Eleazar? Surely not I. Not even when I lost my two eldest sons and nor should you question why the children of some dark-hearted Kushite queen died prematurely. Only Yahvu can explain why things are meant to be."

Eleazar knew better than to pursue that line of questioning any further. His father's cryptic answer was not so cryptic after all. One merely had to read between the lines to understand that Moses' other children never had a chance to survive to manhood. They were a much greater threat than his Midianite wife, Zipporah. She was merely a chieftain's daughter, but Tharbis represented a power and force far greater, considering their eldest son still sat on the throne in Saba.

"Yahvu or you father? Who really determined how things were meant to be?" his son questioned, already knowing the answer.

"What was done, needed to be done. I knew it, Miriam also was well aware of it. We did what was necessary."

"So go on father, tell me now of my aunt Miriam. How does she fit into all of this?"

"Your aunt was a very special person to Moses. They had a bond I could never explain but still when it was necessary, she would defy him."

"But she never lost faith in him father, not like you."

1372 BCE

"The mud pits stink here," Ahrown covered his face with his cotton scarf trying to filter out the odours of the decaying vegetation.

"It makes for good bricks," Thutmoses quickly responded. "And good bricks build lavish temples where you and your kind have been residing for centuries, brother, so I shouldn't complain if I were you."

"Why did you need me along on this journey," Ahrown continued to complain despite the comment. "I have avoided travelling into the delta for a decade, swearing never to return. It is nothing but a land of squalor and mosquitoes."

"You are here because you know exactly what I should be looking for in the Temple of Isis and I don't," the Prince explained for the countless time.

"I could have written you a list," Ahrown growled. "It's not that complicated. There's something else you're not telling me."

"Plus I need someone that can keep the High Priest off my back while I search through their library."

"And exactly how am I supposed to do that."

"From what I understand, the High-Priestess is not a true follower of Seth-Ptah. In fact she has been overheard to say that Isis is still the pre-eminent goddess of this land and has made efforts in the north to restore the old faith amongst the people. Which would suggest the High Priest is of a similar ilk to your Nebwenenhef."

"Which is logical considering that in her beliefs Seth is the enemy of her goddess. Your father's choice in a godhead has not gone down overly well with a large segment of the population. So you think he may be there to watch over her."

"Exactly why you are the one to occupy his time while I search for what I need to know. If she truly wants to restore the beliefs in Isis and since you are dedicated to a mysterious creator God and use Atum-Ra to conceal your own intentions, then I think you are best suited to uncover where the High Priest's loyalties lay. If he supports the High Priestess then I would think that both of you have a lot in common on how to keep the old beliefs alive and thriving while my father continues his father's experiment in spreading the southern Theban beliefs across the entire land."

"And if he's not?" Ahrown wanted the prince to |be specific regarding what he should do.

"If he's not, then I need you to handle him the same way you keep Nebwenenhef under control," Thutmoses suggested.

"What do you want us to do, eliminate any threats and foment a revolution," Ahrown responded sarcastically.

"Remember, the day is coming when I will be Pharaoh. So though you may not believe it now, a revival of the old religion may be possible."

Ahrown grew quiet for the rest of the journey to Behbeit-al-Hagar. The young Prince's response troubled him. He was joking when he spoke of a religious revolution to deal with priests like Nebwenenhef and this High Priest for the Temple of Isis but he knew that Thutmoses had already been giving it consideration. For two years they had studied together, discussed together and argued the true meaning of the ancient texts, but this was the first time Thutmoses had ever inferred that he was considering imposing his own religious views upon the two lands. Which religion? That of his grandfather Yuyu, or what he had learned in the Temple of Atum-Ra. Then why was he now seeking answers in the Temple of Isis? Clearly there was more to his talks with the long dead Yuyu. From the first day they met he knew the Prince was on a mission. He thought he understood what it was, but now that understanding was not so clear. Even his true intentions of why he wanted Ahrown on this mission were shrouded in mystery. Keep the High Priest occupied? Unlikely! Perhaps he would find the answers once they had reached Behbeit-al-Hagar, or maybe there would only be more questions. He would have to wait and see.

As they rode along the dirt roads that crisscrossed the delta and wound like enormous snakes as they followed the numerous rivulets that threaded the marshes and mud pits for which the northland was famous, the people came out from their mud-brick houses in ever increasing numbers to line the streets and greet their young prince. At first they came as a trickle, then a stream, until finally there was flood of people cheering them on as their entourage of horses passed by their communities.

"They love their Prince," Othni commented as the small party moved steadily north.

"If that is the case Captain, then why did you insist that I have an armed escort of four men to accompany us," Thutmoses teased his protector.

"Because it only takes one man who does not love you my Lord to jump out of a crowd. Better to eliminate the threat before it occurs."

"Always the cautious one Othni. But you should remember that these are my mother's people and they all love Tiye. I share their blood. They share our dreams."

"Except my Prince," Ahrown cautioned him, "While you live in the gold-trimmed palaces, I don't think their *raswet* were actually to come to this land and work in the mud and sweat of this swamp. Your father uses them as slave labour to rebuild the temples of New Avaris and the palace in Thebes. No one appreciates being forced into slavery."

"As I once told you, my father's quest to build monuments and cities will not create for him an everlasting legacy. For nineteen years he has been Pharaoh and not once has he walked amongst the common people. Who is it that you think they will remember?"

"A *nehseyt* only remembers one thing," Ahrown remarked. "He remembers who is holding him in chains and that is whom they will hate no matter whether you're the one that made them slaves or not! Unless you think you're going to find an answer at Behbeit-al-Hagar that tells you differently, then why are we here?"

"If you must know, we are here to find the answers behind these cataclysms that have befallen the empires in the north. My grandfather claimed there was a pattern to these events and if I can establish what it is, then I will be able to tame its outcome."

Ahrown laughed loudly. "Only the gods can tame the natural occurrence of events. Not even your grandfather would think he could master the forces of nature. We can turn back now because I can tell you this is a colossal waste of time."

"For a priest that believes the cosmos is a multitude of discs circling at the edges of even greater discs, you don't appear to be totally convinced of your own teachings. If the events of our world revolve around these discs then that means they must repeat. And if they repeat then there is a pre-determined pattern that may have been recorded."

Hitting the side of his head with the palm of his right hand, Ahrown shot his eyes skyward. "I was speaking figuratively, painting a picture for you in generalities. There aren't actual discs that we physically circle upon. There is no guarantee that the cosmos is determined by patterns of repetition."

"But what if there is," Thutmoses shot back immediately. "What if there are certain laws by which our universe is bound? I must know for certain," the Prince demanded.

"Take a look at this place, Thutmoses! Even the gods have abandoned it. We travel between mud-pits and sink-holes. Not even the mighty Nile knows how to flood this delta and inundate it evenly. This is not a land where any true Kemtu wants to live. That's why the nomads and the people of other nations build there huts here, and only a blind man would see it otherwise."

Thutmoses branded the priest with a menacing stare. "So now I'm a blind man," he inferred an insult had just been cast his way.

"Should I pluck his eyes out, my Prince?" Othni interjected a matter-of-factly.

"Ha..Ha…very funny," Ahrown scoffed at the captain of the guard's suggestion.

"Perhaps just cut off his ears," the young prince suggested.

"Actually, not funny at all," Ahrown was not enjoying the intended jest at his expense. "I still object to the stench of this place and wish we could just go back to Onu."

Thutmoses pointed to a building just ahead. "Too late. There's the Temple of Isis. No turning back now."

"Where?" Ahrown responded.

"Look, you can see the Temple's pylons through the trees." The rows of white plastered pylons lining the outer court were now clearly visible.

Othni gave the order for everyone to dismount and take up positions outside the temple gates while the Prince and the priest from Onu entered and walked towards the marbled portico. They approached the double doors that led to the inner court, their feet thumping against the heavy tiles that formed the portico floor. Before they could even reach the massive brass rings that served as both handles and knockers, the doors pulled apart, providing the visitors with a yawning entrance into the inner court and a view of the assembled hosts awaiting their arrival.

Thutmoses immediately addressed the elderly man standing at the centre of the assemblage. "Most honourable Meryptah, high priest of Isis, I am Thutmoses, Crown Prince of Kemet, son of Amenhotep and Sem-priest of Atum-Ra. Will you welcome myself and my companion into your temple?"

Before the old man could say a word the copper-skinned woman to his left responded. "Yes, you are welcome here son of Pharaoh. Enter as our guests. The goddess Isis welcomes you." The woman that spoke was easily in her mid-twenties, not unattractive but neither would you describe her as beautiful. She still retained a slim figure despite her advancing age.

"Why do you speak for the high priest?" Thutmoses sounded angered by the sheer audacity of the lady. "I had not addressed you!|

"Perhaps you should have," she responded defiantly, not showing the least bit of being threatened by the Crown Prince. "I am Meri-amun, High Priestess of Isis. This is my Temple and Meryptah is merely an overseer of your father. He ensures that the temple treasury pays its fair share to Thebes and nothing more, though he does bear the title of Priest for reasons I can't fathom. I guess it to be a most unfortunate circumstance of the government's bureaucracy of assigning meaningless titles."

Thutmoses glanced quickly over at Ahrown. Perhaps he had this all wrong and it was the High Priestess that needed to be kept preoccupied.

"So you are Meri-amun," the prince expressed his comment as if it were a criticism. "I have heard much about you."

"And I'm certain none of it was very complimentary," she laughed. "So be it. The world is a changing place where suddenly the High Priestess of Isis can be a source of derision. Do not try to deny it. I have already heard most of the derogatory comments they make about me."

"I was only going to say that the comments suggest you are a very powerful and forceful woman," Thutmoses attempted to reduce the intensity of their verbal exchange.

"And they say you are a master of words, *Itey* of Kemet. Able to sweet talk your way out of any situation, even if it is an outright defiance of your father's will. Is that not so, priest of Onu?"

She had caught Ahrown off guard, not having had the opportunity of introducing himself as yet. "You know me priestess?"

"I know of you, son of Amun-Ramuse. My condolences on the removal of your father as High Priest. A most unfortunate turn of events but one which I can assure you that we all have been suffering from similar experiences. I suggest that we have a lot in common to discuss over the duration of your visit."

Before she could continue, the Crown Prince interjected. "Yes, regarding our visit," but before he could continue his sentence he was cut off by the High Priestess, a discourtesy rarely afforded to a member of the *savov* family.

"As you can determine, this was a not an unexpected surprise to be graced by the presence of the royal magnificence, the god incarnate, the Crown Prince of the two lands and his loyal *Wab-tepi* of Onu. But as yet, I do not know to what do I deserve this honour," the High Priestess greeted her guests, a hint of sarcasm dripping from her tongue.

"Had you not interrupted me, I would have told you," the Prince admonished her. "Remember who I am and hold your tongue unless you wish to lose it."

"Oh, I am so sorry your highness. Please forgive me. Shall I prostrate myself on the floor and crawl forward to kiss your divine feet," she taunted him, much to the chagrin of Meryptah, whose pained expression suggested all this would be in a report to Pharaoh Amenhotep.

"It might be a start in learning your place and demonstrating humility- Thutmoses suggested.

"I put my faith in the goddess, Prince, not in the divine right of men. There is much that men in power must be held accountable for and very little of it is good. But if you wish that I change my tone, then most honourable Crown Prince, future *Nesew* of Kemet, divine incarnation of the god Amun-Ra, bringer of light to the world, all seeing and all-knowing *Herey* of the two lands, *Neb* of the horse and Guardian of the *Ka*, etcetera…shall I go on….I am most honoured and humbled by your deigning our insignificant Temple worthy of your presence."

Thutmoses outstretched the palm of his hand cautioning the High Priestess that it was enough. "I am not my father, High Priestess, so it is not necessary to pretend that you are glad to see us, but neither is it necessary to mock us," Moses established the groundwork for negotiation immediately. "I need you to speak honestly with me, and therefore formalities will only get in the way as much as you obviously see no need for the courtesy in any regard. Your disdain for the *savov* family is obvious and you certainly have no fear today that your mouth will eventually find your head detached from your shoulders because I would not be here unless I was in need of you, so that being the case, you have no further reason to disrespect me. You are exactly like whom I was forewarned. You are what they say you are, and although most may find it irritating, I at least can appreciate outspokenness, so I do not need your fidelity, nor your formalities, nor even your liking; I only need your honesty."

"You wish to speak privately and openly?" she was both confused and intrigued.

"I do."

"You care not if my tongue lashes out with the truth and burns those it turns against in the process."

"I don't."

"You wish for me to do something for you that no one else can provide," smiling as she made the latest remark.

"That is correct."

"Shouldn't you be speaking to one of your sisters in this manner," she challenged his intentions followed by a girlish giggle in an obvious mocking tone. "After all, most in the *savov* family are betrothed at your age. I hear that your sister, Sitamun, is quite the beauty. Then there is always Iset, perhaps not as beautiful but rumoured to be as clever as your mother."

"I'm not interested in taking a wife at this time, nor is that a topic for your discussion at this time," Thutmoses quickly interrupted her. "Let's get back to the issue that brought me here."

"Oh, I'm sorry," Meri-amun apologized apathetically. "Usually when a man starts a conversation with a woman by suggesting they should become informal then there is an intent and should that be the case then I must stop you now, I'm much older and I still have eleven more years to serve the goddess in her temple." She winked and smiled devilishly. "Men your age can't wait that long if you know what I mean. Although it is the season for the fertility ritual and once again your father is noticeable by his absence. Perhaps you could stand in as the god's representative?" She still mocked the young Prince but his openness and honesty with her had definitely laid the groundworks for a bond between them.

"Ahhh..." Thutmoses became speechless, not knowing how to respond to the priestess's last comment.

"Relax, my Lord. I'm making a little joke at your expense. After all, you want us to relax formalities. And your father hasn't exactly been our greatest benefactor of late, as you can see from the condition of this temple, so a little levity is warranted, don't you think."

"Yes, yes, exactly how I hope we can base our discussion," Thutmoses sighed with relief and gave a little laugh to acknowledge that he was amused by Meri-amun's jest and had not been offended, though he was concerned that he just might have to perform the ritual, so the farmers had their blessing for abundant crops in the coming year. As if all the tension had been released at once, Ahrown started to smile and laugh as well.

"I see *Wab-tepi* that you are not mute after all," she commented. "Talk says that in Onu that he is only answerable to you which has upset his master, Nebwenenhef, greatly," She commented to the Prince. "Not that I mind, the old toad deserves to be upset any way possible. You know that he constantly reports your misdoings to your father. He's worse than a nagging old hag. At least that's what my sources at the court say. Anyway…" the priestess continued, "if I was looking for a matrimonial partner then that one over there is more my type." She pointed in the direction of Othni, Thutmoses' captain, waiting beyond the double doors. "Perhaps he will be available in eleven years when I am retired?" she winked once again. "I could use a good man to steal away my virginity and give me children. I won't be a spring chicken at that time, so having a companion with a little more potency may be what's required, if you know what I mean," she followed with another wink.

"It may be possible to arrange," Thutmoses responded with a smile, only to have Othni wince upon hearing his answer. "In the meantime I have more urgent matters to discuss with you."

Meri-amun took a closer look at the young prince in order to assess what his true motives might be. "You are aware young *Itey* that your father has severely curtailed any authority the Temple of Isis might have. You may already have placed yourself in conflict with him once again just by your being here. Now that he has instituted that blasphemous Festival of Mut each month of Phaophi, he doesn't even bother to come north to have us perform the ritual of the Nile inundation and fertilization of the valley. Abandoning such a sacred tradition will only lead to a tragic ending. I can assure you of that."

"It made more sense to perform the fertility ceremony and the prayers of the Nile inundation in Thebes," the Prince tried to explain on behalf of his father. "After all, the nourishing waters of the Nile do come from the South."

Meri-amun shook her head profusely. "You mean more convenient, don't you? It certainly ensured he did not have to listen to me tell how his father and his father before him understood the sanctity and the importance of the ritual to keep the country from famine and starvation. There won't be another *heru* like your mother's father rescuing us the next time. But still if he thinks that in some manner having the people drink alcohol until they're practically comatose, all the while performing every conceivable sexual act under the guidance of the priests within the temples is an acceptable practice to supplicate the gods then he is sadly mistaken. When the people don't have enough food to fill their bellies that is the time Pharaohs learn that it is the people that have the power and royals die. So if you've come to make some excuse for your father, then I'm afraid we have little to talk about young *Itey*."

"Wait…" Thutmoses insisted, "True it may be seen as being extreme, but the old ceremony of having Pharaoh travel north to the Delta in order that you can shake his penis until he spreads his seed onto the land provided nothing meaningful to the people. You'd read the nilometer and then Pharaoh would go back to his palace, proclaim to the people that he had done his duty and all was well with the Nile. Why should the people believe in something they didn't even see? That they themselves didn't experience? As much as I may disagree with my father, at least this permitted the people to participate and commune with the gods on their own behalf. The people need to know that the gods do listen directly to their prayers and Pharaoh is not always required to intercede on their behalf."

"And that is why we have priests and priestesses young *Itey*. So that the people do always have a means to communicate with the gods without Pharaoh. We were there to witness the spreading of Pharaoh's seed and the farrowing of it into the soil to ensure the bountiful crops in the coming year. We are there to read the nilometer and spread the word to the people that the flood waters of the Nile are coming once again. Kemet does not need a drunken orgy to let the people talk directly with the gods but then again, you are a young man, so seeking pleasure would be your way of life. But know this, it is nothing more than a heresy"

"On this point we will always disagree, Priestess. On routine matters of daily life, the people do not need and should not need anyone to intercede on their behalf. Of what use are the gods if they cannot hear an individual's prayer? Of what use is mankind if neither man nor woman feels empowered to plead upon their own behalf and express their own needs?

Meri-amun looked impressed by Thutmoses' defence of his convictions. "How radical! There may be more substance to you yet young *Itey*. In one moment you go from defending your father to inviting the wrath of the gods in the next. Astonishing but I agree with you that change is necessary. But how those changes are to be made must be done carefully and controlled. The ribaldry of your father's changes are neither. If you truly believe in your father's position on holding his festival of Mut, then I must assume you have certainly participated in this debauchery of Mut yourself."

"Who's to say that I have or I haven't?" Thutmoses was somewhat annoyed that the Priestess was implying that she had the right to disapprove of his lifestyle.

"I say, young *Itey*. Do you think that because I am consecrated to a temple in Behbeit-al-Hagar that I do not have eyes and ears in Thebes? And I say you haven't. Not once have you displayed your manhood. And I know this because you rarely leave Onu and you almost never return to the palace in Thebes. So I know you have not participated in this flawed festival. Which still leaves me wondering young *Itey*, what are you motives? You haven't laid with any of your sisters, you have shunned the religious orgy of your father's making, and now you are here seeking answers to questions you haven't obviously found answers for. You sound more like your grandfather Yuyu than you do from any descendancy of these heretic Theban Pharaohs."

"What would you know of my grandfather?" Thutmoses challenged the high priestess. "He has been gone for several years now before you even held your position."

"I may have only been a young initiate into the Temple when he first came, but do not make the mistake of thinking that your grandfather would only leave an impression on a high priestess and no one else," Meri-amun scoffed. "When your grandfather spoke, even the birds and the animals harkened to his voice. That was the extent of his power of the mastery of this world which lay in his hands. Those are things not even a young initiate will forget. I recall he expressed his concerns and his worries regarding the incestuous relationships within the royal family. He expressed his concern that in some way even you would be horribly affected by the bad blood."

"Me?" Thutmoses questioned incredulously.

"Yes, even you, son of a man who married the daughter of an aunt whom was sister of his grandfather. Or do you forget that your mother Tiye is actually your grandfather Thutmoses' niece because both he and your grandmother Tuya were siblings. Or are you fully aware of that fact and that is why you have avoided impregnating one of your sisters? Do you see the distorted features of your mother's dead offspring and wonder what monsters your seed might spawn? I can assure you that the great Yuyu was aware of such concerns and expressed them more than once."

"Enough! You seem determined to draw me repeatedly into a conversation concerning my relations with women. I can assure you that when it comes time for me to choose a wife then I will do so but now is not that time. I have more compelling reasons not to do so at this time. Yes, my grandfather spoke to me but he spoke of a mission I must fulfil before I can ever consider assuming the obligations of a Pharaoh of Kemet."

"What can be more compelling than fulfilling the obligations of a Pharaoh," Meri-amun wondered while still taunting the prince.

"Secrets that your Temple possesses," Thutmoses responded. "Secrets surrounding the Nile, the valleys and the mountains that Yuyu said were documented in records that only the *Herey* of Min would have access to."

Upon hearing the reference to the master, Meri-amun burst into laughter, once again to the chagrin of Meryptah, whom obviously had no idea what the strange secret bearing the code words mentioned revealed. "Is this something you wish to share with us, High Priestess," Meryptah asked impatiently as he anxiously waited for the laughter to subside. But when Meri-amun gazed upon his scowling face, she couldn't help but to engage in another fit of laughter.

"Can you show me to the *Herey* of Min; which priest in your Temple holds this title?" Thutmoses interceded when Meri-amun took a moment to catch her breath.

Holding up her hands, she held them out towards the prince. "Here are the *Herey* of Min, my *Itey*. What would you like to say to them?" Barely able to release the words from her mouth, she began laughing loudly.

"I don't understand," Thutmoses could not decipher her meaning.

Wiping the tears from her eyes, the high priestess attempted to restore a calm but found it difficult as every few seconds another titter would escape through her lips only to have to be immediately suppressed.

"Stop this behaviour immediately," Meryptah insisted, "and answer the Crown Prince."

"Are you certain you want to know what your grandfather meant?" she asked, the tears rolling down her cheeks.

"Yes! I must know," Thutmoses demanded.

"Don't say I didn't warn you," she cautioned. "As you are aware, your grandfather was designated the *Hemneter* of Min. And as you also know, Min as one of the elder gods was responsible for the creation of all the other gods and mankind." She had to take a moment to catch herself once again as she felt the laughter welling up from her chest. "My *Itey*, have you taken a good look at the statue of Min recently?"

Thutmoses shook his head, indicating that he hadn't.

"You have to appreciate that to be the creator god of all things, you have to have certain endowments."

Thutmoses suddenly caught her meaning as everyone in Kemet was familiar with the uniqueness of a Min statuette.

"In Min's case, he has this huge erect phallus. Now you have to appreciate that as an inductee into the Temple, I was only twelve years old when I arrived. Like all the other girls, I was scared, I was naïve, and I certainly had not been educated regarding the sexual arts. Yuyu was the first to be designated as the *Hemneter* of Min, which made him very special to our religious beliefs. You also aware that your father was tiring of the fertility ritual held each year at this Temple and he proposed that it would be better suited that the *Hemneter* of Min, the representative of the creation of all life on Earth be the one to fulfil the duties of the ritual."

"Aw…maybe I don't want to hear where this is leading." Thutmoses was having second thoughts.

"I'm certain you do," Meri-amun continued her story. "So that first year when your grandfather arrived, we as the newly initiated to the Temple were assigned to prepare Yuyu for the ceremony. We had to wash his body and dress his phallus with fine oils and scents as is customary. But with all our manipulations he grew erect and like the statuettes of Min, his penis was huge. It was so large that the other girls thought he must be the god incarnate and they became frightened and ran away."

"But obviously you did not," the prince finished her sentence.

"No, I did not, and I continued to dress him with the oils and fragrant ointments. Once I had completed the task he turned to me and said, 'You forever after will be known to me as the *Herey* of Min.' And every year that he came, he would call for me and only me to prepare him for the ceremony."

"Why wouldn't he just tell me to seek you out? Why this cryptic message to seek some master that played with his private parts? My grandfather was not one for games."

"Because," she continued, "One year he gave me a key to hold on to. He said there will come a day when someone will come asking for the *Herey* of Min and I was to give him that key. I did not know why or whom he was talking about but I held on to that key exactly as he instructed."

Thutmoses was excited by the revelation of a key. "Ahhh…and now we both have our answers to riddles that he left behind. Do you know what the key unlocks? "

Meri-amun shook her head. "All I know is that he kept a special room in the Temple that no one else has ever entered. I believe the key opens that room but what is inside I do not know as I never dared to unlock it."

"Why was I not made aware of that," Meryptah voiced his objection. "As Pharaoh's representative, I should have access to all the rooms in the Temple. Any treasure that the *Etaty* Yuyu left behind should have become property of Pharaoh upon the vizier's death."

"And now as the first-born son of Pharaoh, I will take delivery of anything my grandfather has left behind, so you need not worry about it High Priest."

"This is most unusual," Meryptah continued his complaint. "I think it will be best if I join you when you first enter the room."

"I think it would be best High Priest if you don't interfere in business between myself and my late grandfather. Whatever it is he wishes for me to have, it is for me alone, am I clear?"

Standing upright in a militant posture, Meryptah remained defiant. "As representative of Pharaoh I must report this event and your refusal to cooperate to a simple standard request."

"Go ahead. You can add it to the list of complaints that I'm sure my father keeps on hand to address me with should I ever return to Thebes. Better yet, tell it to my mother. I think she would be overjoyed to know how you insisted on meddling with a bequest from beyond the grave from her father. Ahrown, why don't you sit down with Meryptah and explain to him how the universe works over the next few days while Meri-amun and I begin researching whatever secrets I am to uncover within this Temple."

"It would be my pleasure to explain it to him," Ahrown responded, knowing now exactly why the young prince had brought him on this journey. Obviously it was his job to run interference, just as he had said.

"But that all can begin tomorrow," Thutmoses continued. "For now, let me suggest that we all sit down for a meal. I'm certain my escorts outside would be pleased to have their horses tended to and to come in from the outside for refreshment."

Clapping her hands, servants to the Temple suddenly appeared and surrounded their High Priestess. "We have guests that are hungry," she informed them. "Prepare the tables with whatever food we have available."

Not long after, the guests were led into the dining area where the pillows had already been neatly arranged around the knee-high tables where the acolytes of the Temple would present their meals. As was customary, Meryptah took his seat at the head of the table with Thutmoses to his right and Ahrown to his left. The remainder of the escort sat around the sides of the table and Meri-amun ensured that she sat right next to Othni, much to his chagrin. Like Ahrown and Meryptah, Othni knew that it would be his job to see that Meri-amun did not feel rebuffed in any way as her happiness was essential to the success of his master's mission.

As evening was fast approaching, the servants first went about the room, the embers of their burning reeds used to light the oil lamps that were positioned strategically for maximum illumination. Once that had been completed, then the young priestesses carried in the trays bearing the meal. Bowing before Meryptah, each laid their tray on the table before him, opening lids and removing covers so that he could first inspect and then provide his approval. Lentil soup, thick barley bread, figs and dates were the staple of every temple, but this night they also had prepared roasted quail, much to the delight and satisfaction of the guests.

"I hope our simple fare meets with you approval, Crown Prince Thutmoses," Meryptah queried.

Thutmoses nodded his approval as he gnawed the meat from the leg bone. "Most certainly," High Priest. "An excellent meal and most unexpected. I have not had quail in a long time."

"Oh, I am then greatly pleased. This time of year the quail migrate across the delta and everyone in the villages goes to sleep with a full stomach. One of the benefits living so far north and away from the big cities," the priest concluded.

"But that is not the usual state of affairs," the Prince interjected.

"Oh, most certainly, my Lord. It never fails; the quail always migrate during these summer months," Meryptah corrected him.

"I was not referring to the quail, High Priest," Thutmoses responded, sounding a little annoyed. "From what I have been told, the villagers have been reduced to nothing more than the slaves of Pharaoh, recruited at his pleasure to build his monuments. Slaves are fed slave rations, since they no longer can till their own fields and raise their own livestock."

"Not all are slaves, my Lord. There are those too young or two old, the women and the weak, they still work the fields and tend to the animals."

"But it's not the same, is it, High Priest? When you take the most fit and able and force them to make bricks and carve stone, then it is at a cost to their own welfare since those remaining behind are expected to grow all the food but are actually the least capable of doing so."

"It is the will of your father, Prince Thutmoses," the High Priest brushed the responsibility aside. "It is by his command and these *pedtay* should be grateful for the opportunity to give service to our kingdom after taking so much of our good will for the past sixty years."

"And which part of our good will, as you call it, gave them this marshland in which to carve out a home. No Kemtu would live here because the mosquitoes were as thick as moss, the stench of decay filled one's nostrils until a man could no longer breathe and then he would fall over, only to sink below the mud which sucked him down into the bowels of the earth. But these foreigners drained the marshes, built the levies to keep back the sea, and grew the grain crops to fill the bellies of even true Kemtu. Which part of our good will have they not repaid?" Thutmoses was infuriated by the insinuation that somehow the clans of the Levant tribes that now occupied Goshen had taken advantage of their Kemtu hosts.

"They are *pedtay*, my Prince, if we do not control them then one day they will not be content to live in Goshen and their numbers will spread out across Kemet. What will you say then when your precious Thebes is overrun by foreigners. In this matter your father has shown great wisdom. It will keep the populations of these villagers under control and ensures that our great land will never suffer under the yoke of *pedtay* ever again as it did under the Hyksos. After all, it was your family that drove those foreign kings from our lands and returned Kemet to the Kemtu people. How can you disagree with your father's policies if they ensure that our future remains within our own hands?"

"Perhaps you forget that one day I will sit on the throne of Kemet and I am one quarter Khabru or have you forgotten that Yuyu was my grandfather? What will you say then High Priest? That I must be overthrown too because I am no different from the Hyksos." Thutmoses gritted his teeth as he glared into Meryptah eyes.

"My Prince, I would never think such a thing. Never!" The High Priest was sorely afraid that he had crossed the line and now there would be consequences. Perhaps as Pharaoh, this prince would think himself more as foreigner than Kemtu. What if he thought exactly alike to his dead grandfather? What would be the fate of all the temples in the land if that was true? It was imperative that he send a communication to Nebwenenhef in Onu. Perhaps together they could find a way to prevent the unimaginable from ever occurring. "Forgive me my Prince. I meant no reflection upon yourself. It is just you father's policy and as his loyal servant I have no choice but to support his undertaking. You can appreciate that. We live to serve."

"Yes, I understand very well High Priest. I understand more than you think." Thutmoses rose to his feet, a signal to all his men to do likewise. "I thank you Meri-amun for your hospitality of the meal but I'm afraid I have grown tired and wish to retire. Please have your attendants show us to our rooms. Tomorrow will be a busy day."

"Of course Prince Thutmoses." Meri-amun flourished her hands about in a series of waves which were immediately interpreted by the temple servants to escort their guests from the table. "Until the morning, my *Itey*. May the goddess watch over you."

It was now four days since Thutmoses had arrived at Behbeit-al-Hagar and began his search within the Temple of Isis. Along with Meri-amun, he had entered the locked room that had been kept in secret by his grandfather but it proved to be nothing more than an archive of documents that Yuyu had considered of primary importance but to anyone else would appear as nothing more than a hoard of personal notes that referred to the Vizier's life prior to his arrival in Kemet. But just in case there proved to be a significant clue intended for Thutmoses buried somewhere deep in the contents of some papyrus, it was necessary that he read each one in its entirety.

"Ahhh," Thutmoses moaned.

"Did you find something?" Meri-amun immediately reacted.

"Yes."

"What did you find?" she eagerly inquired.

"I found that I have a headache," the Prince joked.

"Not as big as one as Meryptah now has," she quickly responded, and they both laughed. "Can you imagine," she continued, "Before you even had a chance to lay down that first night he had already dispatched a *webwety* to Thebes to tell your father that there was a hidden chamber of Yuyu's within the Temple and you were securing it for yourself. And then the very next day he has to send another dispatch clarifying that the room contained nothing but worthless manuscripts. I will be surprised if he's not banished to some forgotten temple in the hinterlands by the end of the week."

"Now that's funny," Thutmoses laughed aloud. "Although searching through this endless pile of papers appears to be a worse fate."

"Perhaps we're missing something," Meri-amun bemoaned as she wiped the sweat from her brow.

"What do you mean," Thutmoses was curious. So far Meri-amun had proven herself to be a treasure trove of ideas.

"Perhaps what we're looking at actually is the clue. We just aren't looking at it in the proper perspective."

The comment heightened his curiosity. "What are you thinking Meri-amun? Just say what's on your mind." After so many days, he was hardly in the mood for more riddles.

"What if the stories contained in what are obviously your grandfather's memoirs are the clues you're looking for. You told me yourself that he had repeated these stories over and over again to you through your childhood, so it's not likely that he though you needed them written down in order to remember them, right?"

"You're right. This does appear to be far too elaborate an exercise just to ensure that I don't forget some childhood tales about my grandfather's family. Secret rooms, code words, and keeping everyone in the dark, that's far too strange, even for someone like my grandfather. There must be a simple explanation"

Scratching her head, Meri-amun pondered the situation. "So you've read through most of the material."

"Practically all of it now," Thutmoses corrected her.

"What was different?" The question was quite simple but one that the Prince had not taken into consideration.

"What do you mean?"

"Exactly what I said," Meri-amun thought it was obvious. "Any differences may be what he wanted you to notice. So, what was different?"

"Well, he added a few details to some of the stories, changed others, but that's what an old man does when they tell stories. They embellish them over time. Every good story teller does that." The prince wasn't clear on where her question was supposed to lead.

Meri-amun shook her head in disagreement. "Your grandfather wasn't most men. If he did something, he did it for a reason. I thought you of all people would have known that," she practically scolded him.

"You know, you're a lot like my mother when you say it that way," he chided her.

"Tell me what was different," she drew him back on to the topic.

"I have to look through the papers again," Thutmoses snapped back, somewhat annoyed that he would need to reread all the documents and secondly that he had not thought about the possibility that the subtle changes to the stories were the clues he had been seeking the first time through them."

"Well you better get on with it," she instructed him. "It's not like I can help you do it since I've never heard most of Yuyu's stories before."

"So what are you going to do then?" he inquired.

"I'm going to go and check on how Ahrown is doing in his attempt to keep Meryptah occupied and not meddling in our business and then I'm going to bring back some dates and ale so that we don't starve while you read through these huge piles once again." She purposely emphasized the word 'huge' as she gave a little laugh.

"You drink ale?" Thutmoses was surprised by the revelation.

"I'm a priestess my dear, that doesn't make me any less thirsty than anyone else in this land." With that parting comment she was gone from the chamber and out of sight.

Sitting back down on the flagstones, the Prince began the arduous task of reading each story but this time more carefully in order to identify any changes from his childhood recollections.

It was an hour or so before Meri-amun returned with a plate of dates and a jug of ale along with two clay cups.

"Certainly took you long enough," Thutmoses immediately complained.

"Did you miss me?" she batted her long eyelashes at him.

"You really don't know how to behave around the *savov* family and maintain some level of decorum, do you?" The Prince tried to sound threatening but Meri-amun paid it no attention and his frown quickly transformed into a broad smile.

"Listen," she informed him, "for twelve years I had to grab your family's genitals, wash them, roll back your foreskins and stimulate you any way I could until you ejaculated your seed into the fertile earth of the delta. So you will have to forgive me if I have trouble envisioning members of your family as being far superior to us mere mortals." All the while she smiled and tittered as she provided her explanation. "And honestly, other than your grandfather's appendage, I can't honestly say I was impressed by any of your other family members."

"Are you suggesting great Pharaoh isn't so great after all," Thutmoses jested, knowing that he finally found someone he could talk freely with about his father.

"Not his, nor your uncles. Trust me, after handling your grandfather's, we're talking about the difference between snakes and worms." As soon as she made that comment they both burst into uproarious laughter. Once she calmed down, she spoke once more. "If you would like, we can perform the ceremony while you're here and I can let you know which side of the family you take after," she flashed him her mischievous wink that Thutmoses had grown accustomed to.

"I think I will forego the opportunity, High Priestess. I'm in enough trouble already with my father that I don't want him to start thinking that I'm usurping his religious authority as well."

Like a shot out of the blue, Meri-amun fired the question that she had been wanting to ask since he arrived. "So why are you really here, *Itey* of Kemet?"

"I told you, I came seeking answers," he responded coolly and calmly.

"Answers that I'm afraid will only lead you down a path of serious trouble," she warned. "You already know there is talk about your defiance of your father by seeking out your own temple to serve and train as Sem-priest in Onu. And then you choose a *Wab-tepi* to teach you whose father has fallen from grace. A *Wab-tepi* that we all know still clings to the old religion of his forbearers and not the cult of Amun-Ra as it is taught now. Then you appear here, searching for something based on a parting phrase from your grandfather, a man who had his own god and never adopted our culture and beliefs fully. You want answers from me, yet still you have not provided me with your questions, so I cannot possibly provide you with any. Yet here you are, sitting on a cold stone floor, shifting through page after page of papyrus while your *Wab-tepi* occupies your father's high priest with tales of a circular universe, which I'm certain Meryptah doesn't have the foggiest notion of what Ahrown is talking about, but even should he wish to leave I noticed that you have Othni and his men stationed at every exit from the room. I somehow doubt it is to prevent people from entering but more likely intended to keep the high priest from leaving. Are we engaged in something that we should be worried about?"

"Would that bother you if I was?" he questioned, staring directly into her dark sanguine eyes in order to gauge her answer.

"It's actually 'we' by this point in time," she corrected him. "I'm too far involved to back out now."

"And what exactly is it that you think I'm doing?" Thutmoses inquired, "That would be so upsetting to our world?"

"I believe you are at a crossroads; your father's world with that of your grandfather's. In order for one to survive the other must be expunged."

"That's a little harsh don't you think?"

Meri-amun shook her head. "It is the truth. You merely have to look at how well the establishment of your Theban religion of Amun-Ra is doing amongst the people here in the north. The people still cling to their old gods in this part of the country. Isis, Horus, and Osiris. These are the gods that served their ancestors well, why should they change now? Pharaoh ignoring this Temple does not make it any less holy to them. Their statuettes of the goddess will still line the ledges in their home. I guarantee they will not be quick to trade them for one of Amun."

"I only seek answers to what is happening to the world at this time," Thutmoses assured her. My grandfather promised me that if I seek them out, they will be found."

"But what will you do with those answers, young Prince? If they fall outside the boundaries of the religious framework your father is trying to create, what will you do then?" She crossed her arms below her bosom, highlighting the outline of her nipples through the sheer linen gown, and stared back at Thutmoses, challenging him to answer.

The young Prince looked away, he would not provide any further statements, as he busied himself shuffling the papers and preparing to read the next one in silence.

"By the goddess," Meri-amun exclaimed gleefully. "You're going to do exactly what your ancestor Ahmose did, aren't you?"

"Quiet woman," Thutmoses snapped at her. "Keep your voice down and don't speak of things you know nothing about!"

"That's exactly what you intend to do," she continued. "Just like him you want to force the old order out and introduce your own religious brand and ideologue. He forced your Theban rites on all of us and now you're seeking an alternative."

"Voicing such foolishness will get us all arrested," Thutmoses tried to silence her once more. "Who knows if Meryptah can hear you from this room? If he even has a hint of religious sedition he will peddle it to my father in order to save his own neck."

"But it's true, isn't it?" she leaned over him and whispered just above his ear.

"The only thing that is true is that my grandfather wanted me to understand the universe in the same way that he did. To be able to predict events before they happen because everything in our universe follows a set pattern. Ahrown has confirmed that for me and somewhere in your Temple are the templates that will prove it to me."

"Wonderful, let me help you," she insisted.

"Why would you want to involve yourself in such an undertaking? If anyone finds out, you will forfeit your life."

"It is my life to forfeit, my Prince. You on the other hand will be Pharaoh one day, which means that whatever we find, you can make a reality once you are in power. I want to be part of that."

"You don't even know if there's room for a mother goddess in whatever we should find. Ahrown speaks of chaos at the beginning of time; that this first creator god is nothing more than a cosmic conflagration that spews out lesser beings at a later time.

And for every world in which we exist, there may be a multitude of other worlds that are intangible to us but nevertheless are just as real. And all the lesser beings, and other worlds, and even us within our own world, we merely follow a never ending cyclic pattern that is repeated over and over again. Like the sun follows the moon, each day, unfailing and never ending. Like the stars circle in the great river across the heavens, their patterns repeated season by season and never ending. But even the gods in their own world follow a cycle in which they ascend and decline, replaced, forgotten, only to arise again at some distant future once again. Yet the *Potohikap neter*, Creator god at the centre, within the chaos, he will never change, he will always be there and by some means my grandfather and his ancestors could communicate directly to that inner sphere that is beyond the reach of the rest of us."

From the stern look on her face, Thutmoses could tell that he was in for another lecture. "When your ancestors came to our Temples and declared that only the Theban gods would hold *tunkeh* authority in the land, my people wept. When your father abandoned the sacred rituals of Isis and said we were nothing more than servants of a small goddess to appease the country-folk and from then on he held his own set of rituals of renewal in Thebes and Memphis I wept and prayed for the goddess to take back what was rightfully hers. But she did not and I've also come to the realization that there must be a more powerful being that is waiting for our recognition. Do you think all those years when I was spreading your grandfather's semen across the ground that he wasn't telling me of his beliefs and about his god and how he only complied with the ritual for the sake of his daughter? Now let me see some of those papers and perhaps we can find something together sooner than later."

Moving aside a pile of pages stacked on the floor, Thutmoses made room for the High Priestess to sit down. Hiking the hem of her linen dress she proceeded to sit down cross-legged beside the Prince.

"Did I just catch you trying to look up my dress?" she playfully accused Thutmoses.

"I most certainly did not," he refuted her statement.

"Why not," she demanded to know. "I think there is something wrong with you!" she suggested

"Are you going to help or not?" he asked, smiling back at her.

With that last question she sat down and they began to read through the papers in earnest, not knowing exactly what they may be looking for but raising any section of interest or any idiosyncratic point for discussion.

"You don't even know what to look for," Thutmoses commented. "Yuyu probably never told you the original stories so you can't recognize any difference."

"True," she responded, "but what I can recognize is when something seems out of place and for that I don't need to know your family stories, do I?"

The young prince wasn't ready to argue with her. In fact he was grateful for the assistance. Time passed slowly until Thutmoses raised his eyes from the manuscript he just read and commented to Meri-amun about it. "Well this is interesting. A little twist to the story that my grandfather never mentioned before."

"Let me hear it," she responded eagerly, excited that they may have found their first clue.

"And Abraham went with Isaac toward the place that God had told him,' Thutmoses began reading, *"and on the third day Abraham lifted up his eyes and saw the place at a distance which God had told him of. And a pillar of fire appeared to him that reached from the earth to heaven, and a cloud of glory upon the mountain, and the glory of the Lord was seen in the cloud. And Abraham said to Isaac, My son, dost thou see in that mountain, which we perceive at a distance, that which I see upon it? And Isaac answered and said unto his father, I see and lo a pillar of fire and a cloud, and the glory of the Lord is seen upon the cloud. And Abraham knew that his son Isaac was accepted before the Lord for a burnt offering.*

And Abraham said unto Eliezer and unto Ishmael his son, 'Do you also see that which we see upon the mountain which is at a distance?' And they answered and said, 'We see nothing more than like the other mountains of the earth.' And Abraham knew that they were not accepted before the Lord to' go with them, and Abraham said to them, 'Abide ye here with the ass whilst I and Isaac my son will go to yonder mount and worship there before the Lord and then return to you.'"

"What does it mean?" Meri-amun inquired. "Why was he taking his son up an active volcano? He wasn't going to throw him in, was he? Is that what he meant by burnt offering."

"No. It's not about the child sacrifice," Thutmoses insisted.

"You mean you did practice child sacrifice. That's horrible!"

"No, we never did."

"But you just said that it wasn't about the child sacrifice implying that he was going to sacrifice his son."

"Yes, but not by throwing him in a volcano. He was going to burn him on an altar."

"Oh, that is so much better then," she stated sarcastically.

"But in the end Abraham didn't sacrifice his son," Thutmoses was quick to assert, so that it didn't sound as bad as she was making it.

"It's still horrible. An altar? Only the Moabites still practice such an evil thing. A savage, uncivilized people. How could any man even consider doing that to his own son? What kind of god did Yuyu worship?"

"It is horrible, I agree. But in the original story Yuyu told me there was no volcano. No pillar of fire, no dark swirling cloud of ash. Therefore the volcano must be the clue he wanted me to see. Nothing about the sacrifice but the mountain on fire is the key. But why?"

"It's not like you even have any mountains that spew fire in Canaan," Meri-amun critiqued the story.

"That's it!' Thutmoses exclaimed. "He's giving me a place. A place I obviously have to go. Do you have all the records in your temple of all the mountains that spew fire and brimstone? We just need to identify which one it must have been."

"Yes, we've got the records."

"Sound like you're going to say but…" Thutmoses interpreted her tone.

"We have library records dating back over a thousand years of all the mountains in the region that have become volcanoes. Every detail of when and where, and what was seen and what was destroyed, but before you get too excited, I should mention that the records show that there are over sixty volcanoes in Nubia and Kush and just across the narrow sea in Midian another seven. How are we ever going to know which one is the one in your grandfather's story?"

"It has to be in Midian because Yuyu writes it took several days to reach a point where they could see the fire on the mountain, and then several more days to reach it. That gives us enough detail to hopefully identify it in your records. We're talking about an eruption probably no more than two or three hundred years ago. Can we do that?"

"Of course it's possible," she confirmed. "Two centuries ago should definitely be recorded but it may not be as easy as you think."

"Why not?"

"Because each element has its own river and those rivers are constantly in motion. In the *assert* or sky, we have the celestial river along which the stars are constantly moving. On the land, we have rivers of water of which the Nile is the mother of all rivers, constantly flowing from the source to the sea and then winding their way back to the source. And below the earth we have the river of fire, also constantly flowing and venting itself to the surface through the mountains. But just like the other two rivers it is a continuous chain and if the river escapes from one vent it is most likely doing so from other vents in the chain as well. So two hundred years ago you may not find only one mountain spewing forth fire but perhaps all seven. Just look how this ring of fire has been active for the past eighty years, moving from the Aegean to the Anatolian plains, destroying civilization after civilization as it does so."

"Like a wheel,' Thutmoses suggested. "The mountains as you explained are all connected by this underground chain of a river of fire. And if it is a river then it must flow in a direction. From Aegean, to Anatolia; from west to east. If that is true then like a true ring it will turn south into Midian before turning west into Kush. Will your records show that there is a pattern that repeats over and over again through time?"

"How will that help you?" she was curious.

"Perhaps it's not a particular mountain Yuyu wants me to find but to understand how it all works and interconnects, like the discs of Ahrown's universe. He might want me to appreciate the sequence of events rather than a particular event."

"The records should contain that information. As long as the dates of each eruption are recorded we should be able to produce a pattern of the river's flow."

"Which would mean that the time may be coming soon for this mountain of god to erupt again as it did in the time of Abraham and I'm supposed to do something with that information. Perhaps I'm to climb one of them just like Abraham?"

Meri-amun looked at him with a degree of suspicion. "So now even if we have a place and a possible time do you really think your grandfather wanted you to risk your life by climbing a mountain when it's on fire? Doesn't make sense unless you're supposed to be the next sacrifice!"

"I don't think that was his intention," Thutmoses rejected her suggestion. "Obviously there is a purpose. I just haven't found it yet. It may still be buried here in one of these papyri."

"No one climbs a burning mountain. It's insane! You'd have to know every path that the lava flow is going to take, every safe spot, every lahar, every cave offering safe refuge," she lamented.

"So, how good are your records?" Thutmoses questioned.

"They're good," Meri-amun offered, "But I don't know if they're that good. Even so, we still don't have any indication about what you are to do and why you would do it. I think we may have misunderstood the message from your grandfather."

"I don't think so," the Prince shook his head. "The more I think about this, the more I know we are on the right trail. Yuyu gave us a starting point. Now we can look at the rest of the papers with a little bit of advantage in knowing what we are looking for a reason for needing to know everything about this river of fire. So keep reading."

"Yes Master," the High Priestess responded mockingly.

Several more hours passed and this time Meri-amun threw up her hands as if to praise the goddess and shouted excitedly that she found something.

"Listen to this," she instructed the Prince as she began to read the text. *"And in that year there was a heavy famine throughout the land of Canaan, and the inhabitants of the land could not remain on account of the famine for it was very grievous. And Abram and all belonging to him rose and went down to Kemet on account of the famine, and when they were at the brook Kemet they remained there some time to rest from the fatigue of the road. And Abram and Sarai were walking at the border of the brook Kemet, and Abram beheld his wife Sarai that she was very beautiful. And Abram said to his wife Sarai, Since God has created thee with such a beautiful countenance, I am afraid of the Kemtu lest they should slay me and take thee away, for the fear of God is not in these places. Surely then thou shalt do this, Say thou art my sister to all that may* ask thee, in order that it may be well with me, and that we may live and not be put to death. And Abram commanded the same to all those that came with him to Kemet on account of the famine; also his nephew Lot he commanded, saying, If the Kemtu ask thee concerning Sarai say she is the sister of Abram."*

"I've heard that story many times," Thutmoses interjected. Nothing new I'm afraid.

"Well it is for me," she countered. "How interesting that the same event of a famine that brought Yuyu's family to inhabit Goshen also brought his ancestor here with all his family as well. Don't you find that an amazing coincidence?|

"There's always a famine. But Abraham came and he left. I still think it is the mountains of fire that we should be looking at," he advised her.

"Well let me continue because it gets even more interesting. *"And yet with all these orders Abram did not put confidence in them, but he took Sarai and placed her in a chest and concealed it amongst their vessels, for Abram was greatly concerned about Sarai on account of the wickedness of the Kemtu. And Abram and all belonging to him rose up from the brook and came to Kemet; and they had scarcely entered the gates of the city when the guards stood up to them saying, Give tithe to the king from what you have, and then you may come into the town; and Abram and those that were with him did so. And Abram with the people that were with him came to Kemet, and when they came they brought the chest in which Sarai was concealed and the Kemtu saw the chest. And the king's servants approached Abram, saying, 'What hast thou here in this chest which we have not seen? Now open thou the chest and give tithe to the king of all that it contains.' And Abram said, 'This chest I will not open, but all you demand upon it I will give.' And Pharaoh's officers answered Abram, saying, It is a chest of precious stones, give us the tenth thereof. Abram said, 'All that you desire I will give, but you must not open the chest.' And the king's officers pressed Abram, and they reached the chest and opened it with force, and they saw, and behold a beautiful woman was in the chest. And when the officers of the king beheld Sarai they were struck with admiration at her beauty, and all the princes and servants of Pharaoh assembled to see Sarai, for she was very beautiful. And the king's officers ran and told Pharaoh all that they had seen, and they praised Sarai to the king; and Pharaoh ordered her to be brought, and the woman came before the king. And Pharaoh beheld Sarai and she pleased him exceedingly, and he was struck with her beauty, and the king rejoiced greatly on her account, and made presents to those who brought him the tidings concerning her."*
Meri-amun put down the paper that she had been reading and turned to the Prince. "So, is that exactly how you heard it before?"

Thutmoses shook his head. "I knew all about calling her his sister but putting her in a chest is a new twist to the story that he never mentioned before. Could have been that he just forgot it at the time and wanted to ensure the story is complete now."

"Or" she wagged her right index finger in front of his face, "he's sending us another clue. Think about it. Your ancestor put his most precious possession in a box, even though that happened to be his wife and it sounds kind of cruel and not to mention all the lying about her. Seems to be a bit of a coward if you want my opinion."

"Which I don't," the Prince added.

"Anyway, this box is coveted by kings and everyone else. What if you grandfather had an object of such beauty that he kept it in a box and hidden away because he knew everyone would try to take possession of it? What if possession of this object somehow made you powerful and the envy of all the other monarchs?"

"A nice tale but I don't recall my grandfather having anything of value that would warrant that level of protection.

"Well let me read on. Perhaps we'll find another clue. *"And the woman was then brought to Pharaoh's house, and Abram grieved on account of his wife, and he prayed to the Lord to deliver her from the hands of Pharaoh. And Sarai also prayed at that time and said, 'O Lord God thou didst tell my Lord Abram to go from his land and from his father's house to the land of Canaan, and thou didst promise to do well with him if he would perform thy commands; now behold we have done that which thou didst command us, and we left our land and our families, and we went to a strange land and to a people whom we have not known before. And we came to this land to avoid the famine, and this evil accident has befallen me; now therefore, O Lord God, deliver us and save us from the hand of this oppressor, and do well with me for the sake of thy mercy. And the Lord hearkened to the voice of Sarai, and the Lord sent an angel to deliver Sarai from the power of Pharaoh. And the king came and sat before Sarai and behold an angel of the Lord was standing over them, and he appeared to Sarai and said to her, 'Do not fear, for the Lord has heard thy prayer.' And the king approached Sarai and said to her, 'What is that man to thee who brought thee hither?' and she said, 'He is my brother.' And the king said, It is incumbent upon us to make him great, to elevate him and to do unto him all the good which thou shalt command us; and at that time the king sent to Abram silver and gold and precious stones in abundance, together with cattle, men servants and maid servants; and the king ordered Abram to be brought, and he sat in the court of the king's house, and the king greatly exalted Abram on that night."* Tilting her head in thought, Meri-amun had to confess, "It certainly sounds like he's talking about himself and not his ancestor."

"Read on," Thutmoses instructed, "I'm certain there will be some differences."

"And the king approached to speak to Sarai," she continued, *"and he reached out his hand to touch her, when the angel smote him heavily, and he was terrified and he refrained from reaching to her. And when the king came near to Sarai, the angel smote him to the ground, and acted thus to him the whole night, and the king was terrified. And the angel on that night smote heavily all the servants of the king, and his*

whole household, on account of Sarai, and there was a great lamentation that night amongst the people of Pharaoh's house."

The prince listened attentively. "Now that's something he didn't mention before. "It's almost as if he's saying the marriage of our two houses is not to the god's liking. Keep reading, perhaps there's something else."

"And Pharaoh, seeing the evil that befell him, said, 'Surely on account of this woman has this thing happened to me', and he removed himself at some distance from her and spoke pleasing words to her. And the king said to Sarai, 'Tell me I pray thee concerning the man with whom thou camest here' and Sarai said, 'This man is my husband, and I said to thee that he was my brother for I was afraid, lest thou shouldst put him to death through wickedness.' And the king kept away from Sarai, and the plagues of the angel of the Lord ceased from him and his household; and Pharaoh knew that he was smitten on account of Sarai, and the king was greatly astonished at this. And in the morning the king called for Abram and said to him, 'What is this thou hast done to me? Why didst thou say, 'She is my sister', owing to which I took her unto me for a wife, and this heavy plague has therefore come upon me and my household. Now therefore here is thy wife, take her and go from our land lest we all die on her account. And Pharaoh took more cattle, men servants and maid servants, and silver and gold, to give to Abram, and he returned unto him Sarai his wife. And the king took a maiden whom he begat by his concubines, and he gave her to Sarai for a handmaid. And the king said to his daughter, It is better for thee my daughter to be a handmaid in this man's house than to be mistress in my house, after we have beheld the evil that befell us on account of this woman. And Abram arose, and he and all belonging to him went away from Kemet; and Pharaoh ordered some of his men to accompany him and all that went with him. And Abram returned to the land of Canaan, to the place where he had made the altar, where he at first had pitched his tent." At that point Meri-amun put down that papyrus she was reading. "That's all of it.

"I think you might be right," Thutmoses said to her. "He definitely altered the original story to resemble his own life more closely. That Pharaoh's daughter, that he gives as a handmade actually became Abraham's second wife, Hagar. So it's as if he's talking about my grandmother Asenathiye, who was also my great aunt being Amenhotep-Aakheperure's daughter. Then the sister would be their daughter who in turn is my mother. I think my grandfather is saying my family is cursed because of these intermarriages. Perhaps he's warning me not to make the same mistake as my predecessors."

"But I still think he is talking about some object of power that he has hidden away in a box somewhere," Meri-amun insisted. "And when others try to take this object they become cursed and suffer for their covetousness. I wish he had told me more when he visited our Temple," Meri-amun lamented. "All we have are these pieces of a puzzle that don't fit together properly."

"We better keep reading then," the Crown Prince insisted. "It's the only way we're going to determine if there is some hidden mission my grandfather intends for me to undertake."

The hours passed until Thutmoses found himself reading one of the manuscripts that brought tears to his eyes.

"What is it," Meri-amun inquired, "is there some sad tale that you chanced upon."

"Exactly the opposite," the Prince responded. "It is the tale of how we all came to this land. Here, let me read it to you." Thutmoses began to recount the story of how the brothers came before the *Etaty* of Kemet but did not know it was their brother Yusef. After revealing himself, he told them to bring all their families and their father back with them.

He became more intent on reading the next section, *"And Jacob rose up and put on the garments which Joseph had sent him, and after he had washed, and shaved his hair, he put upon his head the turban which Joseph had sent him. And all the people of Jacob's house and their wives put on the garments which Joseph had sent to them, and they greatly rejoiced at Joseph that he was still living and that he was ruling in Kemet. And all the inhabitants of Canaan heard of this thing, and they came and rejoiced much with Jacob that he was still living. And Jacob made a feast for them for three days, and all the kings of Canaan and nobles of the land ate and drank and rejoiced in the house of Jacob."*

"It sounds like Yuyu's father was a great *Iaate* in Canaan," the High Priestess commented. "It makes a little more sense, that being the case, why Pharaoh would give his daughter as wife to Yuyu, if he already was a nobleman."

"Did you actually think that a commoner would be allowed to marry in to the royal family?" he questioned her. "That would go against every precept we have in this land. Of course my family were aristocrats. We just never proclaimed ourselves as kings. But otherwise, let me continue to read the passage. *'And it came to pass after this that Jacob said, I will go and see my son in Kemet ,and will then come back to the land of Canaan of which God had spoken unto Abraham, for I cannot leave the land of my birth-place. Behold the word of the Lord came unto him, saying, Go down to Kemet with all thy household and remain there, fear not to go down to Kemet for I will there make thee a great nation. And Jacob said within himself, I will go and see my son whether the fear of his God is yet in his heart amidst all the inhabitants of Kemet. And the Lord said unto Jacob, Fear not about Joseph, for he still retaineth his integrity to serve me, as will seem good in thy sight, and Jacob rejoiced exceedingly concerning his son. '"*

Thutmoses pursed his lips and thought intensely about that last sentence. "It would appear for all the outward performances by my grandfather to act as a surrogate in your Temple rituals that in his heart he had never abandoned the religion of his forbearers. It would appear that I must have been a great disappointment to him for my embracing of the gods of Kemet. At some point I will have to talk to my mother about that and see if it's true."

"What happens next" she begged him to continue.

"At that time Jacob commanded his sons and household to go to Kemet according to the word of the Lord unto him, and Jacob rose up with his sons and all his household, and he went out from the land of Canaan from Beersheba, with joy and gladness of heart, and they went to the land of Kemet. And it came to pass when they came near Kemet, Jacob sent Judah before him to Joseph that he might show him a situation in Kemet, and Judah did according to the word of his father, and he hastened and ran and came to Joseph, and they assigned for them a place in the land of Goshen for all his household, and Judah returned and came along the road to his father. And Joseph harnessed the chariot, and he assembled all his mighty men and his servants and all the officers of Kemet in order to go and meet his father Jacob, and Joseph's mandate was proclaimed in Kemet, saying, 'All that do not go to meet Jacob shall die.' And on the next day Joseph went forth with all Kemet a great and mighty host, all dressed in garments of fine linen and purple and with instruments of silver and gold and with their instruments of war with them. And they all went to meet Jacob with all sorts of musical instruments, with drums and timbrels, strewing myrrh and aloes all along the road, and they all went after this fashion, and the earth shook at their shouting. And all the women of Kemet went upon the roofs of Kemet and upon the walls to meet Jacob, and upon the head of Joseph was Pharaoh's regal crown, for Pharaoh had sent it unto him to put on at the time of his going to meet his father. And when Joseph came within fifty cubits of his father, he alighted from the chariot and he walked toward his father, and when all the officers of Kemet and her nobles saw that Joseph had gone on foot toward his father, they also alighted and walked on foot toward Jacob. And when Jacob approached the camp of Joseph, Jacob observed the camp that was coming toward him with Joseph, and it gratified him and Jacob was astonished at it. And Jacob said unto Judah, Who is that man whom I see in the camp of Kemet dressed in kingly robes with a very red garment upon him and a royal crown upon his head, who has alighted from his chariot and is coming toward us? And Judah answered his father, saying, 'He is thy son Joseph the king.' And Jacob rejoiced in seeing the glory of his son. And Joseph came nigh unto his father and he bowed to his father, and all the men of the camp bowed to the ground with him before Jacob. And behold Jacob ran and hastened to his son Joseph and fell upon his neck and kissed him, and they wept, and Joseph also embraced his father and kissed him, and they wept and all the

people of Kemet wept with them. And Jacob said unto Joseph, 'Now I will die cheerfully after I have seen thy face, that thou art still living and with glory.' And the sons of Jacob and their wives and their children and their servants, and all the household of Jacob wept exceedingly with Joseph, and they kissed him and wept greatly with him. And Joseph and all his people returned afterward home to Kemet, and Jacob and his sons and all the children of his household came with Joseph to Kemet, and Joseph placed them in the land of Goshen. And Joseph spoke unto Pharaoh, saying, 'My brethren and my father's household and all belonging to them, together with their flocks and cattle have come unto me from the land of Canaan, to sojourn in Kemet; for the famine was sore upon them.' And Pharaoh said unto Joseph, 'Place thy father and brethren in the best part of the land, withhold not from them all that is good, and cause them to eat of the fat of the land.' And Joseph answered, saying, 'Behold I have stationed them in the land of Goshen, for they are shepherds, therefore let them remain in Goshen to feed their flocks apart from the Kemtu.'

"It is a beautiful story," Meri-amun wiped away a tear as it rolled from her eye. "It fills me with happiness and I feel that I too want to hug them and cry."

"Yes it is," Thutmoses agreed, "but it is also very enlightening. I had always blamed my father and his father for keeping my mother's people apart and making them live in the worst part of the country. That is clearly wrong for here Yuyu is saying that it was completely his idea. Pharaoh Amenhotep-Aakheperure actually offered them the best lands to live in and Yuyu refused them."

"Why do you think that is?" she continued to probe the Prince's understanding of the story for evidence that would bring them closer to the reason why they had spent so many days searching for clues to a riddle they still haven't even heard.

"I think he was afraid."

"Afraid?"

"If they were settled in the upper Nile, perhaps even near Akhmim where Yuyu had his estate and land holdings, there would always be that chance that they would never return to their homeland. My grandfather is admitting as much when he says to them, 'You remain in Goshen but I'm returning to the palace in Thebes'. Yuyu saw himself as being separate from them and no longer part of their culture and heritage."

"Then why did he hold on to the deeds to the lands of Canaan if he didn't plan to return?"

"Deeds? Why would you think there would be actual deeds to a land promised by God to Jacob?" Thutmoses knew nothing about what Meri-amun was referring to.

"It's right here, in this document," she answered. Listen, *"And at the death of Isaac, he left his cattle and his possessions and all belonging to him to his sons; and Esau said unto Jacob, Behold I pray thee, all that our father has left we will divide it in two parts, and I will have the choice, and Jacob said, We will do so. And Jacob took* all that Isaac had left in the land of Canaan, the cattle and the property, and he placed them in two parts before Esau and his sons, and he said unto Esau, Behold all this is before thee, choose thou unto thyself the half which thou wilt take. And Jacob said unto Esau, Hear thou I pray thee what I will speak unto thee, saying, The Lord God of heaven and earth spoke unto our fathers Abraham and Isaac, saying, 'Unto thy seed will I give this land for an inheritance forever.' Now therefore all that our father has left is before thee, and behold all the land is before thee; choose thou from them what thou desirest. If thou desirest the whole land take it for thee and thy children forever, and I will take this riches, and it thou desirest the riches take it unto thee, and I will take this land for me and for my children to inherit it forever."

"I've never heard this story before," the Prince admitted. "Continue please."

"And Nebayoth, the son of Ishmael, was then in the land with his children, and Esau went on that day and consulted with him, saying, 'Thus has Jacob spoken unto me, and thus has he answered me, now give thy advice and we will hear.' And Nebayoth said, 'What is this that Jacob hath spoken unto thee? Behold all the children of Canaan are dwelling securely in their land, and Jacob sayeth he will inherit it with his seed all the days. Go now therefore and take all thy father's riches and leave Jacob thy brother in the land, as he has spoken.'

And Esau rose up and returned to Jacob, and did all that Nebayoth the son of Ishmael had advised; and Esau took all the riches that Isaac had left, the souls, the beasts, the cattle and the property, and all the riches; he gave nothing to his brother Jacob; and Jacob took all the land of Canaan, from the brook of Kemet unto the river Euphrates, and he took it for an everlasting possession, and for his children and for his seed after him forever. Jacob also took from his brother Esau the cave of Machpelah, which is in Hebron, which Abraham had bought from Ephron for a possession of a burial place for him and his seed forever.

And Jacob wrote all these things in the book of purchase, and he signed it, and he testified all this with four faithful witnesses. And these are the words which Jacob wrote in the book, saying: The land of Canaan and all the cities of the Hittites, the Hivites, the Jebusites, the Amorites, the Perizzites, and the Gergashites, all the seven nations from the river of Kemet unto the river Euphrates. And the city of Hebron Kireath-arba, and the cave which is in it, the whole did Jacob buy from his brother Esau for value, for a possession and for an inheritance for his seed after him forever.

And Jacob took the book of purchase and the signature, the command and the statutes and the revealed book, and he placed them in an earthen vessel in order that they should remain for a long time, and he delivered them into the hands of his children."

"So even if there were deeds, what makes you even think that they ended up in my grandfather's possession?" he could not appreciate how she made this connection.

"I already told you there was something special about the reference of an object of power being placed in a box. Now, it could be the fact that this deed and book were placed into an old clay vessel that makes me think that I'm on the correct path of finding a solution."

"So why do you think suddenly you're on the correct path?" Thutmoses didn't share in her enthusiasm.

"Because sitting over in the corner of this room appears to be what I'd call a pretty old urn, which I'm certain could be referred to as an earthen vessel."

It was the first time that Thutmoses had noticed the vessel sitting on its own in the corner. It had been such a benign object that they never even bothered to pay it any attention when they first entered the room, concentrating more on the piles and piles of scrolls that filled every shelf and cranny.

Rising from the floor, Thutmoses approached the vessel with some trepidation. "Could be snakes and scorpions in there," he half jested, while the other half was quite serious.

"Just be quiet and open it," she shushed him, deathly afraid that his prediction might be correct.

Peeling back the wax that sealed the cover to the urn, he lifted the lid and reached in his hand. Within seconds he let out a muffled scream and began to writhe.

"Oh goddess," Meri-amun pleaded, "What is it? Goddess help him. Please help him."

Sensing her panic and thinking he may have gone too far, Thutmoses ceased his shaking and smiled. "Just having some fun with you."

"I hate you," she threw one of the rolled manuscripts and hit him squarely in the head but he continued to laugh.

"So what's in there," she was eager to know.

Withdrawing his hand, Thutmoses looked at the leather bound book and smiled broadly. "It would appear to be a deed to all the lands of Canaan," he laughed delighted with his discovery. "It's all here."

"Let me see, let me see," she urged.

"It's written in Phoenician?" he dismissed her.

"What? You think only you royals are the only ones educated in languages?"

Handing over the well preserved book, Meri-amun oohed and aahed as she flipped through its few pages. "This means that your father has title to all these lands if he has this book."

"No, this means the tribes in Goshen have the right to return to their own homeland if I make them aware of this deed. They can go back and claim their inheritance. The Ishmaelites and Edomites have no right to occupy the land since Esau signed it all away. "

"Really?" she looked at him as if he was out of touch with reality.

"They have the right to leave now that they are landholders. They no longer can be considered squatters and landless," the Prince insisted.

"That's pretty naïve," she criticized him. "Do you really think your father cares about legalities? He's not about to give up his labour force because of some old parchment that your grandfather had in his possession. Be serious."

"I will show him the deed. He cannot deny it then."

"No, he won't deny it, he'll just cut it in to little pieces. He's Pharaoh; he already controls all these lands. Do you really think he'll honour a piece of parchment?"

"I guess not," Thutmoses admitted reluctantly. "So what do I do about this deed? It can determine the future for an entire people."

"Right now, you do nothing. Leave it with me. I will safeguard it," she advised.

"Why would you put yourself in such a precarious position," he questioned. "If they should find it on you, they could accuse you of fomenting some treasonous act."

"I'm not sure exactly what you're going to find in all this," she pointed to the rolls and rolls of papyri surrounding her, "I don't even know what direction you're heading. But I do know whatever you do, or wherever you go, it has to be better than this. Do you hear the singing? Do you hear the music and all the priestesses dancing?"

"I hear nothing," he shook his head.

"Exactly! Ever since your father changed the religious hierarchy the worship of the goddess has been in decline. Our rituals and are ceremonies are disappearing. I believe that there's something about you that suggests you will change all that. If it's true, then I am with you. I am yours to command and I will pray each day that you can restore some sanity to this land when the time is right."

"I don't know my path yet," he cautioned her. "I don't know where this will lead or what even my true calling is. All I do know is that I'm compelled to find it and I don't know what that holds in store for you."

"I don't want your concern, I just need your promise not to disappoint me. My sisters and daughters in the Temple need your promise. The priests and the musicians need your promise. Don't fail us and that is all we can ask of you."

"That is a huge expectation considering I have no answers at this time."

"I think by the time we finish reading all these papers we will have at least some of your answers. I merely have to pick up any page and I can already hear Yuyu's voice whispering directions in your ears. Take this one for example. She began to read aloud the first papyrus she picked up. *'For I know that many and grievous troubles will befall you in the latter days in the land, yea your children and children's children, only serve the Lord and he will save you from all trouble. And it shall come to pass when you shall go after God to serve him and will teach your children after you, and your children's children, to know the Lord, then will the Lord raise up unto you and your children a servant from amongst your children, and the Lord will deliver you through his hand from all affliction, and bring you out of Kemet and bring you back to the land of your fathers to inherit it securely. And Jacob ceased commanding his sons, and he drew his feet into the bed, he died and was gathered to his people.'* Do you not find this passage extremely prophetic?"

"Scary, to be more precise," Thutmoses suggested. "It is as if Yuyu knew the affliction that would befall all the people by staying in this land."

"Is it any surprise," she wondered. "Your father dismissed your grandfather from his positions as soon as he came to the throne. For fifteen years he witnessed the changes your father was making within government. He saw the forced conscription of the foreigners into the labour forces to build your father's monuments. And now he's telling you exactly what he expects you to do. You will become Pharaoh and you will undo all the evils your father has done. You will give the slaves back their freedom, you will give them back their homeland, and you will let all the people return to their old religions and serve the gods according to their own beliefs."

"I will need you to keep all these writing safe, not just the deed," Thutmoses instructed. "If my father ever got hold of these manuscripts and his advisors interpreted them in the same way that we have, then we will all be executed for treason. I just wish Yuyu had told me how I was going to accomplish all this. Find me something in all these piles that gives me an idea how I can put everything in motion."

"Think," she instructed him. "You've been through all these papers over the past few days. Something must have struck you as being very unusual when you first saw it. That is the keystone you were supposed to find. That is where you begin your quest!"

The Prince closed his eyes and began reflecting over all the hundreds and hundreds of pages that he reviewed. He was so still that Meri-amun thought he may have fallen asleep sitting up, when suddenly he exclaimed, "Yes! I think I know what it is!" He frantically started searching through a particular pile that he had been through two days prior. "Here it is. How well do you know our recent history?"

"Well enough," she replied but the actual historical archives are kept in Thebes. Why do you ask?"

"Because of this," he began reading. *"And Joseph made unto himself a very elegant throne of an abundance of gold and silver and he covered it with onyx stones and bdellium, and he made upon it a likeness of the whole of the land of Kemet, and the likeness of the river of Kemet that watereth the whole land of Kemet. And Joseph securely sat upon his throne holding the sapphire staff within his hand and the Lord increased Joseph's wisdom."*

"I don't understand why that is important," Meri-amun couldn't appreciate his point.

"Because afterwards it describes my grandfather leading the armies against the cities of Tarshish and Javan. *'And Pharaoh sent Joseph with the mighty men and host which were with him, and also his mighty men from the king's house. And they went to the land of Havilah to assist the Ishmaelites against Tarshish, and Joseph smote the Tarshishites and he subdued all their land, and the children of Ishmael dwell therein. And when the land of Tarshish was subdued, all the Tarshishites ran away, and came on the border of their brethren in Javan and Joseph with all his mighty men and host returned to Kemet, not one man of them missing.'* That's why I asked if you remember your history."

"So…?"

"All the records say that my grandfather Thutmoses-Menkheperure led the armies to quell the uprisings in Syria and Midian. He even set up steles all over the land suggesting the same. In the palace of Memphis he had the walls painted with the scene of his victory over the desert dwellers. But as he stands in his war chariot, he's not holding a sword or javelin. Instead he's raising a staff above his head. A staff that shines a shimmering pale blue."

"It's your grandfather Yuyu in that chariot, not your grandfather Menkheperure," she cupped her hand over her mouth in shock and surprise as she realized what he was describing. "So what's it all mean?"

"It means you're right, there is a hidden object of power. When I was young my grandfather told me stories about the staff. They call it the sapphire staff and it was taken from one of the sacred trees in the Garden of Eden."

"Where is that?" she questioned, unfamiliar with the Garden of Eden legend.

"It's a story. No one knows where it is."

"Then how does one get a branch of a tree from a garden that only exists in a legend? .

Thutmoses was annoyed by the question. "It doesn't really matter. All that matters is that the staff exists and that it is said to have been passed down through successive generations. Really doesn't matter what garden it came from. And finally it ends up in my grandfather's hands."

"So where is it now," she pressed him.

"I have never seen it. Which can only mean that Yuyu hid it away before I was ever born."

Shrugging her shoulders, Meri-amun had no suggestions of what to do next. "Maybe it was destroyed."

"It's been around since the dawn of the world, so I find it unlikely that it can be destroyed," the Prince postulated.

"Do you think it holds power?" The High Priestess was not quite certain of the relevance of the object.

"Somehow, I think it is the key to determining my path. Yuyu obviously wanted to make certain that I took notice of it in his writing. Remember he equated sitting on the throne and holding the staff with being blessed with wisdom. It can only mean that I must find the staff in order to gain the wisdom to deal with my situation."

"Find the staff and I'll understand the connection to the volcanos in Midian. I'll understand everything, I'm certain of it. I'll know exactly what my grandfather intended for me."

"So what now? What should we do?" Meri-amun was excited by the quest that had fallen to them.

"Let's take a few days to comprehend the river of fire. That is obviously important. Then I'll have to set out on the trail of finding the staff."

"Where will you go?" she wondered.

Thutmoses rolled his eyes skyward and his voice wavered with trepidation. "Looks like I have to go home."

CHAPTER FIVE

"A high priestess of Isis," Eleazar could hardly spit the words out of his mouth, the taste being so acerbic. "It was bad enough that you confessed to being some priest of Ra but now I find out that my aunt was a priestess in a temple of fornication."

The high altitude was making it even more difficult for Aaron to catch his breath in order to speak but he persevered. "Let me make it clear he interrupted his son, "there was no prostitution in the Isis Temple. Yes, they had their fertility rite but that had nothing to do with any fornication. So be careful with what you say." As soon as he concluded his sentence he began coughing uncontrollably, signalling to his son to quickly bring him some water.

Eleazar poured from the goatskin into a clay cup and helped his father drink until the coughing subsided. "I am sorry Father. I did not mean to upset you but you have to understand that this is all very difficult to accept. I feel my entire upbringing has been a lie."

Aaron waved his hand back and forth as if to say, 'no, you are wrong'. As soon as he stopped coughing, he sucked in a deep breath and tried to continue where he left off. "Your life is nothing but truth. You have lived the true path in the eyes of God. Yahvu has blessed you and you know no other God but Yahvu. That is why I am telling you all these things now so that you will know how the truth came about, and how the true path followed by all of our people sprang from the earlier falsehoods of our lives. Then you will understand the reason for everything that you do now and will follow it without question because you will know it came from Yahvu. And you will tell your sons, and they will tell their sons forever throughout time, so that they can keep the people on the one true path. There will come those that will challenge our beliefs and attempt to steer the people towards other beliefs but you will know they lie because the truth is in your possession."

"Tell me father, how is it that our beliefs which arose out of falsehoods can provide me with the ability to dispute those having other beliefs" Eleazar still found it difficult to accept that the prior lives of his father, uncle and aunt could so easily be dismissed without anyone else questioning them.

"That is why you must listen closely to everything that I tell you. Once you have heard it all, your heart will be strengthened your faith will become unmoveable, and you will see exactly how Yahvu has brought us out of Mitzrayim with a mighty hand and has selected us as his chosen people."

"I don't even know who we are any longer," Eleazar argued. "Are we Ra worshippers, followers of Isis, or warriors of El? Your three gods have determined our set of beliefs and I don't even know if you recognize their influence!"

Aaron smiled beneath his profuse grey beard. It was a question they had faced a long time ago. "We are all and we are none," he teased his son with his answer.

"It cannot be both ways," Eleazar argued. "The two conditions cannot exist at the same time. There can be no other god but Yahvu. That is what you taught me and that is what all of the priesthood has taught the people."

"It has always been both ways, since the three are actually one." Aaron laughed to himself as he recalled the day that he and Moses and Miriam had made that decision. "Hand me that stick," he ordered his son, pointing to a fallen branch laying in the dirt.

"I can throw it in the fire Father, you don't need to."

"I don't want it in the fire," he dismissed Eleazar's offer. "I want to write with it. Now give it to me."

Handing it over, Eleazar watched as Aaron began etching in the dirt near the fire. "So, now you know that your aunt Miriam was a high priestess of Isis." He wrote the name of Isis in earth. "And much to your embarrassment as you have made it clear, you now know your father was a high priest of Ra." He then wrote the name of Ra adjacent to the goddess's name. "Now your uncle, he went to find his god during his search of the fiery mountains. And as you know, he did come face to face with Yahvu on the mountain top. But the people simply referred to the god of the mountain as El. Sometimes El Shaddai, other times El Gibbor, or El Elyon but whichever name is used, he is still El." Saying that, he inscribed the name El into the ground after Ra. Pointing with the stick at the first name Isis, he asked his son, "What was she the goddess of?"

"She was a false god," Eleazar denied her existence thinking that this somehow had to be a trick question.

"That's not what I asked you. What did the Mitzri believe she represented?"

"Love, family, protection, benevolence," he answered.

"And this one," Aaron pointed at the name of Ra.

"Creation, power, majesty."

"And finally this one," he pointed at El.

"Destruction and a mighty force of nature," Eleazar looked at his father questioning if there was any purpose behind this exercise.

"Put those all together and what do you have?" Aaron challenged him to solve the puzzle.

"You have an omnipotent, all powerful God," Eleazar stated. "You have exactly who Yahvu is," he declared.

"Now read what I have scrawled exactly as I have written it, as a single word," Aaron demanded.

Noticing for the first time that Aaron had written the name of Isis without any secondary vowels, he read the word created slowly. "Is-Ra-El." He looked up, staring into the eyes of his father to see if he had properly interpreted the significance of what his father had done. Looking behind the eyes he knew that it was exactly as he thought.

"Another story Father. Wrestling with the Angel of God was all just a made up tale to entertain the children."

Aaron signalled his son to refill the cup and pass it to him. He did so just in time, warding off another coughing spat that Aaron sensed was about to erupt. "Our goal was to unite divergent peoples, of different beliefs into a unified force. For that we needed a common name, a token of respect for who we were, but at the same time we had to put the past behind us and mould us into a single entity. Calling ourselves a name derived from our various beliefs gave that first generation that we led out of the land of Mitzrayim an identity and purpose and a common goal to unite. As for the next generation and those that followed, they were united by their common experience and beliefs, they didn't need to know the truth behind our identity. They only needed to know that Israel was somehow an ancestor but if you look at our lives, then we did wrestle with our gods. We wrestled with our beliefs and eventually those of us that made the exodus won that battle and were able to commit ourselves to Yahvu."

"So am I to forget all that you are telling me now and pretend it never happened? Is that the burden you are placing upon me now? To forget our origins and preach the stories that you have replaced the truth with?"

Moving quickly for his age, Aaron whipped the stick across Eleazar's forearm with enough force that it snapped in two.

"Ahhh!" Eleazar let out a gasp of pain as he withdrew his arm, rubbing the area repeatedly.

Ignoring him his father continued to speak. "Absolutely not! I'm telling you this, so that you will always remember it. And God will ensure that every member of our family afterwards will always remember until the end of the time. We will carry the burden of the truth until there comes a time that the people will no longer believe in the stories we spun and they will demand the truth and our descendants will be there to provide it to them. And they will be relieved, and their faith will be restored, and they will turn to Yahvu and call out in one voice, 'We understand and we believe.'"

1372 BCE

No one had seen the likes of Malkata before and Thutmoses thought to himself that no Pharaoh would ever undertake such a massive construction project ever again. His father's creation filled him with both awe and loathing. In itself, it was a work of art, an achievement that no one else could have accomplished but the cost was so great, not only in the massive depletion of the treasuries, causing the decline of so many temples throughout the land, but also in the lives of hundreds of labourers crushed by the massive stones or fatal falls from soaring heights. Built on the western bank of the Nile, Malkata was not a single palace but a complex of a half dozen residential palaces surrounding a central festival hall. Around the periphery were the villas, built for all the members and relatives of the *savov* family, along with apartments for the officials, servants, gardeners and tradesmen. The people of Kemet referred to it as the 'Pleasure Palace' but Amenhotep insisted on naming his sprawling structure 'the House of Rejoicing.'

As enormous as it was, stretching from the river towards the western hinterland, and following seven long years of construction, it was still just under half completed. His father blamed the slave labourers in Goshen for the numerous delays, as all the buildings were fabricated from mud bricks that were transported the several hundred miles upriver from the delta. Ignoring the fact that every now and then the giant crocodiles of the Nile would tip over a raft, so that both crew and cargo of bricks were lost, Pharaoh still accused the work teams of laziness and intentional delays. Privately, Amenhotep did acknowledge the fact that the monstrous lizards had severely hampered the construction of his palace by building a Temple on the site to honour Sobek the crocodile deity in an attempt to appease the god to leave the rafts alone. But publicly, it still always remained the fault of the workers in Goshen. Too slow, too lazy, too stubborn, so that over the passing years the whip of the task master became unleashed more freely and what initially was conscripted labour had eventually become actual slavery.

Obsessed with sailing his own small pleasure crafts, Amenhotep had a large ceremonial lake excavated on the east side of the palace and connected it to the Nile through a series of canals leading to the enormous man-made harbour designed specifically to receive the rafts transporting the massive loads of brick. The harbour also made the crossing of the river to the city of Thebes on the eastern bank far less treacherous. By the time it would be completed, Malkata would be bigger than any palace ever built in Kemet; far greater than anything the Hyksos had constructed in Avaris or even the Amarna Palace in Memphis.

The royal chambers, had separate dressing salons off the bedroom, as well as a private audience chamber. Directly across from this audience room was the royal harem where all the foreign wives were housed. But the Great Royal Wife, Tiye, she had her own palace complex, separate but strategically located diagonally across from

Amenhotep's residence. Connected by the central hallway that extended the entire length of the main palace were the separate rooms for all of the royal offspring and at the end of this corridor were built the kitchens where every day incredible meals would be prepared and then served in the main dining hall where the entire *savov* family, down to the most diminutive cousin was expected to gather and eat together.

Along the walls of the interconnecting hallways artists had painted a series of murals depicting the extensive wildlife along the Nile. Between patches of painted reeds lining the banks one could see the likeness of crocodiles lurking, while in the deep waters the hippopotami splashed and bathed in the summer sun. The wooden columns supporting the ceiling were decorated to resemble giant lilies. But the murals on the walls of the bed chambers depicted scenes from the gods in vibrant colours, recapturing the entire tale of their evolution until they reached the present time when all bowed down to Amun-Ra. As far as Amenhotep was concerned, this was the heart of his kingdom, and he ruled from Thebes, much to the neglect of the Northern provinces.

The prince returned to his family home in the company of Othni and a few guards that he had retained. If he had his way, he would have easily not come back at all. There were no happy memories here. Thutmoses was nine when his father announced that the complex had been completed sufficiently that they would be leaving their home in Memphis and moving south, returning to the family's origins in Thebes. It meant that for the next four years, the Prince saw very little of his grandfather Yuyu, who had been essentially dismissed to his landholdings in Akhmim, only to hear from his mother one day that he would never be seen again, because her father had died. The regret that he never was given the chance to say goodbye soured and seethed in his heart constantly. That day Thutmoses felt as if something inside him had died and he had born the emptiness ever since. Returning to Malkata refreshed all the bitter memories of that tragic day and he felt his stomach turn as he approached the main gates.

"Who goes there," the sentry along the main road asked the approaching band of men.

"Crown Prince Thutmoses and his escort," Othni replied as they dismounted from their horses in order to hand their reins over to the grooms that were waiting patiently on the other side of the gates.

"The Pharaoh and the Queen are awaiting you in the great hall, my Prince," the sentry immediately informed him much to the disappointment of Thutmoses who had hoped he would be able to enter the city without any fanfare and leave as quickly in the same manner. Obviously his father had a different idea.

Swearing under his breath the entire quarter hour it took to reach the inner chambers, Thutmoses steeled himself for the inevitable confrontation he knew was looming on the other side of doors to the audience chamber. "You better find you way to your own quarters Othni," he advised, "this is probably going to get extremely messy and you don't want to be around when my father is looking for someone to share in the punishment."

"Thank you my Prince," the captain was relieved to be released from duty and he was pacing down the hall in the other direction before Thutmoses even had his hand on the door.

Slowly letting the carved ebony wood door rotate back on its brass hinges, Thutmoses took a couple of cautious steps into the room. He looked around quickly, surveying the surroundings and was relieved to see that besides his parents, there were only a single herald, the *Weni* and an *anu* to record present. He had been frightfully worried that his father would make his admonishment into a full public hearing, thereby having the entire court in session to witness his humiliation. It was still bad enough that the *Weni* was there, a secret judge that was in command of his own secret police force indicating this was far from going to be a simple father and son discussion.

"Announcing the arrival of the *Suten-Sa*, Crown Prince Thutmoses-Mutenkheperure," the herald shouted as if his parents could not recognize their own son.

'Idiot', the Prince thought to himself. There's only the six of them in the room, why even bother with a herald. Thutmoses walked towards the far end of the chamber where the royal couple were seated on a pair of cedar thrones inlaid with gold and silver and encrusted with onyx, emeralds and ruby stones.

Pharaoh motioned to the herald upon seeing his son walking directly towards him. The herald understood immediately.

"You will approach the *Neter-Nesew*, Son of the God Amun, ruler of the red and white lands, subduer of Asia, in the proper manner," the herald commanded.

Thutmoses was about to say something sarcastic but thought better of it and bit down on his tongue to keep from saying anything regrettable. Crossing his arms so that his hands practically rested upon his shoulders, he bent over at the waist, eyes firmly fixed on the floor as he approached his parents. When he was within fifteen feet of Pharaoh he dropped to his one knee, eyes still downcast as he awaited permission to rise. That permission was not forthcoming and the time kneeling, begging for an audience, felt like an eternity. He knew his father must be enjoying this tremendously.

"Prince Thutmoses-Mutenkheperure, it has been brought to my attention that you may have been engaged in activities that were contrary to the wishes of the crown and the nation these past three years," Amenhotep levelled the accusation against his son. "Furthermore, you have failed to perform the regular functions and actions that are expected of the Crown Prince and therefore are guilty of abandoning your responsibilities to both the Crown and the state. In addition…" at that moment Queen Tiye stamped her foot and gave her husband a look that froze him instantaneously from making any further statements. Eliminating every other accusation he intended to level at his son, he moved to his opening question, "How do you respond?"

Biting down even harder, the Prince winced slightly from the pain but it succeeded in keeping him from saying what was actually on his mind. "Great Lord, Son of Amun, wearer of the double crown deshret and hedjet, favourite of Ra, Protector of the red and white lands, I am your humble servant, unfit to gaze upon *Neter-Nesew*."

Having acknowledged his father correctly, he was finally given permission to rise and talk directly face to face with his king. Thutmoses considered the entire pretence ridiculous but as he raised his eyes, he noticed his mother shaking her head slightly as if to warn him not to behave rashly or do anything foolish. "How should I respond to such accusations Great King if I do not know the specifics of what you have heard?"

Amenhotep cleared his throat in preparation to state the nature of the accusations. "In a series of corresponding letters from the *Hem-netjer-tepi* of Onu, he felt it was his duty to apprise me of your activities within the Temple there. Whereas, it was my intent to have you tutored and trained as the Sem-Priest of Ptah-Set in Memphis, you of your own accord ignored my instruction and instead you committed yourself to be a Sem-Priest of Atum-Ra. But as the Queen pointed out to me at that time, as we are the living embodiment of Amun and he is the chief god that rules over all others, then it was your youthful exuberance to please me as Amun incarnate and therefore you defied the order in order to serve me better. But, the laws and dictates of Amun are very different from the archaic beliefs and scriptures of Atum-Ra in Onu and for that reason, I purposely replaced their High Priest with Nebwenenhef, a man with an extensive understanding of the new religion and its Theban dictates. Therefore, it would have been my expectation that you conducted your tutelage under his guidance but as he informed me, you nominated the *Wab-tepi*, a firm believer in the old order to provide your education and therefore though your intention to serve me better may have been honourable, your actions countermand any such intent. For three years you have resisted any effort by the High Priest to correct your selection of tutor and advisor and in his numerous complaints he even accuses you of studying the heretical practices of the ancients, with their misguided beliefs. What do you have to say in your own defence?"

Looking towards his mother, Thutmoses was hoping for a sign on how he should respond but Tiye sat frozen like a beautiful statue, not giving any hint from behind her dark, entrancing eyes. He realized he was entirely on his own on this matter.

"Look at me when you make your response, not the Queen," Pharaoh commanded.

"May I speak freely?" Thutmoses inquired, buying some time while his mind quickly set about filtering through a hundred different responses he could make, actively searching for the best one."

"That is why you are here," Pharaoh instructed. "To speak honestly and freely, so that we may assess the level of your perfidy."

"It is true your Majesty, I did all those things as my accuser Nebwenenhef states in his discourses. In fact, I probably did worse things that he doesn't even know about," the Prince confessed much to the astonishment of his father, whose jaw suddenly dropped as he was taken by surprise, expecting his son to be more defiant and aggressive. "I not only studied the ancient ways, and the old gods, but I asked the *Wab-tepi* to provide me with an appreciation for all the interactions between the gods and man, because….and I will be very clear on this…because in order to serve Pharaoh, it would be irresponsible and ignorant of me to restrict my learning only to how we practice here in Thebes and based solely on the hierarchical structure of the gods of which Amun is at the godhead."

Amenhotep looked surprised by the answer but the barely recognizable smile on his mother's face told him that he was moving in the right direction.

"We are a diverse people," he continued, "stretching from the delta of the lower Nile to the sixth cataract by Bagrawiyah in Nubia; from the Narrow Sea to the deserts of Libya. A divergent, different and dynamic people that have come together to create the most powerful nation in the world. To unite people, we need a common belief, and in that matter I am totally in agreement with the wisdom of my Great King, but even that common belief requires that we incorporate aspects from all previous beliefs so that each of these diverse people can find a trace of their past, present and future in that new belief. Traditions and customs need to be preserved, providing a safety net of comfort to those embracing new practices. To enforce a belief that is in its entirety completely foreign on a people only encourages resistance and revolt. But by incorporating even a thread of their own past beliefs provides them with a reassurance that they are not completely abandoning the ways of their ancestors and thus have not offended any of their household gods. Therefore my actions were designed entirely to ensure the success of your wise approach by unifying the people through a set of common religious beliefs and rituals, which I believe all your advisors and High Priests have deliberately ignored and misguided you, possibly in an effort to see your great plan fail. Of this truth I can assure you!"

Amenhotep fell silent, contemplating his son's words. They had negated practically everything Nebwenenhef had accused him of and Pharaoh found himself at a loss of what to say next. Pushing his lower lip forward, he turned to his left to look at his Great Royal Wife, who simply tilted her head suggesting that any decision or rebuttal he would make would be his own. Leaning forward, he stared into Thutmoses' eyes to see if there was any trace of perjury in his testimony. When he could not see any, he rolled back into the throne, gripping the arm rests so tightly that the whites of his knuckles began to show. "Out, everyone out," he ordered his staff members. "Get out now!" The officials moved as quickly as they could and were out the door to the chamber within seconds.

Removing the double crown, Amenhotep placed it on the brass table that was to the right of his throne. He used his palm to wipe the sweat from his scalp and then released a huge sigh. "You believe you have bested me, don't you?" he challenged his son. "You provided an answer that I can neither approve of nor deny. If I approve, then I concede that what you have done is correct, my priests and advisors wrong and I in turn send a signal to everyone that defiance of my orders is acceptable thus making myself appear weak. If I refute your answer, then I appear to be a ruler out of touch with his own people which encourages even more defiance. I am in a losing position no matter how I rule on this. Why son are you so determined to vex me?"

"Oh, are we talking father and son now?" the Prince wanted to make certain he wasn't going to be held accountable for breaking protocol.

"Yes, why do you think I sent away the attendants?"

"I thought because you knew that no matter how you responded, they would have recorded an answer that others would have taken offense to," Thutmoses commented cynically.

"Do we always have to play this game of fox and hounds in real life? I make a move, you make a counter move and in the end there are no pieces left on the senet board," Amenhotep sounded exasperated. "Can we not just speak as father and son?"

"Perhaps next time don't usher me directly into a tribunal when I show up at your door and I might be able to be a little more comfortable in your presence," the Prince advised.

"There were accusations. There were matters that need to be adjudicated properly."

"I'm sorry father that I've been such a disappointment to you but the reality is that I'm not you, in spite of your expectations. I don't see the world the way you do. I don't need a pleasure palace to let the world know who I am." Thutmoses knew very well that last comment would send his father into a rage. He was well aware that the common people had levelled that accusation against the royal couple from the day the first tax was collected to finance the project.

"A House of Rejoicing," Amenhotep snapped back angrily, "not a pleasure palace. You make it sound like I've built a brothel instead of the greatest palace in the world."

"To the common people, to everyone that felt the whip in its construction, it is a pleasure palace, tucked away in the southernmost part of the country, far away from the great population centers of Kemet. A place where you can sail your little boats and fill your treasure houses." Now he had done it. He knew he should have bit down harder on his tongue but the opportunity to hurl another insult at his father proved far too great.

"And what would you know of building anything, of achieving greatness!" Pharaoh was practically yelling, his face turning scarlet with anger. "When I was your age, I was married, raising a family so this land has a future. But you can't even take on that simple responsibility. Perhaps you are not a man after all? My only son, and all you think about is yourself! Of all the sons that were lost to us in childbirth why has Amun plagued me with you as the only survivor?"

"Stop it! Enough!" The Great Royal Wife could tolerate their bickering no longer. Rising from her throne, she threw her Atef crown with its ostrich feathers against the tile floor with enough force that the clamour it made caused the *Weni* to rush back into the room thinking there had been an attack on Pharaoh. "Get out!" she screamed at him and for a second time the judge fled from the chamber. "For three years we have not seen our son, our only son and this is how you greet him. With a tribunal to hear complaints from one of your over-pompous snivelling priests. And you," she pointed her finger at Thutmoses, "What kind of son shows such a lack of respect for his parents? You do only think of yourself! Not even a single word for your mother in all that time. Now it is my turn to stand in judgment because I've had a stomach full of you both. The fact is you are both stubborn, self-indulgent jack-asses!"

Amenhotep held up his right hand with index finger extended as if to speak but before he could utter a single word his wife had already cut him off. "Be quiet and listen husband. If you think you can punish the boy and break his spirit, then you are wrong and you have been wrong for a very long time. When your father arranged our marriage we both were only twelve. Do you remember? You objected to your father's attempts to control your life to the extent you swore you would never be like him. And when he died so suddenly, you were a mere boy thrust upon the throne without ever having lived a true childhood. The weight of the world was upon your shoulders and before you knew it, your bride was pregnant but what was I but a child as well. Two miscarriages later we were finally blessed with a child. This child!" she pointed at Thutmoses. "Two children suddenly forced to rule over an empire, raise a family, an impossible task but we did it, together we did it. And as much as you said that you would never become your father, the fact is that the day Menkheperure died, it was the day you did become him. So now you find yourself dealing with a son in the same manner your father had to deal with you. I love you husband but you are blind if you think you are any better than your predecessors."

Hearing his mother berate his father, a smug look crawled across the Prince's face.

"As for you, wipe that look off your face," Tiye scolded, "and try to use some common sense for once in your life. Your father is your father, no matter what he does and no matter what titles he wishes to call himself, he is still your father and don't you ever forget that. You are the *Suten-sa*, next in line for the throne and you know nothing about being a king. Know this well, your father is right about one thing, the same way his father was right and his father before him; we do have a responsibility to this land, to these people, and to do whatever it takes to safeguard those responsibilities. The people need to know that this line of kings will continue on for perpetuity. They need to know that you take your responsibilities seriously and that you can plant the seed that keeps this family in tact through the generations. You are sixteen going on seventeen, it is time you are married and ensure there will be a successor. You can delay it no longer."

"The boy needs discipline," Amenhotep argued. "It is the only way that he can appreciate the enormity of the undertaking to be Pharaoh."

"Now you even sound like Menkheperure. I remember him saying the exact same words about you to my father."

"And your father agreed, and because of that I was held in my cell like a prisoner, while Yuyu tutored me endlessly on the administrative duties and legal precedents within our governmental systems. Day after day I suffered!"

"By all the gods, let it go, your father knew he was dying. He wanted to ensure a smooth transition and that meant forcing you to settle down and begin learning every detail of the task before you. When are you ever going to forgive them for doing what was necessary?" It was obvious they had this conversation many times in the past and Tiye still couldn't make him appreciate that they did what was in the empire's best interests.

"He kept me like a prisoner," Amenhotep cried out. "The only time they let me out of my cell was to see you and even then it was for the sole purpose of planting my seed in your belly. They couldn't even let us forge our relationship in peace."

It was the first time that Thutmoses ever saw his father appear as if he was going to weep.

Stepping to the side of his throne, Tiye laid his head across her bosom, while she stroked his temple. "I know my love. I know what they did to you my sweet Nimnim." It had been a long time since she used the childhood name she fondly referred to him by. The effect was not lost, as he calmed down immediately and nestled between her full breasts.

She signalled with a shake of her head that it was time for Thutmoses to leave as she tended to her husband. She would speak to him later that evening.

That night Pharaoh had retired early, exhausted by the events earlier in the day. It provided the opportunity for Tiye to invite her son to dine alone with her within her private chambers. The servants carefully arranged the pillows for the young prince to make him as comfortable as possible as he sat cross-legged at the edge of the table.

"Are you comfortable," Tiye asked.

"Yes, very" her son replied as he adjusted his short skirt so that it would not ride upwards while he sat.

"That's nice." Leaning over the table she slapped Thutmoses sharply across his left cheek. "Now you can behave properly by getting up and giving your mother a kiss and a compliment. I didn't raise you to behave like an animal."

Recognizing that he had completely overlooked such courtesies, Thutmoses rose quickly and walked to the other side of the table to hug and kiss his mother. "I'm afraid I've been away from using proper decorum for too long, Mother," he apologized. "As always Mother you look radiant and I swear you are looking younger and younger each time I see you."

At twenty-nine years of age, the Great Royal Wife was truly young and beautiful on both accounts. Though Amenhotep had six other wives, two from the Mitanni, two from Babylon, and one each from Ammia and Arzawa, none of them compared in beauty to Tiye. Raven locks fell loosely across her shoulder while dark kohl lined eyes peered teasingly from beneath ochred brows. Her long aquiline nose was the only tell-tale sign of her mixed heritage, but her thick ruby lips were entirely from the southern parts of Kemet. At twenty-nine years of age, she still looked as young and vibrant as a teenager and it was no wonder that she had captivated Amenhotep from the moment he first laid eyes on her. Theirs was not an arranged marriage but truly a marriage of love, which not all the princesses of Mesopotamia sent by foreign kings could erase.

Sitting himself back down on the pillows, Thutmoses began the conversation. "There is much to discuss Mother. It is difficult to know where to begin."

"Start at the beginning," she chided him. "I find it is usually a good starting point. What did you discover in Onu?"

"Perhaps you could tell me exactly why you wanted me to study there, and then I can tell you if I actually discovered what you intended me to do. You arrange these things for me Mother, and then in front of Father you support his actions against me. I really don't understand you."

Tiye appreciated his concern and knew it was time to divulge everything she had concealed from him. "Know this, that the tribunal was entirely your father's undertaking. I had advised against it but he no longer listens to me as he did before. His fits of melancholy and depression come more frequently and his rages has manifested itself more physically than ever before. So you must be careful from now on."

Dropping the bread back on to his plate, the Prince became concerned. "He has not hurt you, has he?"

"No, I don't think he would ever hurt me but the servants, the maids, they have all suffered under his heavy fist. Everything he sees as an attempt to undermine his authority and that is why I am so afraid for you." She reached across the table and patted the top of his hand softly. "I fear that the more you challenge him, the more he will forget you are his only son and see you more as a rival. At night his sleep has become so fitful that I hear him cursing out your name. That is why you must start behaving more dutifully and avoid challenging his instructions."

"Mother, how can I suddenly give up everything that you had me set a course upon? Without being offensive, my best years have been when I am away from you and father."

"I am sorry you feel that way," his mother commented apologetically.

"It wasn't as if you were ever there for me mother. I was raised by my nurses and then by a series of pedagogues. Whenever you did come to see me it was with father and he was either ridiculing me or beating me but you never interceded. Not once."

"I could not," Tiye explained. "You had a rebellious spirit, much as he did when he was young and he did to you what his father did to him."

"That explains his actions mother but it does not explain the lack of yours. And now you suggest I return after sending me away for most of my life."

"It was never me, these were the wishes of my father and as you witnessed today, the memory of Yuyu grows more and more sinister in Pharaoh's mind each day. Yes, my father was a hard task master when it came to tutoring your father, but there was never a moment he did not care and love his nephew. But the bitterness grew within your father like a poisonous serpent and by the time he became Pharaoh, Yuyu was guilty of all the injustices within the land. Not even I could persuade him otherwise and although he would never lay a hand on my father, after a few years he banished him from office and practically exiled him to his estates in the south. For those first ten years of his reign, Yuyu was still a welcome guest in our Memphis palace but once we moved here, he was not permitted to visit me any longer. That is why you rarely saw your grandfather but his influence was never very far from you. But Nimmureya knew the people still loved Yuyu and he considered that love a threat to the throne as well. My father no longer was permitted to partake in the Temple ceremonies, no longer able to wear the gold chain that Amenhotep-Aakheperure had given him. But most of all, the day he was no longer able to see you, I believe he gave up all reason for living and that is why he passed away. His heart was broken."

Thutmoses was saddened by what his mother had revealed. Saddened but at the same time he felt the anger rising within him. Tiye could see the same expression in his eyes that she had witnessed so many times before in her husband and for the moment it frightened her. "You let his hatred for Yuyu infect his actions towards me. The more time I spent with Yuyu, the more my father's resentment towards me festered and grew. And you knew that, all this time."

"You must not let your father's rage take control of you as well," she cautioned him. "That is the bad blood of which your grandfather spoke and if you are to become as Yuyu intended than you must learn to master it."

"Intended? All I have is riddles but no answers. Why all these clues and yet none of them lead me to the truths of which you speak? Why not just tell me what it is he wanted from me." The swelling anger was quickly replaced by an even higher degree of frustration.

"Because my father would tell you if he was here, you cannot be told who you are, you must learn to be who you are meant to become."

"Another riddle," the Prince rolled his eyes.

"Not a riddle; a journey," she corrected her son. "One that Yuyu had to make himself. His transition from Yusef to Yuyu was a long hard struggle but he succeeded in doing it on his own. Only once he approached death did he think that perhaps it was time for Yusef to re-emerge. He wished to have himself and my mother buried in the family cave of Machpela in Canaan. Your father refused to let that happen."

"That makes no sense at all," Thutmoses challenged. "He had his tomb in the Valley of Kings. The embalming, the ceremony, he chose to be buried as a King of Kemet."

"That is the story spun by your father. Yuyu never had a tomb constructed. He avoided doing so because he realized that after Pharaoh began enslaving the foreigners in Goshen, there could be no place for his people in Kemet. How could he have his remains buried in a land where his people were suffering? But your father realized that if Yuyu and Asenathiye were returned to Canaan for burial then it would send a message to all the people in Goshen that they should leave this country and that obviously would prevent him from completing his undertaking of his grandiose building projects. My father's tomb in Canaan would become a beacon enticing everyone in Goshen to return to their homeland. Fearing this, Pharaoh appropriated one of the noble's tombs and ensured that your grandfather and grandmother were buried in this land. No one else knew that it had not been Yuyu's desire to be entombed in the Valley of Kings."

"So why not just tell me all these things rather than having me search for pieces of the puzzle without even knowing what I was looking for?" Thutmoses was confused as to why his grandfather and mother kept all these secrets from him until now.

"If your grandfather had told you all this it would have no meaning. They would just be stories on top of the numerous other stories he had already told you. But by having you do your initiation into the priesthood under the guidance of a Lebu *Wab-tepi,* he knew you would start seeing reality on your own accord. You would begin to see how all events in our world interrelate and depend on cycles that have their own timelines in which to repeat. By putting the pieces of that puzzle together in your own mind it would take on a life of its own and lead you to the next step in your search for answers."

"You mean it would lead me to the Temple of Isis." The Prince was beginning to realize that everything he had done over the past three years had been carefully orchestrated.

Tiye smiled benevolently as she witnessed her son's enlightenment. "It was not by chance that Meri-amun had become the High Priestess of Isis," his mother advised.

"She sort of explained their familiarity to me," Thutmoses face flushed as he thought back to the first encounter between Meri-amun and his grandfather. "So you know the High Priestess too?" he was surprised.

"Of course my dear son. After all, I was dedicated to the goddess at birth, as was my mother. Do you forget that your grandmother was a priestess of Isis too, as her name Asenathiye would suggest? Tuya was the shortened name by which my father affectionately called her but I think he did so more because of his dislike of calling out the name of the goddess each time he called his wife."

"And all this time I thought it was to give her a name that would refer to his personal god," the Prince surmised.

"Not for her. That he did for me. Your grandparents actually named me Batiya suggesting that my house would always be their god's house but when my uncle asked what was my name they thought it best to say it was Tiye, thereby honouring my mother's and his mother Tiaa. It sounds almost the same and it is the proper abbreviated form of Batiya, so it achieves both goals," she laughed thinking back to all the times her mother would call out her name and she would answer, 'here I am' to the confusion of all the other children.

"But still you kept your connection to the Temple of Isis even though you didn't believe." Thutmoses sounded somewhat confused that during all that time, he had been unaware of these secrets that concerned his mother.

"This is Kemet and being connected to a temple will always serve its purpose. As when Pharaoh had made it known to me that he was no longer going to perform the fertility rites, breaking centuries of tradition, I suggested to him that my father could take his place. Your father thought it amusing that an old man would have his genitals given a good workout by a horde of young girls, or as he expressed it to me, 'Let that withered old cock have its last whirl.' But it was all designed to have a safe place, far from the reach of your father for Yuyu to have a repository of his documents to leave behind for you to read. Though I did not know his exact arrangements, I did know that he moved many of his personal papers to the Temple of Isis a long time ago. And as he suspected, you would find your way there eventually when the time was right."

"But I happened on finding that room only by chance," Thutmoses asserted. "And if it had not been for Meri-amun insisting that we go through the documents one more time looking for differences from my grandfather's initial telling of the stories, then I never would have put any of the pieces together."

"You underestimate your grandfather. He never had a doubt because he had already seen it happening. "It was your destiny to follow this path. Your grandfather believed you will change the world and told me so repeatedly."

"Not if father has his way," Thutmoses warned her.

"You must be smarter then. You must let Pharaoh believe he has convinced you to be the dutiful son, while at the same time you pursue your own direction."

"How is that even possible mother? We can't even stay under the same roof without going for each other's throat."

"Then don't. Do what you must while here but then a soon as possible task yourself with a mission on behalf of Pharaoh that takes you far away."

As soon as his mother mentioned a task his mind swept immediately of thoughts of the sapphire staff. "There is something I need to ask you mother. The murals in Memphis of grandfather Thutmoses-Menkheperure in his war chariot, they really weren't of him, were they?"

Tiye's lips parted into a broad smile as if to say, you are beginning to understand. "I see the journey to Goshen and the Temple of Isis has provided you with its forbidden fruit."

"So they were of grandfather Yuyu after all," Thutmoses deduced.

"And your father despised those murals but I would not permit him to alter them in any manner. He swore he'd build his own palace where he didn't have to gaze upon Yuyu any longer."

"As he has done," the prince making reference to the construction of Malkata.

"What else did you learn there?" she inquired.

"The staff! Where's the staff now?" he blurted out.

"Menkheperure rarely fought his own battles, especially when they were only to deal with minor skirmishes by the local tribes. For those, he always had my father deal with them. That is the role of being *Etaty* and *Herey* of the Horse. Sometimes Yuyu could negotiate a settlement, other times he had to crush the opposition in battle. With the Tarshishites, there was no such thing as negotiation. Not then and not even now. They had to be defeated down to the very last man."

"But what about the sapphire staff?" he repeated his question.

"Let me show you what I know." Tiye rose from the table and walked towards the door leading to her bed chambers. She opened the door slightly and a silvery-blue blur raced through the opening, across the room and leaped into Thutmoses' lap.

The prince became ecstatic as the sight of his cat that he had left behind these past few years. Suddenly Thutmoses felt like a little boy again as he hugged the cat to his chest and cooed endlessly "Ta-Miu", her name over and over again.

"Careful," his mother urged. "She is very old now and very delicate."

"I have missed her so much," Thutmoses confessed.

"I think more than you missed your own mother," Tiye criticized him.

"Never!" the Prince quickly responded but the truth was that he had given his parents little though during his years away in Onu.

"And I can tell that she has missed you very much too," she watched as the old cat purred loudly, pawing her master's face softly as if trying to determine it was really him and that he had come back for her.

"Thank you for taking such good care of her, Mother."

"Of course. When you are away, she is all I have left of you to shower my affections upon. Ta-Miu will always be a part of you and in that way there is always a part of you with me," the words provided a confession by Tiye about how much she had missed her son but at the same time Thutmoses questioned her sincerity. She may have showered affection on his cat but she certainly didn't do the same to him while he grew up.

"But what does Ta-Miu have to do with the sapphire staff?" Thutmoses remembered why his mother had risen from the table in the first place and now the matter had become confounded by the sudden entrance of his cat.

"Do you remember how Ta-Miu became your cat?" his mother questioned.

"Of course," he answered. "She was one of the kittens from grandfather's litters."

"The last litter to be precise," his mother corrected him. "Just about two years before Menkheperure died, he sent my father on one last assignment to put down a minor revolt in Kush. It wasn't much of a rebellion since the queen was still loyal to us and it was merely some tribal *Iaate* trying to overthrow his own local governor. But nonetheless, it needed to be subdued quickly and in appreciation for doing so, the Queen of Kush gave my father a pair of cats native to her country. Sometimes the kittens born were a fiery brown, other times a pale lilac, but on rare occasions there would be a kitten born in a litter that was a silvery blue, just like Ta-Miu."

"Silvery-blue just like the sapphire staff," Thutmoses made the connection between the two. "So Ta-Miu is the key to finding the staff's location. Once again, my grandfather's riddles point me in the direction of Kush. But why would he have the staff hidden in a land so far away."

"I can't confirm that is where you will find it. All I know is that Yuyu said that you would find the answer when you search through his papers," Tiye advised.

Nodding his head, Thutmoses confirmed his grandfather's deduction. "I believe we did. When you have something of exceptional beauty and power, you must hide it from those in power that will covet it," the Prince reflected. "I'm presuming there were those that would like to have taken the staff from Yuyu."

"None more than your father," she confided. "Whereas Amenhotep-Aakheperure recognized the great power that the staff possessed but knew only Jacob could wield it, already his son Thutmoses-Menkheperure began to wonder if it was bonded to a single person. When he witnessed that Jacob at the time of his passing did not grant it to his eldest son, or his strongest son, but instead bequeathed it to Yuyu he began to think that anyone holding it would possess the power it possessed. After the Tarshish campaign, Pharaoh began to talk about the staff at almost every occasion. Such talk of magic and power easily captured the imagination of Nimmureya and Yuyu could sense that the staff was being coveted and eventually he would be asked to offer it to Pharaoh without argument. My father swore that would never happen. When he returned from the battlefields of Kush, he no longer had it in his possession. He claimed that it had vanished as soon as the enemy had been vanquished."

"But it hadn't", Thutmoses interjected.

"I had no idea what really happened to it," Tiye admitted her father wouldn't even confide in her. "You know more than I ever did from what you already read in the Temple. I'm presuming from whatever you found out that he hid it away somewhere where no one would look."

"But where?"

"All he ever said to me was that you would know the answers when the time was right. He told no one what really happened but he always knew without question that you would uncover the truth. All he ever left me was the name of a cousin to pass on without ever explaining why."

"What is so special about this cousin?"

"I know very little about him other than he was a merchant trading along all the ports of the Narrow Sea. That is all I know. My father was a man of too many secrets."

"Well, he certainly had more faith in me that I do in myself," Thutmoses sighed. "How am I even to find an excuse to journey into Kush without father becoming suspicious of my intentions?"

"You still don't understand," She shook her head, "All these things will happen naturally because my father saw them happening in his visions. The reason for you traveling to Kush will become evident in time. Patience is the key."

"And in the meantime…."

"You will remain here and perform your duties so that Pharaoh doesn't grow suspicious of you."

"And by duties..."

"Everything that is expected of a Crown Prince, including providing a future heir."

"You know that it is not right," Thutmoses insisted. "Yuyu spoke of all the dangers that it represents."

Waving the index finger of her right hand in his face, the Queen took exception to her son thinking he needed to remind her. "I know better than anyone what price is paid for such relationships! I don't need you to tell me of such things. Eleven pregnancies in eighteen years. One son and four daughters that are able to walk this earth and six sons that Anubis carried over to the other realm. No! You don't need to remind me of such things ever! Every day of my life I remind myself." The anger contorted her beautiful features into a rabid mask. "And still your father comes to my bed chambers and begs me for another son. How many more will I bury before my womb runs dry?"

"I am sorry mother," Thutmoses begged for her forgiveness for reminding her of such matters.

"I don't need your sympathies," she snapped back. "I need you to protect your sisters. Already your father talks about how it will be necessary for him to bed Sitamun and Iset because of your failure to do so. Praise the gods that Henat-taneb and Nebetah are still too young for his attentions. It would kill me to see my darling daughters laying with their father. How would they ever forgive me for letting such a thing happen to them? You must save them from this."

"But I am still their brother," he attempted to dissuade his mother.

"Better a brother's half seed than a father's full seed. If you love your sisters, then you will do this for them. You will not let them suffer for your father's compulsions. Promise me that you will do this. For their sake if you cannot find it in your heart to do it for mine!"

"None of this is right," Thutmoses still objected. "It is exactly what Yuyu wanted us to avoid. Now we are saying otherwise."

"How many dead babies must your sisters bury before your heart weeps for them? Sitamun loves you very much. She knows that whatever happens you did not mean to hurt her. But your father, that thought fills her with revulsion because it is an unnatural lust that will only result in the death of many offspring."

"And if she cannot give birth to a child from me?"

"You still will have protected her because your father will not touch her after you have taken her maidenhead."

"Of that you are certain?"

"The priests of Amun have already told him that he must not lay with any woman that is married to another, otherwise it would contaminate his *ka*. Your father would not dare defy their foretelling of a bad omen."

"And what of Iset?"

"Let us worry about Sitamun first and Iset later. If you lay with Sitamun and then we make the announcement of your marriage. That should be enough to forestall your father about thinking upon any of his other daughters."

"Very well mother, do what you must. It is not as if you have ever given me much choice in my life."

"Resent me all you want my son, but one day you will see that I do care about you."

"I pray that day comes in this lifetime," Thutmoses commented somewhat cynically.

CHAPTER SIX

Eleazar's thoughts became totally focused on the staff of Moses. "Is it true? Did you feel the power when you held the staff, Father? The young priest grew excited about the prospect that one day he may carry the staff.

"The staff is not what is important," Aaron criticized his son. "I told you that story so that you would see the path your uncle had to undertake to finally arrive at his true destiny. When he returned to me in Onu after his stay in Thebes, I knew then that he had become a different man. He had been changed. The events of those sixteen months that he was away changed him forever."

"How so father? Was it because he found the staff?"

"Enough with the staff! If you must know, it did have power but I never got the chance to wield it. Perhaps not in the sense that you perceive power but in a way that others react to the staff when they saw him carrying it. But the staff was not in Thebes and that is not what influenced him to become a changed man. The man that returned to Onu was more intense, bitter and far more connected to his Khabru heritage than I ever thought was possible."

"Why, what happened?"

"Some of it I know, but much of it I must surmise. I think that for the first time he was directly touched by the ghost of his grandfather Yuyu. Events took place exactly as Yuyu had predicted and this fact frightened Moses because he knew then that his destiny was already inscribed in the book of life."

"You mean he discovered that he too was a prophet of God?"

"No, I mean that he discovered that he, himself was not a god. The mythos of being more than human was shattered. All the false pretences, two thousand years of the history of lies within Pharaoh's house were destroyed during his visit to Thebes. That part of him that may have still tied him to the old beliefs of the Mitzri were decimated by a single stroke."

"So tell me what happened," Eleazar urged his father.

"Patience, I'm getting to it."

"Did Yahvu speak to him at that time?" Eleazar searched for an explanation.

"Not Yahvu," Aaron shook his head. "Fate spoke!"

1372 BCE

Not everything in Malkata was considered to be bad by Thutmoses. The cascading pools were a favourite diversion for spending his leisurely time. Water was channelled through a series of clay pipes into the first pool, which then overflowed into the next and the next, each pool successively lower than the last until it fed back into the Nile through a return pipe. The system was designed so that the water was always being freshly replaced while the series of screens ensured the wildlife of the Nile stayed in the river where it belonged. Every night before he made his initial journey to Onu, Thutmoses would swim the pools until he became exhausted and would then easily fall asleep after returning to his room. Today had proven itself to be most stressful and if ever he needed to find that point of exhaustion in order to sleep, then tonight was it. Past sunset, no one else ever came to the pools and he never had to worry about privacy, the servants having returned to their quarters hours ago. Having removed his loin cloth, he enjoyed the feeling of the cool water making contact with every part of his body. This was his private world, where he had the luxury to escape the trappings of royalty and pretend he was a million miles away from Thebes.

Approaching the pools from the gardens, Sitamun let the sheer linen gown slip from her shoulders and fall silently to the ground. Dipping her toe into the water she reflexively pulled it out, chattering her teeth in a manner suggesting the water was too cold for her liking. Upon hearing the noise, Thutmoses stopped his swim, stood and turned to see his sister standing there, the fading light of the evening passing through the window and surrounding her with a glimmering halo. Gazing across the pool, Thutmoses noticed for the first time what everyone had seen a long time ago, Sitamun was not just beautiful but it was a beauty that was so beguiling that it appeared surreal, as if she truly was a goddess. Her skin was copper coloured but in the reflection of the pool, it shimmered and glowed like polished onyx.

It was as if he was viewing his sister for the first time. Her pear-shaped breasts hung enticingly above her narrow waist and curvaceous hips. The intoxicating lure of her body drew him across the pool before he even realized he was walking towards her. Like a true goddess her breasts were surmounted by upturned nipples, standing proudly with the firmness of youth. Her stomach was flat, her legs long like those of a gazelle, while every muscle of her body was well defined like those of a prowling lioness.

"I must be in the presence of the goddess Hathor," the Prince mused.

"She has the head of a cow!" Sitamun feigned insult. "How could you compare me to her brother?"

"When not in her cow form she is the most beautiful of the goddesses," he defended himself.

Sitamun thought about it for a moment. "Hmmm...I will let you get away with it this time Muti," using his childhood name which quickly brought back treasured childhood memories.

Sitting down at the edge of the pool, she lowered herself slowly into the water and walked towards Thutmoses, who had now come half way across to meet her.

As soon as they were within a few feet of each other, Moses reached out to embrace his sister. "I have missed you very much sister." He meant it sincerely. Only Sitamun had been there for him while growing up in the Royal Pleasure Palace. She knew how much he hated being there, and she took every opportunity to comfort him and assure him that one day they could return to Memphis. He appreciated all the time they had spent together but in his heart, though he knew not why, for some reason he knew he'd never be returning to Memphis.

"It has been a long time, brother." Her voice was soft and lilting, each word so light that they practically floated on air.

"Yes it has sister. Too long perhaps. I'm sorry I left you all alone here for so many years."

"You should be Muti." she scolded. "Father has become even more uncontrollable after you left. Everyone in the household fears him. His moods swing like a pendulum and he will unleash his fury against anyone that stands in his way."

"I never thought about how he would vent his anger on the rest of you. I only cared about myself and moving as far away as possible from this place. Can you forgive me?"

"It was not your duty to take care of the rest of us Muti. Remember, I knew how unhappy you were living here in father's house. How many times did you cry on my shoulder Muti after father had you beaten?

"You were always there for me sister. I always felt as if you were the older sibling because I always looked up to you. Whenever I needed you, you were there for me. So how can I feel conflicted about helping you, the one time that you truly need me? I feel so ashamed." Hanging his head, Thutmoses admitted his guilt.

Placing her hand under his chin, she lifted his head and stared directly into his eyes. "There should be no guilt, Muti. It is what we were meant to do. We have been paired," she cooed. "From our childhood it was always intended that we should be mated. It is time we fulfil our obligations."

Thutmoses was still hesitant. "It's just that Yuyu said it was wrong for us to pair within the family. He believed it led us down a path of death. It was god's way of punishing us through the death of our children. How could you bear to see their deaths should grandfather should be right? It will tear us apart!" he warned her.

"I am yours," she insisted. "I have always been yours. You always knew that. Don't push me away now because it will not save us. It will only force me into father's bed. That would be a horror to me and I could not bear it. I don't think you could bear it either. I think I would rather seek death than let it happen."

Grasping her shoulders, Thutmoses shook his sister forcibly. "Don't say that! Don't you ever say that! If you should take your life then the best part of me would die as well. I will not have you talk like that."

"Then you must do something about it Muti," she instructed as the back of her hand softly brushing against his cheek.

Thutmoses slowly nodded his head. "Yuyu was wrong. He thought the worst thing that could happen was for us to watch our babies die. But thinking about you pinned beneath father while he forces his member inside you that would even be worse for me. I would want to die with you."

"If we do this Muti, then neither of us has to die. We will have one another to live for. And look, father married his aunt's child and you are fine, I am fine, and our sisters our well too. Grandfather Yuyu did not know everything," she explained her reasoning to support their union.

"But there were many more that Mother told me about that never survived. We were the few lucky ones."

"Then let us use that luck to make our world better. One day we will rule this land and we can make it a better place for everyone. If that is not sufficient to take solace then what more can I offer to convince you this is right?" Having made her point she led him slowly to the side, pushing back against the tiled surface in order to hop out onto the reed mats that edged the pool. Thutmoses did the same and for several minutes they simply let the water drip from their prone bodies while they stared into each other's eyes without saying a word.

Sensing the time was right, Sitamun rolled on to her side and reached over to take his hand into her own. "Your touch is still as soft as I remember it. I have missed the simple feelings I have every time we held hands."

"What we are about to do sister goes far beyond holding hands. I don't want to hurt you."

"Poor Muti, always worried about someone else. You cannot hurt me. This is what men and women do and Mother has taught me how to serve and please."

"But it might hurt," he insisted. "You still have your maidenhood?"

"Of course I do!" she snapped. "How can you ask such a thing?"

"I only meant that because you have your maidenhood this will cause you pain"

"You are such a fool Muti," she responded while placing her hands behind his head and lowering his mouth against her breasts. She held him tightly, seeking an unspoken promise that he would never leave her again.

He noticed for the first time how cool and smooth her skin was, smelling faintly from the essence of persimmons. The slight breeze blew her satin hair across his face, and its touch reminded him of the Nile mist. His eyes wandered across the landscape of her breasts until apexing beneath the caps of brown turgid nipples. The pace of his breathing became more rapid and heavier as he felt the hunger rising within. He could not explain how it happened but he felt as if he was no longer in control of his actions. The scent and sight of his sister had seized possession of his every thought and function, like a puppet on a string and Sitamun was the puppeteer.

His tongue lolled across the top of her breasts, tasting the saline sweetness that made her skin shimmer. His right hand automatically began searching the cleft between her legs, fingers probing into an unexplored world. With each flick of his finger, Sitamun released a muffled moan, rocking her hips slightly so that his fingers journeyed deeper within her. At the same time, she began kneading his manhood until it became turgid and erect, each of his grunts emitted as a short puff of breath against her shell-like ears.

Sitamun broke away from his embrace, returning to a position of laying on her back. She then spread her legs invitingly, while flexing her thigh muscles so that Thutmoses could sense the tautness of every sinew. His eyes became focused clearly on the path leading to the tight patch of curled auburn hairs. Kneeling between her legs, he grabbed the chiselled cheeks of her hips, elevating them slightly above the ground while he slid Sitamun forcefully towards him so that the shaft of his penis disappeared behind the spread lips of the outer labia until he felt himself hitting against an almost impenetrable wall. Thrusting her hips back and forth, he pushed forward, persevering until he felt the thin membrane rupture, allowing him to fall forward as he slipped through into a cavernous place. Sitamun tried to stifle her whimper by biting her lip but it was not enough to silence the pain. Her muffled scream in turn only excited Thutmoses further and in response he began thrusting harder and faster.

The sound of their hips slapping together drowned any other sounds of discomfort she may have uttered, only to find that her own cravings were now vanquishing any sensations other than intense pleasure. Moans of ecstasy replaced any that originated from her loss of virginity and without fully understanding what was happening to her body she began to shake and quiver under Thutmoses' continuous thrusting. Only when she felt her back arch involuntarily did she finally understand what her mother meant when she said to those whom the gods favour, they had blessed women with an indescribable gift from their heavenly realm. The grunts and groans emanating from Thutmoses only made her utter similar sounds in an echo of an unintelligible language of which she had no control. Squeals of delight, incomprehensible words, and shivers that ran from the top of her head to the tip of her toes. These were things that Tiye had forgotten to tell her about and she found herself craving them more and more, reaching behind Thutmoses, in order to grab his buttocks and force him deeper inside.

Over and over her body grew taut, then relaxed, tensed then released, as each sensation built like a crescendo extending towards its climax, at which time Thutmoses poured his seed inside her, roaring like a lion as he did so. Having spent himself, the prince collapsed upon his sister, his head flopping onto her left shoulder, his breath panting, his heart pounding inside his chest, exhausted and unable to remember why he had been so resistant to his mother's insistence that he lay with Sitamun.

"Thank you brother. I know this is not what you wanted but if it helps you in any way then you should know that it is all that I wanted. And even if you can't love me in the way that I love you, and should you ever want to take another as your Great

Wife, I will not hold it against you, for my love for you is enough to compensate for whatever shortfall I might have in your eyesight."

"You know sister, sometimes your tongue wags too much," and he silenced her with a sudden kiss of such intensity that the pleasure and longing caused her to start crying. "Was it that bad that you now cry?" he asked after releasing the pressure on her lips.

"You love me too," she blurted through her tears of joy.

"Of course I do," he wiped away her tears with his fingertips. "I love you so much that even if this is wrong, I will find some way to make it right."

"We are married now Muti," she said excitedly.

Thinking about it, Thutmoses knew that she was right. By the laws of Kemet if a man brought a woman to his home and made love to her then it was considered to be a conjugal knot. Technically it was their father's home but the law did not differentiate. "Yes, you are my wife and I am your husband. We will let Father and Mother know in the morning."

"Thank you Muti," she whispered before bursting into tears again.

"What is it now Sitamun?"

This time it was a flood of relief that released the tearful onslaught. "You have saved me Muti," she spoke through the river of tears. "Now Father will never touch me. Even if you were to go away, he will not lay with a woman that is another man's wife. It is not permitted for Pharaoh to do so. I have been freed by you tonight."

"Enough talk about Father," Thutmoses silenced her by forcing his lips against hers in another never-ending kiss.

CHAPTER SEVEN

"I did not know he had a third wife?" Eleazar looked surprised by the revelation made by his father.

"Not a third wife; that was his first wife. The first woman he ever loved and as much as he knew the love between a brother and sister should never manifest itself physically, he still yielded to the old beliefs. There are many things you do not know about Moses," Aaron forewarned. "His first wife is the least of the secrets that you don't know about and by the time I finish telling you all these things it will be far from the last."

"Why did he not go back for her?" Eleazar wanted to know more.

"He did," his father replied but by then the circumstances were out of his control. You just have to be patient and I will explain everything in its proper time."

"It is hard to be patient, while sitting on a mountain top and knowing that my father is dying at the same time."

"Why? Are you concerned for me or worried that I will not finish telling you everything before I die? Perhaps then you should have your men carry me back down," Aaron suggested. "After all, we are only up here because you were in such a haste to separate me from the people so as to conceal where you were going to let my flesh rot and my bones get picked clean by the birds."

"You know that is not true father. We all agreed it was the proper time."

"Yes, you're right, it's not true. More likely that I get eaten by the wolves before the birds peck my flesh apart. But the truth is that you're just going to let me die up here all alone and that is a fate that no man should be faced with when he edges towards the abyss. It is the time when one should be surrounded by family, not abandoned."

"We have made it comfortable for you up here father. And you know as Yahvu's servant He will not let you suffer, so you cannot play on the guilt to make us change our decision."

"Then you better be prepared to be up here a long time my son," Aaron warned. "It is a long story and I have a feeling that Yahvu will not take me until I have finished it. He wants you to share the burden of carrying the truth that you can never reveal to anyone except your own sons when it comes your time to depart this world. Yahvu will not let us ever forget our birth as a nation. Thousands of years from now we will still be retelling the story of our exodus from Mitzrayim, it just may not include these particular stories that I'm telling you now."

1370 BCE

"Where are we going Thutmoses?"

"South my brother, and you are coming with me as my advisor."

"You only returned to Onu a fortnight ago and already you want to leave," Ahrown attempted to persuade Thutmoses to delay making any hasty decisions.

"And what are you suggesting? That I have not taken the proper time to grieve? That I have not asked the gods to relieve me of the pain that crushes my heart? Is there something you wish to say more?" Thutmoses face contorted into a mask of pure fury.

"Something like that Thutmoses. My only concern is that you should give time for all the scars to heal before you dive headlong into another quest. It is practical advice meant for your benefit. You know I am only concerned for your well-being."

The anger fled from his body almost as quickly as it had flared and Thutmoses rested a reassuring hand upon Ahrown's shoulder. "I know brother that you are only expressing what you think is in my best interest. I appreciate your concern. But right now the inactivity is the worst thing I can do for myself. I cannot erase the image of my wife holding the deformed body of our child in her hands. The sheer horror that I saw in her eyes. The blame with which she looked at me as if somehow I had cursed our offspring by my earlier talk of such matters."

"It was not your fault Thutmoses," Ahrown tried to console him. "We cannot be held responsible for the will of the gods. These are matters beyond our control."

Withdrawing his arm, the anger flared instantaneously for a second time and Thutmoses unleashed his pent up anguish. "The gods had nothing to do with it! It was the bad blood of mixing seed too familiar to the womb, exactly as my grandfather had described it. He warned me from his tomb and I did not listen and now my wife suffers, disconsolate, abandoned and afraid, yet she cannot even stand the sight of me in the same room. Yuyu knew, and I should have known better as well. I let myself be lulled into a false illusion that somehow I could be happy in my father's palace. I had my beautiful wife and for one of the rare times in my life I had a father rather than a Pharaoh at least trying to exhibit some pride in his only son. I allowed love to rule over logic and in so doing I abandoned the journey my grandfather had set me upon and now I and the one I love have suffered dearly for my failure to protect her. I could have stopped it! I should have listened! It is my fault!"

Ahrown tried again to calm his Prince down. "I don't believe it was ever Yuyu's intent to bring this suffering upon you and your house. Nor is it wrong to love. Life is not always as simple as being wrong and right. It is far more complicated than that."

"Of course it is that simple!" Thutmoses snapped back. "He was warning me about what would happen and I chose not to listen. I brought this curse upon myself. Eventually Sitamun will forgive me but the truth is that I do not know if I can ever forgive myself. As long as I am consumed by this guilt, I cannot bear to have her look at me the way she did. It crushed me inside. Do you understand?"

"So exactly how is running away going to earn you her forgiveness," Ahrown challenged him to provide an adequate answer. "You should return to your wife. You should try to make this better between you both."

"What do you know of women?" Thutmoses sneered. "Have you ever loved one so much that you feel every pain that they suffer? A feeling every time that you are apart your heart beats like a hollow drum because of the emptiness? That whenever you close your eyes, her face is all that you can see? Tell me priest, do you know what that is like?"

Shaking his head with eyes downcast, he responded. "No, I cannot."

"Now imagine that world being ripped away from you because the woman that is the sole cause of all those feelings runs away whenever you step into a room. And at night you cannot sleep because all you can hear are her wails and anguish as she relives the nightmare of that moment of birthing a monster over and over again. No-o-o, I am not running away. I'm running to a place where I can make others suffer for the pain I currently feel. Do you understand?"

"I understand that you want to rant and rave against the world. You want to extinguish the anguish in your soul by beating it from the flesh of someone else. But that is not going to stop Sitamun's suffering nor your own. Whatever relief you think you might find by going on this journey, it will only be temporary at best. You still must return to this world and face the reality."

"Get in the cart," Thutmoses ordered him.

"I don't think this is a good idea," Ahrown tried to restrain him from making a rash judgment.

"Get in the cart!"

"This could be a big mistake."

"Get in the cart or I will throw you into it!

"But my duties. Who will take care of my responsibilities in the Temple while I'm gone?" Ahrown fretted about his absence from the temple more than the realization that he still had no idea where they were heading. "What about my belongings?"

"Don't worry," the Prince responded. "Othni has already packed everything you will need. Just climb in the cart and get ready to go."

"Go where? You still haven't told me."

"Sure I did. South! We are going to war."

"War? I can't go to war. I'm a priest. What do I know of battle?" Ahrown laughed nervously, not knowing if the prince was merely teasing but somehow the emotionless mask that Thutmoses wore told him that he was deadly serious.

"I have studied with you for three years, Ahrown. How many books on the art of warfare have we discussed in that time? A hundred? Perhaps more? You, my brother are an authority on warfare though you don't even realize it."

"I think you exaggerate my value, Thutmoses." Ahrown trembled, his body shaking at the thought of going to war. Under the emotional strain the prince was under, the thought that this was an attempt at intentional suicide on the part of Thutmoses was highly likely.

"Nonsense! I know an expert when I see one. You knew practically every one of the strategies and achieved outcomes before we even finished each papyrus. Every manoeuvre, every command that the great Thutmoses gave, you already knew by heart. That makes you an expert and that is why it is essential that I have you on this mission with me."

"Perhaps we should reconsider," the priest was hesitant. "We aren't exactly professional soldiers. Furthermore, these Nubian uprisings are always happening. They flare up, we send in one or two battalions, they scatter and that's the end of it. By the time we get there, it will probably be all over." Ahrown thought that perhaps a more rational approach would persuade the prince to change his mind.

"They say this revolt will last for some time. So no worries, we will have plenty to still vanquish when we arrive."

This did not feel right. Every bone in his body screamed that something was wrong. "Does Pharaoh know about your going to war?" Ahrown inquired.

"It is with his blessing that we are going on this mission. As the Crown Prince of Kemet, I will be riding in Pharaoh's war chariot but it will be my uncle Chenetothes that will be the supreme commander."

"Why would your father be so eager to send you onto the battlefield, especially so soon after the loss of your child? Think about that. Something doesn't feel right." Now his inner senses were really troubling him. It was very unlike Amenhotep to entrust Thutmoses with any regal responsibility, especially one that could garner him honour and accolades.

At the mention of his dead son, Thutmoses became enraged a third time. "For exactly that reason," he shouted at Ahrown. "His House of Rejoicing has become a House of Sorrow. He cannot suffer it any longer and he presumes the separation from my wife will give her a chance for the healing to take place. And perhaps her worry about my taking part in the conflict will restore her concern and feelings for me. For once in my life, I have to actually agree with my father. Now get in the cart!"

Ahrown still couldn't let the conversation end without having the last few comments. "Do you really believe that slaughtering a few Nubians will make all your anguish disappear?"

"No, but it certainly will help," Thutmoses stated emphatically.

"I can tell you now that it won't. We cannot mask our pain. We cannot hide our pain. The only way you can deal with your pain is learning to master it and then use it."

"Enough talk, get in the cart!"

"If this talk offends you, then so be it. I tell you this not as your tutor, not as the *Wab-tepi*, but as your friend and brother."

"So what would you have me do then brother? Should I stoke the fire of the memory of my deformed son until my nightmares become my reality? Is that what I should do? Let myself be consumed by the darkness while I go out of my mind?"

"Of course not, but if you can take your anger and your rage and turn it into a force with which you can do something good, then you will find peace," Ahrown advised. "Right now it is a weakness that blinds you."

"I am channelling it into a force for good," Thutmoses asserted. "I am going to channel my rage and through it master my fighting techniques. I will take all that uncontrolled fury and turn it into a disciplined strength. And then I will take that mastery and strength and slaughter my enemies. That I can assure you will feel good!"

"You want to slash and stab in an effort to kill the pain within you and that in turn will make you careless and you cannot afford to be careless going into battle," Ahrown cautioned him.

"See," the prince turned Ahrown's own words to make his argument, "I told you that you that you had the qualities of a military strategist. I will take your advice and continue to hone my skills on the trip to Kush. Now, get in the cart. I won't ask you again. Next time I will throw you in."

"Just don't get us both killed," the priest commented in a barely audible tone.

"Remember this, at my age, my great-great grandfather was already conquering the crescent. A small rebellion in Kush should be child's play for someone with your knowledge of tactics but at least it will give us both something to cut our teeth on."

The situation of going to war was still too much for Ahrown to accept and he began pleading with the young prince. "Think about this, if your father truly wanted you to be with the army then he would have given you joint command with your uncle. But as supreme commander, Chenetothes acts as an extension of Pharaoh's own power. Any conquests, any spoils taken by your uncle belong to your father but what happens when you are present on the battlefield? Who is likely to get the credit for the victory then? Unless you're willing to remain in the shadows, this arrangement steers us towards disaster. You can see that, right?"

Ahrown's hesitation and vacillation had become intolerable to Thutmoses but this last comment struck an ill chord as he recognized the truth behind it and in so doing he vented his frustration. "Well perhaps if Pharaoh wants to claim all the victory for himself then maybe he should climb down from his golden throne and actually put himself on the battlefield where he belongs. I have no intention of concealing myself back at the camp while the army engages in battle. My father is too busy constructing artificial lakes so he can boast about sailing his boats from the Nile straight to his palace in Malkata without his feet having to touch a grain of sand. That's not the legacy I want for myself. I want more! I need more! I need to fight! Are you ready to get into the cart now?" Thutmoses began moving toward his companion prepared to seize Ahrown and forcibly toss him into the back of the wagon.

Stepping backwards to avoid being manhandled, Ahrown held up his index finger. "On one condition," the priest tried to negotiate an outcome that would reduce the threat that Thutmoses' appearance on the battlefield might raise with Pharaoh, as well as reduce the current tensions between them.

"And what would that be exactly?" the Prince inquired.

"That you let me send a letter to your father explaining that while serving in the Temple, we received a prophecy from Amun-Ra, his namesake, in which the great god commanded that the presence of the blood of Pharaoh must be actively involved on the battle field in order to ensure a victory against Kush. In that way, should there be those praising you for the victory, then you can always claim you were merely the shell or *khat* hosting the *khu* and *ka* of Pharaoh."

Thutmoses couldn't stop himself from laughing. "You priests are so full of crap but you know what, it just might work. And if writing this makes you happy enough to get in the cart then go ahead. What else do you intend to say in this letter?"

"I'd address it in the following manner so that he's bound to forgive you for any transgression…"

"Go ahead."

"Praise be to Amun-Ra, bull of Onu, the beloved one who rules over us all. Hail to you Amun-Ra, *Neb* of the thrones of the two lands, who rules in Thebes, great art thou in heaven known as *artu*, wisest on earth, lord of all that exists. The nations fall at your feet, knowing that you are lord, mighty in appearance, *pursofe* and merciful to whom all the gods give praise. Lord who gives his hands to those whom he loves and hurls his foes into the flames. He who hears the prayers of prisoners and rescues the frightened from their oppressors. The usual addresses, and so on. Then I mention the prophecy and describe how we will perform a ritual to infuse your *khat* with his soul and spirit so that there is no doubt that you are merely a puppet and Great Pharaoh is pulling all the strings."

"That is so much crap," Thutmoses continued to laugh, "He will probably believe every word. So go ahead, write your letter. Now, get in the cart."

Having at least won this small concession, Ahrown climbed into the back of the cart where the others were waiting impatiently all this time. "Find a seat anywhere," Othni instructed, while taking his seat comfortably on the driver's bench alongside Thutmoses. Before Ahrown even had an opportunity to squeeze into a spot between the other passengers, there was a sudden jerk on the reins and the twin horse drawn cart jolted along the uneven road heading north.

Leaning back on his seat, Thutmoses turned his head so that he could speak directly to Ahrown. "Allow me to introduce you to everyone. That one," he pointed to a handsome young copper skinned man with a broad round face," is Hur, my weapons instructor. Though you may have thought I never properly trained while we were together, I had already been taught the use of the sword and spear by that man; one of the best. And that smiling gentleman to your left is my cousin Machir, son of my uncle Anen. He was captain of Yuyu's personal guard and has fought on the previous campaign against the Nubians. Youngest man ever to rise to the level of captain. He knows the terrain, their tactics and still retains his connections in the southern lands. Of course you may already know that grumpy looking soldier on your right. Caleb has been awarded the gold necklace twice for his campaigns against the desert tribes, and through marriage to a rich older widow, is now Othni's uncle. Isn't that right, Othni?"

"He's younger than me," Othni grumbled. "How can he be my uncle?"

"Because he's smarter than you," Thutmoses was quick to reply. "He married for money instead of love." Ahrown picked up on the stinging rebuke that the prince was making regarding his own marriage, but the others simply laughed thinking it was merely a joke at Othni's expense.

"A pleasure to meet all of you," Ahrown responded, "But can someone tell me why we are heading north if Kush lies to the south? The harness rattled to the steady beat of the hooves as they churned the dried dirt road beneath them.

"There is someone in Goshen that I promised my mother we would add to our little party," Thutmoses replied. "Apparently he's a relative on my mother's side and he was entrusted with certain information by Yuyu that he can only impart to me on conclusion of our victory. Another twist in my grandfather's little game."

"Sounds very mysterious," Ahrown checked the expressions of the other companions to see if they thought it sounded as strange to them as it did to him. "Is that all you know about him? Does he have a name?"

"Zelophedad."

"A Khabru name, how strange indeed!"

"If you knew my mother, then you don't ask questions, you just do as she says. You don't really have a choice. So that's what I'm doing," Thutmoses explained. No sooner had he finished his explanation, then a clump of earth flew through the air and struck the side of the prince's seat before exploding in a shower of dirt.

Before the prince could even react, Caleb had leapt from the moving wagon and was forcing his way through the throng of people that had gathered to view the procession. Within minutes he resurfaced from the crowd of faces towing a young lad by the scruff of his tunic. "So my Prince, what shall we do the little ruffian?" Meanwhile the crowd closed in around the wagon to see what the disturbance was all about.

Stepping down from the carriage seat, Thutmoses stood in front of the boy while the urchin continued to struggle to break free of Caleb's grip. He towered over the lad menacingly as he weighed out the options. "Now we all know the crime for striking a member of the *savov* family," Thutmoses spoke loud enough for everyone in the crowd to hear. "Is there anyone here that will speak on behalf of the boy?" His question was met with silence, most too afraid to become involved lest they too become a target of the prince's vengeance. "I guess if I'm going to pass sentence, I better know whose life is in my hands. Wouldn't you agree boy?"

"Get your stinking hands off me?" the boy screamed at his captor.

"He is a feisty one my Prince," Caleb laughed.

"How old are you boy?" Thutmoses asked.

"Let me go," the child tried to kick Caleb in the shins but the swing of his foot missed by a huge distance.

"Simple question boy, how old are you?"

"I don't know," the lad answered, still swinging and kicking in an attempt to break free up to the point he became exhausted and stopped his resistance.

"He's one of the street children that steals from our stalls," someone obscure in the crowd shouted. "Take him away." Others in the crowd took up the chant to take the boy into custody.

"Doesn't appear like the people here like you very much," Thutmoses noted.

"Doesn't matter," the boy said defiantly. "I don't like them either."

"Someone must care for you. Where are you parents?" Thutmoses asked.

"They're dead," he exclaimed, "You killed them!"

"I killed your parents?" Thutmoses asked blankly, having no knowledge of what the child spoke about. "I think you are wrong," Thutmoses advised the child. "Whatever has become of your parents, I have had nothing to do with their disappearance. Does anybody know this boy's parents?" Thutmoses asked the people gathered around their wagon.

The question was met with nothing but silence.

"So how is it that I supposedly killed your parents?"

Whereas most children would have broken into tears by this time, the boy still remained defiant, jutting out his chin as he challenged the prince to deny what he was about to say. "The soldiers came and took most of the men and women in my village away to work in the quarries and the mud pits. They took my parents and they never came back."

Looking at his companions, Thutmoses didn't know how to assess this statement for its credibility. "Any of you know anything about this," he asked them.

"I heard there was a policy of forced labour for those that couldn't pay a head tax," Hur commented. "But I never knew if Pharaoh went ahead with it or not. I guess maybe he did."

"Is that true boy, is that what happened," the Prince asked him.

"They were taken away," the boy responded. "That is all I know. Your men took them."

"Definitely not my men," Thutmoses denied the accusation. "But nevertheless, men I am still responsible for. I am sorry. I hope you can forgive me for what others have done to you."

There was the sound of shock and awe as the people in the crowd overheard the Crown Prince apologizing to a street urchin. It was followed by a steady hum of the people mumbling something indistinct amongst themselves but on occasion Thutmoses could distinguish the name of Yuyu being bantered about.

Kneeling down, Thutmoses reduced his imposing size so that he was level with the boy. "Do you have a name?"

"Why should you care if I do," the boy remained defiant.

"Because I like to know the names of my friends," Thutmoses stated with a broad smile on his face. It was enough to finally win over the boy's trust.

"Hoshea," the boy replied.

"Well Hoshea, if I ask my man Caleb to release his grip on you, do you promise not to run away so we can talk some more."

The boy nodded his agreement.

"Good. So I need to know more about you if I'm going to help you find out what happened to your parents. So you are Hoshea son of whom?" the Prince asked for more details.

"I don't know," Hoshea replied. I was too young to know my parents name when they were taken away.

"Ah, then you are like Ra," Thutmoses placed his hand on the boy's shoulder. "You know Ra had no knowledge of his parents either. He emerged from the primordial shapeless ocean. Do you know what the name for that ocean was?"

The boy shook his head.

"She was called Nun. I think it may have been your mother as well. So from now on you will be known to all as Hoshea son of Nun. Is that name acceptable to you?"

The boy nodded his agreement once more and the slightest sliver of a smile split his lips.

"Do you have anyone taking care of you, Hosea? Family or friends?"

Once again the boy shook his head.

"Everyone listen," Thutmoses shouted to the crowd. "I agree that the boy should be taken away so that his thievery does not afflict your stalls any longer. Hoshea son of Nun will no longer be a problem for you. He is now a ward of the crown and my personal responsibility. You can all disperse now, the matter is settled."

As the throng broke up and returned to their previous tasks, the Prince explained to his companions that Hoshea would be joining their party. Ahrown was first to provide his approval. Knowing how much the prince was still grieving internally over the loss of his son, he could only think that the sudden appearance of Hoshea into Thutmoses' life was a gift sent directly by the gods. Everyone in the wagon was in agreement.

"So Hoshea, do you think you can hurl a stone as well as you can throw a piece of dirt?

Proud of his accuracy, Hoshea answered, "I can hit anything I aim at."

"Do you think you can do it on a battlefield? I need a valet in my camp. Keeping my sword and spear polished takes a lot of care and dedication. But I'll need you to be able to defend the camp as well. Does Hosea son of Nun think he's ready to be a soldier?"

Older far beyond the handful of years since he had been born, Hoshea puffed out his chest and stated without any hesitation, "I am ready."

1367 BCE

Kemet was ancient but the lands at the Nile's headwaters, they were beyond recorded time. Many a Kemtu traveller had claimed to have visited Kush, but very few had ever been further than the fifth cataract, still situated in Nubia. The Kemtu governors ruled from the city of Napata but buried deep in the desert, far beyond the highlands that was where the heart of Kush lay. That is where its fabled city of Saba was situated, high on a hill, surrounded by impenetrable walls that were themselves surrounded by the branches of the Nile, Astapus and Astaboras Rivers. Beyond the rivers were foreboding wastelands, where the sandstorms could be equally as dangerous as any spear bearing soldier, and where the living inhabitants of the desert resented any intruder and would protect their homes with every fang, stinger and claw in their possession.

"This is madness," Thutmoses told his companions. "Chenetothes will get all of us killed if he keeps pursuing this strategy. We have been playing this cat and mouse game for almost three years now, except we're the mice and they're the cats."

"Be careful Thutmoses, just outside this room there may be those that are the ears of Chenetothes," Ahrown whispered nervously.

"Let them listen," Thutmoses raised his voice. "Let them report. It is now three years since we started this campaign and here we are, sitting in Napata, stuck at the fourth cataract, while the Nubians and their Kush allies hold on to Bagrawiyah. How can anyone call this a success?"

When they had first began the move upriver, there was a rousing farewell from the populace lining the western bank of the Nile as the eight hundred barges cast off their tie lines and over ten thousand oars made a thunderous splash as they sliced into the water. The smiling faces of the soldiers beneath their leather helmets, their laughter as they began this great adventure, electrified the communities they passed from the time they left Karnak. The populaces of those small river towns would sail their little rafts as close as possible to the military barges, in order to sell their variety of wares, and fruits. The atmosphere was more carnival-like than the austere expectation of an army about to stare death in the face. But that was three years ago. Most of the villages they passed along the way had remained untouched by the rebellious Nubian forces, but that did not stop Chenetothes from giving the order to tie up and go ashore, where the men would partake in the ribaldry offered by the wine and beer sellers and the dancing girls that saw the profit in entertaining so many soldiers. Even the local priests seized the opportunity to sell their vast variety of sacred trinkets, offering protection of the various gods, and for those that were willing to pay even more, a prophecy of their future success and return safely home.

Further up river they arrived at those cities where the Nubian forces had for a period of time subjugated the inhabitants, but the resistance they offered was minimal as their leader Kikiani was more than satisfied to sound the retreat and take his forces further south, retreating city by city, leaving behind a ravaged and raped populace.

To the young Prince, this was madness, claiming success in battle for cities that had essentially been abandoned. They had saved no one, many of the people that had suffered under the occupation of the Nubians were unable to ever recover their lost livelihoods or the sanity of their daughters that had served the whims of the occupying forces.

It was time for Machir to intervene and see if he could get the young prince to calm down. "It is the same old strategy and Chenetothes is doing what every general has done before him. Take back our cities and then advance and take Nubia city by city. So in his reports to Pharaoh everything is under control. We took Semna, then Soleb, then Kerma and now Napata, the way it's done every time."

"And that's just it," Thutmoses rebuked his cousin. "We do it time after time, over and over again. We launch a campaign and take back our cities. Then they wait a few years, rise up in rebellion and take those cities back. Then we do it all over again. Do you really think that is winning?"

"It's not about winning. Caleb don't you agree? It's just about maintaining the status quo. The same with the desert tribes. You beat them down so they stay quiet and as soon as they raise their heads up, you beat them down again."

"That is an absolutely ridiculous way to fight a war," the Prince criticized the strategies exercised by his companions. "If you don't fight with the purpose of annihilating your enemies then you might as well not fight at all. The purpose of war must be to end war, not maintain a perpetual cycle of battles and skirmishes that never end."

"A world without war," Caleb laughed. "That's a good one. Never going to happen."

"Certainly not if we keep fighting this way," Thutmoses hammered his fist on the table. "It's time to do something different and end this once and for all!"

"Remember Thutmoses," Ahrown cautioned him, "We can't make Chenetothes look impotent, otherwise he will report back to you father that you're attempting to seize control of the army. So whatever you have in mind, you have to make it look like it was Chenetothes' plan."

"He has no plan," Thutmoses wanted to scream. "What does he do now? He sends a boat with scouts past the fourth cataract and when he doesn't hear back from them in a week, then he sends another boat. How many times has he done that now? Five? Six maybe? They're not sending back messages because they're all dead. Anyone with any sense could figure that out. At this rate we will be sitting in Napata another few years before we actually make the next move. Between here and Bagrawiyah the river bends twice. All the Nubians are going to do is conceal squads of archers on the banks at each bend and then pick off our boats at their leisure and there's nothing our men can do to stop it. This is absolute madness!"

"What are you proposing then," Caleb asked.

"We don't do what they expect us to do for starters," Thutmoses advised. "Like us, they're so used to fighting this war with the same strategies over and over again that they can't think of us doing anything but sailing up the Nile. So we don't do what they expect, we come at them over a land route."

"The terrain is treacherous," the others argued back in unison. "It's virtually impossible to cross with an army."

"If the Nubians can figure out a way to move through the deserts, then surely we can do the same. There has to be trails that they're using. They must know where every watering hole is located. We just have to find them."

"It's all stone or shifting dunes and that means no chariots," Machir wasn't liking the idea. "Our chariots are our major advantage over their units. Without them we are on equal footing but they have the advantage of knowing this land."

"But we will have the advantage of surprise," Thutmoses countered. "The city as I understand it was built in two halves. One being Meroe the other is Shendi. If we invade through the corridor dividing Bagrawiyah into those two halves then we have effectively cut their defending garrison in half. They will be in total disarray, unable to reform their units. We cut them down as easy as straw."

"And how do we ensure that we can achieve the element of surprise. They will see us coming out of the desert before we ever reach the corridor," Caleb argued.

"Not if they're still busy watching the river for more of our boats trying to make it through the fourth and fifth cataracts," the Prince advised them. "They won't anticipate a two pronged attack."

"We'd have to convince the General to coordinate his sailing times on the river to correspond with us reaching our targets over land," Ahrown thought. "It would be possible if he was to agree. But getting him to agree is not going to be easy."

"I've given thought on that already," Thutmoses indicated that he was already thinking well ahead on that issue. "From past sailing logs and the maps we have, we know that to go by the river to Bagrawiyah will take approximately forty days to cover the three hundred and fifty mile length of the route. Going straight through the desert is a shorter distance by almost half, but will probably also take us from thirty to forty days on foot as long as we find a guide to show us the watering holes. Does that not sound like a plan to everyone?"

"They collectively nodded in agreement.

"You still haven't said how you are going to obtain Chenetothes approval of the plan," Ahrown raised the challenge once again.

Thutmoses rubbed his chin as he contemplated the matter. "My uncle is a practical man. As long as he can receive all the credit and glory for the plan and taking the city then he won't really care where the strategy originated. And should it fail and we end up all dead or captured then I will give him a good story to feed back to Thebes that frees him of any responsibility. The only objection I can see him raising is when I suggest he forgets about sending out these scout ships and instead sails the entire flotilla up the river immediately. He may see it as too great a risk but as long as we can find a way to reduce his losses then he should find it acceptable. Are we all in agreement that I discuss this with Chenetothes?"

"How many men are we talking about?" Caleb wanted to know.

"What do you think Ahrown?" Thutmoses turned the question towards the priest.

"It won't be easy moving across those dunes," Ahrown contemplated. "Too many men and it will slow us down too much. Too few and we won't have enough to take the city. Plus being away from the river we'll have to ensure we have enough supplies, especially water but at the same time not too great a load that it slows us down even more."

"So how many are you thinking we will need? Give me a figure."

"Assuming there will be some resistance once we have entered the city, then a thousand well trained infantry would be sufficient," Ahrown calculated.

"A thousand!" Caleb was shocked by Ahrown's calculation. "The city has tens of thousands living there. We will be like lambs heading to the slaughter."

"Forty or fifty thousand citizens in Bagrawiyah represent no threat, Ahrown, rebutted. "What's left in the city are women, children and the elderly. All the men will be miles away watching the river for signs of our flotilla. Almost all the warriors will be absent. Whatever remains behind as their garrison will probably number only a few hundred."

"And if you're wrong?" Caleb was still not satisfied by the response.

"Then pray that Chenetothes arrives in time to rescue us," Ahrown answered calmly. "If the timing is correct, and Chenetothes arrives shortly after we've entered the city then we should be able to trap the Nubians between the north wall of Meroe and Chenetothes army," he surmised.

"I think this is utter madness," Caleb objected. "We need a full contingent. At least five thousand men," He argued.

"What do you think Machir," Thutmoses directed the question to his cousin.

"Taking away our chariots means we've already lost our speed and manoeuvrability. The only way we gain some of that back is by attacking with an elite small force. As soon as you have a full contingent you not only slow down the ability of the army to attack and move in rough terrain but you decrease our ability to communicate effectively, not to mention any watering holes probably couldn't handle an overly large force. I have to agree with the priest. Go in light, go in fast and take the city before the people can even react."

"Othni?"

"I'm here to serve you my Prince. You tell me to go in with ten men and I will do it. It doesn't matter to me. I will fight to the end."

"Hur, what are you thinking."

Flicking his sword back and forth between his hands, Hur stopped and planted its point firmly in the ground. "There's a lot of men I trained out there. I know who has the set of skills to pull this mission off. Let me select the thousand and they will be the fighting equivalent of the five thousand."

"Anything to add Zelophedad?" the Prince asked the last member of the group who was sitting in the shadows of the room, keeping his own counsel.

"Not my area of expertise on which to comment," he responded while tugging on his thick black beard.

"Exactly what is your area of expertise?" Caleb wanted to know.

At that moment Thutmoses interjected himself before Zelophedad had the opportunity to make a response. "I ask all of you to have trust in me and believe me when I say Zelophedad's purpose is highly significant but for now it must remain secret. I apologize if some of you don't like this answer but please trust me. In time it will all be made clear to you. But for now we have to focus on this strategy to take Bagrawiyah, which means we have to present a detailed plan to the general and we have to do it quickly.

"I can prepare the plan within a few hours," Ahrown offered.

"That's good," Thutmoses commended him. "As soon as you're finished we can take it into general headquarters and present it to him. Agreed?"

All the companions within the room provided their consent. They would win or die but this is what they were going to do.

That night when they set off to the general's quarters was no different from the previous nights in Napata. With hardly a trace of a breeze the air was hot and humid. The sounds of soldiers around every corner fornicating with the city maidens ricocheted through the stillness, only to be buried beneath the boisterous songs of drunken infantry men stumbling through the streets as they desperately tried to find their way back to the barracks. A flock of young girls ran by feigning terror with their mock screams and exaggerated arm movements, followed closely by a group of chariot drivers laughing excitedly as they hunted their prey. Thutmoses ignored all the events circulating around him, numbed by these same scenes which have been played over and over again day after day, month after month.

"If just once," he turned to comment to his companions, "the Nubians decided to attack us here in Napata, they would wipe our entire army out in a single night. The only good graces we have is that they are probably just as inebriated and just as preoccupied with raping the girls of whatever city they're hiding in now. The state of our army is truly embarrassing and I can't send a word about it back to Thebes, otherwise my father will think I'm trying to usurp command of the army for myself."

"Certainly not the way it was back when I was fighting," Machir agreed.

Slapping Machir on the back, Caleb added his voice, "Same for me brother. This army is ripe for the pickings. We have to thank the gods that all our enemies are in an even worse state than us, or else Kemet would be overrun by the foreign armies once again."

Stopping in front of the general's quarters, Thutmoses instructed his companions to wait outside until he summoned them. He wanted the opportunity to speak alone with the General Chenetothes off the record in order to gauge how responsive to their plan the general might be. Knocking on the door, the general's orderly, Hophni, opened it a crack but as soon as he recognized the Crown Prince, he ushered him inside. Chenetothes was sitting glumly at his dinner table, cup of beer in hand while the shadows cast from the oil lamp skipped across the room in an eerie and somewhat frightening dance. As soon as he saw Thutmoses he rose to greet the prince and pointed for him to sit down opposite at the table. For a while the two men sat there in silence each one waiting for the other to begin the conversation.

Finally, Chenetothes broke the silence. "What is the occasion nephew that you picked tonight to finally see your old uncle? I can only surmise there is something serious that you wish to talk about."

"Can't a man wish to be in the company of family without having a purpose?" Thutmoses inquired.

"Certainly not in this family," the grizzled general joked. "You know what my half-brother said to me the night your mother convinced him to have me take you with on this campaign?"

Thutmoses shook his head not knowing what had been exchanged between them but what he did notice was how his uncle could never refer to his father by name or even by title. It was always my half-brother, a sad fact he concluded of being born to Nefertari but Thutmoses-Menkheperure had been convinced by Yuyu to select the son of the lesser wife Mutemwiya to become the next Pharaoh. While he waited for his uncle to respond to his own question he momentarily pondered Yuyu's possible justification for pushing Pharaoh Thutmoses in that direction and for the first time he realized it was in order for his grandfather's prophecies to be fulfilled. All his predictions counted on his daughter's son being the son of a pharaoh. Yuyu had been moving them all like pieces on a senet board.

"So he said to me," the General continued, "try not to let the young fool get killed while he's there, but if he does, so be it, it is the will of the gods."

Thutmoses actually chuckled upon hearing that. "Yes, that sounds like my father."

Upon hearing that, his uncle poured another mug of beer and handed it to his nephew. "A toast! To family!" he shouted.

"To family," Thutmoses responded. "Think of all the things we could do without them!" the prince finished the toast and they both laughed heartily.

"You certainly won't end up a broken old warhorse sitting on the border of nowhere with no past behind you and no future in front of you."

"So why did you do it uncle?"

"Do you really think I had a choice?" he scoffed. "Think about it nephew. If I had chosen the life of a courtesan, had a wife, had sons of my own, how long do you think any of them would have survived with my half-brother sitting on the throne?" His voice softened as his thoughts sailed back to a time when he actually did think of marriage and raising a family. The innermost flicker of his memories reflecting on the image of a woman that he once loved.

Thutmoses gazed upon the sad and lonely expression that crossed Chenetothes' face. "Surely you don't think my father would have slain your family?"

"As sure as I'm sitting here this sad specimen of a man you see before you. The day you began to defy your father was the day I celebrated the fact that finally he would be paid back for the wrongs he had done to me. The only thing worse than having no son is having a son that totally disrespects you."

"So glad that I didn't disappoint you uncle," Thutmoses raised his cup in salutation and the two men clinked mugs and laughed once again.

"Over the years I began to think of you as my own son," he continued and the prince was beginning to wonder how much beer had his uncle already consumed that night. "I know it sounds ridiculous but I looked forward to the day we would be marching on a campaign together. Had I had my own son, I could think of nothing that would make me prouder but alas, you are the son of a *Neter-Nesew* and I must do everything I can to protect you and keep you out of harm's way."

"But what if I don't want you to protect me uncle? What if I agree with my father and say, 'roll the dice' let the gods decide if I should live or die? What would you say then?"

"I would say that you are a bigger fool than I am Thutmoses. No man should ever wish to die before his time. It is our hope and duty to live!"

"But does the dove wish to live its life in a gilded cage?" the Prince questioned, "or does it dream about soaring through the skies like the eagle? As you mentioned, I have disappointed my father from the day I could speak, why should I suddenly stop now?"

"And what of your beautiful wife, do you forget you have a responsibility to her as well?" Chenetothes challenged the prince.

"The day our child died was the day she forgot our marriage and forgot about me," Thutmoses answered.

"That is not true," the old general scolded him. "Do you know how many soldiers are told by their wives how much they hate them when they tell their wives they're off to war? But I know for a fact that every day their husbands are away on the battlefield, they grieve and worry that they may never be coming back to them. Take it from this old fool, love is often expressed through anger but it only means that once the anger fades, the love is even more intense."

"I did not know you were such a philosopher, uncle."

"When your life is spent sitting in occupied villages or at the war front, then you find you have a lot of time to philosophize. So why don't you go back to your wife young Prince? Take her in your arms and recapture the true meaning of life. In the three years we have been on the march you have never asked me for leave. Don't you think it is time to do so?"

"Not yet uncle," Thutmoses replied. "That is part of the reason I am here tonight."

"Go on," Chenetothes encouraged him.

"What if we actually try to win this war and put an end to the fighting with the Nubians once and for all?" Thutmoses put the mug of beer to his lips and gazed over the rim to watch the general's reaction.

"You're saying that I haven't been trying to win this war," he was perturbed by the accusation. "That would suggest that I have been behaving thus far treasonously. Are you certain you want to make that statement?"

The Prince watched as his uncle's grip on the mug tightened until his knuckles turned white. "Not at all," he reassured him. "I'm saying your campaign has been as successful as all those that preceded you. We will chase them back past the fifth cataract, force them to return to their city of Bagrawiyah, take hundreds of prisoners back to Thebes and we probably earn you another gold chain."

"Sounds like you are going to say but…"

"As I said, this scenario has been repeated over and over again but I believe we can break the circle once and for all. I believe we can wipe out the threat of the Nubians forever."

"That's crazy," his uncle insisted. "No one has ever taken their ancient capital. It is too well fortified and has the river on two sides. Chariots in case you haven't noticed don't move over water very well," his uncle laughed at his own joke.

"That's why we can't let them return to their city and fortify themselves," the prince argued. "We need to take the city before they can return and lock them out, so we can crush them between our forces and their own walls."

"Can't be done," Chenetothes insisted. "As soon as they see our barges turning beyond the fifth cataract they'd be racing back to their city like a herd of gazelles. That is what they have done every time. They are smart enough not to challenge us on the flats beyond the cataract."

"If I can show you a way it can be done, will you consider it? The prince laid the temptation before the old general.

Rocking back and forth, Chenetothes wrestled with the idea. "Total annihilation you say?"

"Yes!"

"You mean this old warhorse could finally hang up his sword for good?"

"Yes!"

"There is the down side though. If you get killed, I'm certain my half-brother will have me executed just to show the people how remorseful he is over the loss of his son."

"That is why we will stage it as a rescue mission. I will disappear with my forces under the cover of night and in the morning you will make the announcement that the Nubians raided the section of the town we inhabit and carried myself away as a prisoner. As the Crown Prince, you had no other choice but to launch a rescue mission. If I should be killed during the battle, it can always be said that I tried to escape my captors and they slew me before you had a chance to perform the rescue."

"Sounds plausible," the general mused. "It will take a lot of careful planning."

"Does that mean you agree?"

"How could I refuse my favourite nephew," the general raised his mug to which Thutmoses immediately responded by raising his and clinking bottoms.

"Good, because I have my cohort of planners waiting outside. Time to let them in," the Prince smiled broadly as they cemented their pact.

CHAPTER EIGHT

"We all knew about the wars in Nubia," Eleazar commented, "but no one ever talks about it. We just know that somehow Moses was there but it is as if you elders purposely shy away from talking about it."

"We can't because we need everyone to understand that our exodus from Egypt was by Yahvu's command, not because of events predicated by our activities in the southern wars."

"What are you saying father; that God didn't bring us out of Mitzrayim?"

"I'm saying that if we talked too much about the Nubian campaign then others might give it too much credence and not realize that every event in our lives had already been predetermined by God. We needed people to see the miracles that Yahvu performed, not the achievements of Thutmoses, the Prince of Mitzrayim."

Eleazar scratched his head as he thought about his father's words, "And that is why you have always downplayed Tharbis's role in our community. She is a constant reminder of Moses's other life as a Prince of Mitzrayim."

"So you understand now?" Aaron questioned his son.

"No, not at all. I think it was a wrong decision. By seeing how Moses sacrificed his entire life, the power he possessed, having the world at his feet in order to pursue God is a greater message than what you've peddled to the people now." Eleazar was angry that the elders dared to control how the people should think and feel. "By presenting him as a man that had already lost everything, then he had nothing to lose. His calling by God didn't start with a burning bush, it began when he sat with Aunt Miriam in the Temple of Isis because that's the moment he knew Yahvu had other plans for him."

"The elders did not see it that way," Aaron attempted to persuade his son otherwise but the effort to do so brought about another coughing fit.

Eleazar sat and waited for the coughing to subside, not bothering to offer his father any water this time. "You claim I do not really know the man who is my uncle because of all these stories you finally are willing to tell while you sit waiting at death's doorway. I think you're wrong. I think I know him very well and whether he's this young man riding in the chariot of a Pharaoh, or an elderly prophet leading us through the desert, your stories only confirm that he is the man he has always been; a leader, a believer, and a man that willingly sacrificed everything to follow the voice of God!"

1367 BCE

The battle for Bagrawiyah had to be postponed until the month of Tybi, when the rains finally stopped and the banks of the Nile finally dried sufficiently that they could be traversed safely. There was much Thutmoses and his companions had to learn about the deserts that covered much of southern Kush. Fortunately, there were always those enterprising inhabitants within Napata that were not ashamed to betray their fellow Nubians if the price was right. Finding a pair of expert guides proved not to be a difficult task as first thought.

One of the first lessons Thutmoses and his companions learned was that amongst the inhabitants there was a distinction between the land referred to as Nubia and the one they called Kush. Whereas the Kemtu referred to everything south of their country as being Kush, in the southern lands they made a distinction. Those lands west and north of the fourth cataract were Nubia but everything else which lay to the east and south of the cataract was Kush. And as Thutmoses came to learn, it was not a geographical separation but a political one. Whereas, it was his own people, the Kemtu, that had made Napata the nominal capital of Kush, as far as the natives were concerned Bagrawiyah was the capital of Kush but Napata was only the capital of that part they referred to as Nubia. But then there was the city of Saba, a city so ancient that the belief was that the gods had built it themselves. It ruled no lands directly, though both Nubia and Kush paid it homage and filled its treasury. In governance, the city was a state unto itself and as long as anyone could remember it had no king, ruled only by a queen, generation after generation. The male offspring of the royal house were given the title of Queen's Consort, and they had the choice of remaining in the city in an administrative role, or they could leave the city and fight for the right to rule over the city of Bagrawiyah but they were never to call themselves King of Saba.

The current war against the Nubians arose because their latest commander dared to break that rule. Kikiani was not content to be known as anything less than King of Kush. But to earn this title he knew that he had to take back all the lands of Kush and Nubia from the Kemtu and only then could he challenge the Queen sitting in Saba. He would return victorious, claim the right of the Queen's hand in marriage, and then he would have himself declared as King even if he had to tear down the walls of Saba to do so. No leader of the Nubians had ever succeeded in the past because each time the Pharaoh of Kemet sent his armies south and defeated the rebels long before they ever had the opportunity to attack the legendary capital. But this time Kikiani swore would be different. This time he would employ a different tactic from all of his predecessors. Rather than face Pharaoh's armies on an open battle field he would draw them further and further away from their home base, stretching their supply lines until they could not be maintained, eventually exhausting the supply of fresh food and water, and then he would strike with the full force of his armies against a weakened adversary. Thus far the Kemtu forces had been playing into his hands, advancing city by city, town by town and village by village, each time finding that the Nubian rebels had fled further south. All along the way, Nubian raiding parties would dart out from the hillsides and the rock formations that lined the banks of the river, fire there volley of arrows and then disappear as quickly as they had appeared.

Kikiani recognized that he was winning this war of attrition. His scouts would report back daily that the Egyptian soldiers were becoming more unruly with each base camp they set up along the way. He heard the stories of the almost continuous drinking their soldiers did each night, the repeated raping of the village girls, and the numerous fights that erupted between their different squads and battalions. The streets smelled from sex, vomit and blood and the thought of his adversaries succumbing to the debauchery made Kikiani smile as his goal neared fruition.

The latest reports indicated that General Chenetothes was preparing to move his troops out of Napata and begin sailing further up river as one massive flotilla. Kikiani had already anticipated that this would be the General's next move having lost several scouting crews already. By sailing the hundreds of ships up river all at once he would be thinking that he could overwhelm the Nubian forces and that would permit the majority of his barges to break through the bottleneck unscathed. As far as Kikiani was concerned it was a desperate move that had little chance of success because he would place enough archers, slingers and spear throwers on the riverbanks to pick off the Egyptian soldiers one by one as they sailed by.

The march of the army began in earnest, first heading northeast from Napata towards the fourth cataract. Charioteers and elite infantry traversed the hardened mud along the banks that remained behind after the summer flooding of the river, while the supplies along with the officers, administrators, archers, and general foot soldiers sailed on the barges rowed by the hundreds of slaves. The relentless sun and flying clouds of insects tortured slave and officer alike the further they sailed up river. Upon reaching the fourth cataract all the barges had to be pulled ashore before the foaming, churning waters concealing the deadly rocky outcroppings could shred the keels of their reed-bundled boats. Unloading the skiffs of all their supplies, then raising both containers and barges onto their shoulders, the slaves struggled to move their heavy loads beyond the treacherous rapids before they could set them down and prepare to return them to the river to continue the voyage southward. It was arduous, merciless labour adding days to the overall march which already felt like an eternity. Delays were common and the cloudless skies made it possible for the scorching rays of the sun to ignite the short tempers and increasingly frayed nerves of the soldiers. Many began to grumble as to why they had to leave Napata in the first place. In the past, reclaiming that city and reinstating the governor in the province was enough to conclude the war and return home. None of the generals of previous expeditions bothered to march on Bagrawiyah and talk circulated amongst the men of the futile effort to rescue a prince who was probably dead already. When the discourse between the troops became too heated and some started shouting out short bitter retorts, then Chenetothes would make an example of the trouble makers, having them whipped publicly, then staked to the earth to be seen by every one of the soldiers as they marched by.

Past the fourth cataract began the long stretch northeast, reaching an apex where the river would take a sudden turn southeast towards the fifth cataract. It was the bend that worried Chenetothes the most. The sloping terrain on either bank of the river with its heavy growth of brush provided the ideal conditions to set a trap. The hundred miles from there to the fifth cataract would be perilous and fraught with danger. But the general had prepared a plan well in advance during his discussion with Thutmoses' advisors. Those barges carrying the archers were moved to the front lines of the flotilla. Each barge had at its centre a cauldron filled with pitch and a second one filled with the dried twigs and plants that they scrounged from the soils on either side of the river to serve as fire pots. At the bend the river was only a fifth of mile wide, necessitating that the boats sailed close to the river banks, thus making them susceptible to any arrows and missiles fired from the surrounding hills. The small, narrow tracts of land on either side of the river would force those marching on foot and accompanying the chariots to fully expose themselves to any enemy concealed above, who could easily roll down boulders, thereby crushing the unsuspecting Kemtu forces. In the narrow confines of these tracts, all it would take was for one pair of horses to panic and the ensuing chaos would send the army into disarray. If such a scenario was to be avoided, then Chenetothes knew that the hills and crevices on each river bank had to be cleared of the enemy, well before his men were within easy reach of their missiles. When Ahrown described the strategy it made perfect sense but now visualizing the shape of the terrain Chenetothes smiled to himself recognizing that the task might prove easier than he first thought. The steepness of the banks could very easily prove to be the seal of doom for the Nubians.

As soon as the boats approached the bend, the order was given to ignite the fire pots. Once at the bend another order was given for the archers to dip their arrows into the pitch. Before turning the bend the next order was shouted to touch the arrows to the fire pots thereby setting the pitch ablaze. Turning the bend the last command was given to let hell rain down upon the terrain on either bank. The dry shrubs and straw-like growth covering the hills burst into flames as soon as they were in contact with the fire arrows. Another volley of arrows lit the next tier of scrub that provided excellent incendiary material upon the hills and the archers continued to launch projectiles until their surroundings were nothing but two great walls of fire between which they safely passed both by land and by river. The screams emerging from the crevices and concealed areas cut into the sides of the hills let Chenetothes know that his strategy had been successful. By firmly entrenching themselves on the slopes, the enemy had left themselves no escape route. He would never know the exact number of the enemy he slaughtered that day but he was comforted in knowing that the rest of the journey towards the fifth cataract would prove to be relatively uneventful.

Kikiani had not anticipated the magnitude of the setback. In absolute panic, his men that he had seeded into the hills were now scattered to the four winds. He knew that many if not most of the survivors would never return to the base camp, instead fleeing to their villages and their homes, choosing not to participate in a fight that no longer concerned them. He knew there would be only one last opportunity to restore the advantage he had maintained for the past four years over his enemies and that meant bringing the entire strength of his forces to bear at the fifth cataract. It would require raising a pitched battle on the open field and success rested entirely on stopping the Egyptians from deploying their chariots. If they failed to do so, then the lightning charge of those chariots for which the Egyptians were renowned would put a swift end to the war.

An ill wind blew over the desert, whipping clouds of sand that tore into any exposed flesh. Despite the searing heat, Thutmoses ordered his forces to wrap their skin with any extra clothing they might have in their packs. Time would not afford them the opportunity to set up tents and take shelter; they had to press on. "Damn this wind," the Prince shouted in an attempt to be heard above the howling sandstorm. "How much longer do we have to deal with this?" The question was directed at the pair of guides hired in Napata.

"Only a little storm," came the reply from one. "It will die out soon, my Lord."

The black skinned Nubian didn't seem to mind it at all, merely wearing a head scarf and leaving the rest of his body exposed to the swirling grit that stung like a thousand needles.

"The gods have cursed this land, I'm certain of it," Ahrown grumbled as he pulled his head scarf down over his eyes.

Moving headlong into the wind slowed the elite force accompanying the Prince even more than the sliding sands of the dunes they crossed for days, had already done. They'd be lucky to have marched five miles by the end of this day and Thutmoses and his companions were growing concerned that they may not make it to Bagrawiyah within the forty days maximum they planned and coordinated with General Chenetothes. The concern was enough to keep them pressing forward, struggling against the wind and the merciless sandstorm as best as they could.

Hur had kept his promise and the men that he selected to comprise the thousand-man force were the best of the Kemtu army. Because they were so far from the supply trains the battalion had to bring their armour packed on their backs along with their shields but not a single soldier complained about the sixty pound burden he had to carry. Every man was armed with a sword and a half dozen javelins. They were all war hardened and tested veterans of the border skirmishes with the Bedouin. Lifelong professional soldiers that chose this life willingly and would stand with their Prince to the very end.

During the day they baked under the desert sun and at night they huddled together to find any warmth available beneath the cold waxing moon. They ate the dried bread and figs they kept in the pouches hanging from their corded belts, drinking only occasionally from the goat skin canteens swinging around their necks. Reflecting upon their situation Thutmoses recognized that in this barren desolate inhospitable land, the gods of Kemet had no power just as Ahrown had forewarned. If they were going to survive the endless monotony of this forsaken wasteland, they were going to need to do it on their own. There'd be no divine intervention to save them this time.

Before the sun set each third evening, his guides new instinctively how to find the few watering holes that were bored into this land of nothingness. The Prince was amazed at how they could distinguish the most insignificant landmarks in order to identify the precise locations. Without his guides he knew they would have never made it this far and in appreciation of their efforts he spent each evening forging an ever closer relationship with these two coal-black men from Kush. As they set in their pole-framed cloth shelters around the remaining embers of dying fires that fought off the encroaching darkness, he would ask an ever increasing number of questions regarding their land, their customs and their history.

"I can't understand how your people could ever live in this land?" Thutmoses asked, the question being rhetorical and not expecting an answer but such nuances were lost on their guides, as one of the Nubians chose to answer.

"We don't Lord, that is why we covet your lands and constantly expand our country northward. We want to live in your Egypt where the living is soft." Thinking he had made a good joke, the guide smiled broadly as he laughed, showing off his set of perfectly white teeth in the reflection of the dying flames.

"Why do you insist on using the Hyksos terminology for my land? We are Kemtu, men of the black lands, not these Egyptians you refer to."

"You are the people that break open your dead and then wrap them in linen bandages," the Nubian replied, "*ua-geb-ptah*. No one else is like you, Egyptian."

"I know what the word means," Thutmoses replied, "I just don't understand why you continue to call us by it when you know we are Kemtu."

"It bothers you then, Egyptian?"

"Yes," the prince replied.

"Now you know why we call you that." Both Nubians laughed at their explanation but Thutmoses merely brushed it aside.

"Yet here you both are, guiding a Kemtu Prince through the desert while your king tries to expand your kingdom to the land to the north for your people. Does that not bother you in some way?"

"You are mistaken my Lord. Firstly, he is not our king. The Kush have no king. We have never had a king! He has broken our sacred laws and that is why so many of us have chosen not to stand with him. If he had the support of all of Kush then we would have been fighting in numbers too great for even the Egyptians to withstand. This land is vast. Our people number like the stars in the heavens." Saying that he pointed towards the night sky with its celestial river of stars that circled overhead.

"Then praise Amun that was not the case," Thutmoses responded. "But tell me, if he is not your king then why do so many still fight for him?

"Know that the majority he reigns over are Nubians. But look at us Lord. Our noses are straight, not broad. Our foreheads are high and our faces are long. We are Kush and we are not the same. For thousands of years we have traded with those across the Narrow Sea and they intermarried with us until we became a different race from the Nubians. There are few of the Kush in his army but they are not many."

"Yes, I can see that now," Thutmoses acknowledged that they did look different. "But they say this Kikiani is from Kush and is King of Kush. That seems to contradict what you say."

"No Lord, not at all," the other guide responded. "Even amongst the Nubians there are those that want change, especially those that want what Saba has but because they are not of the Kush people that cannot partake in the wealth of Saba."

"What does Saba have that they can't receive in Bagrawiyah?" By this time the Prince could see very little difference between any of the cities they had already occupied in Nubia. "One day I will have to visit this Saba for myself."

Both of the guides began to laugh as soon as Thutmoses said he would visit. "No my Lord," they were quick to reject the Prince's notion of entering their mysterious capital city. "No one visits Saba unless they are invited to Saba."

"And who invites these guests to Saba," Thutmoses was very curious as to how the city had not been at least scouted in the past by any Kemtu spies. "Any time a delegation from Saba met with the Kemtu it was either the case that they arrived in the city of Pharaoh or else the ambassadors met in Napata. In all the documents he had reviewed in both Onu and Behbeit-el-Hagar, he could not remember a single reference describing the interior of the city of Saba.

"Entry is only upon the Queen's invitation. The only foreigners within the city are traders from across the Narrow Sea and even they can only remain within the city with an issued permit from the Queen for a limited time."

"Are you saying that not even the Crown Prince of Kemet could enter the city unless the Queen gives her permission?" Thutmoses was quite intrigued by this revelation which sounded like a deliberate challenge to his authority.

"Not even the Queen's brother is permitted entry which is one of the reasons Kikiani is attempting his revolt. If he can defeat Pharaoh's armies, he will get all the tribes of the Nubians under his control as well as many of the Kush. He will then demand entry or take the city by force."

All of the Prince's companions looked surprised. "He's the Queen's brother?" Thutmoses was astonished to hear this particular piece of information. No one had ever mentioned it prior. Looking at the faces of his cadre of advisors and offices he searched for anyone that may have known this. "How is it that none of us could not have known this? This information changes everything. I need this Kikiani alive."

"There is no way we can inform General Chenetothes before they engage in battle," Machir advised.

"Then it's up to us to ensure that as soon as we take the city we then pull Kikiani into the city and keep him from getting killed. I think I know a way to ensure that this war ends once and for all at Bagrawiyah."

"We will do what we can," Machir could not guarantee anything further.

Turning back to his guides, Thutmoses pushed them for more information. "The part about his uniting all the tribes in order to take Saba after he supposedly defeats us has been explained to me in the past but you are the first to tell me he's the Queen's brother. So why can't he simply return to the city and be welcomed as their King, especially since he is one of their royals? That's what I don't understand."

Both of the guides looked at each other as if to suggest the Prince was not very well informed about the politics of the region. "Because it's the law," one of them replied.

"Fine, it's the law," Thutmoses agreed with them, "but exactly what does the law say about royal brothers? Clarify it for me."

"He can't return because he's intact," the one Kush guide attempted to explain it simply. "He made that choice when he turned thirteen."

"Oh, I see," Thutmoses digested what he had said. "If I stay in the city, then I'm neutered but if I leave the city I get to keep my testicles. Is that what you're telling me?"

Both of the guides nodded in affirmation.

"So how exactly does this queen or any queen have children if her brothers are all eunuchs? Can't really fulfil the role of being the Queen's consorts, can they?"

Again the two guides turned to face each other and talked between themselves.

"He doesn't understand," the first commented.

"No, he doesn't understand it at all," replied the other.

"So why doesn't one of you explain it to me," Thutmoses was growing impatient.

"They are merely given the title of Queen's consort but not because they have actually performed any act of procreation with the Queen," replied the first guide.

"Heavens no!" the other guide emphasized. "As her administrators and advisors, they are her chief counsel but they are all castrated at their thirteenth birthday before they ever have a chance to lay with the queen."

"But," the other guide interrupted, "if they refuse to accept their castration willingly then they are shut out from the city and they must learn to survive on their own never to return to Saba."

The Prince reviewed their comments, rolling over the statements in his mind. "I can appreciate why Kikiani might be a little upset," Thutmoses laughed but the jest was lost on his two guides. "Any way, how does the Queen have any children then?"

"Only the queen knows," came the reply. "Some say she selects the strongest and most handsome man in the city,"

"I even heard that the chief god Atum descends from Jebel Barkal and ravishes the Queen one night a year to gift her with his children."

"The uneducated masses say she always sleeps with one of the foreign merchants that she allowed into the city," replied the other, "but that is used as an insult."

"Surely, at some point there is some man in the city that goes around boasting that he slept with the queen. I can't believe there's a man in the world that wouldn't say something while sitting and drinking in a tavern." The Prince was awed that these offspring would appear out of nowhere and no one would be the wiser as to who the father might be.

"No, never," the one guide was shocked by Thutmoses' insistence that there would be men in the city boasting about their night with the queen.

The other was more reserved in his reaction. "Though I still choose to believe the children come from Atum, I have heard it said that if there should be a lucky man that is chosen to impregnate the Queen, then he is slain as a religious sacrifice the next morning to ensure that the conception has taken place."

"Lucky man indeed," Thutmoses shook his head. "Everyone get some sleep. We have a long march tomorrow to make up for the time lost today."

It was the middle of the month of Mechu when Thutmoses and his men finally reached the border of the desert. Between the fifth and the sixth cataract the landscape began to change dramatically. For five weeks the elite force had seen nothing but rolling dunes and sun-seared rock formations. Any vegetation was scarce as hen's teeth and was highly prized for its value to light a fire each night. The only time they saw green plants were within the thin circles of life surrounding the wells that the two from Kush were able to guide them to. Now suddenly they were marching across little clumps of dry grass and the occasional tree stood proudly alone, declaring itself to be a survivor. The days seemed incrementally cooler and the nights were definitely warmer. In the distance they could see swarms of birds flying in circles and herds of gazelles running away long before they ever approached. The winds would blow from the south, carrying with them the sweet taste of moisture on the tip of the tongue. Their guides indicated that they must move directly west in order to meet the Nile at a place known as Sabaluka-pluton. There they would find themselves above the sixth cataract, where the water pooled over a shallow stretch and they could cross safely, simply by walking across the river. From there they would turn northward and cover the fifty miles to Bagrawiyah, striking quickly while the populace all were preoccupied looking in the other direction.

Four days later Thutmoses and his men found themselves staring at the cities of Meroe and Shendi from a position tucked safely behind a series of low hills. The corridor between the two cities was clearly visible, appearing to be used mainly as a gate for moving livestock into the cities. A single guard performed sentry duty but his attention tended to be preoccupied with watching the women passing through the gateway more than looking for intruders. Likely the result of centuries of no one ever attacking the city of Bagrawiyah thus causing anyone on guard duty to grow complacent over time.

There was a constant stream of cattle, sheep and goats being herded through the corridor and Thutmoses perceived this as a gift from the heavens that they never could have foreseen. Assembling his council and officers around him, he described his plan for taking the city. They would wait until one of the farmers was shepherding a large flock of sheep into the corridor. When over half of the sheep were past the gateway between the two cities that's when they would rush the gap, screaming as loud as they could. Thutmoses described how this would panic the sheep, which would then charge in every direction, scattering people, knocking over vendor stalls and creating massive chaos in both cities, so much so that the people will pay less attention to their assault on the city until it was too late. The soldiers were to split in half, five hundred to follow himself and Machir into the city of Meroe and the other five hundred to follow Caleb and Hur into Shendi. Once each party had reached the midpoint of the cities, they would split again, Thutmoses and Caleb taking the eastern half of their respective cities, while Machir and Hur claimed the western halves. Whatever resistance they met was to be killed immediately, no prisoners.

Having finished the details of his plan, Thutmoses asked if there were any questions. Ahrown had one. "What about me?

"You my brother will stay here and safeguard Hoshea. I'll leave Othni to watch over you both. Zelophedad will stay with you as well. Should we fail in taking the city of Bagrawiyah, then our two guides here will get you all out of harm's way and back safely with the army as soon as it approaches. You can let my uncle know what we did and perhaps that will provide him with an opportunity to devise a better plan than mine."

"Officers, have the men count off from one to four. All the ones and twos will follow me into Meroe. All the threes and fours will go with Caleb into Shendi. Once the order is given within each city to split in half, then the twos and fours will go east while ones and threes go west. Pass the word."

The instructions went quickly down the line until every soldier had his orders. The plan was simple enough and now all they had to do was wait for that ideal flock and then watch for a wave of the Prince's hand to approve the launch of their attack. They didn't have to wait long. Approaching the twin cities from the south several shepherds with their dogs were moving a flock of about three hundred head towards the corridor.

Getting ready to give the signal, the plan suddenly went awry as a second guard appeared at the entrance of the corridor. It must have been time to change sentries, but rather than perform the exchange quickly the two guards began to discuss matters of the day and neither seemed in a particular hurry to move on. "Damn!" Thutmoses exclaimed. "I wasn't too worried about the sleepy one; we could have cut him down before he even lifted his head to see us approaching, but now that there are two, there's a chance at least one of them will be able to sound a general alarm. We're going to have to wait."

"But this is our best chance," Caleb disagreed. "Look at the size of the flock! We haven't had any others pass by that were even close to this size. It's perfect for causing the confusion we need. I think we should still go. All we need are two javelins to hit the targets quickly and just look at them, they're pretty big targets."

"But if they don't go down immediately," Thutmoses objected, "We might find ourselves in a fight with the full garrison if they have time to assemble. I don't like it."

Before they had the opportunity to discuss it further, Hoshea interjected with a parting comment of "Leave it to me!" Thutmoses was about to respond but Hoshea was up on his feet and darting towards the gateway before a single word could roll off his tongue.

"The little fool is going to get us all killed," Caleb grumbled. "We better attack immediately before all hell breaks loose."

Placing a hand on Caleb's chest, Thutmoses urged him to sit back down. "No, wait. Let's see what he does."

"This is insane," Caleb continued his rant. "We're placing our lives in the hands of a child."

"A very clever child that managed to survive on the streets for years," the Prince added. "We wait!"

Charging directly towards the larger of the two guards, a tall black man almost four cubits in height with a massive frame bulging with rippling muscles, Hoshea palmed the small blade he kept hidden beneath his tunic. By the time either guard noticed the boy running alongside the flock of sheep, he was practically upon them. A quick slice of his right hand and the target of his attack fell neatly into the outstretched palm of his left without ever breaking stride. With a laugh and a taunt of "Got you!" Hoshea raced through the gateway and into the twin cities.

"That brat stole my purse," the guard shouted to his companion. "After him, we must get it back!" Without any hesitation, both guards tore off down the corridor in pursuit of Hoshea who zig-zagged between the animals and the merchants, continually increasing the distance between himself and his pursuers.

"Smart boy," Thutmoses uttered to himself, as he started to count back from ten. Reaching zero he raised his hand and waved it in a circular motion and the race began. Charging from their concealed positions behind the hills, the battalion of elite soldiers covered the quarter mile in just over a minute. With swords in one hand and javelins readied in the other, they released their blood curdling screams as soon they were within fifty yards of the last stragglers of the herd. A volley of javelins flew through the air and within seconds all of the shepherds lay dead on the ground. The horrific noise of their war cries sent the sheep into a frantic stampede, running in every direction, exactly as Thutmoses had predicted. Bowling over people, tables and anything else that was in their way, the thunderous bleating of the sheep was even louder than the shouts and screams from the soldiers but not even close to the screams and shouts emerging from the mix of angry or frightened denizens of the city.

With the sheep charging through the streets and the alleyways, the city garrisons didn't even look around to see what else might be happening, instead joining in the mad chase with the throngs of people trying to corral the runaway animals. By the time the guards in the elevated sentry houses noticed that their cities were being besieged it was far too late. Blowing on their rams horns the alarm went out but by then Thutmoses men were fully in control of both Meroe and Shendi, slaughtering every man from the city's garrison they chanced upon. Most of the defenders were too preoccupied wrestling with the sheep to even notice the swords swinging down upon the backs of their necks.

It only took a couple of hours to eliminate any remaining resistance in Bagrawiyah, the elite force performing clean up duty after the initial slaughter, moving from house to house to see if there were any of the city's defenders hiding in the homes or commercial buildings. Once satisfied that they had found and executed every armed threat within the twin cities, Thutmoses posted men to man the north wall of Meroe, keeping an eye out for signs of the advancing armies under Chenetothes. Orders were given to seal all the gates to both cities. There would be no one leaving or entering the city until the Prince lifted the ban. Signs were posted forbidding the people to congregate anywhere in the city and a curfew was announced that all people had to be in their homes by the ninth hour after the noon or they would be immediately executed.

That evening as they sat around the table in one of the four taverns they permitted to remain open to serve their men. All of the citizens were absent, stringently obeying the curfew. After a month in the desert, Thutmoses and his companions took a well-deserved rest and quenched an overriding appetite for beer.

"A toast!" the Prince shouted as he rose from the table. "Someone put a mug of beer in the hands of that boy," he pointed towards Hoshea sitting at the far end of the table. Six mugs immediately slapped down in front of the lad as each hoped he would select theirs to drink from. "To the hero of Bagrawiyah; to the lad who's got balls bigger than that guard he stole the purse from; to Hoshea, the man!"

"To Hoshea!" they all shouted, clinking mugs and swarming the boy to pat him on the back.

"Any thing you'd like to say?" Thutmoses asked Hoshea.

"Do I get to keep the purse?" The question was met immediately with a chorus of laughter and cheers.

"That and many more," the Prince shouted above the din. "With courage and bravery like yours, you may end up the richest man in all of Kemet."

"To Hoshea the brave," Caleb began another chorus of cheers.

Waiting for the adulation to die down, Thutmoses continued to stand in order to speak. "Taking Bagrawiyah was a tremendous accomplishment that will earn us our own pages in the royal archives. Maybe," he added, "that is if my father doesn't erase all our names and insert his instead." This too was met with laughter until everyone realized that the Prince may have been genuinely serious.

"No other armies have ever taken this city, but holding on to Bagrawiyah becomes our primary concern now," Thutmoses cautioned them. "Our sentries have still not sighted the main body of our forces under General Chenetothes. I fear that if he does not arrive soon, the citizenry of these two cities may realize that they outnumber us by over thirty to one. Odds like that give even the most cowardly of men thoughts of being heroes. We need to have plans on how to deal with the situation should it arise. I don't want us taken by surprise but we also have to worry if Kikiani in some way was able to defeat our army and Chenetothes is not coming. What will we do then? I'd rather we discuss all our options now rather than later."

Ahrown cleared his throat to speak. "I am not a military man but I do have knowledge of a similar situation taking place under the reign of Kamose."

"Your right!" Caleb shouted out, "You're not a military man. Nonetheless, I will give you some credit of knowing about tactics."

"As I was saying," Ahrown continued, ignoring the interruption, "Kamose when he began his move north against the Hyksos, he took the town of Nefrusy by wiping out the garrison but his attack northward stalled while he awaited reinforcements from his brother which failed to arrive. This was due to the Hyksos King Apophis rallying his Nubian allies to attack the Thebans from the south, requiring that his brother settle the southern front before moving northward. Being caught in Nefrusy, a hostile environment meant that Kamose had to institute drastic measures. You have to remember that the garrison he slaughtered were actually his fellow countrymen that preferred to be ruled by the Hyksos and were therefore loyal to his enemy. You can imagine that many of the townspeople felt the same way."

"Get on with it already," Caleb grumbled.

"You need the background detail," Ahrown shot back. "So to make a long story short, Kamose had his men seal the gates of the town. No one could enter and no one could leave for a very long time. In that way, the Hyksos could not sneak any spies, agitators or warriors into the town and no one from inside the town could run to the Hyksos and inform them of the size, condition and strength of Kamose's army. That bought him the time to start recruiting a new regiment from within the town. He offered any young man from amongst the civilian population the opportunity to start military training. That meant those recruits got the best of the food and drink in the town, the warmest beds, and the promise of payment from the spoils of the town and future campaigns. Thousands took up the offer and swore an oath of loyalty to their new king. You put food in their bellies and you have an army that will be loyal to the very end."

"Sounds like that strategy could work here," Thutmoses suggested.

"I hate to say it but the priest has a good idea," Caleb admitted begrudgingly.

"So how are we going to spread the word?" Hur inquired of the rest. "They'd sooner run in the other direction than talk to us."

"We post notices in all the plazas and we use our two guides to talk directly with any young men they see. Being Kush, they'll be able to achieve a lot more than we can."

"People aren't going to like the fact that we're keeping all the gates locked and refusing to let them exit the city," Machir contemplated how the townspeople might react. "When people start thinking that they're trapped animals they start getting very nervous. And nervous people become very dangerous people!"

"It might not be too difficult to convince them that it's for their own benefit," Thutmoses responded. "We tell them that there are thirty thousand crazed blood thirsty Kemtu soldiers bearing down on this city with orders to slaughter anyone they find on the roads that looks like a Nubian. We're making certain that everyone in Bagrawiyah stays safe. So what we're doing is for their benefit. They can thank us after Chenetothes arrives and they see the size of the army marshalled outside their city."

"You mean if he arrives," Caleb voiced the concern that the others were sharing.

"He will arrive," Thutmoses had no doubt. "My uncle is the best there is. In a few days he will be here. You will see. In the meantime we start doing as Ahrown suggested."

"So assuming that Chenetothes will arrive, what's our plan then?" Machir was looking ahead to the next step.

"We keep the gates closed even after his arrival," the Prince instructed. "Kikiani will have his back up against the wall. He'll think the gates will open for him but instead we raise our flags at that moment on the towers so he realizes he's trapped. He won't be able to retreat and he certainly won't be able to advance on the main body of our army. If he's smart, and I believe he is, considering he's stayed alive this long, he'll throw down his weapons and surrender. At that point we will take him into custody. I can't let him be executed and I won't let him be sent back to Thebes to perform in some ceremony showering Pharaoh in accolades for his successful conquest."

"Your father definitely isn't going to be happy with that," Othni finally spoke up. "Are you certain you want to challenge him on this?"

"Our mission is far from over gentlemen," Thutmoses advised. "I have plans for Kikiani. Big plans."

CHAPTER NINE

"You were there during the fight to take Bagrawiyah," Eleazar sounded impressed. "Moses must have had a lot of faith in you to be heeding your advice."

"He was a different man back then," Aaron rebuked his son, knowing exactly where Eleazar's comments were leading.

"Not that much different from what I can tell," his son expressed his opinion. "Seems as if you were the one that was a different man back then. Did you ever think that perhaps you were the problem, not Moses?"

Aaron reached for the stick but Eleazar had already anticipated his father's movements and kicked it away before he could reach it.

"I see that Caleb still had your measure, even back then," Eleazar taunted his father. "I think I understand it though," Eleazar tapped the tip of his index finger against his temple. "You were just a priest back then but Moses, he was far more. He was the Crown Prince of Mitzrayim. You pretty much had to do everything he said, even to the point of going off to war, and you had absolutely no choice in the matter."

"You don't know what you're talking about," Aaron sputtered, his heart pounding in his chest as his son riled him.

"Oh, but I think I do, father. As a member of the royal family, he was on a level you could never aspire to. He had power simply because of his birth right. And as you admitted, the Lebu were in their waning years, and you were witnessing the loss of any authority of an ancient family of priests that had been made irrelevant. So you had no choice but to chain yourself to him with the hope that somehow his success would turn in to your success as well. The only way you were going to gain back any power and authority was by being tightly associated with Moses. So when he led the people out of Mitzrayim that was your big chance to obtain power once again through a hereditary priesthood. Especially since Moses had absolutely no intent to institute a monarchy, so that provided you with the perfect opportunity to institute a theocracy and that's exactly what you did."

"Enough of this," Aaron shouted.

"Really father? You've had enough of being challenged by the truth? I'm only getting the truth tonight, sitting on this mountain waiting for you to die. Where was the truth the past thirty-odd years of my life? So what is this all about tonight, perhaps your own guilt? Are you feeling guilty for your resentment father? You've resented Moses so much that you have purposely erased our history to replace it with fables that you've created along with your team of scribes. The only part I don't understand is why Moses let you do the things you are doing. He had to know your intentions, they were so obvious!"

"Your uncle was far from sinless," Aaron mustered the strength to argue with his son. "He's committed sins, atrocious sins, but there was no one to hold him accountable. I was the only one that could raise an objection without fearing severe repercussions. Any resentment I might harbour has nothing to do with who he was but because of things that he did. You will see. By the time I finish telling this story, you may actually agree with me and understand why I did what I did."

1366 BCE

Everything went exactly as planned; precisely as the Prince had proposed that night along with his cadre of advisors. The moment they raised their troop's colours on the flag-masts erected on Meroe's corner towers, the remnants of Kikiani's forces lost heart and threw down their weapons. Chenetothes archers quickly advanced to the forefront of the army preparing to finish them off quickly, but at the same time Thutmoses and his men rushed out from the city, establishing a wall between Kikiani's men and the advancing Kemtu forces. General Chenetothes immediately called a halt to his march forward.

For what seemed to be an eternity, no one on either side moved a muscle. Turning to the largest of the black men wearing a prominent bonnet of assorted feathers attached to a circular band of gold that rested across his forehead and a leopard skin draped over his left shoulder, the Prince addressed him, "You must be Kikiani."

"I am," the man who was a head taller than Thutmoses responded.

"I suggest then you stay behind me if you want to stay alive," the Prince advised, while they watched to see if there was any movement from the front lines of the Kemet army.

"I don't understand," Kikiani was not sure of the prince's intentions.

"I'm going to try and keep you and your men alive but you have to tell them to remain perfectly still, say nothing and leave it to me."

The front lines of the body of the army split open and from behind the front row of archers a single chariot emerged. Rolling forward, the General's chariot driver charged towards the gates of the city, covering the half mile quickly and then pulled up directly in front of Thutmoses as he brought his team of horses to a sudden halt. Stepping down from the rear of his chariot the war-weary general opened his arms to embrace his nephew. "I see that my Prince is well, and the grace of Amun has blessed his mission to take the city."

"I see my Lord General is well and the grace of Amun blessed him with victory over his enemies," Thutmoses responded with an equivalent salutation.

"Let us finish this now, my Prince, and we send what remains of the enemy's army in ropes back to Thebes to parade before Great Pharaoh."

"I think we have to talk Uncle."

"The General hung down his head and lowered his eyes to the ground. "I was afraid of this," he muttered. "Nephew, can you not be satisfied with this great victory and let the world for once continue as it has always done without trying to change the course of history?"

"I believe we have a far greater destiny Uncle. We've been handed an opportunity to do what no other Kemtu army has ever done before. The doorway to all of Kush has been opened for us. All of its lands can be ours for the taking. All of its riches we can lay at Pharaoh's feet."

"And then what, my Prince. Will you want to conquer what lies beyond Kush? Will there be an end to this campaign or do you seek to conquer all of this continent?"

"Uncle, once you said to me you wish I was your son. I ask this of you, stand by me as if I was your son. Already we have raised a force of five thousand young soldiers from this city, willing to fight for our Pharaoh. That is more than enough to replace any losses we have suffered in the past four years."

"If they are loyal, then you do not need to have their leader remain here." Pointing towards the tall black man behind Thutmoses, Chenetothes assumed correctly that he must be Kikiani. "Let me send him in bonds back to Pharaoh to show your good faith and loyalty to your father."

"It's not that simple uncle."

"It never is with you nephew. So tell me, what are your intentions?"

"Kikiani is of the Royal House of Saba. He is a brother to the Queen."

"You know this for a fact?" the Generals interest was pricked. "Why did we not know of this earlier?"

"Only the Kush know this. When he proclaimed himself as the King of Kush, the Nubians accepted this as a result of his victories, not based on his pedigree," Thutmoses explained. But he was actually exiled from Saba because he refused to become a eunuch like his other brothers."

"This you swear is true?" Chenetothes directed the question to the leader of the Kush forces.

"I am Kikiani," the man stated proudly, "the one they once referred to as Ikheny of Saba, Prince of Kush."

"See uncle, it is all true. If he returns to Saba at the head of an army, even if he is nothing more than our lap dog, then the gates of Saba will be opened to us. Imagine, no foreign army has ever taken Saba. No foreign King has ever walked the streets of Saba. What riches must lay there are beyond comprehension. The wealth of centuries, gathered from around the world and all ours for the taking. How could Pharaoh ever refuse such a gift? We are standing at the doorstep of the greatest victory known to man. We will be legends. Just say the word Uncle and we can do this."

"Why would they bother to open their gates for a defeated leader that they didn't want in the first place," Chenetothes struggled to see how the young prince could be so certain of their opening the gates.

"Because they will see him standing alongside an army that seriously threatens their existence. An army if necessary that will lay siege to their city and starve them into submission. They will eventually open those gates, of this I am certain!"

"There is a reason no army has ever taken Saba," Chenetothes intervened at that moment. "They say its walls are as high as mountains and thick as a ship's keel. The stone from which they were erected has never been seen before by outside eyes and only the masons of Saba have the knowledge of how to cut it."

"Stories to frighten children," Thutmoses dismissed them. "Designed to prevent armies from even considering an attack. I have no intention to breach their walls. As I said, they will open their gates to us."

"Just like your grandfather Yuyu," Chenetothes sighed, "he too was a dreamer."

"True uncle, but can you deny his dreams came true?

Nodding his head, the general acknowledge that much was true. "He had a gift, I will certainly give him that. Yuyu knew things that none of our own seers could even predict. But that was Yuyu and he is dead. Now you want me to believe you have his gift too?"

"What if I was to tell you uncle that this war, our victory, our being at the doorstep of Saba was all part of a prophecy that Yuyu made? This isn't my *raswet* we are fulfilling, it was his and he handed it down to me before he died. I am just playing the role he wrote for me, the same as you. Will that convince you that we should continue our march south?

"You know it was your grandfather that denied me the throne and convinced my father to offer it to my half-brother instead."

"I know," Thutmoses said apologetically.

"But it was your grandfather that accompanied me on our previous excursion into Kush to fight the war for Thutmoses-Menkheperure."

"I know that too," the Prince acknowledged.

"But did you know that we were heavily outnumber that day on the battlefield and by all rights we should have lost but your grandfather had some religious artefact that he held above his head and somehow it turned the tide of battle?"

"I know about the sapphire staff," Thutmoses informed his uncle.

"Then you also know it also disappeared shortly after we won the battle and hasn't been seen since. A good thing though because your father intended on seizing that artefact as soon as he became Pharaoh. I don't know if it really did possess the *wasur* it was rumoured to have but had my half-brother been able to lay his hands on it, then I know we would have been heading towards disaster."

"Yuyu knew that too," the Prince agreed, "and that's why he made certain it disappeared after the battle."

Taking a deep breath, Chenetothes prepared himself to ask the next question. "Now if you were to tell me you knew where it was, then that would certainly influence my decision to support you in the taking of Saba. So do you know where it might be?"

"Maybe," Thutmoses grinned. "I have a man heading across the Narrow Sea as we speak. He was with Yuyu the night the staff was sent into hiding."

"How did your father not know of this man? He interrogated practically everyone that took part in the battle in an effort to find it."

"I doubt whether this man was ever on the battlefield. He was a cousin of my mother that operated a merchant vessel."

"The one that was in your company when you set off to take the city," his uncle figured out whom he was talking about.

"His mission was to retrieve the staff. I don't know how long that will take but he is the only man that has any knowledge of its possible whereabouts."

"If we do this," the General cautioned, "I need to put everything in the report to your father. You know that. You understand that. We just can't take off on this adventure of yours without doing the proper paperwork. If Pharaoh disagrees with our plan then we have no other choice but to return to Kemet and forget about Saba. Agreed?"

"It will still take months until we have his response," Thutmoses calculated. "A lot can happen over a period of several months," he grinned.

"You will be the death of me I fear, my Prince," his uncle joked.

It was the month of Pharmuthi, a time when even the desert showed brief signs of life by sprouting flowers on the shrubs and trees that sparsely dotted the hills. It was two and a half months since they had taken Bagrawiyah and during that time the adjusters attached to the commissions' office had been busy writing the manifest, assigning values to all the plunder and treasures that had been looted from the city before packing them into crates in preparation to sail them down river back to Thebes.

At the same time, the new recruits from the city had undergone an intensive training program to make them battle ready for when they reached Saba. The Nubian division consisting of the remnants from Kikiani's army and the raw youths from the twin cities now numbered close to ten thousand men. Added to the thirty thousand units in the regular army, they were now a sizeable threat to any enemy they might encounter and General Chenetothes' confidence in taking Saba grew proportionately to the size of his army.

Over the years, Chenetothes had become a wizened old general and knew the value in rewarding his men with their expected dues. Part of the treasure trove from the city of Bagrawiyah he had melted down in the city's metalworking furnaces, hammering them into silver and gold plates from which portions were cut and distributed to the men in proportion to their level of service. The officers received their payment in gold, while the regulars in the army were more than satisfied to receive their bits of silver. Even the new recruits from the city received a minor share, a payment in good faith as Chenetothes described it, in anticipation of the great expectations he held for them in the coming battle.

The doling out pay to the ranks did not go without some objection from the commissions' officers who felt that every last scrap of precious metal should be sent to Malkata and then afterwards whatever was deemed as fair payment would be returned by Pharaoh. Chenetothes had been in that situation too many times in the past, and he was not willing to undergo it again. It was often the case that Pharaoh, having no first-hand experience of waging war would often under-value the rank and file in the army, which meant by the time the soldiers did receive their money, they were riled, disgruntled, and flushed with anger when they saw that they had been underpaid, receiving only a pittance of what they deserved. Leading angry soldiers into battle was certainly not a situation the Chenetothes desired and one that he refused to let happen under his watch. Therefore, he personally supervised the payment of the troops, ensuring that every man got his just deserves. For three days the men lined up to receive their payment but once it was completed, only then did the General give the order for the remaining plunder and treasure to be loaded onto several boats that were then sailed down the river towards Thebes.

Along with the prizes from the war, the General sent his personal letters to Pharaoh Amenhotep, describing the battle and the army's future intentions. It was a dangerous gambit, especially since there was no other way to describe the changing circumstances without mentioning the significant role that the Crown Prince had played in the decision making process. The situation regarding Kikiani was handled delicately, describing him as a trophy of war that was on loan for the purpose of drawing the troops of Saba into a pitched battle. He made no mention of the mission that Thutmoses had sent Zelophedad on, knowing that any reference to the sapphire staff would send Amenhotep into an uncontrollable rage. He prayed that Amenhotep wasn't already aware of how the rescue mission of his son had been a ruse, otherwise there would be no consoling Pharaoh, who would immediately see treason from both his one and only son and his half-brother.

The very next day the march on Saba began. Spearman to the front with archers and slingers behind. To their rear paraded several rows of chariots, followed by the regular infantry. Trailing behind rolled the wagons of the supply train, the non-military administrators and the hundreds upon hundreds of slaves, carrying crates of supplies and the barges that they would reload on to the river once they had passed the sixth cataract. The precision of their movements, the beating of the drums, and the thumping of spear shafts hammering against the leathery skin of their shields was an impressive sight to behold and hear.

Over the hundred or so miles to Saba they witnessed a dramatic change in the terrain, shifting from desert landscape to ever increasing patchworks of vegetation over the short distance marched that first day. By the end of the next few days the slow, sloping ascent brought them to what appeared to be an endless plateau rippling under a sea of knee-high green grass. Even the air felt different, cooler, and sweeter, the soldiers filling their lungs with the heavenly fragrance. A cool moist wind traversed the plain, blowing the white-lace clouds overhead across a pale blue sky. In the distance they could see the purple mist covered mountains ringing the horizon.

To the Kemtu, they had no idea that there was a land like this so far to their south. The sixth cataract was always a barrier in the minds of the people, as no Kemtu ever returned to inform them of what lay beyond the last cataract and therefore the realm of their imaginations was let loose, filling this unknown land with monsters and other-worldly creatures. To a people that spoke of themselves as being masters of the world these soldiers suddenly recognized how little of the world they actually knew. Now they found themselves marching on a legendary city, advancing through a mysterious land that filled them with awe and wonder.

The regiment of Nubians added a new dimension to the army of Kemet. In unison with their steps, these black warriors chanted hypnotically, a rhythmic, almost lyrical tune, "uba cha cha, uba cha cha" that made the march feel less onerous. The chant was infectious, and before long the Kemtu picked it up and were chanting along with their black brothers-in-arms. The noise they were making was so loud that they startled flocks of nesting hornbills that hid in the tall grass, taking to flight and circling menacingly overhead should the men march too close to any of their nests. Looking skyward, the soldiers could see swarms of other birds that they could not immediately recognize; quetzals and trogons, sungrebes and finfoots. In the distance flocks of ostriches raced across the plateau as if something large and menacing was in pursuit. A few minutes later they witnessed a cheetah leap through the air, landing squarely on the back of one of the enormous birds, bringing it to ground.

As they continued their journey south, the children from the nearby villages would run behind the tail end of the army, shouting profanities at the lighter skinned Kemtu, but Chenetothes kept his troops in line, ensuring they did not break ranks from the main force in pursuit of their youthful tormentors. He knew it for what it was, a trap. He had seen it used by the Bedouin hundreds of times before. The same way he knew they were not alone, their advance being closely watched by hidden eyes dispersed throughout the tall grass. They would love nothing more than a small group of soldiers to tear off in pursuit of the urchins, distancing themselves from the main body of the army, only to find a hundred knives ready to cut them down, unseen, unnoticed and ultimately forgotten.

"The men are doing well," the General shouted from the back of his chariot to Thutmoses who rode in Pharaoh's chariot to his right. Besides his charioteer, Hoshea also accompanied the Prince in the royal chariot, his job to ensure that the spear rack was kept full and that Thutmoses' long laminar horn bow was kept well-oiled and ready for battle.

"I am surprised we have not seen the enemy as yet," Thutmoses replied.

"Have no worries," Chenetothes assured him, "They certainly have seen us. They have been watching us for days now."

"You have seen them?" Thutmoses asked surprised, having not been aware of the enemy's presence.

"These are things you will eventually learn, my Prince. One does not need to see the enemy in order to know where they are. You will learn to watch when birds scatter and where they choose to land. You will hear sounds that repeat too often and are too regularly spaced to be from the animals they're intended to mimic. Listen and learn, my Prince. One day you will be leading the army on your own and their lives will depend on you anticipating the movements of your enemy."

"That day will be a long time in coming," Thutmoses replied, "When I have such a wise and capable general to lead my armies for me."

Chenetothes laughed. "This old warhorse is thinking it's time to lay down his arms. After this campaign there will be nothing left that will capture my interest. The Mitanni and Hatti are at peace. The Bedouin have been subdued. Nubia has been wasted. All that remains is the greatest prize of all, the legendary capital of Saba. Once we have taken that, there is nothing else to keep me riding on the back of this chariot."

"Perhaps I will not let you retire uncle," Thutmoses countered the remarks.

"Do you think you can stop me," Chenetothes raised the challenge.

"Probably not," the Prince conceded, "But I and the men will certainly miss you."

"There will be other generals to follow," Chenetothes assured him. "Some even greater and others not so great, but that is the nature of warfare. But we have entered a time of relative peace and I pray that your reign remains that way."

Thutmoses was amused by his uncle's comments. "How is it that a general can hope for a lifetime of peace? What would be the point in that?"

"When you have shed as much blood as I have," Chenetothes hung his head, "Then you will understand. As a young man, we will always seek glory and the rewards of conquest. But as you get older, you begin to see the error in that belief. Glory is a passing, ephemeral concept that only lasts until there comes an enemy more determined, more confident and better armed to erase everything you ever achieved. And as for the riches, just remember that there is only so much that a man can spend in a lifetime. You will be a wise Pharaoh, Thutmoses, and you will know when there is nothing more that you need. That is the time when you think about your people and provide them with what they need. And what the people want more than anything else is peace, and the ability to live their lives without having to worry about the threat of war hanging over their heads."

"I will remember the wise general that told me that," Thutmoses smiled as he saluted his uncle with his right hand while holding on the side of the chariot with his left. "So what about our unwanted guests that are watching us?" the Prince returned the conversation to where it had begun.

"Let them watch," Chenetothes advised. "I'm certain they have already sent word back to their city regarding your captive king riding along with us. Not as if you can miss him with that plume of ostrich feathers on his head. He stands there like a proud peacock and I don't think he even realizes he belongs completely to us now."

Thutmoses glanced to his right to see Kikiani poised on his chariot exactly as his uncle had described him. "It will definitely send a message to their Queen," he commented. "She has to know that he is returning to claim her throne"

"More importantly," the General suggested, "The people have to know it. If they believe that we are here to install one of their own on the throne then there is going to be an element of the populace that will see that as a good thing. We need them to agitate from within the city. If we can create a disruption in Saba that the Queen must quell, it will divide her defences and weaken her hold on her army. Divide and conquer, my Prince. That's the *tept* or first rule of warfare. Remember it well!"

CHAPTER TEN

"So much that you have kept secret from us," Eleazar criticized. "Why should you and the elders be the ones to decide what we should know and what we shouldn't know?"

"Because this was not the Moses that you know," his father responded. "The man known as Thutmoses did not come out Mitzrayim with us. The Moses I knew as a young man had a love for life that was infectious, he cared about people and valued friendship. But the Moses you know is a vindictive and bitter old man. During his own personal journey, he transformed into a man I could no longer recognize. God help you if you should find yourself on the other side of an issue from his personal viewpoint. That's when you need to fear for your life."

"Are you certain you're not describing yourself father? Do you think the people respect you out of love or is it fear? If a man violates the Sabbath and you should find out, then his life is forfeit according to your laws. Moses gave us Yahvu's ten commandments to live by but you and your elders, they have generated over six hundred commandments. How can any man remember that many without committing a sin, even if it is by accident?"

"The people need laws, they need order and structure," Aaron insisted.

"Yes they do," Eleazar agreed, "But they also need forgiveness and mercy, something which was absent under your theocratic authority."

"Then give it to them," the old High Priest shifted the onus of responsibility back on to the shoulders of his son. "After all, you are the High Priest now. You can do as you please. But I should warn you that when people know that they won't be disciplined for their transgressions then they push harder to break even more laws and rules. You think I was too harsh, yet I don't believe I was harsh enough. You will see for yourself."

"Maybe so, but we cannot enforce the beliefs in Yahvu as a god that loves and protects us, if all the people experience is a god that punishes them harshly for even the most minor of infractions."

Aaron shook his head in disagreement. "Only a fool believes that love is a solution rather than a problem. Everything that Moses did was a result of the disappointments he suffered as a result of love. Listen to my story and you will see that what I'm telling you is very true. The bitterness that love leaves behind can destroy even the strongest of men. There is a fine line between love and hate and if you don't learn how to deal with it properly then the hate will consume you in the end."

"So you're suggesting then that Yahvu is a vindictive and spiteful god and that is what has influenced your harsh judgments," Eleazar sought clarification.

"I will let you decide for yourself," Aaron advised his son, "But if you choose to believe that discipline is performed without love as the reason for its implementation then you fail to appreciate the true relationship between a parent and child. We are children of Yahvu and what you consider harsh judgments are essentially a father's love."

1365 BCE

It was already the beginning of the month of Epiphi when the Kemtu army first glanced upon the city of Saba. Elevated on a high butte, the massive white stone walls surrounding the city reflected the sunlight like a giant mirror, dazzling and overwhelming all that beheld the city. The sloping sides of the butte led steeply downwards to a manmade channel funnelling the waters from the surrounding three rivers into cisterns that were carved into the bedrock deep below the city. This manmade moat provided a considerable barrier to reaching the city walls, but the additional fact that the waters had been populated with crocodiles from the Nile made any attempt to cross the barrier far more treacherous.

Kikiani explained how the only entry to the city was on the city's eastern side, where the natural rock formations provided a sloping ramp to the city gates but the ramp itself was only twenty feet wide, thus limiting the amount of traffic moving up and down at any one time. He described to them how the channels were fed by all three of the neighbouring rivers so that an attempt to dam any one of the rivers was a futile effort and trying to dam all three simultaneously was an impossible task as the waters would flood the plain below the city drowning the attacking army as a result of their own efforts. The cisterns beneath the city were the size of buildings, three in number, able to hold enough water to sustain the city for over half a year if by some impossible means the enemy did find a way to stem the flow from the rivers. There were storehouses of food and warehouses below the city containing salted meats that would last for several months as well. There was good reason Saba had never been conquered in the past; it was impenetrable. The city's garrison was only ten thousand strong but that had always been enough the few times the city defences had been tested. From their perches on the battlements, they would rain down their arrows in a continuous torrent and should the supply of arrows be exhausted then they had an equal number of javelins to launch with amazing accuracy. For good measure they also had a regiment of slingers, able to hurl their stones a considerable distance into the enemy camps constructed far away from the city walls. As they listened to the King of Kush describe the situation, some of

Chenetothes' officers became disheartened, witnessed by the expression of their frowning countenances.

But none of this appeared to concern Chenetothes, who simply nodded as Kikiani provided the details. "Then we might as well start now digging in for the long haul." The General had heard it all before. A long list of cities that were supposedly impenetrable but in the end they all eventually fell. They had said the same about Avaris but his ancestor Ahmose broke through its supposedly impenetrable walls.

Thutmoses discovered that his uncle was being quite literal with his comment concerning a long haul. The forests laying between the three rivers provided a valuable commodity. Initially the wood provided the perimeter wall constructed around the circumference of the camp. Cut as long poles, they were dug into the ground, buried at least six feet, while that part above ground extend a further ten or twelve feet, culminating in a sharply carved point. Within their compound the men set up the tents and constructed a stable area to house all of the chariot horses. Foraging through the local villages, the Kemtu soldiers forcibly seized the supplies they required, often leaving the families they raided without any remaining food in their stores on which to survive. Thus were the wages of war.

General Chenetothes needed to ensure that the people of Saba saw that their enemies weren't going to be leaving for a very long time. During their construction there was very little resistance provided by the garrison of Saba. The distance from the city and the perimeter wall of their compound rendered any projectiles from their slingers ineffective. The palisade was merely the first of the defensive strategies designed to unnerve the citizenry of Saba.

Next on Chenetothes' list was to make the Queen recognize how isolated her city actually was. More trees were cut down, many now having to be hauled from miles away as the Kemtu had already cleared the nearby forests. This time, he ordered his engineers to design and construct a containment wall that would completely surround the butte, with massive gates mounted on the north, south east and west. Beside each of these doors, a tower was built so that any activity that the Queen might instigate outside her own walls could be easily monitored. But the towers also served as podiums from which Kikiani would make his daily speech, urging the people of Saba to open the doors of the city to their rightful King, who had returned at the head of this massive army to liberate them from the oppressive hand of their Queen. It would take months to fully complete the containment wall, so the towers were erected first, thereby making it possible for Kikiani to begin his daily diatribes almost immediately. The proximity of the towers did place the Kushite king within striking distance of the garrison's projectiles but the guards standing on the platform alongside Kikiani ensured that their shields deflected every missile launched in his general direction, while the Kemtu archers and slingers managed at the same time to strike back as soon as any of the garrison soldiers raised their heads above the parapets.

Day by day the people of Saba watched as the enemy increased the stranglehold it held on the city. This time they faced an enemy that had come prepared to lay siege for years if necessary. They knew in a war spanning numerous seasons that eventually the city's supply stores would be depleted unless they found a means to secure a new supply line but that would necessitate somehow breaching the containment wall, which extended its ominous length with each passing day. They prayed to their city gods, a pantheon of goddesses that had protected them for over a thousand years, but even the good news being preached by their priests seemed hollow as the hammering sounds from the enemy's carpenters rang out constantly, reminding them of the impending doom waiting just beyond their city walls.

With the passage of weeks desperation ensued, seen by the increasing numbers of the city's populace attempting to flee the city, many finding novel ways by which to descend the walls because their Queen had ordered the city gates to remain sealed. Those that didn't injure themselves in the fall from the dizzying heights, had to weave their way through the criss-crossing moat with its ravenous reptiles. If by some miracle they managed to survive these two trials, then they quickly discovered that in those areas where the enemy had not yet erected its walls it still had patrols in the vicinity with the sole purpose of capturing anyone that managed to escape. Those detained were promised they would be released as long as they provided information. There weren't many that managed to make it into enemy hands but those that did provided a wealth of information of conditions within the city, current strength of their military, and the general sentiment of its citizens. Overall, it provided a horrific picture that the siege of Saba was proving itself to be highly effective and time was the greatest weapon in the hands of the Kemtu.

"In the name of the Great *Neter-Nesew,* Amenhotep-Nimmureya, I welcome you all to our latest tactical meeting," Chenetothes began. "There is talk that some of you are becoming bored and restless. My advice for you is take some of your men and go hunting. Find something to keep you busy because we are going to be here a long time. Patience is the greatest weapon in our arsenal. Remember, the backbone of any resistance can be broken if you apply the proper strategy. We could storm the walls as some of you have suggested; we may even have some success with our men scaling the ladders and making it over the walls to engage the enemy within their own city. But ask yourself, to what end? Is it worth the hundreds, even thousands we'd lose in doing so? If we were successful in taking the city, would there be enough of us to hold on to it? As your commander it is up to me to use our resources wisely.

The battle of the mind is the fiercest confrontation any of us needs to master. If we can gain the advantage over our opponents and get in to their heads, then we've already won the war. Some of you have been with me on other campaigns. For others this is your first time you have fought with me. Then let me make it clear to all of you, we are not here to win the battle, we are here to win the war. If we sacrifice the lives of our men foolishly, then ultimately we have lost because we will never sustain our victory. The gates of Saba will be opened to us; not tomorrow, not the next day but eventually they will open. That I can assure you!"

Thutmoses rose to stand by his uncle. "I have no issues in the manner in which this campaign is being conducted. As representative of the crown, I think that should be sufficient to put to rest any of you that may be thinking otherwise. If some of you have something to say, then speak up now."

Rising to his feet, one of the senior captains named Epher prepared to speak. "Let me be clear from the onset I am one of the most loyal officers to our general and I have no doubt that he speaks correctly, but I need to tell my men something more. We have been fighting this war for five years. Many of the soldiers in my unit are not career military men. They are farmers and they are concerned what has happened to their farms and their families while they have been away."

Some of the other officers in the tent grunted in agreement with the sentiments expressed by their fellow officer.

"Do we have any idea when this war may be ending and when we can return home?" Epher asked bluntly.

"Look," Chenetothes had a slight tinge of frustration in his voice, "It's Epher, isn't it?" The officer nodded. "Everything we have done, is what we have done in siege operations conducted for centuries. I have not changed the proven strategies in any way. But our adversary, the Queen of Saba, she knows her city is not like any we have encountered before. We have no other choice but to eventually starve them out but as we heard from Kikiani, their stores are large. But know this, they are not endless."

"My concern," Epher pressed the matter further, "is that should we experience a single setback then we could very well have a mutiny on our hands."

The hairs on the back of Chenetothes neck could be seen to visibly rise upon hearing the word mutiny. "That is not going to happen in this army!" he hammered his fist against his desk. "I will have anyone speaking of rebellion in the ranks whipped and flayed in front of the troops. Let your men know that now so that they don't make the mistake of even whispering the word."

"Your words will be passed through the ranks General," Epher hastily returned to his position and sat down.

"I have heard that we do not fight this war with Pharaoh's approval," a voice emanated from several rows back of officer's faces.

"Who said that?" the General quickly turned on the hidden critic. "Stand up now!"

Sheepishly, one of the captains rose to his feet.

"Where did you hear that?" Chenetothes verbally assaulted the young officer.

"My apologies General but it was voiced by others and I am merely repeating what they are afraid to say."

Thutmoses could see that his uncle was about to respond harshly, which would only play further into the hands of whomever was spreading this rumour. He knew that he had to intercede immediately. "General, if I may address the officers," the Prince requested.

Chenetothes was aware that he was about to lose his temper and conceded to his nephew. "Please go ahead, my Prince," he acknowledged the request.

"Yes, it is true," were Thutmoses' first words of his response caused many in the tent to gasp in astonishment. "The decision to attack Saba was my own," he continued. "The opportunity to capture the greatest prize of any war the Kemtu had ever fought was one that I could not resist. I had a choice, to send word to my father, the great *Neter-Nesew* Amenhotep, of my intentions, to which we would have sat in Bagrawiyah for half a year, awaiting his response, or march on Saba and while we awaited Great Pharaoh's response, we already lay the groundwork for laying siege to the city."

Many of the officers nodded their heads in understanding, seeing the logic in what Thutmoses had just said.

"Now I cannot speak as to what decision Pharaoh will make but until I hear otherwise, I am the voice of Pharaoh and any man that thinks otherwise, let him identify himself now."

Not a single person within the tent stirred, fearing that any movement might be interpreted as an objection.

"Good," Thutmoses commented, "the matter is settled. Until I hear otherwise, we technically have Pharaoh's approval to continue this war. What you think you hear does not matter. What you might have heard does not matter. What you hope to hear does not matter. Only once I have my father's written response in my hand will it matter! Are we clear?"

To a man they all responded in the affirmative.

"Now that I have your attention, I'd like to discuss the many options we can use in hastening an end to this siege," Thutmoses looked over to Chenetothes to see if he still had his consent to continue, "Of course with your permission, General…"

"Of course my Prince," Chenetothes consented, wishing himself to hear what his protégé was about to say.

"My discussions with Kikiani have provided me with a greater insight into the architecture of this city. What I always wondered was how do they manage to keep the crocodiles from entering the culverts into their cisterns? Apparently there are a series of grates within these culverts that will not even permit a new-born crocodile to pass through. Each grate consists of openings approximately two inches square. You have to admit, that is pretty small and we have no way in which to remove these grates so these lizards can gain access to the city. But, let me tell you this! Whereas, they may be too small even for the baby crocodiles, they are large enough for young puff adders to pass through."

"No insult intended, my Prince," another of the officers spoke out, "But how are we to obtain these snakes."

"We don't," Thutmoses responded with a big grin. "Personally, I have no desire to even touch one but apparently young adders are a delicacy to the men in our Nubian regiment. They have learned to hunt nests from the time they were young boys, smoking them out and bagging them without a second thought to their own safety. Apparently these boys made good money removing the glands to sell to their military for preparation of poison to paint on their arrow tips. Then the boys would go home and roast the rest."

"Tastes like chicken," someone shouted from amongst the officers.

"Could be," Thutmoses laughed again. "But what is most interesting, is adders love to swim. And they instinctively swim away from crocodiles finding the places where the big lizards can't go. So, with your permission General, I will charge the Nubians with the task of bringing back as many of the baby adders as they can find. We then dump them into the canals and let them find their way into the culverts. We will let nature fight our battle for us!"

"You have my permission," Chenetothes readily agreed. "Does anyone else have a better strategy?" The question went unanswered. "Then I defer to our Prince and may the gods bless his plan with success for us all.

Within weeks the results the adders were having within the city of Saba became clearly evident. For ten days the Nubians hunted the adder nests and then loaded the snakelets into the water supply to the city. Once bitten, without proper medication the venom spread slowly throughout the body destroying those cells it came in contact with. Death was a slow and painful process. Unable to bury or burn the bodies within the city, death patrols drawn from the garrison, collected the corpses, raising them to the battlements on the walls and then unceremoniously tossing them over the side. Crashing down on the slopes of the butte, the bodies then rolled down the hill towards the canals, the scent of rotting flesh alerting the crocodiles to the presence of their next meal.

The spectacle actually provided sport and entertainment for the soldiers of the Kemet army. As soon as the monstrous lizards crawled out onto the land to retrieve the corpses, the Kemtu archers assigned to the containment wall towers would take aim and unleash a hail-storm of arrows. The majority of the projectiles failed to penetrate the thick hides of the animals, bouncing off harmlessly, but the few that did manage to hit a tender spot caused the beasts to unleash their terrifying roar before racing back to the safety of the water to nurse their wounds. Day after day the bodies were rolled down the hill reaching such numbers that the crocodiles became too bloated to eat any more, leaving piles of corpses to rot where they fell until the stench of death even filled the nostrils of those in the Kemtu camp.

Each day Kikiani made his usual rotation from tower to tower, beseeching his people to abandon their Queen and open the city gates for a new glorious age under Saba's first king. "I implore you my brothers and sisters of Saba, let not your foolish pride lead you to death's doorstep," he shouted. "My sister sits in her palace unmoved by the depths of your despair. I have come with my army to liberate you from the yokes around your necks. My Egyptian allies promise that they will not harm you. They only wish that we join their empire and share in the bounty and wealth that only Egypt can offer. Take this opportunity to ring in a new age for our city. An age where we are no longer isolated and alone. Where we become part of something bigger than ourselves. An age where Saba and its ally rule the world!" Stepping beyond the extended cover of his shield bearers, Kikiani spread his arms wide as if to embrace all the citizens of the city. It was at that moment the blur of an arrow slid by the corner of his eye, lodging in one of the tower poles behind him. Seeing that the arrow had missed its target, Kikiani laughed at his unseen assailant. "You cannot kill me my brothers. You cannot kill the truth. I…I…" Suddenly feeling a little weak, Kikiani reached out grabbing the arm of one of the shield bearers in order to steady himself. It was then he felt the throbbing pain in the left side of his neck. Raising his left hand to a point under his chin, he felt the thick, moist, oozing blood attempting to coagulate but unable to do so. The wound wasn't very deep, little more than a nick but the damage had been done. His knees began to buckle, unable to support his wait and the Kushite king fell backwards on to the platform. How ironic he thought. The same strategic solution that he had provided to Thutmoses on how to bring Saba to its knees had now become the vehicle of his own demise. Poison arrowheads had always been a favourite tool of the hunter in Kush, the concentrated toxins a hundred times more potent than an actual snake bite. He failed to calculate that there were those in the city that still knew how to prepare the toxin. A most serious miscalculation.

It was a week before Kikiani finally succumbed to the deathly effect of the venom. Before he died he requested that all the men from his regiment be assembled to hear his last words. A bier had been constructed on which he lay, resting on a mattress of combustible materials until such time that he drew his final breath. Barely able to speak, his second in command leaned over the king, listening intently to the last few words Kikiani mouthed and then repeating it to the assembled host. "My brothers-in-arms," he began. "It was always my dream to have a free an open Saba, where all men were welcome. Where Kush and Nubian lived side by side, sharing in the wealth of our land. Where any man with a dream could find that special place where he could make it a reality. I will go to join my ancestors now but I do not take this dream with me. I leave it with you. It is now up to you to make it a reality. Liberate our city. Free the minds of our people. But you need a king to lead you, a man of honour to guarantee your trust, a god to bring you to your promised land. I name Thutmoses-

Mutenkheperure as my successor." Pulling his second closer, Kikiani repeated over and over again "Thutmoses, Thutmoses," until he breathed his last.

The chant quickly spread through the Nubian regiment. "Thutmoses, Thutmoses," they repeated, banging the shaft of their spears against the ground in unison. The Crown Prince acknowledged their support, waving his hand in appreciation to all of them. The second handed him the flaming brand and Thutmoses stepped forward to light the bier in a final farewell to the man who wished to be King of Kush. The flames quickly spread to the incendiary materials packed beneath the body, the searing heat forcing everyone to step back and watch in silence as the fire consumed the massive black man dressed in his regal finery.

Few could remember a month of Choiak where it rained so much. The rains had come early this particular year and although it meant that the citizens of Saba had an alternative source of drinking water, replacing the demand on the cisterns which still had issues with a few remaining snakes, these heavy rains also managed to seep into the grain stores, causing mold to spread rapidly, destroying a large percentage of the food supply. This was welcome news when Thutmoses heard it from the latest group of escapees that had lowered themselves over the side of the wall using ropes, then nimbly negotiated a route through the sleeping reptilian giants that floated just below the surface of the canal waters. Not only was food in a shortage, so was morale they reported, large numbers of the population holding the Queen responsible for the current situation. In response, the Queen tasked the garrison with rounding up any of the trouble makers and hauling them off to prison. The action fuelled resentment and for the first time in the history of Saba there was talk that a king would be welcome within the city if it meant an end to the siege.

Thutmoses read the signs as being a strong indication that Saba was nearing its breaking point. A few more pushes towards the edge and the city would definitely fall over the precipice. It was at a time when he was formulating a new strategy, thinking of a means by which to divert the rivers rather than damming them that he heard the scouts had returned with news of an approaching army from the east. They were still too far away to be identified properly but it was estimated the advancing force to be only about seven thousand strong. The officers ran to the eastern tower to see if they could discover more from the sentries posted there. Still too far away came the reply, but it was obvious that it couldn't be a hostile army for two reasons Chenetothes informed his men. Firstly, they were moving out in the open and secondly who would attack a force almost six times greater in number. That only left two possibilities, either its commander was a fool, or this was possibly a regiment sent by a foreign chieftain to join their army in sacking Saba, a not unreasonable expectation since the Bedouin were well known for being wartime scavengers.

Thutmoses questioned the General about a third possibility, that being a delegation from Pharaoh but Chenetothes quickly dismissed such a possibility, replying that they were coming from the wrong direction and they had no chariots according to the scouts. Therefore definitely not from Thebes. The only thing east of Saba was the Narrow Sea, and thus the General guessed they were most likely to be one of tribes from the Arabian Peninsula that made the short voyage across the waterway.

As Chenetothes guessed correctly, once the approaching force neared the main body of the Kemtu army, it became clear that this legion of soldiers was neither Kemtu nor Kush. Their grey turbans and face scarves over heavy bearded faces easily identified them as Midianites. It was well known that the Midianites were one of Saba's biggest trading partners. Had they come to rescue the city from the clutches of the Kemtu? Unlikely, though the possibility played on Thutmoses' mind as he watched them approach.

A delegation consisting of General Chenetothes, Thutmoses and a couple of senior officers rolled their chariots forward under a white flag to intercept the strangers a quarter mile away from the camp. They brought their chariots to a halt and then waited for a corresponding delegation from the Midianites to approach.

"You are a long way from home," the General Chenetothes called out across the expanse between them but the actual interpretation and intent of his words were 'stop where you are and identify yourselves'.

Not wishing to appear as a threat, the leading Midianite at the forefront of their forces signalled the officers to stop the march, each in turn signally the cohorts of men under their command to halt their advance. Like a fine oiled machine, each man landed on his right foot and swung his left foot forward until it was firmly planted in parallel with the other foot. Their leader then flashed a signal over his head and immediately three of his men stepped forward to join him, two of them carrying a long crate. The Midianite spoke in the language of the Kemtu. "You also are a long way from home General. But we have been waiting a long time for this day to arrive," his last comment sounding strange and mysterious. "I am called Jethro, tribal chieftain or as you would say *Iaate* of the Midianite confederacy."

Clearing his throat, General Chenetothes greeted their arrival in a traditional manner. "In the name of the Great *Neter-Nesew*, Amenhotep-Nimmureya, Pharaoh of the two lands, *Herey* of the Levant, right hand of Amun-Ra, we welcome you in peace."

"All very well," Jethro replied, "But it is that one we have come to see." He pointed at Thutmoses as if they had known one another for a very long time.

"May I introduce the Crown Prince of Kemet, Thutmoses-Mutenkheperure," Chenetothes continued his introduction, "Son of the Great *Neter-Nesew*, future Pharaoh of the two lands, and recently proclaimed as King of Kush."

"And grandson of Yuyu," the chieftain added. "It is only this last title which matters to me. Let me return one of your men to you." At that precise moment the one

Midianite beside Jethro lowered his scarf and Thutmoses immediately recognized the face of Zelophedad.

"You have returned cousin," Thutmoses acknowledge Zelophedad's safe return. "Am I to presume your mission was successful?"

Pointing to the crate resting on the ground between the other two Midianites, Zelophedad was beaming with pride as evidenced by his wide smile. Thutmoses tried to recall if he remembered Zelophedad having a missing front tooth when last they were together but he dismissed the thought almost as quickly as it appeared.

"Yes, my Prince, it has been very successful. The Lord Jethro has been the guardian of the staff since it was presented to him by Yuyu. I only knew the name Jethro, which was all our grandfather indicated to me, but it was the one name that took me directly to what we sought."

"When a stranger comes to our land and starts asking the people about Jethro," the Chieftain interceded, "then obviously word is going to reach me and I needed to investigate."

"You mean you needed to have me apprehended," Zelophedad rephrased the sentence adopting a slightly malicious tone.

"Investigate, arrest, it all amounts to the same thing, does it not?" Jethro laughed. "Your cousin is a brave man," Jethro related more of the story. "Following his detainment, my interrogators tried to find the intent of his mission but he would not say a word to them, only repeating that his message was only meant for the one called Jethro."

"You mean they beat me for three days," Zelophedad provided a more detailed version of the events.

"It is how we interrogate, my apologies Prince Thutmoses. I love your cousin like a son. Not a word did he say after three days of interrogation. He amazed all of us. I had to see for myself what kind of man was this to withstand such intense questioning."

"Beatings," Zelophedad reiterated while flashing his now gap-toothed smile. "Let's get this correct, they were beatings!"

"When finally I said to him, I am the Midianite known as Jethro, he began to cry with such happiness to see me that I knew he was an honourable man."

"I cried from the pain your men inflicted upon me, my Lord, to be more precise."

"That too, but you were happy to see me."

"Only because I thought the beatings would finally stop."

"A slight difference of opinion but as soon as he told me he was Yuyu's grandson my heart was filled with joy. I had been waiting a long time for the grandson of my greatest friend to appear. We celebrated his arrival."

"Until you found out I was the wrong grandson and then you had me thrown back in your prison."

"Again, a slight misunderstanding. I knew of only one grandson that I was supposed to speak to. Your grandfather never mentioned that there may be another grandson involved. I thought perhaps you were an imposter."

Thutmoses had tolerated enough of this back and forth bickering. "What matters is that I see in the end you did recognize my cousin was speaking the truth and you did believe him when he told you I would be waiting for you at Saba."

"Of course, Excellency. As soon as he started talking about the sapphire staff then I knew that he truly was a grandson of Yuyu. It was a simple mistake any of us could have made. But in the end, El Shaddai cleared my vision and we both saw eye to eye."

"You threatened to use a red hot poker to remove my eyes," Zelophedad protested. "Thankfully, my god put the words in my mouth to talk about the staff before you had the chance to torture me further."

"It is a shame he did not come with a letter from you, young Prince. It would have made the process to verify his story so much easier but as soon as he told me he was on a mission for the Crown Prince of Kemet then I knew that the time had truly come. It had all been foretold by your grandfather."

"Alright then," Thutmoses, "my cousin is relatively unharmed. Right Zelophedad?"

"I survived," Zelophedad responded begrudgingly.

"And you, Jethro, have brought the staff to me, and my grandfather's prophetic vision has been confirmed. So we're all happy now, correct?"

"I only wish to go back to my home," Zelophedad expressed his one and only desire after his ordeal.

"And you will certainly do so cousin, with my blessing and tokens of my appreciation. But that we can do tomorrow; today we must celebrate the arrival of the sapphire staff. Will you and you men be my guests?" the Prince addressed that last question to Jethro.

"I would be honoured, Excellency. We crossed the Narrow Sea, marched several hundred miles to this spot, and now a feast would be a most welcome reprieve."

"Good," Thutmoses replied. "I have so many questions regarding the staff. I hope that you can answer them for me."

Jethro bore a quizzical look on his face. "Excellency, you will learn that if you are the chosen bearer of the sapphire staff, then it will answer those questions for you."

"Did you experience that yourself," Thutmoses asked.

"No, never," Jethro sounded horrified by the thought of holding the staff. "Only the chosen bearer can touch the staff."

"Why, what happens to anyone else that takes the staff in their hands?"

"They die," Jethro replied succinctly in a very serious tone.

A huge bonfire lit the Kemet encampment casting terrifying gargantuan shadows of their celebration against the walls of the city. The unlimited drinking from the kegs of beer, dancing to the sounds of musicians visiting the camp, the singing and caterwauling that continued into the early hours of the morning had their effect on the citizenry of Saba as they watched from their domiciles or from the battlements of their city walls where the bravest amongst them had gathered. To some, it fuelled their anger against the invaders and they prayed in desperation to their goddesses to bring down the wrath of heaven upon the heads of the revellers, but to others they interpreted it as more evidence of their impending doom.

Within the Queen's palace her advisory council sat huddled in the palace conference hall discussing in a highly animated manner what actions they should take next. Sitting upon her carved ivory throne, the Queen sat impatiently, listening to the monotony of their constant squabbling. The advisors tried not to gaze upon her in her regal splendour, draped in a silver and gold threaded gown that scattered the torchlight into beams of fiery illumination, radiating in all directions and penetrating into every corner of the room. Upon her head she wore a bejewelled tiara ringed by golden antelope horns from which little gold and silver bells hung from the tips. She was young and beautiful and just like so many of queens before her, no man was her equal in either the level of power or influence that she wielded. Hers was the final word in the land of Kush, inviolable and omnipotent. Long ago the goddesses that ruled in Kush had declared that the land controlled by Saba would be a matriarchal society, where the sole purpose of men was to serve and protect the women of their civilization. Tonight, the Queen was demanding they do exactly that, 'Serve and Protect.'

"But my Queen," Nebuti, her military advisor began, "We cannot hope to win a confrontation with the invaders. As you saw this day, even our staunchest allies have joined their forces. If the Midianites join our enemies, how long until the Kenites and even the Ishmaelites come to pick the flesh from the bones of Saba? Our only hope is to sue for peace."

"Since when did you become my advisor for trade relations? If I want to know the price of capitulation then I simply have to ask Rikenzi how many wagons of gold we should give this Prince of Kemet to go away. All week he has been increasing the number." Upon hearing her comment, the one known as Rikenzi hung his head in shame. "You are my military advisor, so give me some military advice or is it time to replace you?"

"Queen Tharbis, no one here is more loyal to you then I am, but we all know you cannot stop the flooding of the Nile with a single bucket of sand. That is what we are compared to the numbers of the invader. Their chariots will mow us down as soon as we reach the level of the plains and that is assuming that we make it past their containment wall which hems us in."

"It is a wooden wall, Nebuti. Surely you could burn it down."

"Oh, if was only a matter so simple my Queen but how are we to do that? If my archers assemble on the walls with fire arrows, then their archers and slingers will pick off our men as soon as they raise themselves to release their projectiles. If we try to roll down burning bales, they will only be extinguished as soon as they fall into the canal system that we purposely dug in order to protect ourselves. If we roll them down from the gate, the only place where the canals do not circle our city completely, then we expose the interior of our city to a counter attack. I am sorry to say my Queen but I cannot see any effective way for our troops to free ourselves from the prison this city has now become."

"Saying it cannot be done is not acceptable!" the Queen voiced her opinion loudly as she rose from her throne. When she stood, her crown made her seven feet tall, but nonetheless she was easily six feet without it. The shape of her body, outlined beneath her dress showed the firmness of every muscle. Sculpted like black marble from the heels of her long legs to the broad strength of her shoulders. "I want a strategy, and I want it soon," she commanded.

Without even glancing at her military advisor she moved on to the next topic of discussion. "Cantis, you are my minister in charge of the city's harmony, what is the mood of the people today?"

A middle aged woman rose to speak, wearing only a beaded grass skirt and a pair of sandals made from twisted reeds. "I would like to tell you that the people are happy and support you wholly, my Queen, but I'm afraid I cannot say these words. Many have heard that your brother has named the Egyptian Prince as his successor. They ask why Saba shouldn't become part of their Empire."

"They are fools to think this, Cantis. I need you to have men in the streets to tell the people there is no sharing of the Empire with the Egyptians. There is only slavery beneath their heels. They will make our men work in the mines and they will rape our woman to feed their sexual appetites. Our children will be made to work as domestic slaves in their homes. That is what awaits them if we do not liberate our city. I need everyone to know this or else those who continue to spread this seditious talk in the city will find themselves in our prisons."

"There too, I'm afraid I must tell you otherwise my Queen," Cantis continued. "Our prisons are unable to take any more inmates. There are already too many behind bars. And those that have had their loved ones locked away are clamouring for their release. They infect the other people with their tales of woe, claiming the government has falsely incarcerated their husbands and sons."

"You can speak more plainly Cantis. What you really want to say is they blame me for it. It is all right to say so; I know they do. But what I do is for their own protection and the goddesses approve for they have preserved us and kept us safe thus far. Shiragu, how are our supplies of food and water? I pray that you can give me some good news."

The thin man rose while the matronly Cantis returned to where she was sitting. "Our cisterns are safe once again and they are full to the brim," he smiled.

"Well done, Shiragu," she congratulated him. "When this war is done and the Egyptians have left, I want you to ensure that we have another layer of grates installed that even a water flea cannot pass through. We will never have our water system used again as a weapon against us.

"Of course my Queen," Shiragu bowed. "My men are working on it already. As for our food stores, they are dwindling but as long as we ration out the grain we should be fine for perhaps another six months."

"And what of our dried goods?" she inquired.

He hesitated to reply, "Our dried meats will be gone in the week and our dried fruits have been depleted."

"Are we to live on bread alone? And after the six months, then what," Queen Tharbis mocked his incomplete report.

Shiragu was momentarily caught off guard, needing a moment to compose himself. "We can hope that before the six months expire that Commander Nebuti can free us of the stranglehold on the city."

"Right now, we have as much hope of that as all of us sprouting wings and flying away from this city. I need answers now! Is there anyone in this room that has any good news to report?"

Clearing his throat, chief engineer Mombasi rose to give his latest report on any structural damage to the city. "We uncovered a tunnel being dug under the wall on the north side of the city, your Majesty. We weren't able to identify those that were perpetrating this act but it was clear that they intended to use it to try and escape the city under the cover of night. The tunnel leads to a wooded area on the northern slope that conceals the opening from the outside. We're guessing that they assumed now that the Egyptians are marshalling a large number of their forces on the eastern side of the city, expecting that one day we will open the gates and try to rush their wall, the northern side will not be as closely monitored. That might give them enough time to go unseen to wedge blocks between the posts of the barrier the Egyptian built and then they could escape into the grasslands to the north. We've started to fill in the tunnel and should have it completely blocked and sealed within a couple of days."

Tharbis listened intently to the engineer's report. "Stop what you're doing immediately!" she ordered. By the goddesses, this might be the answer we have been looking for."

"You Majesty…" chief engineer Mombasi was confused.

"Can't you see," the Queen attempted to explain it, "What you consider an escape tunnel could be the very means by which we launch an attack? I need you to work closely with Nebuti and devise a strategy."

"Yes, your Majesty," Mombasi nodded his head.

"You say it emerges under cover on the northern slope…how much cover does it afford? I need to know how many men can be moved through the tunnel, concealed by the wooded cover, and how quickly from there to the northern barricade they can move without being detected and still able to avoid the canal system."

"But your Majesty, the tunnel is very narrow and low, we couldn't move a large number of men through it quickly."

"Are you my chief engineer or not?" she snapped at Mombasi.

"Yes…" he replied cautiously.

"Then do what engineers do and enlarge the tunnel and design portable bridges they can use to cross the canals. Is that so difficult to understand?"

"No, your Majesty."

"Nebuti, you figure out what your men will need to wedge apart the poles once they reach the barricade. Monitor all activity on that north tower that the Egyptians man. There has to be a time when their guards are not focused on that section of the wall immediately across from where the tunnel emerges. I need a detailed plan as soon as possible so that when the opportunity arises, we're ready. The Egyptians will get careless one of these nights and that is when we will pounce upon them."

"And what should the rest of the council do," Cantis asked.

"Pray," Queen Tharbis remarked. "Pray like you never prayed before.

CHAPTER ELEVEN

"Are you expecting me to condemn my uncle for what he did? Is this your intention for telling me all these stories? You were at war. During war decisions are made that appear controversial but they have to be done." Eleazar knew that his father had always been critical of Moses whenever his uncle engaged in an act of mass killing. He would hear him rant and rave at night, practically yelling at his mother, Elisheba, but the fact was that his father was always complicit in these executions as well.

"If you keep telling yourself that lie then eventually you will actually believe it. But that still doesn't make it the truth." Aaron rebuked his son. "A large percentage of those bodies that they threw over the wall were children."

"And how many children have we lost as we wandered through the desert. How many children died when the lava flow swallowed them up at the base of the mountain simply because they stood with their parents beside Korah? How many did you put to death because they went into the fields and gleaned grain along with their parents on the Sabbath? There is always a price to be paid and more often than not it is the innocents that pay it. There's just as much innocent blood on your hands as there is on his."

"Yes, but when our children died it was at Yahvu's command."

"Keep telling yourself father. I'm sure you believe it."

"But that time had nothing to do with Yahvu. It was Moses making that decision all on his own. He wasn't intending to harm the rulers of the city. It wasn't even intended to inflict suffering upon their garrison soldiers. Those aren't the people that go down to the cisterns to fill their pitchers with water every day. Almost always it's the women or the children of the city. The innocents of warfare and your uncle knew all along what would happen."

"So what would you have done differently if you were in charge?"

"We could have continued the siege without resorting to a level of barbarism that was beneath us but Moses wanted to accelerate their downfall. He needed to take the city before his father could put a stop to his actions."

"So now you play the moral high-ground. Where was you morality when you had Moses eliminate all those that challenged you for the priesthood? Why can't you admit that when the situations were in your favour, you had no issues with how you retained your power but when it comes to Moses, anything that promoted his authority, or increased his power over the people you were set against. Admit your hypocrisy father and perhaps your legacy can be preserved as well. Here on this mountain top is the time to confess your sins to Yahvu before it is too late."

"I grow weary of this discussion," Aaron complained. "I think I need to rest."

"Take your rest then father. You can continue telling your story when you awake. We will stay on this mountain until you have nothing more to say. Then I will leave you and you can wrestle with whatever demons haunt your soul on your own."

"He is not who you think he is," Aaron insisted.

"And who is that," Eleazar wanted to know.

"He still thinks he is a god," the High Priest warned his son.

"The reality is father that he is about as close as any man could ever get to being one. How many other men can say they stared God directly in his face and survived?"

"I did," Ahrown was quick to correct his son and add his name to the list.

"And so you say," Eleazar confirmed. "Except you were kept at a distance and somehow I think you've always resented that you were never as close to Yahvu as is Moses. That has stained your entire perspective. You've been too busy intentionally blinding yourself to recognize that it tainted your relationship. So go have your sleep. Perhaps once you've had a rest you will see more clearly and just maybe then you will be given the opportunity to pass from this world peacefully."

1365 BCE

"Why have you summoned me to your tent Uncle?" Thutmoses was confused by the sudden urgency with which the *webwety* said he must go immediately and see the General. "Are you not well?"

Reaching beneath his tunic, Chenetothes pulled out a rolled papyrus scroll and slammed it down on the top of the desk. "It depends on how you define 'not well.'"

"What is this," Thutmoses asked, staring intently at the scroll with its broken seal that looked ominously like his father's cartouche had been pressed into the clay.

"Read it!" the General commanded.

Picking it up with a level of trepidation, Thutmoses unrolled the scroll and began to read the lines of hieroglyphs. Examining the broken seal more closely, he knew immediately that it had come from his father. As he continued to read, his eyes became glazed and soon afterwards a few tears managed to roll down his cheeks, only to be wiped away as quickly as they appeared.

Chenetothes didn't wait for the Prince to respond. "I once told you that I wished you were my son. Now more than ever I wish that was true."

Still fighting back the tears, Thutmoses responded. "And I wish it were true too Uncle. You are more of a father to me than Pharaoh has ever been. What father could actually order the execution of his own son?"

"Pull up a chair my Prince and sit down. We have a lot to discuss."

"But what about the siege?"

"Don't worry, we are not foregoing the siege as he ordered. We will still be here tomorrow and the day after tomorrow and the day after that. We have been at it for over seven months already. A good general doesn't quit when he's this close. So sit down."

"I think I should stand."

"Sit down, you are looking pale," the General ordered.

Thutmoses pulled the three legged stool up to the desk and then sat down. "Are you going to kill me Uncle?"

Chenetothes shook his head. "Don't be so melodramatic. Of course I'm not going to kill you. You may not be my son by flesh and blood but you are my son in my heart. Now pull yourself together and remember who you are. You are the Prince of Kemet, a god incarnate, and no man can raise his hand against you. Is that clear?"

Collapsing his face into the palms of his hands, the Prince tried not to weep but he was not successful. "No one but my father, you mean. How could Pharaoh order such a thing? What kind of man does that to his own son?"

"Now listen to me," the General ordered. "You are the Crown Prince, so stop your whining immediately. And in answer to your question, my half-brother is a sick man. Always has been but he's been getting worse over the past few years. He's been seeing and hearing things that tell us he's suffering from madness but he is the *Neter-Nesew* incarnate and there is nothing we can do about it but tolerate his dementia. I know your mother has mentioned this to you but she's hidden from you the degree of his derangement. But in truth, we all knew the day would come when the madness would overcome his rational thought. I guess now we know that day has finally come."

"But if you don't follow through on his instructions then he will have you executed as well," Thutmoses was concerned for his uncle. "The *webwety* he sent will surely inform him of your failure to stop the siege once he returns to Thebes."

"He won't be returning," Chenetothes informed the Prince.

"What do you mean?" Thutmoses inquired.

"He's dead," Chenetothes replied without any trace of emotion.

"You killed him?" Thutmoses was somewhat shocked by the news.

"Let us say that he had an accident along the way and he never delivered his message as far as we both are concerned. That does change our present predicament."

"That will achieve nothing but a delay," the Prince began to panic again. "There will be other messengers and you can't make all of them disappear. Eventually you will have no choice but to carry out his orders or you will die alongside of me. There are no other options and you and I both know it."

"Yes, that is true. Others will follow but only a member of the *savov* family can take the life of another member of the royal family." Smiling, Chenetothes offered the alternative, "So as the only other member of the *savov* family on this battleground, what if I choose not to do as instructed? What happens then?"

Thutmoses already had the answer ready, "Then he will send other members of the *savov* family to carry out his orders and they will kill both of us. We cannot avoid that eventual outcome."

"Yes, that is probably what he will do, it is what I would do, but he won't be successful."

"How can you know that?" Thutmoses needed an explanation of how the General could be so certain that he was right.

"Over these past five years I have taught you a lot about commanding the army. You aren't reliant on that powderpuff of a priest any longer to devise tactical strategies. You are your own man when it comes to that now." Effortlessly, Chenetothes had diverted the discussion away from his nephew's last question.

"Ahrown is still very useful uncle. He knows as much about warfare as anyone could who is not a regular in the army," the Prince defended his companion.

"Reading about strategy is very different than actually implementing it during an actual battle," the general validated his original comment. "You have been on the battlefield, even if technically it was the taking of a city and therefore a different sort of operation. But you've tasted battle and that is what counts. That is something he will never appreciate no matter how many histories of warfare he reads. You understand that?" Chenetothes waited for confirmation before continuing. "The second thing you've learned is loyalty. It goes both ways. For your men to be loyal to you, then you must be loyal to them. I've seen you interact with the troops and I can tell you these men would march to the ends of the earth for you. They love you and that is worth far more than simple respect of rank."

"Not as much as they love you, uncle."

"They respect me, they fear me, but they do not love me. There is a difference and you have seen it, so don't try to deny it. When Kikiani named you as his replacement as King of Kush, he did so not because of your rank but because of the man you are. That is far more than respect that is love."

"I'm not certain of that," Thutmoses still was not willing to accept the General's evaluation.

"You will learn the difference. Loyalty has its limits, but love does not. That is why you must never fully trust even the most loyal of your allies. Only trust those that love you."

"Is this another lesson you are making me aware of?"

"Of course," Chenetothes smiled, his eyes twinkling with insight. "In life you will learn there may be one or two men that you can trust explicitly. You can trust them because they do love the person you are, not because of some sense of loyalty, or because you hold rank on them. No, it is because of an actual love. You have two that I already see having that devotion to you and you must prize it because it is invaluable."

"Who are they uncle?"

"I think you already know Thutmoses. There is Othni and there is the boy, Hoshea. Those two would go to the ends of the earth for you without even questioning why. Take care of that boy. He needs you and trust me, at some point you will need him."

"And who was your person of such loyalty that they loved you Uncle?"

"My orderly of course. Hophni come in here."

Upon hearing his name, the general's orderly entered the tent and stood attentively. "Is there something more I can do for you General?"

"Did you take care of the *webwety*?" the General asked.

"Of course Sir. There won't be a trace of him by tomorrow."

"You see, my Prince, that's more than loyalty. That's a priceless devotion that goes beyond the call of duty. I would give my life for Hophni and he would do the same for me. So when you have people like that, then you must cherish it and nurture it until if fully blooms. Those others that you call friends, can just as easily be your enemies tomorrow. Remember the first time I took you hunting?"

"Of course I do," Thutmoses responded excitedly. "How could I forget? I would have been killed if it wasn't for you."

"What you need to remember from that day is as much as the lion thought you were his enemy, you had to understand he was your enemy as well. That lion was willing to kill you as much as you were trying to hunt and kill him." The General leaned back as he reminisced about that day thirteen years ago.

"I really did think I was as good as dead when he sprang at me," Thutmoses recalled.

"Because you failed to remember that a wounded enemy is even more dangerous than one that you've never harmed. Our enemies in life are no different from that lion. They come at you constantly, and most of the time they can be beaten back easily because their hearts aren't fully into it. But wound them in some manner and now you've raised their enmity to an entirely different level. Now they have hate and they want revenge. Same as that lion. He would have been equally as happy to just have disappeared into the forest and left you alone until you threw your spear. It may have only been a glancing blow but it cut him and suddenly running away wasn't an option any longer. Even a lion can want blood for blood."

"But it made no sense Uncle. There were five of us in the hunting party. Even a lion had to know that he was not going to take down five men on horseback and survive." Thutmoses thought back to that day and suddenly recognized how strange the lion's behaviour had been.

"I'm certain the lion did know he was going to die but he was so obsessed with paying you back for wounding him that his instinct for survival was overridden." Chenetothes held out his hands as if to say do you understand now.

"Is this a lesson for the future," the Prince wondered, "Or are you saying something about Pharaoh as well?"

"I'm saying both my Prince," the wise old general explained. "Your entire life you've been wounding your father. Yes, my half-brother is seriously ill but that only amplified his resentment for you. He sees himself as a great builder, probably one of the greatest in the history of Kemet. Who can disagree? Certainly not me but you on the other hand, dismissed all his great works and even went so far as to criticize him as building nothing more than a pleasure palace."

"That is exactly what it is," Thutmoses was not about to apologize. "One man's ego displayed for all to see in monuments of stone and mud."

"Maybe it is, but it is still magnificent but his own son could not afford a single word of praise. Instead you talked endlessly of Yuyu, your grandfather, a man that your father resented because of his hold over your mother and the influence he had on my father and grandfather. Once again the more you talked about your grandfather, the greater the wound you inflicted on your father."

"Am I to feel sorry for a man that couldn't even show the tiniest amount of love for his children? I don't think so," Thutmoses answered his own question.

"Nor am I here to make excuses for my half-brother but I need you to see the lesson here," Chenetothes wagged his finger at the Prince.

"He was going to rape his own daughters because I wasn't prepared to take them as my wives," the Prince flared as his anger began to well inside.

"Yes he was and as much as you or I find that despicable, he would not be the first Pharaoh to do so and he will probably not be the last. So what did you do? You took your sister Sitamun into your bed and married her. For what reason? Because you loved her? Or was it because you didn't want you father touching her?"

"Uncle, why are you provoking me," Thutmoses was now directing some of that anger he bore for his father towards the General.

"Because you need to understand that wounded animals will strike out at one another without thinking, without logic. Solely focused on one thing only. Harming the other at any cost. That lion was so focused on killing you for what you had done that it didn't even pay any attention to me with my spear in hand. It lost its life because it was no longer rational.

"And you're suggesting that I'm now being hunted by my father because he is no longer rational in his attitude towards me," the Prince began to calm down as he began to put the pieces of the puzzle together that his uncle had laid out.

"Now you are beginning to understand what it takes to be a great leader," Chenetothes congratulated him on the sudden growth of insight. "If we look at this entire campaign that we've been on for the past five years, then you have to acknowledge a large part of why we are laying siege to Saba is because you want to shame your father for failing to be one of the great *kefaw* that existed in your family. You may say it was to escape the misery that you and Sitamun had suffered with the death of your child but if you loved your wife as much as you claim as your reason for marrying her, then you would not be here right now. You'd be home in her arms and working on the children to come."

"I may have let my feelings for revenge against my father get the better of me as well," Thutmoses admitted now that the facts had been laid out before him.

"And I do not condemn you for it, nephew. Two wounded lions, each trying to take down the other. Very few men in your position would have reacted any differently."

"But you would have," the Prince was quick to defer to his uncle's better judgment.

"Your father gave me good reason to master my anger and resentment. Do I resent the fact that I was overlooked to be the next Pharaoh? Of course I do. Do I resent the fact that I knew I could never have a family of my own because eventually they would be seen as a threat to Pharaoh and he would have them killed? Of course I do," he repeated his answer to his own questions with a wistful look in his eyes. "Do I resent the fact that I fight Pharaoh's wars and every inscription and stele commemorating those victories are in Pharaoh's name and I am not credited anywhere in the Royal Archives for achieving those victories? No, I do not. Because if I let that wound penetrate into my heart, it would have made me irrational in my judgements on the battlefield and I would have been slain a long time ago. You must know and learn where to draw the line before seeking revenge. One wrong decision and you will bring yourself down!"

"So how could you accept all these things that your brother did to you without seeking revenge?" Thutmoses wanted to know.

"Because I recognized that I had something even better than revenge. Yes, I did not become Pharaoh, but I've lived a life of freedom and adventure that few men will ever experience. No, I never had a family of my own, but who took you on your first hunting trip? Who oversaw your weapons training with Hur? Who tutored you in the art of warfare all those years you spent in the palace alone because your grandfather was no longer permitted to see you? I did have a family; I had you! And I realized I had something my half-brother will never have; your love and affection. And lastly, all the steles and memorials in the world are not going to replace the fact that it was my name the troops shout after victory. It is me they salute as I send them home after the wars. The inscription in stone are hollow and so those I could easily overlook. They are lies that will erode with time and weather but the truth is inscribed on the hearts of my men and that will never be erased."

"I am a fool uncle. I have let my emotions rule my mind and now I see that to be the man I truly want to be I must have my mind rule my emotions."

"The fact that you now understand this most important lesson means you have attained a level of awareness that makes you one of the wisest men in the kingdom," Chenetothes congratulated him. "A wise king will remember this lesson and ensure that every decision is made with calm and reason. Like the lion, ruling by emotion will get you killed."

"So you have a plan on how to deal with the situation of my father wanting my death?" the Prince determined that the General was already several steps ahead of the game.

"Of course I do," Chenetothes assured him. "One more lesson for today. You must always take proper care of your weapons. Let me see your sword."

"Withdrawing his sword, Thutmoses prepared to hand it over hilt first but his uncle insisted on seeing the blade, running his thumb across the edge.

"Not bad," Chenetothes evaluated the edge but it still can use a little work.

"I have been training Hoshea to take care of all my weapons," Thutmoses explained. "He is learning quickly."

"That boy will prove to be your greatest asset with time," the General reiterated how important Hoshea's loyalty and devotion to Thutmoses was. "Here, take a look at my blade." Laying his sword flat on the desk he encouraged the Prince to run his fingers over the edge. "You feel the difference? That is the work of a master craftsman. Hophni takes care of all my weapons. I will have him spend time with Hoshea until he's able to do the same for you."

"Thank you uncle. I'm certain that Hoshea will appreciate that."

"So are you ready Hophni?"

"I am my General."

"So let's see that sword again," he instructed Thutmoses to pick it up once more. At the same time Hophni had moved behind the Prince and shifting the full weight of his body, he forced Thutmoses to stumble forward so that the sword in his hand pierced the General's chest and ran him through.

"What have you done," Thutmoses screamed at the orderly hysterically, succumbing to the shock of realization. "What have you done?"

"Help, help," Hophni began screaming, "Save the Prince. The General has tried to kill the Prince. Help save him!" Running out of the tent, Hophni continued to scream the exact same words repeatedly calling attention to the General's personal guard and everyone else in the vicinity of the tent.

As Chenetothes collapsed and rolled off his stool, the Prince attempted to catch him, holding on to the bear-like frame of the man until he was practically buried beneath it. "Uncle, uncle, why have you done this? What did you make me do? I need you! Don't die on me!" This time the tears could no longer be held back and they streamed from his eyes like a river.

Blood gathered at the corners of the General's lips but he still was able to speak though the sound of the air and bubbling blood hissing from his chest made it hard to hear. "Now you can cry my son," he attempted to raise his arm to hold the Prince by the shoulder but he was too weak.

"Why, uncle, why?" Thutmoses repeated, still in shock.

"Remember, when someone truly loves you, they will be willing to die for you. That is the test of a true man."

"We could have worked this out uncle. You didn't need to die," Thutmoses wept.

"I have done what needed to be done. You are free now," Chenetothes gasped. "Pharaoh owes you his life now."

"What are you talking about," the words made no sense to the young prince.

With his dying breath, the General completed one last sentence. "I wish you were my son."

"I am, uncle, I am," Thutmoses cried as he held the now limp body in his arms, tears flowing uncontrollably as he cried for the one man he truly could call father.

CHAPTER TWELVE

Sleep had not improved his demeanour at all. Aaron sighed heavily after recounting that part of the story concerning the death of General Chenetothes. Clearly, it was a turning point in the relationship between himself and Moses. "Following the death of his uncle, Moses was never the same."

"What do you mean father?"

"Exactly what I said; he was a changed man. None of us really knew all the details of what happened that day in the General's tent, but afterwards your uncle became more withdrawn. He was less reliant on our council, often making decisions completely on his own. The only one he appeared to confide in was the young boy, Hoshea."

"By Hoshea you mean Joshua, don't you?" Eleazar wanted to confirm that they were talking about the same person.

"Hoshea, Joshua, what's the difference? You know whom I'm talking about. Something happened and Hoshea got drawn into his confidence and the rest of us were set aside."

"More resentment father?" Eleazar was still analysing what the burning issues between Moses and Aaron were. He knew his father had been jealous of the fact that Joshua had been appointed as Moses' heir apparent. A man with no hereditary privilege, no background of any significance, was now appointed to be the supreme commander over the tribes of Israel. That was almost too much for Aaron to bear.

"I was his most trusted companion and he ignored that. I don't know if you call it resentment as much as feeling displaced. We were brothers and that all changed." At that moment Aaron spat up a wad of red-stained phlegm, shooting it into the flames where it crackled and sizzled.

"So what are you suggesting," Eleazar inquired.

"I may not be suggesting anything," his father denied any significance to his comment. "All I can say is that following the death of the General, Moses was then supreme commander over the entire army. Months earlier he had been proclaimed as the King of Kush. He had over forty thousand men under his command. An army large enough to march on Thebes if he so decided. That kind of power is bound to change a man.

"Of course it would but he didn't march on Thebes. He didn't make himself a king in the true sense either then or now."

"Only because of what happened next," Aaron was quick to point out.

"Whatever you're about to tell me father, if you examine it with a wider perspective, I think you will see that it actually made the man we now call Moses," his son reflected on all that he had heard so far.

"Nonsense," Aaron spat once again. "Just listen and learn otherwise."

1364 BCE

The entire month of Pharmuthi was declared a period of mourning for the deceased general. The soldiers were incredibly moved by the display of grief that the Crown Prince still paid towards his uncle even though the letter concerning the plans to assassinate the prince and the Great *Neter-Nesew* Pharaoh was fully exposed and in possession of the officers of the commission detail. As the story unfolded from the initial hearing after the General's death, his orderly, Hophni had found the letter that Chenetothes had written to his unidentified allies in Hattu, detailing how he was preparing to assassinate the Crown Prince as part of plot conspired along with certain officials within the palace in Thebes in a manner that would be beyond any self-incrimination. The remainder of the letter explained how they would carry out the rest of the plan to eliminate the royal family.

Firstly, he would return with the body of Thutmoses to Thebes, being accompanied by an honour guard that was totally under his command and knowledgeable of the coup they were undertaking. Aware that Pharaoh would attend the commencement of the burial preparation according to the standard practices, having the body embalmed and the vital organs removed and placed in the canopic jars, there would be ample opportunity to carry out the second phase of his plan. During this procedure, only Pharaoh and the priests conducting the embalming could be present. That would be the moment when Chenetothes and his men would rush the mortuary and slay Pharaoh. As Pharaoh's older brother, he would then lay claim to the crown and as there would be unlikely any resistance, he would be the next *Neter-Nesew* and able to reward his northern allies afterwards. Just to be certain, his captains would return with his army down river, arriving in Thebes at about the same time that the coup was being completed. The women of Amenhotep's family would be given a choice to either become his royal wives or perish should they refuse.

The plan was perfect, except for the fact that he left the letter on his desk where it was discovered by his orderly who was loyal to the crown. Seizing the letter, Hophni took it immediately to the Crown Prince who then returned to the General's tent to confront his uncle. A scuffle ensued and fortunately with the blessing of Amun-Ra, the young prince was able to best the general and end the plot to eliminate the *savov* family.

Despite the seditious plot, here was their Crown Prince, providing the benedictions and blessing over an uncle that attempted to kill him and then assassinate Pharaoh Amenhotep of Kemet. If ever there was a living embodiment of the true spirit of the gods, capable of demonstrating a forgiveness that exceeded all expectations of piousness and righteousness to a level that no one else could even imagine to achieve, here he was, Crown Prince Thutmoses, a god incarnate.

The Prince ordered the camp carpenters to construct a sarcophagus in which to place the body of his uncle. The task of finding a tree large enough from which they could carve the sarcophagus they knew would not be easy, resulting in scouts being sent south towards the *dehnet* ranges far in the distance to find one that was suitable. It took several days but they eventually returned dragging the massive tree behind them.

Knowing that his uncle would be classified as a traitor, and therefore refused the customary embalming practice to prepare him for the afterlife, the Prince instructed the army medics to do whatever they could to simulate the practice that would have been performed in Thebes. After what Chenetothes had done for him by making the ultimate sacrifice, it was the least he could do to repay that act of unselfish love, but sadly, he could never talk about the true nature surrounding the events. Instead he had to promote the lie that was exposed in the letter, all the while accepting the continuous stream of praises for his magnanimous nature.

The final breaths taken by his uncle laying in his arms would haunt him for the rest of his life but the real nightmare was knowing that behind it all was his own father's desire to have him killed. There would always be those that were completely loyal to Chenetothes who would never believe that their commander could have been formulating a plot to overthrow the Royal House, but others in the commissions' officer were focused on the issue of the killing of a Kemtu aristocrat. Even though Thutmoses was the Crown Prince that still did not empower him to be both judge and executioner. Only Pharaoh had that authority and Thutmoses had already anticipated that at some point in the future he would have to account for his actions. How he could manage this to his own advantage was critical.

Meanwhile, the Prince had other concerns to deal with as he felt a dark shadow crawling over soul. No matter how hard he tried, no matter how much he paid attention to his uncle's final words of advice, he could not shake the feeling of desolation. With Hophni's assistance, he had moved his belongings into the General's tent, taking only Hoshea with him and leaving his cabal of advisors behind to share the officer's tent without him. All of his uncle's mementos and awards presented to celebrate his various victorious campaigns were scattered about the tent as a reminder of the greatness of the man. Only Thutmoses knew now that the true measurement of greatness was actually achieved only when you are willing to sacrifice everything, your reputation, your possessions, but most of all your life for a cause or purpose you believe in, even if it means that no one will ever know. Of all the lessons that Chenetothes had imparted to his nephew, that was the one which impacted the Crown Prince the most. How was he ever going to live up to the expectations of a man that could make such an unselfish sacrifice? Thutmoses feared that when there did come a time when he faced a similar situation that he would fail in the eyes of his dead uncle.

For the time being, Saba became a non-issue in the minds of the soldiers during the month long mourning period. Normal daily routines were interrupted by rotational visits to the sarcophagus where the troops would pay their last respects to their departed general. When some would question why it was still expected for them to do so for a man that was clearly a traitor, it was Thutmoses who immediately replied that they do it for the great general that for almost three decades spearheaded their forces to victory after victory, making no mention of his supposed final betrayal. As they paraded past the podium most did have a cherished memory of a leader that inspired them when they needed it most and in their silent prayer they praised his spirit and wished his soul a safe journey. They prayed that Maat would weigh his existence fairly and recognize that he good deeds of the man far outweighed the madness that afflicted him in the end.

At night Thutmoses would unfurl the papyrus that had come from his father, the one that ultimately led to Chenetothes taking his life. As much as he tried to recall that one particular lesson from his uncle on replacing emotion with logic, foregoing thoughts of revenge for peaceful resolution, as soon as he read the instruction from Amenhotep to murder his son, the fury in his heart would rise to the surface, becoming inflamed until there were no other thoughts other than revenge, not so much for himself but for his uncle. It would take much longer to master his emotions but he knew that he owed his uncle to do so.

Numerous times, Caleb, Hur, Machir, Othni and Ahrown would come to the tent to check on their Prince's condition but after exchanging a few pleasantries he would dismiss them all. The melancholy had taken hold and not even the thought of Saba's fall could relieve the feeling of gloom that enshrouded his waking hours. Repeatedly he thought of exposing the lie in its entirety, detailing the full series of events to his colleagues and explaining how his uncle had willingly sacrificed his own life in order to rescind Pharaoh's decree, but he knew that would render Chenetothes' sacrifice meaningless. He would live only because the belief that he had killed his own uncle in order to protect the lives of the royal family prevented Pharaoh from taking any further action at that time. Yet, it was the underserved praise that he received from those thinking his action was noble and honourable that cut him the deepest. His was still the hand that held the sword when it was plunged into the General's chest and though it was through no intent of his own, he still felt the unbearable burden of the shame for not preventing its occurrence.

Caught in one of his moments of reflection, the prince did not notice that Hoshea had entered his tent. The boy was now a young man, perhaps twelve or thirteen years of age, though no one truly knew, showing the first evidence of a few hairs sprouting on his chin. Training with the troops had provided him with a muscular frame and even at this young age he was of equal height to most of the other men. Picking up the Prince's sword, he took the sharpening stone from the small pouch around his waist and walked over to the stool where he regularly performed the ritual of sharpening the edges, exactly as Hophni had shown him, until they could slice a hair in half. The sound of the stone sliding and scraping along the brass blade aroused Thutmoses from his brooding thoughts.

"Hoshea," Thutmoses sounded surprised to see his ward. "I was not aware of your coming into the tent."

"I wished not to disturb you my Lord," the boy responded.

"Take good care of that sword. It was one of the points that General Chenetothes made me promise to do. It was very important to him."

"I know my Lord,"

"What else do you know Hoshea?"

"What do you mean my Lord?"

"Exactly what I asked, Hoshea. Do not be afraid to answer truthfully. The only way you could know about the sword is if you somehow overheard it." Thutmoses tone was without any malice and reassured the boy that he would not be punished for answering truthfully.

"Most don't pay attention to a young boy moving about the camp," he answered. "I hear a lot of things. I see a lot of things."

"And somehow you overheard everything that happened in this tent the night that the General died. True or not?"

Hoshea hesitated but then decided to answer honestly. "I heard some of it only my Lord. I was not close enough at the beginning of your conversation."

"Then you know what happened at the end."

"I know that you did not kill your uncle," Hoshea admitted to hearing the most crucial part.

"And yet you have kept that secret all this time," Thutmoses was surprised.

"If you were not going to tell anyone, my Lord, then I assumed you had your reason and I was not about to betray your confidence."

Smiling, Thutmoses found the words strangely reassuring. "It is funny. The General was very right about you. He had a rare talent to assess the people around him properly. You obviously impressed him."

"I would never betray you my Lord."

"It was six years ago that I took you into my care," Thutmoses reflected. "Do you still blame me for the death of your parents?"

"You are not one of them, my Lord. You are the man that they say you are in the streets," Hoshea confided.

"What do you mean that I'm who they talk about in the streets?"

"Permission to speak freely, my Lord"

"When have I had it any other way?" the Prince reassured his ward. "Most of the time I can't stop you from saying what's on your mind."

"They talk about things that your grandfather said."

"You mean Yuyu?"

"Yes. He often visited us in Goshen but he would never live amongst us. He would tell us that he was not the one to lead us back to our homeland. He said that man will be coming soon."

"Lead who? The people in Goshen are from everywhere. If I was to count the nations living in Goshen I would run out of fingers and toes," Thutmoses joked.

"All of us," Hoshea replied. "The one to come will take all of us back to Canaan."

"Impossible!" Thutmoses rejected the idea. "There is no way you could all live together. Shasu, Khabru, Apiru, Nabu, as well as all the rest cannot live together in peace. Your blood feuds would never permit it."

"But we already do live in harmony in Goshen," Hoshea pointed out.

"Only because you are under Kemtu law," Thutmoses pointed out. "If any of you tried to revive your old feuds, the security forces would be on you so fast and whipping your bare backs that you wouldn't even have a chance to deliver a second blow."

"That is very true," Hoshea admitted. "But the man to lead us out of Kemet will also be a disciplinarian that will keep us in order. He will give us laws to live under. "

"He'd have to be prepared to whip you constantly. You are a stubborn people. All of you. What man would ever want to undertake that role?"

"Yusef said that man was coming soon. We all believe him. As I said my Lord, they talk about that man in the streets of Goshen."

"No, you said they talk about me in the streets." Upon making that statement, Thutmoses suddenly stopped in his tracks and stared intently at his young ward. "No, no, no, no. They have that wrong. I'm a Prince of Kemet. In fact I'm the Crown Prince. I'm going nowhere except back to Thebes. That's where I belong. Your talk in the streets is nothing more than a myth. People want to believe in legends and if that keeps them happy then so be it, but I'm not part of it."

Looking up at the Prince, Hoshea's broad smile suggested that he knew better.

"You're a young boy. I understand you have your dreams and fantasies and you may even believe that I'm the answer to those, but it is not going to happen."

"Yusef said it will. Everything that Yusef has said in the past has come true. That is undeniable," Hoshea purposely used Yuyu's Khabru name.

"You mean Yuyu," Thutmoses corrected him. "The moment he put the *worret* of the vizier upon his head he was no longer Yusef. He was part of the Kemtu aristocracy. He wouldn't even live with his own people, preferring to stay on his estates in the south. I'm surprised he even found the time to visit the people in Goshen."

"He was never Yuyu," Hoshea insisted.

"What do you know? You were probably no more than one or two when he died. You never saw him, you never heard him, so how can you know anything?"

"He still lives in the streets of Goshen," Hoshea explained. "His prophecies are recorded on the hearts and minds of the people. His flesh is gone but his teachings will never die. He promised the people that everything he said would be fulfilled."

"Yuyu was a dreamer," Thutmoses insisted.

"Yusef was a *hemneter*, a prophet," Hoshea was adamant in his beliefs.

"I can't believe this," Thutmoses began pacing around the tent. "I'm actually arguing with a boy about what my future is going to be, based on some prophecy from a foolish old man."

Hoshea didn't respond but instead simply pointed at the crate in the corner of the tent.

"What?" Thutmoses demanded to know what he was suggesting now.

"Take it out," the boy instructed.

"I'm not taking it out," Thutmoses refused. "And who are you to tell me what I should do? This is ridiculous. I'm not listening to you. No staff in a box is going to determine my destiny. Absolutely ridiculous. Stop pointing at it!"

"Then take it out," Hoshea repeated.

"There's no reason to," Thutmoses made the excuse. "Anyway, from what I know it is only used at time of battle. Plus Jethro said that if you're not the right person to hold it then you will die."

"I may be a young boy but I know that if my grandfather sent me on a mission to specifically retrieve that artefact then I wouldn't hesitate in picking it up."

"It's a staff. Sure it may be an unusual colour and people believe it can manifest magical properties but it's not going to bring back my uncle."

"No, nothing is going to bring back you uncle. But it's your choice to do nothing or to ensure that his death had a higher purpose. He believed that he had to die in order to ensure that you stayed alive. He believed you were going to achieve something of great importance to change this world. So you can sit here in your tent most days and do nothing, wallowing in self-pity, or you can pick up that staff and be the man that he anticipated you would be. The one that your grandfather Yusef proclaimed was coming. Be that man!"

"I can't believe I'm listening to some youth who is hardly old enough to wipe his own ass telling me what I should be doing with my life. How do you even know what self-pity even means?"

"Because your uncle said that I know you well." Hoshea reminded Thutmoses of comments made that night.

"You are distorting my dead uncle's words from a conversation you shouldn't have ever heard."

"Your uncle also said you should recognize there are very few people that are totally dedicated to you and that I'm one of those people."

"You definitely shouldn't have been listening to us that night. What happened then was very private and you violated that privacy.|

"Be grateful that I did because I'm too young to know better not to speak what's on my mind. Right now you need more people that will do that and not give a crap that you're the Prince of Kemet and tiptoe around you."

"I can have you punished for your insolence," Thutmoses threatened.

"Go ahead, but do it after you open the crate."

"You are a pain," the Prince relented. "Okay. I will open the crate. I will hold the staff and when you see that nothing happens, then you will forget this nonsense and not bring up these foolish prophecies of my grandfather again. Agreed?"

"Agreed," Hoshea rubbed his hands together having won this battle.

Nervously, the Prince approached the crate and very cautiously touched the lid, drawing his hand back immediately as if he had been shocked. Recovering his calm, he untied the rope knots that held the lid closed, taking an overly long time to do so. Hoshea put the sword down and walked towards the crate in order to peer inside as Thutmoses slowly raised the lid. As soon as the lid was removed, both of them released a loud, audible gasp.

Lying on a bed of cotton cushions, the staff practically glowed in response to the intensity of the shifting lights within the tent. The colour was difficult to describe, sometimes a shimmering blue, then a silvery frost but practically never the same in response to the battle between shadow and light as the sun passed over the tent during the course of the day.

Hoshea was the first to speak. "It's beautiful," was his first response.

"It is remarkable," were the first words to come to Thutmoses' lips.

"Go pick it up," Hoshea practically commanded the Prince.

"I think we should just watch it first," Thutmoses was very hesitant to lay his hands on it, remembering the stern warning that those undeserving will die.

"You're the only one that can," Hoshea said in response.

"We don't know if that's true," Thutmoses was still appraising the situation.

"Well I'm not about to touch it in order to find out," Hoshea refused to even approach any closer than he had already.

"I want you to know," Thutmoses warned, "that if I die upon touching it, I will never forgive you for making me do this."

"I understand completely," Hoshea nodded. "I won't forgive myself either."

"Are we sure about this?" Thutmoses performed a last second check.

"It's your family's staff," Hoshea explained. "I guess that means you have some bond to it."

"It's glowing!" the Prince commented. "Why's it glowing?"

"That's just reflected light," Hoshea commented.

"Are you some sort of mystic now that you can explain the properties of light?"

"Are you going to touch it or not?" Hoshea asked impatiently.

Closing his eyes, Thutmoses reached into the crate and grabbed the staff with his right hand. Immediately he felt a strange sensation course through his body. It was as if a peaceful calm took hold, immediately replacing the melancholy he had suffered from for days. His mind was clearer, his perceptions sharper, and though he could not explain it, there was a feeling inside his head as if he knew things that he had never known before.

Hoshea grew concerned by the immobile stance of his Prince, a total lack of any perceived movement for what felt like several minutes. "My Lord, are you alright?"

"What," Thutmoses responded as if snapping out of a trance. "Did you say something?"

"I asked if you were alright my Lord. You were standing there like a statue for the longest time. I didn't know what to make of it."

"Hoshea, summon the officers quickly," the Prince's tone had a ring of urgency.

"What is it my Lord?"

"I can't explain it but I think we may be under attack. Move quickly. We must get everyone prepared for the onslaught."

Hosea ran from tent to tent as fast as he could, sounding the alarm that the enemy may have broken out of the containment palisade.

The officers assembled in front of Thutmoses' tent awaiting instruction. As soon as the Prince emerged from the tent holding the staff, they were initially overcome by a strange sensation of awe and wonder. "Prepare the troops immediately for battle," Thutmoses shouted his orders. "The enemy has broken through our wall. I want shield bearers with javelins to the front. Archers behind. Charioteers, get your horses reigned up and ready to roll. I want that city by tonight!"

At first the officers hesitated to move, caught completely off guard by the prince's commands.

"Now people!" Thutmoses conveyed his sense of urgency.

There had been no indication of any breach of the wall from any of the sentries posted on the towers but that was easily explained by the reduction of those on duty within the towers since many had come to pay their respects and prayers at the sarcophagus of their deceased general. In fact, this was the perfect time for their adversaries to launch countermeasures.

The trumpeters blurted their series of notes sounding general orders to prepare for battle. As the horns rang out the troops assembled in formation, swords, javelins and shields in hand. Archers strapped their quivers to their backs and raced into pre-set positions according to the battle plan. Within minutes the entire army under Thutmoses was ready for action.

The squadron of archers charging towards the northern tower were the first to encounter the enemy which was pouring through the large opening they had created in the palisade like a tidal wave. Hundreds of the enemy had already made it through the breach and were charging in both directions in an attempt to hem the Kemtu soldiers in on the eastern and western sides of the city, thereby restricting their movements and preventing them from using their chariots in close quarters lest they accidentally run over their own men. The Kemtu officers immediately shouted the orders to their archers to 'fire'. A hail of arrows rained down upon the warriors of Saba. So many arrows in fact that they practically blotted out the sun.

Word was sent back to the command tent that the enemy had torn down a section of the northern wall and slain all the sentries in the north tower. No one could say how long ago they had made their foray out of the city but already their numbers had swelled into the thousands beyond the breach and they were inflicting a heavy toll on both the eastern and western flanks of the Kemtu army.

Thutmoses ordered his forces to separate into six legions of approximately five thousand men each. Midianites were ordered to stay behind at the main camp and serve as an auxiliary force if called upon. Knowing how hungry the Nubian troops were to battle their brethren that had denied them equality for so long, he sent them ahead of the legions as his shock troops. Still unable to bring his chariots into close proximity of the battle due to the limited space to manoeuvre, he commanded the chariots to take a more defensive position, forming an outer ring that encircled the combatants, eliminating any of the enemy that tried to run into the forest and flee from the scene of battle.

"How did they get out of the city?" Thutmoses demanded an answer.

"I don't know my Prince," the captain responded nervously.

"Well find out. If there's a way out then there's obviously a way in for us as well. I need men assigned to no other task but finding me that opening into that city. As soon as you locate it, I want the engineers determining how we can use it to our advantage!"

The captain immediately barked orders to his subordinates who then ran off to assemble a search team to scout for the concealed access point.

While discussing the situation with his officers, Hoshea was busily strapping the Prince into his polished brass armour. Completing the grieves, breastplate and forearm guards, Hoshea reached up to place the blue war helmet Khepresh with its prominent golden uraeus upon Thutmoses' head.

"Where's my chariot driver?" Thutmoses asked his captains as he looked around but couldn't see the driver anywhere.

"His division was housed on the north side, my Prince," came the reply from one of the officers. "They were caught by surprise by the enemy. None of them survived. I believe your driver was amongst the fallen."

Turning to Hoshea, Thutmoses looked his ward in the eyes. "No time to find another driver. Do you think you can do it?"

"I've ridden with you enough times that I think I could handle it," Hoshea did not sound overly confident.

"Strap up the horses then and bring my chariot around. Today's as good a day to learn as any."

"Right away my Lord," Hoshea responded, eager to take part in the battle.

"My Prince," one of the captains objected. "He's just a boy."

"He's far more than a boy captain. I have every confidence in him. This is one battle I'm not going to miss. Tell the men, tonight we dine in Saba."

The warriors of Saba enjoined the battle with mixed feelings of fear and loathing. Having suffered for so many months at the hands of their enemies until their supplies had dwindled to the point of exhaustion, watching their loved ones starve and die from malnutrition and disease, the hate swelled in their hearts and pushed them forward with little regard for personal safety. Fear stemmed from the fact that they knew they were vastly outnumbered but fear was also a powerful driving force that made them fight like unleashed demons. There was no semblance of strategy to their attack. Having been directed to engage the enemy as soon as they breached the wall, they fought with the desperation that drives men into a berserker rage, with the hope of taking the Egyptians completely unawares and overpowering them with their fury.

Nebuti coordinated their release through the tunnel on the north side. One hundred men at a time were able to conceal themselves behind the clumps of trees projecting from the northern slope of the butte. The first platoon to enter the tunnel consisted of their best archers. From their concealed positions on the slope they quickly and easily dispatched the sentries in the tower. Immediately afterwards, the group of engineers raced to the palisade with their little bridges to cross the canals and tools at ready to take down the palisade wall. Using huge block wedges and large wooden mallets with leather covers over the hammer heads to silence the blows, they drove the blocks easily between the poles, at first separating them but eventually causing them to crack and topple. At that precise moment Nebuti ordered the regular forces into the tunnel providing a continuous flow of men with no plan other than attack, attack and continue to attack. Charging across the opening from the butte to the palisade there was no opposition, as all the Egyptians stationed on the north side had already been eliminated by the advancing contingent of archers.

It wasn't until they rounded the perimeter of the eastern and western walls that they first encountered the legions of Egyptian forces at which time they unleashed their deafening war cry. It was like no sound that the Egyptians had ever heard before. Hardly describable as human, it was a horrifying mixture of rage and fury emitted by a ravenous beast starved for revenge. The sound made the Egyptians pause momentarily, frozen in their tracks, a fatal error permitting the warriors of Saba to have advantage of first strike with their javelins. From behind the city walls the drummers beat a steady rhythm that drove their warriors into a killing frenzy. As some of the Egyptian new recruits came face to face with their enemies, their only prevailing thought was that this must be what death sounds like, permitting the haunting, otherworldly noise to get inside their heads. Unimaginable shrieks and screams, striking terror in the Egyptian's hearts, petrifying some from fighting back. Though their numbers were far less, the extreme shock of their attack provided the Saba forces with an equal standing on the battlefield. At this early stage of the encounter it was evident that the battle could easily have gone either way.

Watching the events from her palace balcony, Queen Tharbis surrounded herself with her city council members as they witnessed the battle. "I think we are doing well," she commented to her administrators.

"Nebuti is an excellent commander, your Majesty," Cantis agreed with her queen's appraisal. "If anyone can win this battle, it will be him."

"The tide is in our favour, my Queen," Mombasi reaffirmed the previous comments.

"But I don't understand how the Egyptians managed to stem our flow so quickly," the Queen commented. "It's almost as if they had some warning that we had broken through their wall but that was impossible. We had killed their sentries before they could even sound an alarm. How were they able to react so quickly?"

"We still managed to move at least a thousand through the gap before they discovered our attack," Mombasi was delighted to emphasize the work performed by his engineering team. "And we are still pouring thousands more through the tunnel as we speak, your Majesty. The Egyptians can only stop us if they seal off our tunnel and that is unlikely as our forces beat them back from the breach so quickly."

"Well done, Mombasi," the Queen complemented his engineering team. "It won't matter if they reach the tunnel or not," she suggested, "once we have all our fighting men beyond the wall and that should happen shortly."

"And anyone of our soldier is worth two or three of theirs," Shiragu interjected himself into the conversation. "The goddesses smile favourably upon us, your Majesty."

"We can only hope it is so," Tharbis responded.

"It is a certainty," Shiragu comforted his queen.

"I have learned that nothing is ever a certainty," the Queen dismissed his comment. "If we were so certain that my brother Ikheny would not pose a threat, then how did we underestimate him so badly before we exiled him from our city. Instead he raises an army of Nubians and as Kikiani, King of Kush, he has brought us to this moment. If only we had killed him when we had the opportunity we would not be fighting the Egyptians now."

"It is not within our laws, your Majesty" Cantis was quick to defend the decision made so many years ago. "The royal sons either submit to castration or they are exiled; that is the law."

"It isn't our custom to have anyone proclaim himself as the King of Kush either but now we have not only had my brother doing so but his successor, this Egyptian. Perhaps you should read our laws to this Prince of Egypt so that he will know better?"

Cantis bowed her head and retreated from the balcony on which the queen was perched.

"Laws are meant to be changed," the Queen took a parting shot at Cantis. "If we survive this then it will be a priority. Somebody tell me what is happening now. What is that cloud of dust I see rising in the distance," the Queen alerted her advisors to the sudden change in the appearance of the horizon which was now turning brown from the turbulence.

Shiragu was the first to tell her. "It's their chariots my Queen."

"What are they doing?" she wanted to know.

"From this distance, my Queen, it would appear that they are going to drive their chariots forward into the chasm left by our forces when they turned either to the right or to the left." Clever, Shiragu thought to himself. The warriors of Saba were busy beating back the Egyptian divisions on either side of the breach, thereby leaving the hole they made in the wall as the thinnest point of their forces. Having recognized this, the Egyptian commanders were ordering their soldiers to step back slowly in a slow, controlled retreat, thus increasing the yawning chasm between the two main bodies of the Saba forces, rendering them even thinner at that point of the breach. By deliberately separating them into two bodies moving in different directions, they wouldn't be able to come to each other's aid. Divide, separate, and conquer, one of the first rules of warfare. And now the chariots were heading directly towards the chasm thereby being able to attack the rear of both segments of the Queen's army as well as seal the flow of any further soldiers passing through the breach. "I'm afraid I have some bad news…" Shiragu began before being cut off by his Queen whose attention had been caught elsewhere.

"What is that?" she pointed out the window towards the lead chariot.

"It is their Prince, my Queen," Shiragu recognized the blue helmet with the golden insignia of the uraeus.

"Not him," she dismissed his answer. "What is in his hand?"

Looking more closely, all the advisors standing on the balcony alongside their queen could see it. The pale glow radiating off its surface had a ghostly, haunting appearance that mimicked the dying flames of a campfire. None of them could identify what it was.

Only Nebuti recognized it and he was down in the tunnel with the last of his men preparing to exit the city. Picking his last man from the line-up, Nebuti gave him a message to run back to the Queen as quickly as possible.

Queen Tharbis was just stepping down from the balcony when the messenger came charging into the room. He immediately ran up to the queen, going down on one knee in front of her with head bowed.

"Speak" she commanded. "What is the word from your commander?"

"Commander Nebuti is concerned, my Queen. This rod held by the Prince of Egypt, he has seen it before. Thirty years ago when merely a soldier fighting alongside the Nubians, the Viceroy of the Egyptians held it in his hands. He said, 'suddenly our army felt ill and we could not fight any longer and the advantages we had gained that day were all lost. We were on the verge of victory and in a matter of minute we were being slaughtered.' He says this staff presents a bad omen from the goddess."

"Is he saying all is lost?" she demanded an answer from the messenger.

"He did not say, your Majesty" The messenger was fearful of suffering the Queen's wrath.

"Get back down there and find me an answer," she shouted.

"Yes, my Queen." The messenger shot from the room, relieved to be returning back to the battle rather than face the Queen another moment.

Returning to the balcony the Queen watched the actions of the Egyptian prince intently. His chariot swerved wildly, rolling from right to left and then left to right, incapable of holding a straight line. In his left hand the Prince held the sapphire staff aloft while he reached with his right hand for javelin after javelin, tossing them with pinpoint accuracy into the backs of the Kush warriors as his chariot careened by. The only means of remaining upright was the leather tether that tied him to the chariot rail. The chariot driver weaved his horses through impossible gaps, much of the time the wheels barely touching the ground.

"I've never seen anyone able to do such things with a chariot before," the Queen commented. "They roll back and forth like men possessed."

"The driver must be a master charioteer," Shiragu commented. "To manage the horses like that and still maintain the chariot upright takes years of practice. Few men could accomplish such a thing. And the way their Prince can still throw and hit his targets while in constant motion; an incredible feat. The pair are absolutely fearless. Surely the gods are protecting him!"

"Not incredible! Impossible!" the Queen ranted. "He is taking down our men without any resistance. The tide of battle is turning against us. We must do something."

The army of Saba was in a state of confusion. Infantry to the front and now chariots to the rear, no matter which way they turned they were being cut down before they were even able to engage the enemy. The mass of bodies in the army of Saba were so tightly compressed that the javelins tossed from the chariots could not miss. Some did manage to turn and attempted to attack the chariots, only to be buried beneath the thrashing shod feet of the horses or the bone grinding wheels of the chariots. All around the Prince's chariot the other chariots circled and drove headlong into the remnant of the Queen's army. Having loosed all his javelins, Thutmoses used the sapphire staff like a war club, its dense wood smashing skulls with ease as they drove by.

The Queen could not remove her gaze from the Egyptian Prince. Both he and his driver were covered in blood from head to toe but none of it theirs. The pair of coal black horses were lathered with the white creamy foam of their sweat. Her own warriors were seen fleeing in every direction from before him, as he wielded his staff with deadly efficiency. This was not a man, this was a god as far as she was concerned.

"Enough," the Queen cried out. "Someone have Nebuti sound the retreat before we lose every single soldier in our army. Draw whatever men we have left back inside the city." From the time she had spoken until the sounding of the retreat was only a matter of minutes. The warriors of Saba quickly ran back through the gaping hole they had made in the north wall. It was obvious that the Egyptians could have easily blocked their retreat and slaughtered the remnant but she knew it was also evident that their Prince had given his men an order to let them retreat to safety. He was giving her men the opportunity to survive but at the same time they had to live with the ignominy of their failure and loss. To some in her army, they would have preferred death to the shame they must now live with.

"He is a man with honour," Shiragu commented, seeing how easy it would have been for the Egyptians to butcher what remained of their forces but choosing not to do so.

"It is not honour," Queen Tharbis disagreed. "He is a man that wishes to negotiate for the remaining lives he has spared. He is calculating on us trading for the privilege of saving our lives. Send word to him that he can bring a delegation along with a squadron of his own men for protection through the eastern gates. We will open our doors to him and welcome this Prince of Egypt."

"Are we offering terms of our surrender, my Queen," Shiragu wanted to know exactly what he was to say to entice the Prince of Egypt to accept the invitation into the city.

Tharbis took offense to her advisor's question. "I am offering him terms of our peace. Arrange for us to meet in two hours. Now go!"

CHAPTER THIRTEEN

"What did it do? Obviously the staff had some unworldly power," Eleazar insisted on knowing. As he had suspected, the sapphire staff had been imbued by the touch of Yahvu with special properties.

"Moses obtained an insight that came directly from the central sphere of creation that I had spoken about with him the first time we met," Aaron tried to explain.

"Exactly what does that mean?" His father's explanation was hardly satisfactory.

"When I first talked to the Prince, I told him that his family had some special gift that gave them a conduit to the inner sphere of the Creator. The belief amongst the Lebu priests was that they were born with it and that is why we wondered if was in the male line and if the Crown Prince possessed it. Because his mother did not possess the gift, we didn't think it could be anything else to explain this gift of prophecy and prognostication."

"But now?" Eleazar was beginning to appreciate where his father was going with this line of thought.

"It was not a gift they were born with. It was the staff. Somehow the staff communicated with them when they held it. Yahvu became present in their thoughts and their actions when they held the staff."

"But that can't be correct father," Eleazar challenged Aaron's explanation. "Yusef was able to prophesize long before he came into possession of the staff."

"You are not listening," Aaron scolded him. "I'm not talking about prophecy. I'm referring to this direct line of communication between a man and the Creator. One can be born a prophet, but that is completely different from what this staff could do."

"Did Moses tell you that?" Eleazar wanted to know if it really was true.

"In so many words," his father answered. "He claimed that it provided a link between God and his family but with no one else."

"Is that true?"

"I do not know. When I asked to hold the staff he refused to let me do so. He said anyone but his family would die if they held the staff," Aaron's tone suggested that he did not necessarily believe what Moses had told him.

"You never touched the staff? Eleazar was surprised that in all the years that his father and Moses had been together he never once held the sapphire staff.

"No."

"But the stories say that you did hold it." Eleazar thought back upon all the stories that they have retold to the Children of Israel.

"Never, it was always my own staff that I used to perform some of the feats they speak of. If anyone was to try to hold his staff and defy Moses then you would end up dead like your two brothers. I knew that would be my fate if I ever challenged him. Even if I had held the staff and survived, I doubt I would have had lived long enough to tell anyone."

"You truly believe that father? Do you really think that Moses would have put you to death if you held the rod? After all, you had committed other infractions, such as moulding the golden calf and he still forgave you."

"I know it to be true," Aaron was adamant. "All else could be forgiven but not attempting to hold that staff!"

1364 BCE

There was no time to clean up properly after the battle, so Thutmoses did the best that he could, splashing water over his arms and face in an effort to remove as much of the dried blood as he could. The death splatter still covered his armour and exposed legs. Looking down at his current condition he had to admit that he still looked a mess but it would have to do. Climbing into his chariot he gave Hoshea a nod to give the reigns a flick and begin the trot up the ramp towards the giant brass covered gates that guarded the eastern entrance. Riding at the head of his delegation, his chief officers and his group of advisors followed in chariots of their own. Behind the chariots marched a division of five hundred armed infantry. Under a flag of truce they entered beneath the gates and into the main plaza of the city. A raised dais had been erected at the far end of the plaza but for the most part the area appeared abandoned. Thutmoses gave the order to his men to stand at the ready. He also ordered fifty men to guard the gates to ensure that they remained open and would not be closed behind them.

"There is no reason not to trust us Prince," a discombobulated female voice sailed in from somewhere behind the dais. The voice was sweet and melodic, immediately putting the Prince at ease. It was soon followed by the Queen and all of her retinue assuming their places on the raised stage. Queen Tharbis had taken the time to prepare for their meeting, her dress of gossamer shimmering like a summer lake. Every outline of her body could be visualized through the practically invisible garment;

statuesque and carved from dark ebony. The Prince was enthralled by the sheer grace she exhibited as she settled into her throne-chair. Her attendants remained standing, split almost evenly on either side of her.

Thutmoses removed his blue war helmet and tucked it under his left arm. "Excuse the size of my escort but there's much I need to learn about Saba from you Queen Tharbis and how we were to be received was one of those questions. Best to be prepared for all possibilities."

"Your concerns are understandable, Prince of Egypt, but you should know that any that are invited to enter Saba at the behest of the Queen are guaranteed protection under the crown. No hand will be lifted against you and your men."

"Your invitation then is graciously accepted," the Prince responded. "I do prefer to be referred to as the Prince of Kemet, though. Egypt brings to mind some negative connotations of the Hyksos invaders that conquered our land. It is a term we do not find very flattering."

"As you know we were allied to the Hyksos, young Prince, so it will be difficult for us to change words that have been ingrained into our culture."

"As it obviously is difficult for your people to see us as anything but the enemies you considered us back in those days as well. I had expected to see the people of your city upon our entry but it would appear that they are still all in hiding." The Prince looked around at all the closed shutters and still he could not see a single citizen watching from even a rooftop, which made him very suspicious.

Queen Tharbis had a ready answer for that question. "You are the first army to ever enter our city in over a thousand years. They have no prior experience regarding what you might do next, only stories of the raping and pillaging of conquering armies of the Egyptians. You inspire fear, so in response they hide."

"I can assure you Queen Tharbis that my men, the soldiers of Kemet, will not lay a hand on any of the citizens. It is not our intention to harm any innocents."

"What is your intention then Prince of Egypt?" the Queen was very deliberate with her question while still playing her game of words knowing that she had already struck a chord of irritation with Thutmoses.

"I would say that my first intention was to see if the beauty of the Queen of Saba matched the stories that they spread in distant lands."

"That is an odd justification for launching a war on my city," she did not know if she should be flattered or upset. "So what is your verdict?"

"The stories did not do you justice," Thutmoses complimented her.

Speaking in a hushed tones, Ahrown leaned over the side of his chariot so that only Thutmoses could hear him. "What are you doing? Talk of beauty? Really?"

"Buying us time," the Prince responded. "All the shutters are closed for a good reason. If these talks don't go well I suspect that we will find behind them that there's an arrow pointed directly at your heart and everyone else's. Now spread the word and see to it that we have several more legions ascend the ramp and ready to storm the city."

"Is there a problem Prince of Egypt," the Queen asked as she watched him speaking in confidence to his colleague.

"No problem," Thutmoses smiled broadly. "I have merely asked my chief advisor to return to the camp and arrange for my gifts to be brought to you. Some of the treasures that I gathered along the way which will serve to adorn your beauty."

"You are most gracious Prince."

"Ahrown," Thutmoses turned to his priest, "Bring the golden necklace from my tent along with the gold and pearl earrings. They are the Queen's now. Now do as I have commanded."

Ahrown stepped down from his chariot and taking a small escort of men with him exited from the city.

"Are you certain that you do not wish to give them to your wife?" the Queen suggested. "Even this far south I have heard that you are married to your sister. Is that not so?"

"You are well informed Queen of Saba. I am surprised that you received news of events from Kemet this far to the south."

"There are many traders that come to Saba," she explained. "They bring us information from all around the world. There are very few secrets that we have not heard in Saba. After all this city is the centre of the known world."

"Then you should already know that I have not been with my wife for many years and that now all I see before me is your indescribable presence. These gifts I am about to give you pale in comparison to the beauty of the woman that they will adorn."

"So tell me of this beauty that you behold," the Queen finally weakened to his flattery though still weary of her would-be conqueror.

"Your coal-black hair plummets to frame the grace of your long delicate neck. Rarely have I ever beheld such a finely sculpted figure of a woman with its tapered waist and full ripe bosom. Your heart shaped lips are red like precious rubies, only to part and expose gleaming white teeth that radiate like the stars at night."

"Enough," she stopped him. "This is talk that belongs in private and not in a public forum from a Prince. So tell me Prince, what is your real intent for Saba?"

"Shall we take a walk to discuss," Thutmoses was determined to have her descend from the dais.

"Whatever needs to be discussed I'm certain can be done in this forum," the Queen was reluctant to leave her throne.

"As one royal to another," the Prince began, "the issues of diplomacy that need to be discussed are best done with full disclosure. We are under a flag of truce, which means no harm will be done to either party while we conduct these talks. If that is so, then let us discuss these matters in a less austere environment."

"There is nothing wrong with this environment," she insisted.

"Everything is wrong with how this meeting is being conducted," Thutmoses disagreed. "You and your advisors are situated upon a podium high above us. We are standing in our chariots while our horses beat their hooves impatiently against the flagstones. Before long they'll cover your forum with excrement. This is not how to conduct a truce."

The Queen's features showed her obvious displeasure. "Are you suggesting that I have not been sincere in my intent to arrange this truce?"

"I am only suggesting that if we really wish to make progress between our two nations then you should stand by me and we go to a place where we can talk openly without the concern of intrusions."

"We can speak here," she insisted.

"I don't believe we can," Thutmoses disagreed. Looking to his left and right, the Prince barked out his next command. "Men, back to the camp. The men at the gates will remain in position there to ensure the gates remain open." Turning their chariots, the captains started marching their men away from the plaza.

"Wait," Tharbis sprung from her chair, arm outstretched in an effort to stop anyone from moving. "What are you doing?"

"I thought it was obvious," the Prince replied calmly. "We are going back to our camp and will wait for you to change your mind as to how we will conduct these talks."

"Wait," she pleaded. Lifting the hem of her dress, the Queen began to descend the first step of the dais.

"My Queen, what are you doing," Nebuti reached out in an attempt to grasp the Queen's wrist but she shook him off.

"We have a flag of truce, commander," she explained to Nebuti and everyone else in her council. "He will not harm me."

"This is most unusual," the Council was in agreement. "This is madness. The Egyptians will take you prisoner. You cannot do this."

"In case you haven't noticed," she spoke harshly to her advisors, "We are already their prisoners. There is no choice, I am doing this." Descending the steps one by one, the Queen strode gracefully towards the Prince's chariot. Reaching down, Thutmoses took her hand and helped her into the back of his chariot. As soon as she was safely on board, he helped place her hands on the rail and then gave the command for his force to leave the city.

"Hoshea, take the horses around our encampment, I want the Queen to see the extent of our forces."

Having gained a degree of mastery over his horses, Hoshea reigned his horses into a high-stepping gate as they paraded through the gates.

"Is that intended to be a threat," she turned her head to face the Prince while still holding on tightly to the rail.

"No, I just wanted you to see what you were up against, should you have given the order for your archers concealed behind your shuttered buildings to fire upon us."

"They were only there in case you reneged on our truce," she explained.

"It made it difficult to conduct any negotiations when you know that at any moment you could be the target of hundreds of arrows."

"We are a people of integrity. I would not have given the order unless you violated the truce," she insisted.

"And I am a man of great honour and integrity and I swear you will not be harmed and neither are you my captive. I will return you to your city as soon as we complete our talks."

"That he is your Majesty, a man of great integrity." Hoshea confirmed.

"You let your subordinates address us like that," she was surprised by Hoshea's impertinence.

"Allow me to introduce my ward, Hoshea. He speaks when he shouldn't but I wouldn't have him behave any differently."

"An honour to meet you, your Majesty," Hoshea broke protocol again.

The Queen did not know how to respond to this boy that had no respect for class positions. "How did you know?" she asked.

"Know what?" Thutmoses questioned back.

"How did you know my men were stationed behind the closed shutters?"

"I could tell you that it was natural instinct gained from being in similar situations a thousand times, but that would be a lie. Yours is only the second city I have ever taken. If you wish to know the truth, then I think it was the sapphire staff," he confessed to her. "Ever since I held it I've had this ability to sense events about to happen. Some voice in my head told me what was concealed within your buildings."

"Why are you so willing to tell me about your most sacred weapon? What if I should take possession of it? It was foolish of you to tell me this." She was surprised by the prince's openness and candour.

"I tell you this because that same voice is telling me that I can trust you. That you and I will have much to share in the future."

"Perhaps you will let me hold it then?" she requested hesitantly.

"Not unless you have a death wish," Hoshea snickered.

"Is he threatening me," she was disturbed by the boy's insolence.

"Not at all. They say that anyone not of my family that touches the staff dies instantly. I think that is Hoshea's way of saying he likes you and he does not wish to see you harmed." Thutmoses gave Hoshea a light kick on his calf muscle to tell him to be quiet and pay attention to his driving.

"Oh," was her only response, not knowing how to properly interact with this impertinent chariot driver.

As the chariot rolled past the troops, all the soldiers shouted their approval of seeing their Prince riding with the Queen of Saba. Some saluted, others hooted but none showed any display of emotion other than the excitement of believing their war was soon to be over.

"Obviously, my men wish to believe that we will successfully negotiate an end to our hostilities."

"You declared this war upon us," she corrected him. "We had no reason to go to war with the Egyptians."

"Keep referring to us as Egyptians and we may very well start another war," Thutmoses taunted her. "We did fight and removed the Hyksos from our land. That also removed that name the Asiatics used for us as well. So please, from now on we are Kemtu."

"I promise," she agreed.

"Good, we have just had our first successful negotiation."

"I guess we have," she smiled, the first time that she had shown any other emotion other than the sternness with which she first greeted her occupiers.

"I knew I was right," Thutmoses sighed.

"What are you talking about," she was confused.

"I was right that behind your red ruby lips lay gleaming white teeth that sparkle like the stars at night."

"You certainly seem to be in a strange, happy mood," she laughed, once again showing she was capable of displaying emotions not too different from an ordinary woman.

"Certainly happier than I've seen him in a long time," Hoshea interjected himself into their conversation once again.

This time the kick to the calf muscle from Thutmoses was even harder. "Keep your focus on where you going," the Prince instructed his ward. "Don't pay him any attention," he turned back to the Queen.

"So now that we are riding around your camp Thutmoses, what is it that you wish to show me?"

It was the first time she had said his name and he liked the way it sounded coming from her lips. "Exactly what you're seeing. Thousands upon thousands of men, willing to do exactly what I command. Had you done anything foolishly with your concealed archers we would have destroyed your city. I don't want to destroy your city."

"Tell me then, what is it you want," she asked once again.

"Your brother named me King of Kush. I want to be able to say that Saba is now part of the Egyptian Empire."

"And what does that entail," she wanted to hear the details.

"The usual," he replied. "Annual tribute, preferred trading status, support for our military during times of war, and other needs as they arise."

"Other needs? That strikes me as something far more personal," she teased her captor.

"We can let our negotiations determine what those other needs might be," Thutmoses wanted to remain a little mysterious though his intentions were beginning to look obvious to the Queen.

"And in turn you will spare the city," she questioned.

"The city, your throne, even to a degree your independence. I need you beside me, not laying defeated beneath my feet. You have my word," the Prince promised.

"How can you speak for your father?" she wondered. "Word has it that he has not been pleased with your actions on this campaign. You may promise one thing but his is the final word."

"I will convince him that it is in Kemet's best interest to have Saba as an ally rather than an enemy."

"Your words are not that comforting to me. Your ability to convince Pharaoh is tainted by your past relationship. There is even word that you will be arrested for what you did in Bagrawiyah."

"Your ability to know of matters in Thebes is incredible," Thutmoses congratulated her gathering of intelligence. "I'd almost expect that you have a spy in my father's court to know all these things."

All that Tharbis returned was a silent smile, leaving Thutmoses to guess whether it was true or not. "So do you have another suggestion?"

"A matter of fact, I do. Be my consort," she suggested.

The Prince grimaced upon hearing that word. "Not to be unappreciative but we have our ability to gather information as well. What I've been told is that those that become your consorts don't live through the next day."

"Ridiculous! Of course they make it to the next day," she rebutted the statement. "But…"

"Perhaps not through the following month," she clarified. "My physicians first have to determine that I'm pregnant before we can dispense with my consort."

"I don't think being your consort is a very healthy option under those circumstances."

"Not healthy at all," Hoshea added his opinion.

"Quiet," both of them responded in unison and then laughed afterwards.

"At least as my consort you would guarantee your word and bond to our city. Pharaoh is unlikely to try and change any of the terms of agreement as long as you are here. We can always find a way to change some of the rules regarding the policies concerning impregnation," she stared into his brown eyes beguilingly. "After all, laws are made to be changed."

"And why would you believe that?" Thutmoses wondered.

"Because a woman knows when a man is truthful. I can see it in your eyes. If you swear that you will safeguard the terms of any agreement as well as the people of the city then I will believe you. I've heard enough about you that I know you would actually oppose your father."

"I was actually referring to why you would believe it would be so easy to change your laws regarding your rules of conception and the expected lifespan of your consort." Thutmoses challenged her. "I also definitely have to find out who your spy is in the Theban court. But more importantly, let me make it clear, I have no intention of sacrificing my life as soon as you're pregnant."

"What is the point of being a Queen if I can't make new laws?"

"Well if we're going to change the law then let's start with the one concerning no King in Kush. Have myself declared as king and then we have the equality I seek in our relationship. We can resolve all the issues with that one declaration."

"Saba has always been ruled by Queens. The goddesses ordained that should be the way it is."

"I think your priests need to go back into the temple and hear the latest oracles. I'm certain your goddesses have some new messages for them."

"Does this mean that when you become Pharaoh of Egypt, I mean Kemet, that I will be called Queen of Egypt?"

Thutmoses nodded. "You will be a Queen of Kemet."

"Will I be Great Wife?"

"That will be determined by how well you treat the King of Kush," Thutmoses said playfully.

"I do believe I hear the goddesses summoning the priests," the Queen cupped her ear pretending to listen to the heavenly voices.

"I hear them too," Hoshea turned the horses and headed back to the city gates.

CHAPTER FOURTEEN

"And that is how your Uncle Moses became ensnared by that black harlot," Aaron spat a wad of phlegm into the fire again, listening to it crackle before he continued to speak. "You would have been sickened if you had been there watching them ride around the camp like two lovers mooning over one another."

"I think your eyes are clouded when it comes to Tharbis," Eleazar criticized his father. "She is not to blame for everything that you think has gone wrong in our lives."

"Had Moses not fallen under her spell we probably wouldn't have even have left Mitzrayim. We'd be ruling it!"

"What are you talking about?" Eleazar was beginning to think his father's mind was becoming addled as death approached. "Tell me you are not becoming delusional."

"Had we returned to Thebes as soon as we took Saba and laid all the treasures of that city at the feet of Pharaoh, I am certain he would have forgiven all that his son had done. Moses would have continued to be the Crown Prince and right now he'd be sitting on the throne and we would have been restored as the official religion in the land, and all the foreigners in Goshen would have been granted their freedoms once again to live how and wherever they chose. We could have restored the balance to our world."

"And then what, father? As long as Moses was alive and on the throne we'd all be happy and Yahvu would grant us a world of everlasting peace? Do you seriously believe that is how it would have been? "Do you even think Yahvu would have exposed himself to Moses if he had not been exiled? If you do, then you truly have lost your mind and it is best that you die on this mountain top far away from the people before you poison their minds with your sickness."

"How dare you speak to me that way!"

"Perhaps it is about time someone did. History shows that each new Pharaoh of every dynasty institutes his own religious sect, erases the past from previous Pharaohs and always finds ways to make the foreigners pay for the privilege of living in their lands and it's usually paid for in blood. How are you able to ignore the facts which speak out as plain as the nose on your face?"

"It would have been different," Aaron insisted. "Instead your uncle spent two years fornicating with that witch and forgetting all about his responsibilities back in

Mitzrayim. He preferred to be king of some misbegotten backwater kingdom than protect his own birth right"

"No it would not have been any different father. You were never in charge of your own destiny. Everything that happened did so because Yahvu willed it to be so. I thought you would know that by now. I thought the prophecies from Yusef would have convinced you that you were never in control of your own destinies. We were never meant to stay in Mitzrayim. You have become a fool like all those that followed Korah and Dathan if you think there actually was a choice. Stop this nonsense father before it erodes all the good things that you have done. Do not blacken your memory with talk of such nonsense!"

"He took it all away from us," Aaron actually began crying. "My own father died while I sat in Saba. I never even said goodbye to him. Eight years of my life were taken from me so that he could roll around in a bed with that whore!"

As much as Eleazar wanted to be angry with his father he could not be unsympathetic to the old man breaking down in tears before him. Moving beside his father, he wrapped his arm around his shoulders and held him tightly. "I know father, I know. Life has not been easy for you or for that matter, the rest of us. Yahvu has been testing us from the day He decided to free us from slavery. But you must never think that we were destined for any life other than the one we are living now. I don't know how to explain it to you but I know in my heart that in some way we are going to change the world. This band of refugees, this mixed multitude of nations is going to be talked about for thousands of years. We are going to be a beacon to all the other nations of the world. I don't know why, but I just know that we will be and when they remember you, they will remember that you were Moses' strong right hand and you never lost faith in our mission. Whatever doubts you may have now, whatever disbeliefs you presently hold, all these disappointments and regrets that you have carried for so many years, they will all perish on this mountain top with you. I promise you that father. Just let those regrests from the past be and stop trying to pursue this path you are now following into a pit of darkness. Let me keep your legacy as we know it now and I will preserve it for the people to remember forever. Let go of this resentment you cling to father and maybe Yahvu will forgive you for your lapse in faith."

1362 BCE

Thutmoses rolled over on top of Tharbis, pressing her body down into the soft cushions of their bed. The fingers of each hand interlocked with hers as his lips gently stroked her long neck. He slowly moved his way down from the nape of her neck to the turgid nipples of her breasts.

"Hey," she laughed. "Those aren't meant for you to chew on. Be gentle husband."

"I can't help myself," he confessed. "I am a hungry animal when I'm with you."

"That's very nice but if you start biting then I start biting back and you won't like me biting down there very much," she threatened him.

"Maybe I will," he thought about it before nuzzling her breasts again.

"Are you happy husband," she asked with sincerity.

"Happier than I have been in a long time," he confessed. "I have my beautiful wife, our beautiful son. What should I be unhappy about?"

"I just wanted to hear you say it," she admitted.

"You're not as tough as you try to make people believe," Thutmoses then began to lick her navel, which he knew was one of her most ticklish spots.

"Stop it, stop it," she was practically screaming, crying and laughing at the same time.

It wasn't until there was a knock on their bedchambers door that Thutmoses gave her any relief by stopping his playful torture.

"What is it?" Thutmoses angrily shouted through the closed door.

"You have a visitor from Thebes, my King," the voice from the other side of the door responded.

"Have them wait in the conference chambers," Thutmoses instructed. "I will be there shortly."

Rolling out of the bed, Thutmoses looked around for his tunic. "It is amazing how anytime we just want to be left alone so that we can make love all morning that there's always an interruption."

"You exaggerate husband," she taunted him by displaying the full nakedness of her practically perfect body. Even after childbirth there was not a single line or crease across her belly.

"You are being cruel Tharbis," Thutmoses scolded her as he found it difficult to stop staring at her exquisite form.

"Shall I come with," Tharbis asked as her lithe and naked body slid from the bed.

"See to Ra-Seth-Hiye first," he suggested. "Then join us with our son afterwards."

Hurriedly dressing into a simple tunic, the King of Kush left their chambers and was escorted to the hall where his visitor awaited. His thoughts were still fixated upon the view of his wife sprawled across their bed and as a result he experienced a brief flush of anger towards some unwanted visitor who had robbed him of the opportunity of being alone with Tharbis.

He was already preparing some angry words for this guest when suddenly all that he was thinking vanished. Upon seeing his guest, all formality was abandoned and Thutmoses ran to embrace his visitor. "Uncle Ephra, what are you doing here?"

"Is that any way to greet your uncle, questioning why I bothered to come? I think I should be insulted," he jested. "How many years is it now? Eight," as his uncle answered his own question. "Eight long years."

"Of course I'm happy to see you uncle. I had no idea that you were coming to visit. Or is this official business? Why didn't you send word? I would have sent out an escort to meet with you."

"What would be the point of sending word if it would take just as long for the *webwety* to reach you as it did for me to come here?" His uncle's argument made perfect sense.

Thutmoses nodded his head in agreement. "True, but at least an escort would have protected you on route."

"It was not necessary. I had my own escort of a hundred troops."

"So this is an official visit then," Thutmoses deduced from the size of his uncle's bodyguard.

"Actually nephew I am here for both reasons. And if you were to tell me several months ago I'd be travelling up river past the sixth cataract, I would have never believed you. But your mother can be very persuasive and how could I ever refuse my sister anything she requested."

"Yes, mother does have her ways," Thutmoses agreed. "Please sit." He led his uncle to the sedan chairs at the side of the room where they reclined. "Bring us some figs and dates," he ordered the palace servants. "And some wine. Some very good wine!"

"I see that being a monarch has suited you well nephew," Kheper-Kephrure teased his nephew.

"I think you better refer to me as your Majesty," Thutmoses tried to sound stern and serious. "We don't want the servants thinking that they no longer need to keep a sense of decorum."

"Really?" his uncle questioned.

"Of course not, Uncle Ephra," Thutmoses jabbed his uncle. "But it does sound good when others say it," he laughed. "So tell me everything. I've had no news from Thebes for over two years." Thinking back, Thutmoses grimaced at the thought that sprung to mind, "Not since I had my father sent his instructions to have me killed." He didn't intend to let the words spring out in that manner but his emotions got the better of him.

"What are you talking about?" his uncle sounded shocked by the revelation. "What nonsense is this, nephew?"

"You mean no one in Malkata knew about it?" Thutmoses was as equally surprised. "How's that even possible?"

"No! Of course not! We knew nothing. All we heard about was how you uncovered the sinister plot by General Chenetothes to assassinate the *savov* family. Where did this ridiculous story of an attempt to have you killed on Pharaoh's orders come from?"

The mention of his uncle Chenetothes brought tears to his eyes and touched him with the sadness he had not felt for two years. "Not nonsense Uncle Ephra. I still have the letter signed by Pharaoh ordering it. I can show it to you if you don't believe me."

"No need, nephew. You have never lied to me. This saddens me greatly. I don't know what to say. I am sad and angry at the same time," his uncle confessed.

"Exactly how I feel whenever I think about it. Saddened and angry."

"But what about this plot that you foiled?"

"Lies, all lies," Thutmoses confessed. "A story created by the General in order to protect me and keep me safe. He was the one that received the orders from Pharaoh to have me killed. But he could not do it and instead gave up his own life along with his honour and his reputation in order to save me."

Kheper-Kephrure practically fell off the sedan upon hearing what Thutmoses had to say. "I cannot believe it nephew. I assure you we knew nothing of it. You have to believe that your mother did not know anything about this. She never would have gone along with this. You must believe me!"

"Yes, I believe you uncle but there had to be others that did know about it. The *anu* that wrote it, chancellors, and a host of others in Malkata that were willing to have me killed. I can barely make sense of it. What would have driven father to such a decision?"

"You know he is not a well man. He suffers the madness. That makes a man do things for which he is not responsible. Perhaps when he heard that you were made King of this city, it made his lose his capacity to think properly."

"This was before I had even officially become King in Saba, Uncle. All I was doing was expanding his empire, in his name. How can he accuse me of any crime for doing his bidding?"

"He's not well, Thutmoses."

"He's been ill for a long time," Thutmoses still wrestled with finding an explanation. "What possibly changed three years ago that my father would suddenly decide to have me killed?"

His uncle reached out to grab his hand, holding it securely. "I think I know. Three years ago you say. It must be because of your brother," he informed him.

The mention of a brother hit Thutmoses as if he had been struck by lightning. He collapsed back into the sedan trying to catch his breath. "What? I have a brother?"

"Yes, he was very sick for the first year of his life but he survived against all the odds. No one said anything at first because they feared he would die like all the others. It was just over three years ago. I'm guessing you didn't receive any of the letters. I know you mother tried to send you letters many times. She had hoped that you would return to see your brother and at the same time restore your marriage with your sister and heal the rift with your father." His uncle seemed sincerely sorry that Thutmoses had no knowledge of any of these events.

"He didn't want me to return," Thutmoses put the pieces together. "He obviously intercepted mother's letters to ensure I was kept in the dark and had no reason to return. He wanted me to be killed in Kush so that he could pretend to mourn my loss in battle. What kind of father could even conceive of such a thing?"

"As I told you, he is not well," Kheper-Kephrure presented the same excuse that the Prince had heard so many times before.

"Yes Uncle Ephra, you all serve him, and my mother still loves him, but all I see is a monster. A monster that would devour his own son! How long will everyone cater to his madness and pretend that there is nothing wrong? How many times will you say to me 'he is not well' and I should merely pretend that he did not try to have me killed."

"He is the *Neter-Nesew*, Thutmoses. We must obey," his uncle explained.

"Do you think your father would have said the same thing? I somehow doubt it. Yuyu would say that a Pharaoh must stand for justice for all or he must not stand at all."

"My father had the protection of his God. He was fearless because he knew his God would protect him no matter what he did. But the rest of us don't have a god protecting us. You cannot blame us for merely trying to remain alive."

"Perhaps Yuyu had the protection of his God because he was willing to take a stand against injustice," the Prince suggested. "Perhaps it's necessary for us to first take a stand in order to deserve and earn that god's protection." Thutmoses himself wondered what must come first. Did devotion to the deity without question bind God to the man or did God have to act first in order to bind the man to God?

"I cannot say for sure," his uncle spoke. "I believe my father confided more in you than he ever did in your Uncle Anen or myself."

"And now you have come to take me back to my executioner. Am I your nephew or am I your prisoner?"

"Stop being so pessimistic nephew. I came here because your mother wanted you to see a familiar face and feel confident that you will be safe. Nothing more."

"So why does she think now would be safe when my father would surely have me killed along the way if it were any other time?" Thutmoses still was unwilling to believe that Amenhotep had agreed to let him return to Thebes safely. "How can I go back to Thebes if I don't even know the situation I'm walking in to?"

"Because all is good now," his uncle attempted to calm him down. "Your brother appears to be healthy, the people still talk about your heroism in stopping the supposed plot, and your mother has convinced your father that it is time you come home."

"So he can kill me? Don't you think it is very odd that he invites my return knowing that my brother is going to survive? I suspect another of his nefarious plots. I cannot trust him. I will not trust him!" Thutmoses refused to accept that his father could possibly have had a change of heart.

"I would not have come all this distance if I didn't have a letter signed by Pharaoh guaranteeing your safety and that no harm will befall you now or in the future."

"Shall I put that letter alongside the other and we can see which one holds true?" the Prince chastised his uncle for putting his faith in anything that his father might have signed.

Kheper-Kephrure shook his head in defeat. "I cannot say for certain which will prove to be the true intent of Pharaoh. The fact that he has already tried to have you killed once makes me have doubt even of this mission that my sister has sent me on."

"So what should I do then uncle? Grandfather said that of both his sons, you were always the most clever and jurisprudent. You are a legal counsel in the courts in Memphis. Surely then there must be a solution that you can propose."

"Let me think for a moment," he urged his nephew to sit back and be patient. Resting his chin on a clenched fist, Kheper-Kephrure thought long and hard. "I think I have it. Your father's greatest fear is that he will be judged harshly at the time of his death by the forty-two assessor deities. What if we use the Papyrus of Ani against him in an open tribunal?"

"How would you ever get my father to agree to appear before a tribunal?"

"I couldn't," his uncle freely admitted. "But if you're willing to admit that your hand helped slay an innocent member of the *savov* family, then I could conduct a tribunal that brings you to trial."

"How in the world does this help me?" Thutmoses was very suspicious of the proposal, seeing it as nothing but another trap.

"Because you will present all the evidence of your father's attempt to have you killed and we use the letter of the General's confession to assassinate the *savov* family as his only means to save you. The court will see the love and respect between you and the General and contrast against the nefarious and horrendous contempt that Pharaoh had for his own son."

"If you have the letter of the General's intended coup, then you already know that he refers to unnamed people within Malkata that gave orders to have me assassinated. That was already in the letter from Chenetothes. So if the justices were reviewing that letter, whom did they possibly think the General may have been referring to? The possibilities were quite limited," Thutmoses was very suspicious of this proposed plan for a tribunal.

"It must have been removed from the original letter," his uncle responded. "I can tell you that as a magistrate of the court, there was no reference in that letter of anyone within the palace working with Chenetothes. What we received made no mention of any orders to have you killed. I swear it."

Moses laughed cynically. "See, he has a myriad of court officials doing his dirty work for him. Even letters confessing to a plot are altered upon his orders. You have no idea to what depths my father would go in order to achieve his goals. The only way your plan for a tribunal will achieve any justice is if my father confesses to the crime," Thutmoses objected. "Even when I produce the letter I possess, he could easily deny that the letter was even his, seal and all. Why would he confess?" The Prince could not see the logic of Amenhotep admitting his crime.

"Because he fears the judgment at the time of his death more than he fears any decision of the tribunal," his uncle replied. "If there's one thing I know about your father it's that he has an almost irrational belief in his immortalization following his death. If he thinks in any way that it might be denied to him, he will become hysterical."

"So you need to convince him that it is being denied then?" Thutmoses fathomed from his uncle's reasoning.

"As it clearly states in the papyrus, at the time of having the *ib* of his heart weighed against the maat of the feather of truth, he must declare that he has not lied, robbed, killed, which includes the intention to kill on false pretences, been quarrelsome or quick to anger or shown impatience."

"Ah, so you're convinced his fear of the afterlife is greater than his fear of lying in this world," Thutmoses followed his uncle's argument. "You're going to bring up all of those situations during the tribunal as attacks against my father. He cannot deny them or else he won't be able to pass through the gates to enter the ship to *Artu*."

"Now you understand how we can make this work."

"Only if he actually does fear his failure to join his ancestors in the afterlife more than his desire to have me killed. Are you positive you can succeed?" Thutmoses was still concerned.

"I can't guarantee the verdict of any tribunal. With ten judges, you are at the mercy of their sense of justice, not only mine. But I can guarantee that I can present it in such a way that he will never be able to try and harm you ever again." His uncle held his hands with palms upward as if to say, that is the best he can promise.

"And should I choose not to go with you?"

"There cannot be a renegade king in the south. The fact that the Crown Prince had himself declared as King of Kush, has been interpreted by Amenhotep's ministers as an act of treason. He is raising another army. He is going to march south and take

Saba and I fear he will slaughter all the inhabitants if his army does manage to reach this city. That means your wife and son will not be safe. Why do you think your mother was so insistent that I come here to persuade you to return? But sadly now we know her husband's promise not to harm you is possibly meaningless."

The hairs on the back of his neck stood up as Thutmoses let the anger flush throughout his body. "I came down here with thirty thousand troops and I have added almost an equal number of Nubians to that number over the past two years. If my father wants a battle, I will give him one."

"No!" Tharbis entered the room and heard the last statement of her husband. "No more wars. We must find another way. There has to be another way."

May I present my wife uncle, Queen Tharbis and my son, Ra-Seth-Hiye."

Rising from the sedan, Kheper-Kephrure bowed to the queen. "It is my great pleasure to meet you, your Majesty."

"So please continue," she requested while holding her one and a half year old son in her arms. "If my husband does not return then what is Pharaoh's intent?"

"As I mentioned to my nephew, your Majesty, Amenhotep is raising an army for the sole purpose of bringing Saba to heal."

"Why now?" the Queen was confused.

"That's the easy question," her husband confided. "I now have a brother which means I am expendable. It does not matter if I live or die now."

"This is true?" she asked their visitor.

"Yes, your Majesty. His name is Amenhotep-Neferkheperure."

"How surprising that he would name him after himself," the sarcasm dripped from Thutmoses' lips. "I pray my brother has a better life than I was ever afforded."

"I am saddened for you husband," Tharbis moved beside Thutmoses to console him.

Thutmoses wrapped his arms around his wife and son. "I cannot let him hurt either of you. I have to stop him. Otherwise, Pharaoh will be a constant danger to us."

"War is a greater danger to all of us. Go to him husband. You will find a way to bend him to your will. I know you will. Let your mother guide you."

"My mother over the years has hardly been my best advocate. My uncle has a plan but it cannot be guaranteed to be successful."

"Trust him. He is your family. Trust your mother. No matter what she has done, you must believe that your mother would not betray you as I would never betray our son. We will wait for you husband. As long as it takes I will be waiting for you."

"I will leave Caleb and Hur to manage the army and watch over you. No matter what happens to me you will not be left unprotected. Pharaoh will never lay a hand on my family. I swear that to you."

"I believe you husband." She kissed him deeply without any notice of their guest.

Thutmoses kissed back just as hard, leaving Kheper-Kephrure to look idly around the room in an effort to appear non-embarrassed.

"Is there anything else uncle that you wish to tell me?" Thutmoses remembered his uncle was present only after what passed for an eternity.

"Only a rumour," Kheper-Kephrure added. "There are those that have carried back stories from the warfront that say you know the whereabouts of my father's sapphire staff. Pharaoh has demanded you bring it to him if it has been discovered."

"Never found it," Thutmoses responded. "But even if I had, it would never be placed into Pharaoh's possession."

"Should you have found it," his uncle continued, "I can honestly say that Yuyu would have told you that you must never give it to a man like Amenhotep. So I am glad that you never found it," he winked, suggesting that he knew better. "Shall we agree that we should begin our journey back home in a week's time?"

"Yes, that will give me time to make all the necessary arrangements. I have no intention to arrive without my own means of protection. It is a long journey and if someone wanted to they could attack us easily along the route."

"I did tell you that I had a hundred of my own men to escort us," his uncle responded.

"Uncle, the bandits in this land have larger gangs than your pitiful escort. I think five thousand Nubians should do just fine. They will have no conflicts of loyalty to the royal house in Thebes." Thutmoses was putting his uncle on alert that should his plan go awry, Thutmoses was not going down without a fight.

CHAPTER FIFTEEN

"I had no idea that Moses was placed on trial," Eleazar was surprised by the revelation.

"Of course you did," his father responded. "You just didn't recognize the context of the story in which it was revealed."

"You're describing the episode where you say he had to flee after killing an officer of Mitzrayim, aren't you?" Eleazar was able to draw the connection to the story that Aaron was referring to.

"It was the catalyst for everything that followed," Aaron indicated. "With hindsight, perhaps we could have been a little smarter but the intent was to reverse the charges and hold Amenhotep accountable. In that respect, we probably succeeded but the price we paid was horrendous."

"If by horrendous, you mean we find ourselves in our current situation then I think you still haven't understood Yahvu's intent father. We weren't permitted to stay in Mitzrayim. We aren't to glorify our past lives as if they were somehow better than our lives now. That way of thinking from your generation must disappear. Moses is absolutely correct that the separation from our past must be complete. Can you not understand and appreciate that father?"

"Our family represents over fifteen hundred years of history in Mitzrayim. How does one make that all disappear simply by wishing it so?" Aaron found himself reflecting more and more on the past these last few weeks.

"That past dies on this mountain," Eleazar informed Aaron. "I appreciate the stories you are now telling me but ultimately I will decide what the people hear and what they don't. We are no longer Lebu father but Levi. The Lebu have died. They are gone! The day that Pharaoh outlawed us and forced us from Onu was the day the Levi were born."

"He labelled us as rebels," Aaron coughed as he said those words. "Rebels! Can you imagine that? We, who have served loyally for millennia are suddenly outcast and treated as criminals."

"Exactly as Yahvu intended," Eleazar explained. "When are you ever going to realize that you were never in control of your destiny any longer? God, Almighty determined all your actions, all your thoughts. You wanted to be in communication with that inner sphere but obviously you never wanted to pay the price for what that actually entailed."

"But Moses he was let to do as he pleased!"

"Aha!" Eleazar exclaimed. "Finally, you are willing to admit that your jealousy of Moses has caused this rot in your soul that serves as the infection that is killing you now."

"I said no such thing," Aaron tried to argue.

"But you did father and you don't even realize it. How sad. How pathetic. You think Moses was never restricted by Yahvu, that he did whatever he wished. You were the one that could always connect with the people. He never possessed that quality. To him the people were always a source of discontent and irritation. He was always distant from them but you could interact directly with the people like he never could. Yes, he was closer to Yahvu. Yes, he was the one to intercede on behalf of the people with God. But you were the one that translated God's words into actions. You were the one to establish rules and provide the details that Moses never could do. Don't you see? He had many shortcomings, but God made you Moses' strong right hand to overcome his deficiencies."

"Humph!" Aaron had no immediate comment for his son. "True, I was the one that had to organize everything. Your uncle would bounce from one thing to the next and leave all the pieces for me to pick up. And whenever he upset the people, it would be Miriam's job to try and restore a sense of joy and happiness."

"You see father, it was never a case of Moses doing as he pleased in any true sense. He did things, and left it to you and Aunt Miriam to fix the damage he left in his wake. If anything, I think Uncle Moses was probably jealous of both of you. You and Aunt Miriam could connect with the people, more than he ever could. He ruled by fear, but you ruled by law and Aunt Miriam ruled by love. Yahvu knew it would take the three of you, working together, to unite these divergent people into a single nation."

"He still made a mess of things when Amenhotep held the tribunal," Aaron felt that he still had to get the last word in against his brother.

"Yes, father but you were there to rectify it."

"Yes, I was!"

1361 BCE

"I hear that I am a grandmother," Tiye opened the conversation with her son.

Thutmoses had been sitting in her presence for over five minutes without saying a word. "Yes, I have a son." He said proudly. "His name is Ra-Seth-Hiye."

"It is a beautiful name," she replied calmly as she peeled the cap from a fig.

"And you have a son as well," Thutmoses responded.

"Yes, I do. I have two sons to be correct, but one seems to be very angry with me and I don't know exactly why."

"I know Uncle Ephra has told you about the letter in my possession, so you must know what is on my mind mother." The Prince saw no reason to be anything less than blunt.

The Queen looked offended. "Do you think I could have in any way supported the murder of my own son? How dare you imply such a thing!"

"I did not imply mother but it is an obvious question that one must ask. The same way I need to know whether or not you have mentioned a word of the letter to your husband."

"You mean your father."

"No, I don't," Thutmoses stated angrily. "He gave up being my father the moment he signed the letter to have me killed. He is not my father and I certainly am not his son."

"Do not say such a thing!" Tiye beseeched him. "For a son to deny his father, it will offend the gods."

"The gods are already offended. They will say as much at the tribunal. So I ask you again, you did not say anything about the letter to him?"

"I did not. I cannot even talk about such a thing with him or else I will begin to hate the man I love."

"I will trust you mother, though every bone in my body says that is probably a mistake. Sometimes I think that love you have for him blinds you to the truth."

"He is still Pharaoh," his mother responded in her husband's defence.

"And therein lies the problem mother. As he does these evil things, those that he cares about should turn their backs on him. They should show their disdain they have for his actions. Otherwise he feels empowered to do them over and over again. Who knows how many sins he has committed because no one has had the courage to say how much it disgusts them."

"What do you know of love, my son? As soon as Sitamun was faced with despair, you chose to run away rather than stand beside her."

"I chose to give her the space that she demanded from me. That I did in the name of love. And I regret every day that I have been away from her, but that is what love is all about as well. Pain, regret, and the hollow in one's chest through absence. It is not all happy thoughts and frolicking through life, like you choose to believe it is with your husband. You all turn a blind eye to his madness, and you call it love. That is not love, but instead is self-delusion that you chain yourself with. One day I pray your eyes will open."

"Why have you turned so bitter, Thutmoses?" Tiye began to cry, his words stinging her deeply. "Have I been so cruel to you that you wish to hurt me so much?"

"Cruel? Never mother. You have never been cruel. You were too busy being absent from my life to ever be cruel. You never protected me from him. You never really tried to change him from the path he had taken. Far easier to send me away and keep us apart. That was your solution. You set me upon your father's path I realize now, not so much because you cherished what Yuyu had ordained for me, but because you saw it as a means to keep Pharaoh and myself apart."

"That is not true!" she insisted. "I only thought of your protection. I knew your father could be vicious in his attitude towards you and I did what I thought was best to keep you safe."

"Well you must be happy now that you have a son that Pharaoh actually accepts. It must be so much easier for you now not to have to protect him the way that you did me."

"Your brother is still a young boy. He is only five years old. He has not shown the independent streak that you possessed."

"Then pray he never does mother or else Pharaoh will attempt to eliminate him as well."

"He never would," Tiye rejected the insinuation.

"Like he would never try to have me assassinated," her son challenged, "Or was I so different that you aren't surprised that he tried?"

"He has shown nothing but love and affection for little Neferkheperure," she defended her position.

"So you aren't surprised then that he tried with me. That is what you are saying."

"I did not mean it that way. You are putting words in my mouth," she argued but her words were lost on her son. "Do not be this way, Mutenkheperure. Do not let the hatred overwhelm you."

Remembering the words of Chenetothes, Thutmoses realized his mother was correct. Whatever may happen at the tribunal, he could not let the raw emotions that weighed heavily on his heart, poison his mind. "You're right mother. We must let the judges of the tribunal decide who was right and who was wrong. I bear you no ill will and my brother is but another innocent caught in the web this family spins. I wish him nothing but a happy life."

"Come meet him," Tiye suggested.

"I don't know," Thutmoses hesitated.

"He's your brother. You should get to know him. He needs to know you." Taking her son by the hand she led him down a corridor to a room not far from her conference chamber.

Upon entering the room, Thutmoses realized that his mother also had other intentions. Surrounded by their attendants, the young boy was playing ball with his older sister Sitamun. It was almost nine years later but in his eyes Sitamun had not aged a single day. Her beauty still illuminated the room, outshining all the other maidens.

"Now sit down here," his mother insisted, letting him down easily on the pillows beside Sitamun, while he still remained in a semi-state of shock.

"Who is that?" the young boy asked.

"That is my husband," Sitamun answered sweetly. "Isn't that right, Muti?"

Thutmoses still had not regained his voice and simply nodded. But as he sat in silence he felt compelled to stare at his young brother. It was hard to explain but the proportionality of the boy appeared somewhat irregular. This appendage a tad too long, another perhaps a fraction too short. Individual features that probably would have gone unnoticed on any other child but when combined into a single individual they became more apparent. The boy spoke again, snapping Thutmoses from his preoccupation with examining his physical features.

"Is he coming to play with me?" young Amenhotep asked.

Placing the ball into Thutmoses' hands, Sitamun answered for him. "I think he would love to play with you Nefi. Isn't that right Muti?"

Still gazing upon the sparkling eyes of his wife, Thutmoses reclaimed his voice. "Yes, I would enjoy very much to play with you."

"Don't say it to me, silly," Sitamun joked, "Say it to your brother."

"Is he my brother?" the little prince asked.

Turning to the young boy, Thutmoses flipped the ball to him. "Yes, little one, I am your older brother."

"Why have I not seen you before?" the boy was full of questions.

"That is a long story. Perhaps one day I will tell it to you."

"I want to hear it now," Amenhotep insisted.

"Yes Muti," Sitamun joined in, "Tell us a story."

"Alright then," he began. "Once upon a time, there was this Prince of Kemet, who was married to the most beautiful woman in all the land."

"I like this story already," Sitamun interrupted.

"I do too," little Amenhotep agreed.

"And as much as the Prince of Kemet wished he could live in peace, the gods had other intentions for him. There would be lots of challenges and hardships and sometimes people do and say things during those hard times they shouldn't."

"And sometimes we are so caught up in ourselves we don't see the suffering of those we love," Sitamun, added.

"You know this story too?" the young prince was curious how his sister knew the next line.

"But more appropriately, when those in love feel the pain, they must share the suffering together and not apart," Thutmoses continued the story.

"I am sorry for pushing you away Muti," Sitamun reached out to her husband.

"Not as sorry as I am for not returning before now to find you," Thutmoses embraced his wife.

"Is this part of the story?" the little prince asked.

As the two kissed, it was Tiye that answered her young son's question, "Yes, this is the best part of the story."

It wasn't until the month of Payni that arrangements for the royal tribunal were finalized and the ten judges had been selected to sit in the court. Chief magistrate was Kheper-Kephrure, who was the administrator that brought the charge before Pharaoh on behalf of Prince Thutmoses. When Pharaoh Amenhotep first heard that his son wanted to have a tribunal conducted to clear General Chenetothes of any wrong doing, he could not believe that the gods had granted him such a gift. If Chenetothes was innocent of any crime then it meant that his son had killed an innocent member of the royal family. In doing so, Thutmoses would be placing his neck beneath the executioner's axe all on his own. With that in mind, Amenhotep was more than pleased to grant the request to have the tribunal established and did his very best to have it expedited.

Thutmoses had brought the sarcophagus holding the body of his dead uncle back to Thebes and it now lay in the Temple of Amun, its fate to be decided as well after the outcome of the tribunal. On the opening day of the trial, the Prince had arranged to have the body moved to the centre of the court where it would stay until the conclusion as if it too was listening and judging the words that would be spoken on its behalf. Sitting on their platform on the western wall of the court, the judges dressed in their white linen robes and round linen caps waited for the introductions to begin. The royal dais was located beneath the eastern window that permitted the daylight to flow into the room and determine the time when any testimony must finish for the day once the shadows began to fall across the faces of the royal family. Eager that everyone would witness the demise of his son, Pharaoh had his entire family seated on the dais. To his left sat Great Wife Tiye, to his right were his six other wives, Gilukhepa of the Mitanni, Tadukhepe also of the Mitanni, the daughter of Kadashman-Eilil of Babylon, the daughter of Kurigalzu of Babylon, the daughter of the King of Ammia and finally the daughter of the King of Arzawa. On the tier below the wives sat the royal daughters and his son Amenhotep-Neferkheperure. And on the tier below the children of Pharaoh sat the vizier, ministers and heralds of Pharaoh.

Rising from his seat, Kheper-Kephrure called for attention of everyone gathered in the Great Hall of Audience. Amongst the crowd that had been assembled sat all the nobles and prominent businessmen of Thebes. Space was at a premium as more than three hundred spectators had crowded into the court for what everyone considered the biggest event of their lives. Here was the conqueror of Nubia, the self-proclaimed King of Kush, the supposed hero that saved the *savov* family from assassination about to declare that what they thought was true was possibly all a lie, a fable made up to confuse and conceal a possible crime. "Beneath the eyes of Maat," Kheper-Kephrure caught their attention, "I call upon the wisdom of Ptah, the truth-seeker Nehau, the hater of lies, Bast, the maintainer of just causes Sertiu, the grief renderer Kenemti, the stopper of idle gossip Sekheriu, and the protector of those that cannot protect themselves, Nefer-Tmu, I welcome you to guide us. I call upon Nu, to keep us from making scornful words, Neheb-nefert to keep us from making false offerings, and most of all Amun, to grant us wisdom during this tribunal to arrive at the correct decisions in seeking truth and justice for all." Having completed the traditional greeting for the gods to guarantee a just and honourable trial, the chief magistrate waited for Pharaoh to signal the commencement.

"I, the son of Amun, beloved of Ra, *Neb* of the two lands, Pharaoh of Kemet, the Great *Neter-Nesew* pronounce this court is now is session," Amenhotep had risen from his throne to make his opening pronouncement.

"Great Pharaoh, do we declare that what we hear today will be the truth?" the chief magistrate initiated the official benedictions.

Waving his flail Pharaoh voiced his consent. "It is so declared."

"*Neb* of the two lands, do we declare that no man, whether royal or commoner is above the law and the verdict of this court shall be binding?"

Crossing the crook across the flail Pharaoh again voice hid consent. "It is so declared."

"King of Kemet, do we declare that any man whose guilt or innocence is established by this court shall have no other man take exception to the decision of this court lest that other man be punished by death?"

Uncrossing the crook and flail, Pharaoh shook each three times before saying, "So it shall be. Any man disagreeing with the verdict of this court and chooses to take the law into his own hands shall be punished by death."

"Then let the tribunal begin," Kheper-Kephrure announced. "Let the court recorder read out the case to be tried.

Standing with scroll in hand, the recorder did as instructed. "On this the seventeenth day of the month of Payni in the twenty-ninth reignal year of his Majesty, the *Neter-Nesew* Amenhotep-Nimmureya, son of Thutmoses-Menkheperure, it has been raised before the court that the confession of General Chenetothes, son of Thutmoses-Menkheperure was made fraudulently and therefore his body which lays before us is deserving of burial in a manner of a true hero of the kingdom. Thus so declared the death of General Chenetothes was neither warranted nor appropriate as no crime had been committed."

"Who so makes this charge?" the chief magistrate asked the plaintiff to step forward.

Moving towards the sarcophagus, Prince Thutmoses laid a hand on the sculpted body-shaped coffin while he spoke. "I Thutmoses-Mutenkheperure, son of Amenhotep-Nimmureya make this charge."

"Let it be written that the charge has been brought forward by the Crown Prince of Kemet, the man who is also responsible for the death of Chenetothes son of Thutmoses-Menkheperure. Does the plaintiff realize that should it be shown that the General was innocent of the crimes of which he was accused that you may find yourself on trial for possible homicide?" Kheper-Kephrure looked down upon his nephew to see that he understood the seriousness of what he was doing.

"The ramifications of this charge are fully understood, your Honour and I am prepared to accept the consequences of the verdict." While Thutmoses was responding the smile that spread across Amenhotep's lips went undetected. Pharaoh looked smug and satisfied, two warning signs that should have set off alarms in the young Prince's head had he been looking that way. That overconfident smile suggested that the thorn that he felt prickling in his side for so many years was about to be removed.

"As the plaintiff understands that by proving the truth of his charges it would render him possibly a defendant in this case, and therefore he can be cross-examined, then I rule that this case can proceed and the plaintiff is asked to bring his first witness forward."

"At this juncture your Honour, I ask permission of the court to have the *Wab-tepi* of Onu, Ahrown son of Amun-Ramuse, High Priest of Onu act as my solicitor as he is far more knowledgeable of the law and his speech is far more eloquent than mine."

"Let the record show that Ahrown son of Amun-Ramuse has been named as the acting solicitor for the plaintiff," the chief magistrate had it written into the official record. "Let the solicitor come forward and speak."

Stepping forward until he was alongside Thutmoses, Ahrown bowed first to the *savov* family in the east and then to the judges in the west. "To all gathered here, it must seem strange that Prince Thutmoses would place himself in legal jeopardy by requesting that this tribunal be convened to clear his uncle, General Chenetothes of any crimes against the Royal Family. But what does this say about the Prince? To me it speaks volumes of the upstanding character of Prince Thutmoses. It tells me that his love for his uncle exceeded any reason to conceal the truth. His wishes to see that the subsequent assassination performed on Chenetothes' character be expunged and this far outweighs any ramifications of guilt that may be attributed against the Prince in the death of the General. And what is that truth that he wishes for this court to hear? I summon the General's own orderly, Hophni to step forward and tell us of the events of that night."

Upon hearing his name, Hophni rose from the front row of chairs where he was seated and came forward carrying two rolled up scrolls in his hand.

"In the name of Maat, will you speak the truth," Ahrown asked Hophni.

"I so declare," the orderly responded.

"You have evidence you wish to present to the Chief Magistrate?" Ahrown pointed towards the two scrolls in his hand.

"I do," Hophni replied succinctly.

Stepping forward, Ahrown received one of the scrolls handed to him by Hophni and then turned to walk towards Kheper-Kephrure and handed him the rolled papyrus.

"What is it that I have given to the Chief Magistrate?" Ahrown asked while Kheper-Kephrure unrolled the paper to quickly scan it then passed it on to the seated judge on his right, who then read it and passed it on to the next judge.

"That is the confession of General Chenetothes," Hophni replied.

"The confession in which he claims it was his intent to murder the *savov* family as part of a plot with his Hittite allies. Is that not so?" Ahrown turned to face the assembled crowd to see that they all understood that there truly was a signed confession.

"Yes, that is it," Hophni confirmed while the scroll passed down through the rows of judges, each one quickly scanning it and then showing signs of disgust at what they read.

Turning back to face his witness, Ahrown smiled confidently. "I guess this closes our case," he said. "We have a confession, you confirm that it was signed by the General, so I presume there is not much else that needs to be said," Ahrown stated a matter-of-factly. "Is there some reason we should doubt the veracity of this confession?"

Hophni wet his lips nervously before answering that question. "Yes, there is," he explained. "I helped the General write that confession on the day he died."

"And that is significant because…"

"Because we composed the entire plot at the time we wrote the letter. It is a lie."

"So you're saying there was no plot by the General, it was fabricated in its entirety."

"Yes."

Kheper-Kephrure struck his sceptre against the cap of his podium, signalling that he would cross-examine. "Is it your statement that you along with the General made up this entire confession? Why would you do such a thing?"

Lowering his head, Hophni tried to explain it simply. "Because he loved his nephew, the Crown Prince Thutmoses, as if he was his own son."

"I am confused," the Chief Magistrate shook his head from side to side. "You are saying that a confession to assassinate the *savov* family was completely fabricated because the General loved the Crown Prince. I can think of other ways one could express their love."

A ripple of laughter spread through the assembled crowd upon hearing the Chief Magistrate's comment.

"Explain this to me how this confession was necessary for the reason you stated." Kheper-Kephrure tried to guide Hophni through a logical process.

"General Chenetothes knew that in order to save the Crown Prince he had to be perceived as a hero by the people so that his enemies would not harm him."

"Harm who?"

"Prince Thutmoses," Hophni pointed towards the Prince.

"Solicitor, carry on with your witness."

"You say that this confession was created for the sole purpose of protecting the Crown Prince from someone that wanted to harm him, is that correct?" Ahrown went straight to the heart of matter.

"Yes, by turning the Prince into a hero, as evidence by stopping a plot to murder his family, he would be protected."

"Protected from whom?" Ahrown directed Hophni to move on to the second phase of their argument.

"If you read the confession completely, you will see that the General had been ordered to assassinate the Crown Prince." A shockwave passed through all those within the Great Hall of Audience, the gasps echoing over and over again.

"Oh," Ahrown sounded shocked. "How can that be? In copies of the confession letter that were circulated through Thebes and Memphis there was no mention of such an order. How can you explain that?"

"Because I had purposely left that out of my report back to ministry when I reported the plot to the palace," Hophni confessed.

"You intentionally and wilfully altered a report to the ministry of justice," Ahrown stated for all to hear. "Why would you do such a thing?"

While preparing to give his explanation, the judges quickly circulated and reviewed the original letter of confession to confirm that it did contain this additional statement mentioned by the orderly. They all nodded in affirmation upon finding that specific reference.

"I feared that if I mentioned it to the ministry then the perpetrator of ordering the death of Prince Thutmoses would become desperate to have everyone aware of the letter eliminated including sending assassins to kill the prince."

"Any man that could eliminate anyone that had knowledge of the contents of the original letter must be very powerfully placed. Would you not agree?"

"Yes," Hophni responded without elaboration.

"So you have knowledge of where this order came from. From whom did you learn the identity of this highly placed person?" Ahrown went on the attack.

"From the General himself who was ordered to kill the Prince."

"That's a serious accusation that the General had been ordered to murder Prince Thutmoses. There is only one person that could order the highest ranking general in the army to do such a thing. You will need proof to make such a statement." Ahrown sprung the trap.

"I have that proof here," Hophni waved the remaining scroll in his hand.

"And exactly what is in that scroll?"

"It is the official order to have Crown Prince Thutmoses killed," Hophni exclaimed.

Leading the witness to the Chief Magistrate, Ahrown now had the second scroll in the judges' hands. Before asking any other questions, he watched as the papyrus was passed between all the judges, ensuring that each showed sufficient signs of shock and surprise on their faces. Many of them examined the broken seal in order to confirm the identity of the author, shaking their heads in disbelief as they did so.

"So what happened next? You wrote the confession in order to prevent the murder of the Crown Prince. Then what?" Ahrown purposely led the testimony away from actually revealing the identity of person that gave the order. He knew that the delay would serve to intensify the reaction of all those in the hall once revealed.

"We summoned Prince Thutmoses to the General's tent. Under the pretence of examining his sword, I rushed from behind and pushed the Prince's arm forward so that it pierced the General's chest."

"So in essence, the Prince killed the General entirely by accident and was not complicit in your scheme. Is that your view of the incident?"

"Entirely by accident," Hophni confirmed.

"So, if it was the General's intent to essentially commit suicide, then why bother to have it done by the hand of the Crown Prince?"

"In that way, we could spread the story that the Prince had thwarted the General's intent to overthrow the *savov* family and take the throne for himself." Hophni looked up at the judges as if to suggest that it was perfectly natural to devise such a plan.

"But Prince Thutmoses at no time had any knowledge of what you and the General had been planning."

"None at all. We knew that he would try to stop us if he had prior knowledge."

"And why would he try to stop you? If he knew the General had been ordered to kill him, why prevent the death of the tool that would result in his own destruction?"

"Because the Prince loved his uncle," Hophni responded.

"Ah, there's that love word again," Ahrown emphasized how strange to talk of love during a murder trial. "Everyone involved would rather die themselves rather than hurt the person they love. I guess that truly is love, is it not?" The question was directed rhetorically for everyone in the audience to digest.

Scanning the judges, Ahrown saw that all ten had now completed reading the second scroll and knew its full content. It was time. "You said that papyrus scroll you passed to the judges was the proof of the General being ordered to murder Prince Thutmoses. Who signed that order?"

Hophni tried to answer but when he gazed to the east and saw the murderous look on Pharaoh's face he trembled with fear.

"I'll repeat the question," Ahrown attempted to shake Hophni from the grips of his terror. "Who signed that order?"

About to answer, Pharaoh jumped up from his throne and tried to declare the trial over ordering everyone from the hall but Thutmoses noticed that Amenhotep's theatrics appeared rehearsed, almost as if he had anticipated this moment occurring during the trial.

"Great King, *Neb* of the Two Lands, you do not have the authority to dismiss the tribunal," Kheper-Kephrure argued. "I insist you sit down. Having confirmed the three declarations in the Great Hall of Audience your authority has been passed on to the judges of this tribunal. You are now subject to our authority and so I insist that you sit down."

Reluctantly, Pharaoh Amenhotep sat back on his throne but made no further objection. The Prince tried to rationalize what he had just witnessed. Certainly, it would have been instinctive that Pharaoh would suspect that any trial conducted by the son of Yuyu would have been prejudicial towards him but why was he taking this so calmly? Why raise his objection and then sit down without so much as another comment. His father was never so restrained in the past. That thought persisted to nag at the Prince and why when he looked at his mother she didn't appear to even flinch during her husband's outburst.

"Continue with your examination," the Chief Magistrate instructed Ahrown.

"Who signed the order to have Prince Thutmoses murdered?"

"It was signed by Pharaoh Amenhotep," Hophni was finally able to get the words out of his mouth.

As soon as Pharaoh's name was mentioned, the gallery filled with people became extremely restless and boisterous. Some tried to make their way to the exits afraid that Pharaoh might retaliate in some manner. Banging his sceptre once again, the Chief Magistrate attempted to restore order. "Silence in the court," he yelled. "Silence in the court," a second time but the situation was disintegrating rapidly. Kheper-Kephrure continued to call for order but it was not until the courthouse guard with their spears appeared at the entranceways that the people finally settled down and returned to their places. Holding the unrolled letter above his head, he Chief Magistrate asked the other judges to confirm the identity of the author of the letter. All ten identified Pharaoh Amenhotep as that person.

"Having revoked privilege of distinguishing royal from commoner, then by the power invested in me by this royal tribunal I direct this question to Amenhotep-Nimmureya, who now stands before Maat, is this your letter and your signature?"

Shifting in his throne, Amenhotep looked towards his Great Wife, but she stared blankly ahead, unmoving as if a statue. He then looked across at the judges, only to see that they too were already answering the question in their minds. Pharaoh knew that within the Great Hall of Audience he was not the *tunkeh* authority and anything he said would be used by the gods at the time of judgment when he died. "I can't remember," Pharaoh then explained that there would be many papers presented to him daily with a request to sign and he does not necessarily read each one. It was a simple answer, stated calmly, and one that Thutmoses now realized had been prepared well in advance.

Calling one of the court stewards to his bench, Kheper-Kephrure handed him the papyrus and instructed him to carry it over to Pharaoh for a closer look. Waiting until Amenhotep held it in his hand, the Chief Magistrate asked his next question. "I direct this question to Amenhotep-Nimmureya, who now stands before Nehau, do you concur that is your signature?"

"Yes, it is my signature, but I still do not recall signing this document." A gasp went up from the crowd as soon as he admitted to it being his signature. "Do you intend to call upon all forty-two gods of judgement to examine my *ib* and *ka*," Pharaoh wanted to know, a little bit of humour which appeared to calm the reaction of most present.

"If necessary," the Chief Magistrate replied. "I pray that Pharaoh's memory will be restored long before that, so that when it his time to be weighed on the balance of death that he will be absolved of all sin. Now if we may continue. Call you next witness," the Chief Magistrate instructed Ahrown. Kheper-Kephrure recognized he could go no further in his questioning of Amenhotep as long as he insisted he had no recollection of signing that letter.

"I call upon Crown Prince Thutmoses-Mutenkheperure to speak to the tribunal. In the name of Maat, will you speak the truth," Ahrown asked the Prince.

"I will," Thutmoses responded.

"For the past nine years you have been fighting along with General Chenetothes as his second in command. Is that not so."

"That is true," Thutmoses declared.

"Having taken the city of Bagrawiyah, all of Nubia had been conquered by the army under General Chenetothes and jointly you made a decision to take all of Kush by conquering Saba. Is that not so?"

"Yes," the Prince agreed, "And all that we did was in the name of Pharaoh."

"How can you prove this?" Ahrown challenged him.

"By this," Thutmoses clapped his hands which was a prearranged signal to his Nubian troops that were waiting anxiously outside the Hall. As soon as their captain standing by the doorway heard the clap, he signalled for his men to begin bringing in the boxes they had carried with them all the way from Kush. Crate after crate they stacked around the sarcophagus until there was a mountain of these wooden crates occupying the centre of the room. Thutmoses flicked his right hand in an upward motion instructing the soldiers that carried in the crates to open the first lid. "I bring you ivory from the vast plains of Kush." He motioned to open the next. "Gold from the *dehnet* around Saba." Then the next crate was opened. "Emeralds, diamonds, rubies, that pour down the rivers beyond the sixth cataract." Another lid was flipped. "Lapis lazuli from the fiery mountains. Another crate is filled with ebony from the

African forests. I bring twenty crates of such riches to lay at the feet of Pharaoh Amenhotep. Riches beyond measure gathered from the heartland of Kush by General Chenetothes and myself to adorn the Temples of Kemet. All that we did, we did in the name of Pharaoh." With a wave of his hand he dismissed the bearers from the Great Hall.

Ahrown turned to face the Chief Magistrate to speak directly to the judges. "I ask the court to log in the tribute brought back by Prince Thutmoses in the name of Pharaoh." He then turned back to his witness. "You were summoned to the General's tent the day he died, is that correct?

The Prince responded simply in the affirmative.

"At time did he show you the letter from Pharaoh Amenhotep?"

Again the Prince responded in the affirmative.

"Obviously you would have discussed this with General Chenetothes at the time, especially your feelings on knowing that your own father wanted to have you killed. What was the nature of that discussion?"

"We were concerned that Pharaoh had lost his mental faculties. That the gods no longer blessed him and had stolen his capacity to think clearly."

"Was this something you only identified upon seeing this letter or did you have suspicions of a possible illness for a much longer time."

"I had suspected it for years."

"Did others see the deterioration of Pharaoh's mind?"

"I believe so."

"I object to this," Pharaoh raised his voice. "I refuse to sit here while you debate the state of my mind. I am still the *Neter-Nesew* and I am not to be governed by the laws of men. This tribunal is sadly becoming a farce!" Thutmoses watched his father's reaction and knew that this time Pharaoh had not been prepared for this accusation. He had never discussed his intent to bring up the mental state of his father when he spoke with his mother.

"I summon he who has no name who comest forth from Annu," Kheper-Kephrure began reciting from the Book of the Dead. "Look into Pharaoh's heart to see if he has done iniquity."

"I order you to stop this immediately," Amenhotep demanded but he no longer held any authority within the hall. He knew exactly what the Chief Magistrate was doing. By reciting the ritual he was actually demonstrating how Pharaoh would be denied entry into the world beyond after his death.

"I summon the Devourer of the Shade, who comest forth from Qernet to look into Pharaoh's heart to see if he intended to commit murder."

"You cannot do this," Amenhotep showed the first evidence of real concern and worry since the tribunal began. Kheper-Kephrure had adopted a tactic that would destroy Pharaoh's opportunity to pass peacefully into the netherworld of the gods upon his death.

"I summon He who shootest forth the Flame, who comest forth from Het-Ptah-Ka to look into the spirit of Chenetothes, to see if Pharaoh did cause him pain."

"I object, I object, I object," Pharaoh's voice waned as he slumped back into his throne. "I am not on trial here! It is the Crown Prince that is on trial. It is he whom you must be cross examining!"

"I summon Bast, who comes from her secret place, to judge if Pharaoh has dealt deceitfully."

"Stop. I order you to stop immediately." Pharaoh appeared to writhe in pain as he squirmed in his throne. Fearing that the Chief Magistrate might continue to read out the remainder of the death judgment gods, Pharaoh became silent and let the court continue its operation.

Thutmoses, watched intently, thinking to himself, 'You didn't anticipate this coming, did you, you bastard?'

"You say Prince Thutmoses, that others have seen the mental demise of Pharaoh and therefore can attest that he has been cursed by the gods," the Chief Magistrate returned to the questioning.

"Yes, your Honour. I declare that the Queen Tiye, the Great Wife, knew of his affliction."

As soon as he said that his mother shook her head, not wishing to be drawn into the situation that was taking place. Her eyes pleaded with her son to not make her do this. She felt Thutmoses' own return stare cutting her deeply like daggers. Her own duplicity had now caught her in making a decision between husband and son.

"I direct my question to Queen Tiye, Great Wife of Pharaoh Amenhotep, did you at any time suspect that your husband was being cursed with madness by the gods?" From the tone in her brother's voice, she knew that Kheper-Kephrure was not going to permit her to abstain from answering.

The Queen tried to look away but any direction she turned had hundreds of pairs of eyes staring at her. She felt like an animal in a trap with no opportunity to escape. If she admitted to her husband's illness, she knew that he'd never forgive her and in fact he could possibly become more dangerous to the rest of her children. But if she denied it, then she knew that she'd be losing her son forever and even her own brother might cast her off for doing so."

"I...I..." She could not get the words out."

"I know this is not easy for you to say. But think of all the other lives that are affected by the decision you make," Kheper-Kephrure addressed his sister on a more personal level. "Look to the sarcophagus of General Chenetothes laying before you and know that either he is a violator of the law by defying Pharaoh's command to commit an action, no matter how detestable that command may be, or else he is a hero that saved the Crown Prince by deliberately forfeiting his life. Think about your son, who admits now that he was a conspirator in perpetrating this lie of protecting the *savov* family by being involved in killing the General, or is he merely a victim of a king that lost perspective and tried to command the murder of an innocent. Think of those in your past that have preached truth is the only pathway to salvation."

She knew from her brother's last comment that he was referring to their father and how she would be dishonouring his memory if she did not answer truthfully. The pressure brought to bear was tremendous and the tears began to roll down from her kohl lined eyes.

"Remember this," the Chief Magistrate wanted to give a final bit of advice, "And should it be found that Pharaoh is suffering from madness, then he cannot be held accountable for any crimes he may have committed and therefore the weighing of his *ib* at the time of his death will not be affected. You have it within your power to see that justice is performed."

Staring into the eyes of her son, she could see all the suffering that Thutmoses had experienced for so many years, eyes that were now pleading with her to tell the truth and for once in her life protect him from the years of damage done to him by Pharaoh. She felt ashamed and knew of no penance that could ever make it up to him. "I have seen the possibility of madness progressing," she responded in a hushed tone, tears in her eyes as she expressed his illness in a way that those in attendance could take it both ways without actually humiliating and shaming her husband before the courts.

"Let it be recorded in the court journal, that we have two statements from two witnesses that the mental state of Pharaoh Amenhotep-Nimmureya has been brought into question. As such, in my authority, I declare it to be so. Does the Crown Prince Thutmoses have any further statements to make?"

"He has nothing further to say, your Honour," Ahrown concluded.

"I demand to exercise my rights to ask questions of the witnesses," Pharaoh stood and held his crook and flail above his head as evidence of his divine right.

"It is within the rules of the law for Pharaoh to cross examine any witness brought before the tribunal," the Chief Magistrate deferred to King.

Thutmoses took a deep breath. He knew this is what his father had been waiting for all along. Obviously, he had prepared carefully, with advice from his own counsel on exactly what to ask. And the only way he would have known what to ask meant that once again he had been betrayed by his mother as he suspected.

"That being the case then I ask that my dear brother's orderly come forward to answer my questions." Moving to a spot before the platform on which Pharaoh sat, Hophni took to a knee and bowed his head. Amenhotep requested that he stand and look at him. "You said that the General wished to examine the sword of the Crown Prince, is that not so."

"Yes, you Majesty," Hophni replied.

"Yet, you then say you pushed the Crown Prince forward and in so doing, his sword pierced the chest of my dear departed brother."

"I had been instructed to do so by General Chenetothes, your Majesty."

"But Thutmoses knew nothing of this plan for my brother's suicide, is that not correct?"

"We would never tell him, your Majesty. Otherwise he would have no part in it."

"If I asked you to examine my sword, as an orderly, how would you do it?"

"I don't understand the question, you Majesty."

"I'm certain you must," Amenhotep insisted. "You're an orderly to a general. At least you were. You'd be taking care of his equipment and weapons every day. If he asked you to examine his sword, then how would you do it?"

"I would take the sword and check the edges, make certain there were no nicks or roughness. If there were then I would apply my stone to remove them. I'd also check the hilt to ensure that it had not loosened."

"So in other words, you have the sword in your hands, and you'd examine it thoroughly. Is that not so?"

"Yes, that is correct your Majesty."

"Why then, was the Crown Prince holding his sword, point forward if my brother was supposedly examining his sword?"

"It is how the General intended it," Hophni's voice wavered.

"Don't you think it strange that the Crown Prince presented it blade forward. If I was handing you my sword I would present it with the hilt first."

"The General requested it that way, your Majesty," Hophni attempted to explain once more.

"But the Crown Prince, who had no idea as to your plot supposedly designed by my brother and revealed only to you, yet he's holding the point of the blade against my brother's chest. Why should I not believe it was the Crown Prince's intent all along to kill the General and that perhaps you were in it together with Thutmoses and not with the General as you'd like this tribunal to believe?"

"But your Majesty, there is the General's letter where he expresses his intent to murder the *savov* family."

"Which he could have easily been forced to write under duress if his orderly and second in command were holding a sword to his chest."

"But that was not the case, you Majesty."

"Or so you say," Amenhotep concluded. "You may return to where you were standing before. I now call the Crown Prince Thutmoses, to stand before me."

Reluctantly, the Prince moved to a position before his father, taking to his knee with eyes cast downward. Amenhotep made certain that he left him in that position for an exceedingly long time for everyone in the court to see, before granting him permission to rise. Thutmoses knew that even though his father might be going mad, he was still as cunning and sly like a fox and therefore a force to be reckoned with.

"Prince Thutmoses, we've already heard that you were holding the sword that killed General Chenetothes. There is no discussion in that matter. But after the death of my beloved brother, you perpetrated this hoax that you had slain a traitor to the crown. And you maintained that hoax for years before the guilt of carrying this lie weighed too heavily upon you and you requested this tribunal in order to cleanse your soul. Is that not so

"Yes your Majesty but there…"

Amenhotep cut him off midsentence. It was a yes or no question and you answered yes. I did not request anything further.

"But…"

"No buts. Chief Magistrate, please remind the plaintiff that he is only to answer the questions directed at him and he is not permitted to elaborate unless I request it."

"The Crown Prince is advised to answer the questions as proposed," Kheper-Kephrure reminded Thutmoses.

"Are you therefore prepared to state before Bast that you have not acted deceitfully? Yes or no."

"I did act deceitfully in respect to the hoax but…," Thutmoses had to admit.

"No buts, we've already been through that. As your hand was on the blade which killed my brother, are you prepared to state before the Devourer of the Shade, who comest forth from Qernet that you did not commit murder whether it be intentional or accidental."

"I cannot," Thutmoses acknowledged that it was his hand that took his uncle's life.

"Having made fools of us all with this lie against my brother that he intended to be a traitor and murder the *savov* family, are you prepared to swear before Maat that you told no lies?"

"I cannot," Thutmoses felt the trap that he thought he had so cleverly sprung against his father now closing around his neck.

"Will you swear before Tmu, who comest forth from Tattu, and Nefer-Tmu who comest forth from Het-Ptah-ka, that you haven not seriously harmed a member of the *savov* family."

"I cannot," the Prince repeated his previous answer.

"Will you deny now before Fentiu, who comest forth from Khemennu, that you did not steal the *worret* of Kush which rightfully belonged to your Pharaoh.

Upon hearing that accusation, Thutmoses was prepared to finally object to one of the charges. "I deny it!" he shouted. "The men of Kush placed the *worret* upon my head after their king proclaimed me his successor. I stole nothing!"

"You may return to your prior position Prince Thutmoses. I have no further questions. You may now go deliberate Chief Magistrate, I believe you have several decisions to make." Pharaoh sat back on his throne with all the confidence in the world, nodding appreciatively to his Great Wife, who pretended not to notice, staring only towards the west with eyes focused on the far wall, avoiding anyone's eyes.

The tribunal was adjourned, everyone leaving the gallery talking animatedly about the day's events. All were eager to return the next day at which time the judges would render their decisions on the case. Seeking only peace and quiet, Thutmoses spent the rest of the day confined to his quarters. Only Sitamun was permitted to stay with him though he did not talk much. He knew that Pharaoh had gained the upper hand, casting doubt on everything that he and his witness had stated. Though he had the burden of facts on his side, and the admission that Pharaoh was believed to be going slightly mad, it was the final performance by Amenhotep that everyone would remember. Not even the delicate hands of Sitamun massaging the back of his neck could relieve him of the cloud he felt circling over his head. Despite his wife's presence, he could not shake the feeling of being so very much alone.

The next day the crowd of minor royals and the aristocracy forced their way into the Great Hall of Audience, pushing and shoving to obtain a space providing a good vantage point. Their number in attendance was almost three times as large as the previous day. Everyone knew that the decisions of the Tribunal were going to rewrite history that particular day. The charges exchanged between father and son were quite serious and depending on how the courts ruled, it could be the forbearance of a radical change in governance. Not since the days of Hatshepsut had there been anything like this. At that time, the aunt of Thutmoses-Manahpirya, also known as Thutmoses the Great, used the official capacity of the Tribunal under the authority of Chief Magistrate Senenmut to have herself declared equivalent of male and thereby able to take the position of both King and Pharaoh of Kemet. Whether today's events would rival those of the previous century no one could say but neither did anyone want to miss the possibility of seeing history in the making.

The royal family took their positions on the platform in the east as they did the previous day. One by one the judges entered the Hall, taking their positions on the platform in the west. Kheper-Kephrure moved into his position behind the podium on the judge's platform. In the centre of the room, the sarcophagus of Chenetothes remained unmoved but the crates of treasure that Thutmoses had presented to Pharaoh the previous day had all disappeared. Hardly a surprise to the Prince. He knew his father wouldn't waste any time adding the offerings to his treasury.

It took a considerable amount of time for the judges to move into their positions, as they repeatedly adjusted their seats to find a comfortable position before the Chief Magistrate decided to open the court. Clearing his throat, Kheper-Kephrure had the trumpeter sound that the court was in session. After blasting his short medley of three notes, the crowd fell quiet.

The Chief Magistrate opened with the usual salutation. "Beneath the eyes of Maat, I called upon the wisdom of Ptah, the truth-seeker Nehau, the hater of lies, Bast, the maintainer of just causes Sertiu, the grief renderer Kenemti, the stopper of idle gossip Sekheriu, and the protector of those that cannot protect themselves, Nefer-Tmu,

I welcome you to guide us. I called upon Nu, to keep us from making scornful words, Neheb-nefert to keep us from making false offerings, and most of all Amun, to grant us wisdom that we have arrived at the correct decisions in seeking truth and justice for all."

There was a pause by Kheper-Kephrure as he surveyed everyone in the room assessing what the possible reaction might be once the verdict was read. "Let it be known that the son of Amun, beloved of Ra, *Neb* of the two lands, Pharaoh of Kemet, the Great *Neter-Nesew* has declared that no man, whether royal or commoner will be considered to be above the law and the final verdict of this court shall be binding on any man, royal or commoner. Let it also be known that the King of Kemet, has declared that any man whose guilt or innocence is established by this court shall have no other man take exception to the decision of this court lest that other man be punished by death. So it shall be."

Turning to Pharaoh, the Chief Magistrate requested that the King confirm the opening statements of the court and declare this day's session able to commence. Not having any choice in the matter, Amenhotep crossed flail and crook and made the declaration as instructed.

"I should identify that the original case brought before the tribunal by the plaintiff Crown Prince Thutmoses-Mutenkheperure concerned the legacy of General Chenetothes. For the past few years we were presented with a story that the General had plotted to overthrow the *savov* family through an act of treason and it was only through an act of bravery that he was stopped by Prince Thutmoses whom in an armed struggle killed his uncle. Whether through personal guilt or grief the Crown Prince wished to set that record straight and provide proof that there was no plot of treason and that General Chenetothes had always remained a loyal servant of Pharaoh.

Following lengthy deliberation the judges of this Tribunal came to the following decision. That General Chenetothes, son of Thutmoses-Menkheperure did not make any attempt to overthrow the government nor commit any other act of treason."

Thutmoses at that moment turned to Ahrown and gave a congratulatory nod at the first outcome.

"But," the Chief Magistrate continued, "The General did defy a direct order form Pharaoh and in so doing prepared a scheme in which he intended to deceive the people of Kemet, as well as Pharaoh and in so doing is guilty of fraudulent behaviour in which the Crown Prince would directly benefit. The court is compassionate though and understands that the reason the General did these things was because of his love for the Crown Prince. As such we admonish him for his actions and although we cannot agree that he be buried in his family tomb, we do see a compromise where his body can remain in the Hall of Death for perpetuity.

Those assembled in the hall appeared to be satisfied with that first decision. Overall, it appeared to be fair and appropriate.

Now, in the matter of the death of General Chenetothes, we have the word of his orderly that he wilfully pushed the sword hand of the Crown Prince forward thereby causing it to pierce the chest of the General. As the General is not here to speak on his own behalf, we have no way of confirming that it was his intent to die in this manner, Nonetheless, his orderly Hophni is guilty of murder, by his own confession, whether with the approval or not of Chenetothes, of having taken the life of a member of the Royal Family. It matters not if there was criminal intent or not. For a commoner to take the life of a member of the *savov* family, there can only be one ruling. Murdering a royal is punishable by death."

Upon hearing the pronouncement of the sentence against him, Hophni, began crying hysterically. "I only did what I was told. I am not a murderer. I did as I was told," he yelled, only to be seized by two of the court guards that immediately dragged him from the hall. Some of the people in the gallery clapped their approval of the decision. Being aristocrats themselves, the common people must never be given the opportunity to feel they could raise their hands against their betters with impunity.

This time it was Ahrown glancing at Thutmoses and his eyes were easy to read as if they were saying that man will die because of you. Thutmoses lowered his eyesight, knowing that he was guilty of causing an innocent man's impending death.

The Chief Magistrate continued to roll on. "We have had numerous secondary charges made during the course of the Tribunal. One of these is the authorization by Pharaoh Amenhotep-Nimmureya to have Crown Prince Thutmoses-Mutenkheperure killed. Pharaoh has confirmed that the signature on the order was his but explained that it may have been signed accidentally as he does not necessarily read all the letters placed before him. As we cannot determine the veracity of this claim, but we can attest that the letters at a minimum had to be prepared by the royal scribes and presented to him by the palace vizier, then as a result we have distributed arrest warrants for all those involved and they will be executed for their known participation in this matter."

Thutmoses looked towards his father's face to see if he could detect any emotion upon the pronouncement that the palace personal staff was going to be executed. There was nothing. Not even a single wince to suggest he was capable of any empathy. More people to die because of Pharaoh's sins, but still his father remained unscathed. The Prince felt deeply saddened.

"In the matter that the Pharaoh Amenhotep-Nimmureya may have actually been knowledgeable of signing the command to have the Crown Prince assassinated, it first needed to be determined if Pharaoh was in full retention of his mental capacity to appreciate what he was doing. As the issue had already been raised that Pharaoh may not be in full possession of his mental faculties, an accusation made by the Crown Prince and confirmed by the Great Wife, it obviously was the responsibility of this Tribunal to seek medical advice from the palace physician in this matter to confirm or deny this matter. Under oath, Pharaoh's physician has told us that the Great King's gums are abscessed which cause continuous pain and headaches and that these conditions could result in fits of rage and distemper. When questioned about these ailments, Pharaoh Amenhotep-Nimmureya confirmed that he suffers from these ailments and that at times they cause him to suffer episodes of violent behaviour but of which he has no recollection in his memories, but is only aware of them when he is told afterwards." The Chief Magistrate paused for a significant break to let what he just said settle in the minds of the audience in the gallery.

Still looking at his father, Thutmoses watched with keen interest how this pronouncement questioning his mental health didn't even cause any reaction from Pharaoh. 'Of course you admitted to it' the Prince thought to himself. If you have periods of mental instability then the court will not hold you responsible, even of the crime of attempting to kill your own son. Pharaoh already knew what the outcome of this finding would be. Once again they were playing the senet board and this time his father was winning.

"After long deliberation," uncle Ephra continued, "It was the decision of this court that there is no overwhelming justification to consider Pharaoh Amenhotep-Nimmureya not fit to sit on his throne but to ensure that during these periods of instability, that we have suitable precautions in place to safeguard the continued good governance of the two lands, we establish that a co-regency is to begin immediately."

Thutmoses and Ahrown stared blankly at one another trying to comprehend exactly what the meaning of this pronouncement was. Upon first hearing it, Thutmoses wondered how he could manage to sit in the same room with his father, let alone try to work in a cooperative manner. He had his answer to that dilemma soon enough.

"Therefore it is proposed," Kheper-Kephrure continued, "That Amenhotep-Neferkheperure, son of Pharaoh and Great Wife Tiye will act as co-regent. During the early years of his reign Queen Tiye will act on the prince's behalf until he is old enough to act alone."

Thutmoses watched as the first trace of any emotion finally crossed his father's features. It was a sinister smile, as if to say 'of course I would be consulted by the tribunal in making any decisions you fool.' The Prince thought how stupid he was to have placed his trust in Uncle Ephra. Even with the best of intentions there was no way his uncle would have been able to get the better of Pharaoh. Out of ten judges, how many were puppets of his father. Now, he had to deal with the execution of a number of people on his account while Amenhotep was free to do as he pleased.

"In the matter of the tertiary charges levelled against the Crown Prince by Pharaoh Amenhotep," the Chief Magistrates voice carried throughout the hall, "We must deal with the first matter that Prince Thutmoses-Mutenkheperure knowingly deceived the people of Kemet for several years by maintaining the pretence that the act of killing General Chenetothes was in order to save the *savov* family by preventing a heinous act of treason. In regards to this deceit, it must be noted that although the Prince appears to have been an unwitting pawn in the conception of this plan, he nonetheless played an active role after he realized that it was necessary to deceive and lie to the people in order to preserve the integrity of the original lie.

It has been duly noted that the actual murder of General Chenetothes was committed by the actions of his orderly Hophni, but the hand that actually held the weapon resulting in death was that of Prince Thutmoses. Therefore, though we deem it an accidental homicide, the law is quite clear on the recourse for any royal that causes the death directly or indirectly of another royal even if doing so accidentally. The accused if found guilty is to be stripped of all titles, all land-holdings and is to be sent into exile for the duration of the reign of the presiding king. That is the law."

As soon as that pronouncement had been completed, Sitamun burst into tears, only to be immediately admonished by her father. She ran to her mother's side but Tiye paid her little attention, sitting frozen like a stature bereft of any emotion and ignoring her daughter's pleas.

"Finally, in the matter of being declared King of Kush, the court accepts that the title may have been imposed on Prince Thutmoses but his decision to marry the Queen of Saba was made entirely by himself and therefore in direct opposition to the laws of Kemet that stipulate all royal marriages involving foreign monarchs must be with the permission and consent of Pharaoh. Therefore, we pronounce that the marriage is null and void.

Thutmoses' first thought was 'what a ridiculous decision'. How in the world could they rule that he and Tharbis could no longer be married? Was their son simply to disappear with a snap of the court's fingers?

Stepping away from the podium, the Chief Magistrate prepared to dismiss all those assembled in the Great Hall of Audience. "We conclude the Tribunal at this juncture. All praise be to the Great *Neter-Nesew* Amenhotep, may the remainder of his reign be bountiful." At the conclusion of his statements, the Chief Magistrate stepped down and began moving towards the judicial quarters, closely followed by the ten judges.

At the same time, Thutmoses gravitated to the centre of the hall, not content to leave yet, though Ahrown vainly tried to restrain him. "Hear me Pharaoh, your reign will end before my son, the Prince of Kush, turns ten" Thutmoses declared, loud enough for everyone to hear. "And you," he pointed his finger directly at Amenhotep still seated on his platform, "Will suffer horribly those final few years of your life. Your body will rot from the inside and your *ka* will turn sour. You will beg for death but it will not come swiftly. When I return I will spit on your tomb!"

The crowd was horrified by Thutmoses' outburst. No one had ever spoken to the *Neter-Nesew* in that manner before publicly. It was a terrifying event but rather than leave the Great Hall of Audience, they stayed to watch for any further quarrelling.

"I will have your body splayed so that the birds pick you bones dry," Pharaoh shouted back.

Hearing Pharaoh's threat of retaliation, Kheper-Kephrure pounded his sceptre against the floor with such force that everyone stopped in their tracks. "You will do no such thing Pharaoh Amenhotep. You have sworn before the gods that the decision of this court will be final and no man will lift a hand against any that have had judgment passed, otherwise those that do will be executed whether they be commoner or royal.

That is the law and that is what you have ordained. You are advised to retract your statement immediately or there will be another charge levelled immediately."

"I retract," Pharaoh sneered. "But I will still have my revenge. The name of Thutmoses-Mutenkheperure is to be stricken from every record, erased from every memorial, prohibited from ever being spoken on anyone's lips. There is no law against that, magistrate. From hence forth, you are no longer my son. My firstborn son is dead to me."

"Very well," Thutmoses' response almost sounded as if it was one of relief. "You have never been my father. You have always been dead to me. Hence forth, I am the son of no one."

Ahrown tried to pull Thutmoses away from the direction of the royal platform before the war of words turned into something far more serious.

"Be gone, son of no one. Take your Lebu pet with you. Leave this land and don't return."

"Oh, I will be back. It will not be long. You will not see your fortieth year of reign. That I promise by all the gods. Your years are numbered and I will be back to celebrate your death."

Holding out his hand, Thutmoses begged Sitamun to come with him in a final effort to persuade his sister to spend the rest of her life with him. In silence his eyes pleaded with her.

"Where do you think she is going?" Amenhotep held his daughter back. "You do not exist any longer. Her marriage never existed in that case. I will take her to be my wife and she will bear my children."

"You are a deviant and it sickens me to think I share blood in common with you. Keep your husband Tiye, the two of you deserve one another. When he lays with your daughters you can dwell upon the fact that this is the monster that you supported. Take a good look at your only remaining son and imagine what any offspring from your daughters will look like. This is your own doing as much as his!"

The fact that he called her by her name was not lost on his mother. She realized that her son was also cutting his ties with her as well. The incredible shame of her actions were coming to full realization.

"Thutmoses, I did not do this thing," she pleaded with him.

"This thing has always been your doing," her son replied. "I swear by the gods, he will suffer horribly for the remaining years of his life. He will beg you to put him out of his misery and you will shed your tears into a hollow cistern for you chose to support a creature that will rape his own daughters. Come Sitamun, come now before he can force himself upon you."

"I cannot," she cried. "You are stripped of everything Muti. I cannot live like that. I must stay here."

"She cannot leave," Amenhotep interceded. "I forbid it!"

"I will be back one day Sitamun. I pray that you will be safe until I return. I have always loved you." At that moment Thutmoses felt his heart torn in half and the pain was almost unbearable.

Hoshea and Machir had come to the aid of Ahrown to help separate Thutmoses and pull him away from approaching the base of the platform. Othni was already clearing a way through the crowd so that they could make their escape before Pharaoh tested how enforceable the law restricting him from laying a hand on Thutmoses truly was.

"This is going to get ugly," Hoshea warned everyone as he saw more and more people attempting to push their way into the central area of the hall. "Before long the guards are going to come and they will start clubbing everyone in their way whether they be aristocrats or not. That's when things will get wild."

"Let us go Thutmoses," Ahrown pulled hard on his companion's tunic.

"There is no Thutmoses," the Prince turned on him in his rage. "I have no part in this family. I am the son of no one. From now on I am only Moses!"

CHAPTER SIXTEEN

"What happened father? How did it go so wrong?" Eleazar was alarmed by the events that happened the days of the Tribunal.

"What happened was your uncle's ego," Aaron snapped back. "He thought he could just stand before the judges, say a few words and everything would fall into place exactly as he planned."

"That's not exactly how you described it father. When you told the story you implied that he was betrayed by his mother."

"Oh, did I? Well that happened too."

"But you were standing there by his side. You agreed to be his legal voice in the courts. I know you well enough father, you wouldn't have agreed to do that unless you too thought you had everything under control."

"I agreed to undertake that role because I thought your uncle had a plan," Aaron confessed, "And it wasn't until afterwards I found out his plan was for us to lose our case,"

"I don't understand," his son was confused by the answer.

"Well, I certainly didn't understand either. Most normal people initiate a legal action because they want justice. Moses was seeking injustice so that he could justify every action he undertook afterwards." Aaron rocked his head back and forth as if to suggest the entire episode was insane.

"But that makes sense then," Eleazar pointed out. "If everything we have done to create this nation was a result of losing that trial, then you can appreciate that it was God's will. You had to lose in order to win. Moses must have understood that!"

"Now you sound exactly like your uncle," Aaron admonished him. "It wouldn't have been so bad if Moses had actually explained to us in advance what he was doing but by keeping it a secret, innocent people got swept up in the net and lost their lives as a result. Surely you can see that." Aaron stared intensely into his son's eyes to see if his point had registered.

"I have a better question for you, father. If Moses had told you in advance what his plan was, would you have let him go ahead with it?"

"Trying to stop Moses from doing anything was practically impossible." Aaron reflected on all the disagreements he had with the leader of Israel over the years. "But yes, we would have tried. And failing that, then at least we would have had a choice not to participate in it."

"Presume you did stop him, and all the events that followed afterwards including our exodus from Mitzrayim never happened, then what would have been the point of your life?" Eleazar decided it was time to provide some hard lessons to his father that the old man had been refusing to listen to for a long time.

Aaron looked confused. "What do you mean?" He coughed and cleared his throat several times, an obvious delaying action to avoid answering the question.

"You heard me," Eleazar was not willing to permit his father bypass the question. "If the plan intended by Moses had never been executed, if there had never been an exodus, then what would have been the purpose of your life?"

"I had my own life before Moses entered into it," Aaron tried to defend himself.

"Oh, as the *Wab-tepi* in a Temple where they were already stripping any authority away from your family. Time to take a look at reality father and realize that without Moses, without the course of actions he took, whether you agreed with them or not, you'd have nothing."

"I...I...I..." but Aaron had nothing more he could say. Without Moses he recognized he would have been nobody of consequence. There was no argument, there was no rebuttal. It was a fact.

"Another question for you father. What happened to the General's sarcophagus? Is it still in the House of Death?"

Aaron chuckled though he had little else from this conversation to laugh at. "I told you when we first climbed this mountain that we needed a set of bones to carry out of Mitzrayim."

"I thought so," was Eleazar's suspecting response.

1361 BCE

Just beyond the door to the residence, a squadron of Nubian soldiers stood on guard to ensure the protection of those within the building. They had been provided by the Court, as Kheper-Kephrure still feared that Amenhotep would attempt to finish what he failed to achieve in Nubia but they were equally preventing anyone from leaving as much as those entering. Within the house, the group of men sat engrossed in their own thoughts. Each had to deal with the reality of dreams lost and strange fates that they were about to experience. No one dared to ask the next question even though they knew they must.

"Why do I feel like we are prisoners?" Hoshea finally took the initiative and broke the silence.

"Because we are," Machir answered him. "Don't be fooled by whatever my uncle says, the reality is we are not able to leave until he says so."

The Prince finally spoke up but surprisingly in defence of Kheper-Kephrure. "It is probably a smart decision to have us secured within this building. As soon as we were moved from Thebes to Memphis, the probability of Pharaoh making an attempt on our lives increased substantially."

"You mean your life," Ahrown wanted to be specific.

"I don't know what you issue with me since the trial is brother but the fact is that you have an equal probability of being killed as I do. So I suggest you get over whatever your problem is and we start working together."

"My issue with you is that we are in this mess because of you." Ahrown retaliated, stating his problem as simply as he could.

"And exactly how do you define this mess, brother?" Moses wanted to hear the specifics of Ahrown's accusation.

"Is everyone here blind?" Ahrown couldn't believe that no one else was picking up his argument and agreeing with him. "We are under house arrest. None of us will ever be able to go back to the lives we had."

"Oh, you mean you won't go back to your life," Othni decided he had remained quiet for too long. "My life has been watching over and protecting the Prince. I can't see why that is going to change."

"I haven't really had a life other than the military," Machir confessed. "Perhaps this will provide me with an incentive to actually do something else with my life. Uncle Ephra thinks it has been wasted so far. Perhaps he has work for me as a court official. Oh, wait. He can't tolerate my father," Machir laughed to himself. "I guess that's out of the question."

"I don't want to go back to my life as it was at all," Hoshea declared. "I'm much happier to stick around here. I get a bed, I get food, this is much better than my experiences before meeting the Prince."

"So let's be clear. The only two significantly affected brother are you and myself. I must go into exile as you know, but I have no worries, because I know I will be back as soon as Amenhotep is dead. Your concern is that you won't be able to return to life in your Temple. Perhaps you forgot your father had been stripped of the high priesthood and I'm certain Nebwenenhef already had made plans to remove any Lebu from the Temple."

"How can you be so certain of that," Ahrown wanted to know.

"Because I know. The same way that I know that Pharaoh won't live another eight years."

"The man could live forever," Machir commented. "Are you now a seer, Thutmoses? Seriously, how do you know it's only eight more years?"

"I told you not to call me that. It is simply Moses from now on," he chastised his cousin.

"But that's only half a name," Machir argued. "You have to be the son of somebody."

"That is where you are wrong," Moses corrected him. "I don't need to be the son of anyone. My entire life has been the mistake of trying to be someone's son. I now understand what our grandfather meant when he suggested I must first find myself."

"Well, since you're so certain I won't have a position in the Temple to return to, then why not let us come with you into exile," Ahrown suggested. "That way we don't have to wait for your return."

"Are we done with your brooding over this matter and blaming me for everything that has gone wrong in your view?" Moses wanted to establish where the two of them stood.

"I may have blamed you for more than you deserved," Ahrown admitted.

"What kind of answer is that," Hoshea piped in. "Doesn't sound like much of a conciliation to me."

"It will suffice for now, if it means we can treat each other with civility," Moses accepted the luke-warm agreement from Ahrown. "We need to be on the same side because I have other tasks for all of you while I am gone." Moses informed them.

"Tasks?" Ahrown asked. "You have to stop this. You have to admit it's over? We lost. We lost everything. Our families, our careers, there's nothing left! It's the end!" Ahrown threw his hands up in the air suggesting that anyone listening to this nonsense had also lost their minds.

"Don't be so theatrical," Moses shot back at his long-time companion. "We're just beginning! When we first got together you told me that you hoped we could change the world. Were you naïve then or did you really believe it?"

"That was then, this is now!"

"Yes, you are right, and now is the beginning," Moses asserted. "You keep thinking that our conquest of Nubia and Kush was in some way the crowning achievement whereby we changed the world. We changed nothing! That entire affair was to serve one purpose and that was to lay my hands on the sapphire staff because that is the mission that Yuyu set me upon."

"Yuyu is dead. His missions are dead," Ahrown declared.

"That my friend is where you are sadly mistaken. You say you and the Lebu understand how the world works. I say you understand nothing. Yuyu knew how it worked and that's why your father was so desperate to have me do my initiation in your Temple. He hoped that I would show you how Yuyu did what he did. You never took the time to appreciate that you were really providing me with the information so that I could understand why Yuyu thought the way he did. And I say his mission is very much alive and this is just the beginning." Moses loomed over his companions, his posture almost threatening if anyone else wanted to challenge him.

"Beginning of what?" Ahrown found it hard to deal with Moses' displaced optimism.

"There is much for us to get ready and we only have eight years in which to do it," Moses instructed his companions. "So if anyone of you aren't prepared to do as I say, then now is the time to say so and we can part company."

The others in the room glanced from face to face, looking to see if anyone would take the option to back out. Moses gave them the time to think about it seriously before putting an end to their silent deliberation.

"So what do we have to do?" was the general response from all of them.

"Ahrown, you must go back to the Temple in Onu. Make peace with the departed soul of your father for your own sake. I am sorry you were not there at the time of his passing. I truly am."

"And what am I supposed to be doing back in the Temple? As you mentioned, Nebwenenhef will never accept me back as the *wab-tepi*. Pharaoh has probably seen to that."

"I needed to know everyone's level of commitment to our mission. Now that I know it, I will let you in one something I've heard from my Uncle Ephra. Pharaoh is about to force the Temples of Atum-Ra to adopt service only to Amun from now on. That was the original purpose of having your father removed as High Priest. I suspect many of your fellow priests will be disgruntled with that decision. Perhaps you can encourage them to express their views a little more forcefully but that is already under consideration by some. But first, there is too great a wealth of documents in your Temple archives. I need you to preserve the ones most important for our cause."

"Most important?"

"The one's you Lebu wrote about the *potohikap neter*. Anything to do with the cycles of events since the dawn of keeping records. Of course anything else you believe to be useful, I would suggest you take as well."

"And what am I supposed to do with those once I've collected them?"

"The creator god is common to all the tribes in Goshen. Use them to teach the people about the god of their ancestors. Tell them that I will be coming back for them. Those documents are very important even though you may not realize it yet."

"What are you talking about?" Ahrown was confused and thinking perhaps a touch of the madness was within his friend as well. "Why are we wasting our time with the *nehseyt* in Goshen? We should be thinking about raising the army from Nubia."

"I know I am probably sounding a little crazy to all of you right now but I assure you that I'm not."

"Exactly what a crazy person would say," Hoshea joked but Moses was not amused.

"There are things I never told you before. When I held the sapphire staff it was if it was speaking to me, telling me things, foretelling my future; our future. How do you think I know that Pharaoh will be dead in the next eight years? How do you think I knew to leave my wife Tharbis and my son in Saba and not bring them north with me? I did not foresee all the events of the trial but I did know that we would be at this point in time preparing for my exile and that is why my Queen had arranged to have the staff returned to the care of the Midianites."

"So we are going to Midian?" Hoshea asked.

"Yes, you and Othni will be coming with me to Midian. My Uncle Ephra arranged that I can take an escort of fifty of my Nubians to protect us on the road. So now you can appreciate those men outside are there only for our protection and part of keeping us safe is keeping us in this house. When we're ready to leave, they will be coming with us."

"And what about me," Machir asked.

"You will work with Ahrown."

"Oh, lucky me," Machir responded sarcastically.

"He needs you and you need him," Moses chastised him. "The tribes in Goshen won't be immediately receptive to Lebu priests arriving in their midst. After all, the Lebu have never had a taste of slavery. Those in Goshen will think of them as still being elitist and part of Pharaoh's world until their revolt. So Machir, you must convince those in Goshen that the priests are our allies. I also need you to be the conduit between myself and Uncle Ephra. The Chief Magistrate will be critical in arranging for my return."

"Assuming our uncle is still alive in eight years," Machir had his doubts.

"Don't worry, I have seen his future and he will be around for a very long time," Moses reassured him.

"Me too," Machir wanted to know.

"Yes, you too," Moses reassured him.

"Just a second," Ahrown interrupted. "I understand the part about my teaching the people in Goshen but when did it become all of the other Lebu priests heading to Goshen and living amongst the people?"

"That is a direct result of the revolt," Moses clarified the matter.

"What revolt," Ahrown grew concerned. "You said nothing of a revolt."

"Yes I did," Moses corrected him. "I said you fellow priests will grow disgruntled and you should encourage them, as well as the people won't fully trust you until the revolt. Remember?"

"You said something but it didn't register with me at the time. So what revolt," Ahrown asked for Moses to be more specific.

"Some of them are actually going to try and oppose Pharaoh."

Ahrown shook his head. "Priests don't revolt."

"This time they will. Maybe that will be enough to convince you that I can see what will happen soon in our futures. So you will prepare a safe harbour for them in Goshen because they are vital to our future. They will need you to lead them more than ever. Are you up to the task?"

Ahrown nodded even though part of him still insisted that priests don't revolt.

"And I also need you to recue those documents as soon as possible so they don't get lost in the fire?"

"*Exieti?*"

"Amenhotep won't take too kindly to the little revolt staged by your brotherhood of priests. He will try to burn you all alive in the Temple. But now that you are forewarned, you'll be able to keep them safe."

"And when were you going to tell me all this," Ahrown felt Moses had not been fully transparent in regards to the events of the future he had witnessed.

"I just did tell you. Now prepare yourself accordingly."

"And exactly why are we bringing all the Lebu to Goshen?" Machir was still confused.

"Because after the fire, they won't have anywhere else to go. And I need them to fully undertake Yuyu's prophecy. I now understand everything Yuyu was trying to tell me when I read through his papers in the Temple of Isis. We are going to take back our freedom, we will restore our nation and we will shake the land of Kemet to its very foundations."

"I told you," Hoshea shouted excitedly. "I told you that the talk in the streets was right. Now you finally admit it!"

"We cannot escape our destinies," Moses conceded.

"It all sounds fantastic," Ahrown was still critical of the plan, "But in case you haven't noticed there is only the five of us here. I'm not certain how much shaking of the foundations we're actually going to be doing. It will take a lot more people and an entire army to conduct a revolution."

"More than you can imagine but leave that to me," Moses remained secretive but his sly smile let everyone know that he wasn't going to divulge any further information in that regard. "On your way to Goshen, I need you to find Meri-Amun at the Temple of Isis. She is also holding a wealth of documents for me. They will be crucial for our plan to succeed. Just pass the word on to her that the time is now and yes, we need her to join. She'll understand what I mean. Machir, I suggest you also find accommodation for some of the priests and priestesses from the Temple of Isis should they choose to join us early on."

"Plan? What plan? You haven't told us anything yet," Ahrown growled.

"Trust me, brother. It will all become crystal clear when I return.

"How are we to trust you when you are gone for eight years?" Ahrown struggled with the overriding issue.

"Each day you will see the movement grow," Moses reassured them all. "The people themselves will inspire you. You will be able to take heart from their hope."

"Are you suggesting that tens of thousands of *nehseyt* can wrestle away the government from Pharaoh with his armies?" Ahrown shook his head, still believing that this so-called plan was nothing more than complete madness.

"I will be honest with you brother, I have not seen any visions beyond what I have told you thus far. I can't tell you what the people will do upon my return. But in the meantime, remember that just because a Tribunal says I am no longer the King of Kush doesn't mean I am not the King. I still have my Queen sitting on the throne and an army waiting for my return. Who's to say I cannot march them north at my bidding?"

Machir was still trying to appreciate his role in all this. "So not to diminish your talk about armies and queens, but how exactly am I to convince the people that they should listen to some Lebu priests and a prince that is no longer a prince and who is disappearing for eight years? I've never been that good at public speaking."

"I will give you signs that they can look for to show them that I have spoken the truth and that you are my trusted servant in this matter. Tell them this; in three years they will look to the northwest and they will see the sky across the great sea glow fiery red at night for an entire year. In the morning the ground will be covered with ashes that have blown across the water. There will be a message from Thebes that Pharaoh has fallen ill and all will prepare for his death but he will recover and falsely believe that the worst has passed. And all the people will say, 'how did he know' and you will respond, 'Because he is Moses.'

All will be quiet until the fifth year when the sky will be lit directly in the north for an entire year. And Pharaoh again will fall ill but this time he will not recover. Every day they will prepare for his death but he will not die. Each day he will be tormented by a thousand deaths, and will scream to be released from his suffering, but he still will not die. And the people will ask you, 'How did he know.' And you will say, 'Because he is Moses.'

But in the eight year, the fires in the northeast will be so bright that it will be hard to tell day from night. And the heralds will pronounce throughout all the land that Pharaoh has died and Moses, the disenfranchised prince, is returning to spit on his tomb. And the people will say to you, 'Why did Pharaoh die so young' and you will say to them, 'Because he challenged Moses,' and they should prepare for my return."

"I will try," Machir agreed. "If everything happens as you predict it will, then that should be sufficient to convince most of them."

"The signs will be enough," Moses reassured him. "They are signs sent by the Creator."

"What will we Lebu do during this time," Ahrown inquired.

"Machir will have given you the perfect platform from which to teach them about the Creator. As he tells them everything that will happen because the Creator has spoken directly to me, you will convince them that the Creator speaks to all of them as well. You will instil the beliefs in them so that when I return they will know exactly of what I speak."

"And what exactly are you doing for the eight years," Ahrown wanted to know.

"While I'm in Midian I will contact Caleb and Hur and let them know what is taking place and what their roles will be. I'm sure they've heard plenty of rumours by now. I better let them know the truth so my Queen does not do anything foolish in the meantime and waits for the proper time to play her role. For the time being she must remain in Saba until my son is old enough to rule on his own."

"You sound pretty confident about all this," Ahrown was still skeptical but he was gradually beginning to realize that Moses was very serious about having this ability of precognition.

"I know you probably feel that I've kept you in the dark about much of this," Moses somewhat apologized, "But I had to be certain that what I was thinking was true and not just my imagination. I needed to also know that you were all still committed to my cause."

"Well I'm still with you," Othni gave his affirmation once again. "Been your personal body guard since the day you climbed out of your crib so it's not like I know how to be anything else," he laughed. "Plus I hear the woman in Midian are quite beautiful so I might as well see for myself."

"Not like I have to worry about losing my standing in the community, Machir commented. "They won't understand why a descendant of Yuyu wants to climb into the mud pits with them, so if I talk about freedom at least they'll understand I'm not there to make bricks. So count me in."

"So that's two," Moses took count.

"Didn't think I needed to state the obvious," Hoshea took his turn to speak. "You are the only family I have, so I'm in it to the end. Where you go, I go."

Moses nodded his approval and gratitude to his young ward. "Well brother that leaves only you."

"Didn't I say so, already?" Ahrown still struggled with providing a direct answer.

"Not exactly," Moses responded. "Now that everyone has all the facts, I need to hear it again. I need to hear you are committed to the cause."

"I thought I said so," Ahrown still avoided making a direct response.

"Not at all," Hoshea felt it necessary to add his own criticism.

"He burns down my temple?" Ahrown still sought confirmation.

"A considerable amount of it but specifically the library," Moses specified the details. "Punishment for trying to lead a popular revolt against his religious reformation."

"And there is no way to stop this from happening?"

"You can certainly try," Moses suggested, "But I don't think any of these events I've seen can be changed."

"And in this future world of yours, we Lebu somehow become linked to all the foreign tribes in Goshen?"

"Inextricably. In fact you will instruct them on the correct worship of the Creator God from your Lebu documents. That's part of the reason you have to rescue them."

"So what's the other part of the reason," Ahrown's curiosity had been piqued.

"You came to the land of Kemet and created a religious institution that took a bunch of swamp water farmers and converted them into the mightiest Empire this world has ever seen. I need to know how your ancestors did it, and I'm assuming the strategy is buried somewhere in those documents. You need to find out how it was done and then do it again."

Ahrown thought long and hard about what Moses had just said. It had been his father's dream of a restored Lebu religious practice, but certainly not with the *pedtay* or foreigners in Goshen. But perhaps Goshen was a good starting point from where it could spread once they were in positions of power once again. "Okay, I've been with you this far," Ahrown said half-heartedly, "So we might as well see it to the end together as well."

"Wow, isn't that reassuring!" Hoshea jumped in again only to be stared down by Ahrown, who resented his interference.

"It was a pretty pathetic answer," Othni concurred.

"I still don't know if that was a yes," Machir decided he should get in a dig on the priest as well.

"Okay, okay, I'm with you," Ahrown finally gave in to their criticisms. "Wherever this takes us, whatever happens to us, I'm standing with you. They say your grandfather was a dreamer, Moses. So let's dream!"

CHAPTER SEVENTEEN

"Sounds like you were being very antagonistic towards Moses, even back then." Eleazar commented on his father's past actions.

"We had our disagreements over the years," Aaron admitted.

"Quite a few of them if you actually start counting them," Eleazar started rolling them off his fingers as he started to recount them silently in his head.

By the time he started raising the first finger on his second hand, Aaron stopped him. "Alright, yes we had our disagreements."

"They were more than disagreements," Eleazar challenged Aaron. "Some of them were outright disobedience and you know it."

"Those are the lies of my enemies," Aaron defended himself.

"So it wasn't you who urged the people to give their gold rings and earrings to you so that you could fashion a golden calf for them? Are you still denying that?"

"As I told Moses then, it was the people that made me do it. They would have killed me if I didn't submit to their wishes."

Eleazar couldn't believe his ears that his father was still in denial of his role that he played that day. "Who are you trying to fool?" he chastised his father. "You saw it as an opportunity to seize power. Moses disappeared up the mountain for weeks, you assumed he must be dead, and that was your opportunity to seize control over the people and the first thing you wanted to do was restore the practices of the old Lebu religion. You made a model of the Apis bull, in which your version of the invisible creator god, your Lebu *amenen potohikap neter*, rides between the horns. I may have been a child then but I know what I saw father. You can't deny it."

"I do deny it, the same way I denied it when Moses accused me of doing so. I said it then and I say it now, the people threw their gold into the fire and the statue of the calf emerged from the fire all on its own."

"I saw you with your tongs and hammer," Eleazar was practically screaming. "Stop lying. Stop lying to me!"

"It's true, it's true," Aaron buried his face into the palms of his hands. "Why won't you believe me?"

"Because it is a lie. It was a lie then and it is even a bigger lie now that you try to retell it."

"Haven't I suffered enough for it?" Aaron still tried to defend his actions. "Didn't I lose your two brothers because of it, Nadab and Abihu?" Wasn't the payment in lives of close to three thousand revellers enough for Moses that he had to take my two boys as well?"

"He didn't kill them, father. Yahvu took them for their improper actions before the altar."

"Moses killed them as surely as you are condemning me for making the golden calf," Aaron stated with certainty. "It was the first time we were lighting the altar within the tabernacle. Moses claimed he could not enter with us and like a fool I didn't suspect that there was some other reason he refused to enter. He told my sons they must sprinkle their clothing with the blood of the sacrifice mixed with the anointing oil. They had to ensure that the garments were covered with this strange mixture. Then they were to climb to the top of the altar and light the fire. As soon as they lit their brands the flames leaped upon their clothing as if they were living creatures. There was nothing any of us could do. They were gone before we could even react. Moses made certain that they were the first sacrifice made upon the altar and then said they were killed by Yahvu because they offered strange fire to the Lord. What he really meant was that they intended to offer human sacrifice like the Moloch worshippers. My boys had no intention to die that day but Moses killed them as certain as if he had lit them on fire himself. That was his punishment for my sin. How I wish that he had just killed me instead, rather than making me witness the death of my two sons. Now you know the truth! What do you think of your lawgiver now?"

Eleazar found the truth difficult to swallow but he knew this time that his father was being truthful. "I am now High Priest of Israel father. What would I have done if I found you crafting a golden calf? I think my role as High Priest would have outweighed my role as your son. I would have had you executed. Moses loved you too much. He could not bring himself to have you killed. So instead he punished you and perhaps that punishment was far worse than death. They were my brothers and I grieved for their loss. They should not have been punished for your sins."

"You see now, your great lawgiver is a murderer of innocent people. He thinks himself to still be a god, above all others, and he must be held accountable for his own sins."

"Perhaps. Perhaps not," was all that Eleazar could say. "Perhaps if you had admitted to your sin at the time, he would have forgiven you. Instead you chose to lie. You lied to him and you lied to Yahvu. Now is the time, while you stand before God to have your sins weighed, that it might be best to tell the truth before your final judgment. Shall we review your sins together so that we can clear your slate?"

"What other sins do you want to accuse me of? Was not this one sufficient to satisfy your obsession with finding blame for all I've done?"

"Not me, father. If you wish to clear your slate then do it now before God. Before He comes to claim your soul and you find it is too late."

1361 BCE

Leaving Memphis under the cover of night, Moses and his two companions rode silently from the city towards the North King's Road. Running alongside of their horses, the Nubians carrying shield and spear kept pace, never seeming to tire as they covered the first ten miles without ever stopping. The intention was to cover twenty miles each day. If everything went smoothly, they should be in Midian by the fourteenth day. They would avoid the traditional caravan routes as that would make it too easy to be discovered on the road should Pharaoh intend to try and finish what he started in Nubia. Even so, concealing a party accompanied by fifty Nubian soldiers was not going to be an easy task. By following the mountain passes and the dried wadis, they could avoid using the main thoroughfares for most of the journey. Rather than take the North King's Road through the cities along the Nile, Moses led them directly east across the barren countryside towards the Great Bitter Lake. Here they would encounter a few small, scattered villages where they would refill their water gourds, buy some food and quickly move on. Traversing the Desert of Etham would present some danger should the anticipated wells and oasis be dried up but Moses calculated they could manage to carry enough water just in case of that situation arising. That would bring them to the Gidi Pass in the mountains but beyond that was the Desert of Paran. Once there, things could get a little more dangerous. It was the month of Mesure and Moses was calculating, or better to say that he was praying that the desert rains, as sparse as they were that month would still be collected in the Wadi Al Arish. From there they would cross to the Wadi Jita with the same hope that the late spring rains still had left some trace of rainfall in the river bed. Afterwards, they would travel to the town of Ezion Geber where they could refill their stocks of water and food. Turning south for the next forty miles would take them into the heart of Midian and with a little luck, they'd be able to find the Chieftain Jethro and his confederacy of tribes with a lot less difficulty than Zelophedad had experienced.

Listening intently to the plans for the route, his companions were uneasy every time Moses mentioned the need for a little luck or hope in securing drinking water.

"A little luck is finding a village that has a nice hot bath that we can wash the desert dust off," Hoshea reacted. "Hoping that dried river beds will have water in them that's more than a little luck. Sounds more like we're praying for miracles."

"Don't worry, I described the worst case scenario to you. I doubt we will encounter much difficulty," Moses reassured them. "Can't be any worse than when we crossed the desert in Nubia," he drew a comparison.

"Except we had two guides that knew every watering hold along the way," Othni commented on what he considered to be a significant difference. "We're travelling blind this time."

"Not exactly," Moses corrected him. "We have our horses. And you won't find a better animal able to smell water beneath desert sands."

"How do you know that," Hoshea asked.

"I read it during one of my classes in military tactics," Moses explained.

"Oh, you read it," Hoshea responded sarcastically. "That makes me feel much better."

"You know I can put you back on the streets in Goshen," Moses threatened him.

"You'd be lost without me," Hoshea countered.

"Any way, focus on our conservation of water. Don't drink more than you need and don't start stealing any from the horses' supply. We should be at Gidi Pass before nightfall."

That evening they untied their sleeping mats from the back of their saddles and unrolled them on the few flat pieces of ground they could find. There was an inexplicable calm that pervaded the rock faces of the pass. The few outcroppings of grass and shrubs seemingly growing directly out of the rock provided a serene beauty sharply contrasting the bareness of the Desert of Etham that they had just traversed.

Hoshea became intrigued and fascinated as he watched their Nubian escorts busily scrounging through the bits of vegetation sprouting from the rock.

"What are you doing?" he asked the big burly black warrior closest to him.

"Hunting for dinner came the reply."

"I don't know if those plants are edible," Hoshea cautioned him.

"Not those, these," the soldier replied jubilantly having found a nice fat black scorpion. "Would you like me to find you one too?"

"I think I'll pass on it," Hoshea responded as he watched the Nubian pop the scorpion into his mouth and start chewing."

"Aren't you a little worried about being stung," Hoshea was nervous but still curious about this peculiar eating style displayed by the Nubians.

"After being stung so many times in the mouth," the black man responded, "The venom is no longer a problem. Instead, there is a bit of a euphoric effect from eating them. I think it may be from the venom."

"That's good to know," Hoshea thanked the soldier for sharing his knowledge. "I will keep it in mind if I should be desperate enough to want to eat one."

The Nubian smiled broadly, showing off the set of claws protruding from his teeth, before he spat them out.

Turning to Moses and Othni, Hoshea couldn't block the picture of eating live scorpions from his mind. "That had to be one of the most unappetizing things I have ever witnessed," he confessed to the two of them.

"Don't dismiss it," Moses warned him. "When we're starving and dying of thirst while they're all sitting back crunching on their scorpions, you may actually start begging them to catch you one."

"I think I would rather die," the boy quickly dismissed that idea, causing Moses and Othni to burst out laughing.

"Eat your dried mutton and get some sleep. Tomorrow we start trekking across the Desert of Paran, so expect to be hot and thirsty for the next forty or so miles until we reach Elath," Moses instructed his two companions.

Tapping Moses on his right shoulder, the Captain of the Nubian guard roused Moses from an uncomfortable slumber on the rocks.

"What is happening?" Moses asked sluggishly, using his hands to rub the sleep from his eyes before he looked around and saw it was still the middle of the night, a river of stars still forming a canopy over their heads. The fire that was at the centre of their camp was practically out, all that remained was a pile of glowing embers that cast eerie shadows across the rock faces.

"One of the sentries has heard many footsteps approaching our camp" the captain whispered. "We must be ready for them."

Moses immediately tapped Othni and Hoshea, arousing both of them and informing them that they were possibly under attack. All three of them reached for their swords and sat ready for anything that might happen.

"Where are all our men?" Othni raised his concern, seeing that at most there were only around ten Nubians lying on the ground near the remains of the fire.

Calling the Captain back to his side, Moses asked nervously, "Where did all your men go?"

"Hunting" came the reply very calmly and without any evidence of concern.

"Hunting what?" Moses thought it best to ask.

"Someone hunts us, we hunt them," the Captain responded. "Now, the three of you lie down and pretend to sleep like my men. That way they will come directly into the camp to kill you," he said with his best smile as if there was very little to be concerned about.

"We're the bait!" Hoshea sounded nervous upon realizing what the Captain was doing.

"Have no fear," the Captain said very calmly. "You will be safe."

"That's easy for you to say," Hoshea found it difficult to be calm. "Most likely they're hunting us and not you and your men. They're coming for us first."

"Shhh…" the Captain held his finger to his lips. "Lie down and make as little noise as possible. They are almost upon us."

Listening intently, Moses thought he could hear the occasional stone being crunched beneath a footfall. He tried to close his eyes, to look the part of being asleep, but he could not bring himself to do so. At least with his eyes open, he'd have a chance if one of their attackers made it past the Nubians.

Curling themselves into balls, they had their swords tucked neatly beneath their bodies and ready to use as soon as they leapt to their feet. "What if they don't even enter the camp?" Hoshea raised the question.

"What do you mean?" Hophni asked his young companion.

"They could just shoot arrows from the distance and not even approach us. We're just laying here like three big targets."

Moses thought about it for a second then replied, "Too dark for shooting arrows. We'd have to have the fire going so they could actually see us clearly and the fire is almost out." No sooner did he finish his sentence when a couple of arrows whizzed overhead.

"Can't see us but thy may be able to hear us," Othni said in a hushed whisper. "Everyone be quiet."

The silence was suddenly broken by the familiar war cry of the Nubians. Getting to their feet, the three of them stood at the ready brandishing their swords but none of the attackers ever appeared in the circle around the dying campfire. From the impenetrable darkness that surrounded them, Moses heard the thud of spears piercing leather armour and the horrified screams of men suddenly aware that they were dying far from their homes. The screams didn't last long, replaced by an almost eerie silence where no one moved and not a sound was made.

Stepping out from the darkness, the Captain dragged one of the wounded assailants across the rough ground and dropped him at Moses' feet. "This one is still alive my King. His five other companions are all dead," the Captain informed Moses while at the same time giving his captive a swift kick to the head.

"Thank you Captain. According to Pharaoh, you aren't to refer to me as your king any longer."

"You will always be our king," the Captain disagreed with Pharaoh's edict. "And Tharbis is our Queen. We will serve you both faithfully until the day we die."

"You and your men have served me well tonight, Captain. If I had it within my power, I'd reward you with tribute and honours but all I can do now is say thank you."

"The appreciation of my King is reward enough," the Captain saluted then followed through with another kick to his prisoner.

"If you keep kicking him, I won't be able to question him," Moses cautioned the Captain to restrain himself.

"He is an Egyptian dog, your Highness. He deserves to be treated as one."

"I'm not disagreeing Captain but it would be best to find out if he knows anything of value before you do him any serious harm. And please remember that the three of us are also Kemtu and I don't think we like hearing ourselves referred to as dogs or Egyptians for that matter."

"Your Highness, I only meant that he is an Egyptian dog. I would never say such a think about my King."

Moses indicated to the Captain that he accepted his explanation but stressed that it would be best to utilize a better choice of words next time. Kneeling beside the prisoner, Moses raised his leather capped head to get a better look. There was nothing special about his uniform or the weapon he carried. Everything looked to be the normal ordinance for a regular infantry man in the army. But then regular infantry men don't try to carry out an assassination attempt in the middle of the night and a hundred miles from the closest barracks.

"Anything you'd like to say before you die?" Moses asked the assassin.

The man refused to say a word.

"You know if you talk, I might actually send you back with a message to whomever sent you," Moses tried to entice the assassin to start speaking with a promise of sparing his life.

Once again the man refused to speak.

"Oh well, Captain, see if you and your men can loosen his tongue before you kill him."

"Yes my King," the captain saluted with his right fist crossing his chest and proceeded to drag the prisoner a short distance before tossing him into the outstretched hands of several other Nubians.

"Foolish man," Moses said to his companions. "I would have let him live if he just confirmed what we already know, that my father sent these men in an attempt on my life."

"And if he had spoken, what would you have done then," Othni wanted to know.

"I would have sent him back to my Uncle Ephra with a two man escort. Kheper-Kephrure could then deal with the breach of the agreement regarding not lifting a finger against either plaintiff or defendant after the court decision was made."

"Not like Pharaoh actually cares," Hoshea commented.

"Still, I think it would give my uncle great pleasure to level some new charges at Amenhotep," Moses smiled thinking about it.

Listening to the screams emanating from the prisoner at the hands of his gaolers, Moses just casually shrugged them off, waiting patiently for the last scream's echo to fade. "It would appear that he still doesn't wish to talk," Moses tried to cover up the screams with a mild jest but he didn't need to. The screams ended abruptly and after having his men round up the six horses of the assassins as well as strip the bodies of all weapons, food and water, the party of weary travellers went back to sleep as if nothing ever happened.

The rest of the journey to Midian was without incident, neither from attack nor a shortage of water as the wadis fortunately were not dry. Though the Nubians did supplement their regular tack with the addition of raw scorpions, by the time they reached Ezion Geber, the three from Kemet, other than losing a few pounds along the way never had to resort to eating the scaly invertebrates. The inhabitants of the village were uncomfortable with the presence of the strangers since it was obvious they were neither merchants nor traders, which were the usual sort of travellers they had been accustomed too. They were even more uncomfortable when they saw that some of the Nubian warriors were wearing weapons taken from Kemtu infantry. Their initial thoughts that they were renegades but then they could not understand how they were under the command of three Kemtu if they were military runaways. Still there was business to be had, feeding, drinking and the occasional women for a few of the soldiers after they had had too much to drink and in this world of their everyday reality, the pursuit of money meant that everyone was welcome as long as they could pay.

Moses sought out the local horse trader and received a tidy sum for the six additional animals he had obtained after their assailants were killed. Without taking any of the payment for himself, he handed the pieces of silver he had received immediately to the Captain, asking that he distribute it between himself and the men. There were some lesson he had learned from Chenetothes that he would never forget. When he did so, he let the Captain know that the reward received could never fully express his gratitude for their service.

When it came time to move on and leave the hospitality of Ezion Geber, they were pointed in the general direction of where they should be able to find the Chieftain known as Jethro. Go south along the coastline they were told. It would just be a matter of time because as they said, "You don't find Jethro, Jethro finds you!"

CHAPTER EIGHTEEN

Eleazar searched for anything that might be combustible within the general vicinity of the cave. They had been talking for so many hours that they had consumed most of the small bundles of twigs and branches they had prepared in advance. The few bundles of material that remained weren't going to last very long if they intended to continue talking through each night. But with morning approaching swiftly, it meant that any of the small twigs they could scrounge would last them until the first rays of the sun spread across the mountain, without needing to start on the next bundle.

"I never quite understood what were your issues with all of Moses' wives," Eleazar was curious as to why each one had been condemned by his father.

"Shouldn't it be obvious," Aaron sputtered, a small amount of blood bubbling upon his lips. "He made rules for all to follow but when it came to his wives, he didn't even follow the same laws he imposed upon the rest of us."

"I don't understand...exactly what are you trying to say?"

"Sitamun was his sister. His own grandfather advised him not to marry his sister but Moses did not listen." Aaron spat in disgust. "He went ahead and did it anyway. Then he gives us laws to tell us who we can marry and who we can't."

"But as you told me, there was not much choice. If he didn't marry her she would have been wed to his father and Moses in his mercy actually saved her from that fate. Wasn't that worthy of consideration?"

"Did he? Did he really?" Aaron had to catch his breath before continuing. "Then let me tell you the rest of her story. After the tribunal, Pharaoh kept his threat that he made to his son that he would take Sitamun to be his own wife." He coughed several times but he settled down just as quickly. "While Moses was in Midian, Amenhotep did exactly as he swore he would do. Throughout Mitzrayim they celebrated Pharaoh's thirtieth reignal year. As part of his celebration he married his daughter, Sitamun, and proclaimed her to be Great Wife. By declaring that Thutmoses-Mutenepherure never existed, then it meant that Sitamun had never been married. In that way Pharaoh broke no laws restricting their marriage. It was Amenhotep's way to punish not only Moses but his wife, Tiye as well for siding in part with her son. As much as I condemn the marriage between Moses and his sister, it could only be surpassed in evil by a father laying with his daughter. I think Sitamun believed that Moses in some way would come to her rescue and save her from this fate worse than death but when he did not, she took the only action that was left to her. As soon as she learned she was impregnated by her own father she took her own life. Where was her Moses, her saviour? He was laying in the comfort of another woman. This time with a Midianite Chieftain's daughter. As I have been telling you, he leaves behind him a trail of innocent corpses."

"There was no way he could have stopped Sitamun's death," Eleazar argued.

"No, but if he followed the same laws he imposed upon us he would not have married her in the first place and perhaps she would have been overlooked by her father as a bride."

"You know that's not true," Eleazar dismissed his father's comment. "The Kings of Mitzrayim are an incestuous lot. If they lived long enough they'd probably even bed their grandchildren. So there would have been no hope for Sitamun no matter what Moses did. And what can you possibly hold against Zipporah other than the fact that she's given Moses two sons that will carry on his legacy."

"She caters to his depravity," Aaron screamed but the lack of air in his chest resulted in it being no louder than a shrill bark. "Yes, she provided him with two sons but once Tharbis arrived in our camp he had little time for Zipporah. You've seen that yourself. You can't deny it. Even her father left our camp because he knew his daughter no longer had favoured status. Zipporah is a daughter of our tribal confederacy, she is one of us. She should never have accepted being relegated to a secondary status."

"And you have made your disgust with that situation well known to Moses time and time again," Eleazar reminded Aaron. "But perhaps you should remember that it was you that sent Zipporah and his sons away when you encountered them the first time at Mount Horeb. You told him at that time the people of Goshen would reject him if they saw their deliverer with a Midianite wife because the people still had to think of him as a Prince of Mitzrayim. Do you recall that, or was that some fanciful story you told us all long ago merely to appease your own self-righteous indignation?"

"It was true," Aaron confirmed that he did turn her away for exactly that reason. "It may have been a mistake because by the time we returned to Goshen, Moses knew that Queen Tharbis was already on her way north with his army. Without Zipporah present there was no balance. Every time afterwards he sided with Tharbis whenever she made a suggestion. He no longer sought our advice!"

"And that is the crux of your resentment which you have avoided discussing since we brought you up the mountain. You can't tolerate the fact that between Tharbis and Zipporah, Moses didn't seek out your advice as he had done in the past. You had been relegated to your priestly duties and nothing more. Isn't that so father?"

The accusation by his son was met with another coughing spell. Taking a deep breath he tried to speak again. "I had done everything he requested of me," Aaron became furious. "Every letter he sent to me in Goshen from Midian, I took to heart and did exactly as he requested. Together we calculated the rate of flow of the river of fire. We knew exactly how quickly it would circle from west to east and then spread south into Midian. From the records we secured from Miriam, we knew every event that would take place as a result of the mountains being on fire. Once I had provided all the information he requested he had no further use for me. I was dismissed as if I no longer mattered. He only needed advice from Tharbis!"

"As you said father, Zipporah was merely the daughter of a tribal Chieftain but Tharbis, she is a Queen and she did come with her army to deliver us when we needed it most. So how can you find fault with her or for that matter, with any of his wives?"

"What I provided to him was far more important than any army she provided."

"Yes, it was when he had to face the newly crowned Pharaoh and fight for our right to be set free from bondage. But it wasn't Moses' ability to predict which plague would come next and when it would likely come, or his determination of the logical consequence of each one of those events that saved us from the Mitzri attack by the Bitter Lakes. We survived because Tharbis arrived with Caleb and the army to save us. I may have been young but I remember it well father. It was only five days after we had left Goshen. We were disorganized, untrained, and the only actual fighting men we had with us were the fifty Nubians that guarded Moses and a small band of stone masons that Joshua and Othniel had trained to use weapons. So all the documents in the world, those from the Temple in Onu and those from the temple in Behbeit-el-Hagar weren't going to save you or anyone else from a division of soldiers dispatched by Pharaoh. Not unless you think you could have buried them beneath a mountain of paper. The only thing that saved us that day was Queen Tharbis and her fifteen thousand troops. Praise be to Yahvu that he sent her in time!"

"If we had waited, Yahvu would have delivered us by his own mighty hand," Aaron tried to suggest that they hadn't given God a chance to perform another miracle for their deliverance.

"He did deliver us! He sent us Tharbis and her army. Don't you see, father? She was sent by Yahvu to arrive at that particular time when we needed her most. We are all tools in His hands to be used and he chose Tharbis as his tool for the precise purpose of delivering us."

"Bah!" Aaron could not bring himself to admit that the Queen of Saba had saved them that day. "All it did was blind Moses to the truth," the old man insisted, looking for the moment as if he would start coughing but instead he merely wheezed several times and appeared to set himself right.

"What truth is that?" Eleazar could barely tolerate his father's stubbornness any longer.

"That he was no different from the rest of us. He was not a god; he was not even a king any longer. But as long as she is with him, he still believes he is something more than the rest of us."

Upon hearing Aaron's explanation for why he detested Tharbis so much, Eleazar couldn't restrain the mocking laughter any longer. "You're an old fool father," he could no longer placate Aaron's indulgence in his self-absorbed view of their world. "You want the truth! Then here's the truth. Moses is far more than the rest of us could ever dream of being. None of us will ever come close to being the man that he is. Even if you added us all together we would never equal him in the sight of God!" Eleazar couldn't stop shaking his head as he came to grips with one of the many demons that plagued his father for so many years. "Your entire misguided view of the injustices you suffered is based on your refusal to admit that you had to stop half way up the mountain whereas Yahvu invited Moses to the mountain top. You weren't worthy to go all the way to the top. You weren't good enough. You didn't deserve to meet Yahvu face to face. Unlike Moses, you weren't that special. Do you understand?"

"Why are you being so cruel to me?" Aaron pleaded with his son to stop, the stress bringing about another fit of coughing but this time wads of clotted blood shot from his throat.

"I'm not father. I love you but I need you to open your eyes before you meet Yahvu. You will not be able to enter the Shekinah as long as you remain a blind man."

1361 BCE

Watching from the hills, Moses and his men waited for the shepherds to water their flock from the well and then move quietly on their way. Keeping themselves secure and unnoticed overrode their thirst for the time being. They were resigned to the fact that it would take some time as there were several hundred sheep and only the seven shepherds to care for them, but on closer examination they did not mind at all since it turned out that the seven shepherds were actually seven very comely and shapely shepherdesses, wearing simple skirts and cotton blouses. After so many days crossing the wilderness of Sinai, watching seven beautiful women draw water from the well was a pleasant distraction.

"More coming," Hoshea pointed to the flock of sheep and goats swarming over the hills to the south. This new flock was much smaller than that belonging to the women but that didn't stop the forced intrusion by these new shepherds from trying to scatter the other sheep so that they could gain access to the water immediately for their own animals. The women objected loudly, but the Bedouin shepherds simply ignored their wailing and name calling, doing as they pleased.

Moses could overhear what appeared to be the eldest shepherdess arguing with one of the Bedouins, saying that this was her father's land and therefore she and her sisters had first rights to watering their sheep from the wells. Wells, she emphasized that her father's workers had dug to reinforce her claim of first rights.

The Bedouin appeared to have little respect for traditions or custom, arguing that he and his men would take what they want whenever they wanted it. From their black turbans and maroon coloured robes, they were obviously Amorites and as such they cared little for the rules of Midianites. Tired of her abuse, this Bedouin threatened her that if she continued to object, then as soon as he and his companions were finished watering their animals, then they would seize all the seven women and have their way with them in the open field, shaming them before their father's eyes. There was little love between these two tribes, their hatred for one another spanning centuries.

Rather than be frightened by the threat and retreat, the shepherdess took her staff and struck the intruder on the side of the head soundly. The force of the blow stunned him and he fell to one knee but he did not go completely down. "Hit him again," Moses found that he was talking to himself but he knew that if you don't cripple your enemy immediately, it could prove to be a fatal mistake. The lesson of his uncle's hunting expedition sprung freshly to mind.

Moses could hear the man cursing and swearing as he rubbed the side of his head but as soon as he rose to his feet he lunged at the woman. She easily side stepped his clumsy first attempt to seize her but then he called for his companions to assist and three others quickly came to his aid so that they were able to encircle the woman, restricting her movements. Her sisters saw her desperate situation but before they could come to her rescue, they had been cut off by another five of the intruders, blocking their way.

The Amorite that had been struck was obviously their leader and he lunged forward a second time in an attempt to grab her. This time was able to duck below the arc of her swinging staff and seized her firmly about the waist. As soon as she was in his arms he thrust her to the ground and fell heavily on top of her, pinning her to the grass, while she kicked and screamed.

"Time to put an end to this," Moses instructed his men. "I will go down first and try to settle it peacefully but if it looks like they won't listen, then I will signal for help. Just show yourselves. That should be enough to scatter them. Amorites are a cowardly bunch from what I've heard."

Strolling down the hill, Moses headed directly to the point of confrontation. "Peace brothers," Moses raised his left hand in salutation. "I think you should help the young lady up, don't you?"

"Who are you Mitzri that you bother us? Can't you see we are busy?" the leader questioned this unwelcome stranger dressed in military garb with leather cap and curved brass sword. While he pinned the woman's arms to the ground with one hand, his other hand began to raise the hem of his own robes as he prepared to violate her.

"I am the son of no one," Moses answered. "But I really think you need to reconsider what your course of present action is," he warned. Drawing his sword he waved it back and forth for all to see. "Raise your robes any further and I may have to cut off anything that falls out."

After a brief moment of assessing the threat from this Mitzri son of no one, all the Amorite shepherds began to laugh. "Go away 'No One' before we raise your skirt and circumcise you like the rest of us." The threat of circumcising a Mitzri always resulted in bursts of laughter amongst the desert tribes.

"One last time," Moses warned him. "Let the girl go or I will make you release her."

The threat of a single man with a sword was hardly worth consideration to a group of shepherds armed with their staffs. An experienced shepherd learned from a young age how to fend of foxes, wolves and lions. Therefore, one man with a sword was hardly a threat. "Teach this stranger a lesson," the Amorite commanded his brethren. "Use his own sword to circumcise this unclean foreign bastard." This time the threat to circumcise was no longer meant as a joke. Four of the shepherds started advancing towards Moses.

Signalling with a wave of his hand, Moses stood his ground, while both Othni and Hoshea came over the top of the hill with their swords drawn. "Did I forget to mention that I wasn't alone?" But not even three men with swords was enough to deter the shepherds as they continued to advance on Moses.

"That was a mistake," Moses cautioned them. "I may have been willing to let you go with a simple warning but now you have offended me. You should be quaking in your sandals when you see three sword bearing battle trained Kemtu but you're not even giving us the respect that we deserve."

"Shut your filthy Mitzri mouth and prepare to die," the Amorite shepherd on top of the woman threatened.

"Well, death may be preferable to circumcision," Moses still laughed off his threat defiantly. "Don't say I didn't warn you," Moses reminded them as he repeated the signal for the second time.

With shields raised and spears held forward, the contingent of fifty Nubians ran quickly over the hill until they had completely ringed all of the Bedouin and the shepherdesses. They had moved so swiftly into position that the Amorites didn't even have the opportunity to turn and escape.

"Now, I will ask you again to take yourself off the girl," Moses moved forward to place the edge of his sword against the side of the man's neck, the point making a little nick so that a drop of blood appeared and began to trickle down to his collar.

Rolling off the man quickly got on his knees and pleaded with Moses to spare their lives. "We never meant you any harm, stranger," the shepherd claimed, his voice suddenly quivering in fear.

"Does that mean you no longer wish to have me circumcised?" Moses asked as he placed the edge of his sword once more against the man's neck.

"It was merely a jest, a harmless joke," the shepherd insisted. "We'd never do you any harm, Lord."

"Why do I find that so hard to believe," Moses turned to his companions to see if any of them had an answer to his question. "They don't appear to believe you either."

"Remove his head," the elder shepherdess demanded as she got to her feet and straightened her rumpled skirt.

"You are a feisty one," Moses reacted to her demand. "I think it is a little too early in the day for removing one's head."

"I am the daughter of the Midianite Chieftain of these lands," she stated proudly. "All those who threaten to harm the daughters of Jethro the Midianite are to be punished by death. It is the law of the land."

"I think I know of a much better way to resolve this than by starting a new skirmish between the Amorites and the Midianites, if you permit me to adjudicate." Moses looked back and forth between the Midianite shepherdesses and the Bedouin shepherds to see if they were willing to listen. The Amorites definitely looked eager to have it resolved without losing their heads.

"Now you say," he looked directly at the eldest shepherdess to see if he was paraphrasing her correctly, "That it is the law of the land that anyone threatening a daughter of Jethro the Midianite must die. That being the case, then we would have to perpetrate the execution of nine men, but we can't say for certain that anyone other than this man would have touched any of the other women."

"It does not matter," the shepherdess insisted. "He is their leader, they all must die!"

"Yes, I know, it is the law of the land. You've already said that. But even laws can be moderated to suit the situation. Now I say, what kind of father sends out his seven daughters to tend his flocks and draw water from a well. That is man's work. As chieftain, I'm certain that he has more than enough able bodied men that could perform this task. But still, he chose to send his daughters. Why is that?"

"Our father has no sons to carry on his name. Only by raising his daughters to be the equal of any man can he ensure that no son-in-law will ever take away our inheritance and wrest control of the tribe from our family," she explained.

"That being the case," Moses assessed the situation, "then if you are to be the equal of any man, then you must defend yourself like any other man as well. True?"

"Had he not summoned his friends, I would have defeated him handily," she claimed without any evidence of bravado in her statement.

"I think you most certainly would have. Is that not true?" Moses questioned the Bedouin who was still kneeling beneath his blade."

"It is true, Lord," the man admitted.

"I believe if you lose a fair fight, then you must forfeit part of your possessions as winnings, don't you?" Moses didn't wait for his answer. "And since you admit that had this been a fair fight you would have lost, then what is it that you can offer the daughter of Jethro the Midianite in restitution?"

"We have nothing, Lord. We are only poor shepherds tending our master's flocks. We have no possessions of our own."

"It was your master's animals that caused the initial offense, was it not?" Moses purposely toyed with the man.

"I don't follow you Lord."

"Your animals came charging over the hill wanting to be watered. They forced their way between the Midianite's flock and the well. In your capacity as shepherds, you had no choice but to try and cater to the demands of your master's animals. Hence, the real offence was carried out by your sheep and goats in my opinion. I am willing to hold them accountable for everything that may have happened afterwards, rather than hold you and your crew of shepherds accountable. Is that not fair?"

The Amorite must have thought Moses to be a little addled but with the sword edge still weighing down on the back of his neck he was willing to be very compliant. "Yes, Lord, it was definitely the fault of the animals."

"Good, then it is settled. The lives of all your animals is forfeit." Turning to Jethro's eldest daughter, Moses rendered the verdict. "Daughter of Jethro the Midianite, you say that all those that threaten to harm you must be put to death as it is the law of the land. Correct?"

"Yes," she nodded.

"Since we have established that these men were merely trying to cater to the demands of their master's animals, and it were these sheep and goats that initially threatened you, then their lives are forfeit. Shall I have my men kill them all now for you or would you prefer to simply add them to your own flocks for the time being?"

"At this time I choose to add them, my Lord," she responded.

"Alright then, it is settled," Moses stated as he lifted the sword from the kneeling Shepherd. "You can take your men and remove yourself from this land, minus your animals of course.

"You can't do that," the shepherd threatened. "You can't take our animals."

"I believe I can," Moses signalled for his Nubian soldiers to move closer to the nine Bedouins. "It is the law of the land and you agreed to have me adjudicate that law. So, I would advise you to start running back to wherever you came from," Moses instructed. "I will count to one hundred to give you a head start. Then I will let my soldiers loose. Make it over the next ridge before they catch you and you get to live. A simple challenge, don't you think?"

"We will not play this game," the Amorite reclaimed a bit of backbone.

"If you don't, I will tell my men that now you have chosen to offend the King of Kush and they will slaughter you where you stand. Trust me, they are quite good at doing that."

As the Amorites looked from one Nubian to the next, each one of the black soldiers wore a huge smile, as if they would relish the opportunity to hunt them like wild pigs.

"I will not tolerate your offense for long. I suggest you start running!" The look on Moses' faced showed that he was already losing his patience.

The Bedouin did not have to be told twice, turning tail and running up the slopes of the hill back in the direction from which they came. From behind they could hear Moses counting slowly. One, two,…

Some of them started shouting curses and threats at Moses once they had reached the summit, at which time Moses ordered that a couple of spears be launched in their direction to help them on their way.

Turning towards the daughters, Moses found them all kneeling before him. "What is this all about?"

"Forgive us your Majesty, we had no knowledge that you were the one that our father spoke about," the eldest daughter replied.

"What is your name, girl?"

"Zipporah," she answered.

"Zipporah, I'm afraid I'm hardly the man I used to be but go tell your father that I have come to reclaim that which is mine. But first, let my men tend to your flocks and then you can be on your way."

"You are most kind, your Majesty."

"I would prefer if you simply just call me Moses."

Jethro was overjoyed to see his old friend from the wars in Kush. Inviting Moses, Othni and Hoshea into his tent he instructed all of the servants to prepare a banquet for his guests. It was the first time any of them had seen how these desert dwellers lived, and the enormity of the tent was a pleasant surprise to all three. The tent served as both domicile and great hall for the Chieftain of the Midianites. It was constructed from all the most exquisite and expensive materials that the trade routes between east and west could offer. Hippopotamus hides were used to construct the roof and walls of the tent. Silks from the east adorned the interior, functioning as movable walls, thereby providing a rainbow of colours that danced in the desert breezes that on occasion skimmed over the terrain. Gold brocade and silver tassels streamed from each cedar pole. Huge brass oil lamps hung from copper chains that were strung through a series of pulleys permitting them to be raised and lowered all at once when the oil needed to be replenished or when the wicks needed to bit lit each night. Every inch of the ground was covered by hand knotted woollen carpets, each with its own geometric design dyed in a variety of shades and colours. Around the low tables, common to Kemet, dozens of soft pillows and cushions provided comfortable seating for their meetings and dining.

The three of them were so enthralled by their surroundings that they did not notice the seven dancing girls that entered the room, their bodies covered in layers of veils so that all that could be seen were hennaed hands and dark kohl ringed eyes. It was only when lathe musicians began to play, and the girls took to the centre of the hall that they all became aware of the night's entertainment.

"I have seen to your Nubians," Jethro remarked, "though I doubt they'll sleep in the tent I provided. It is in their nature to sleep under the stars rather than on something soft and comfortable."

"And eat raw scorpions," Hoshea added.

"Yes, I have seen that too," Jethro laughed. "But where is your cousin, my Prince. I miss him."

Moses knew exactly to whom Jethro was referring. "Zelophedad is happily back in Goshen, Jethro. I don't think he was overly thrilled by your hospitality last time he was your guest."

"That is a shame," Jethro commented. "I would have wished to have had the opportunity to make amends. Such is life. But most of all I would like to thank the Prince for saving my daughters from those barbarians. Had they deflowered even a single one of my daughters I would have hunted down every last Amorite and slaughtered them like the dogs they are."

"I was surprised to see Amorites this far south," Moses was curious as to what could have driven them towards the peninsula.

"There is chaos in the north," Jethro revealed the latest news he had received. "Mitanni's flame is extinguished. Hatti is on the march. Babylonia quivers and shakes almost as much as the ground itself is reported of doing. Fire and brimstone has destroyed the cities of the sea-farers. My only surprise is that more haven't fled to the south to escape the death and destruction unfolding."

"And the mountains? Any reports of the mountains spewing fire," Moses wanted to know.

"Nothing that I have heard. But they say that in the plains of Tartarus great clouds of steam are rising from the mountains in the valley. That could be a foreboding of things to come. But enough talk of doom and gloom. Sit back, eat and watch the girls as they dance for you."

"They are lovely," Othni commented.

"Of course they are lovely," Jethro responded. "They are my daughters and they wish to dance for you in gratitude for saving them today. Drink up gentlemen, there is plenty more wine where that came from."

No sooner had they finished one cup of wine, when a servant would rush forward and refill their cups to the brim. The music began to repeat its hypnotic rhythm, faster and faster as the girls twirled and spun around the room, slowly and seductively removing one veil at a time. It was hard to determine which was more intoxicating, the dance of the veils or the wine they were drinking. Both stimulated and captivated the senses simultaneously.

Moses was fixated on one of the dancing girls, whose lithe body contorted and swayed magically before his eyes. But it were her eyes that imprisoned him. He remembered staring into them earlier that day, when she stood so proud and defiant in the face of her attacker. Eyes that glistened with darkness, penetrating like pointed daggers but at the same time warm and intelligent. Now their eyes were locked together and he followed them closely as she twirled, dipped and pranced about the hall.

"You like?" Jethro interrupted Moses' thoughts.

"What?" It took Moses a moment to snap back to reality.

"If you like what you see, then she is yours," Jethro negotiated the betrothal of his eldest daughter in the same manner he sold his sheep.

"I'm not looking for another wife at this time," Moses laughed, thinking that Jethro was not serious and was merely having a little fun at his expense.

"Perhaps you should be, King without a name." This time Jethro sounded very serious.

"What are you inferring," Moses was slightly irritated by the Midianite's last comment which sounded like a jab at his unfortunate circumstances.

"Much has changed since our last meeting," Jethro reminded him. "Even here in the middle of nowhere we hear about the happenings in Thebes. You have been stripped of your titles, you have been renounced and erased from the royal family. Even your title of King of Kush is being absorbed into the long list of titles possessed by Amenhotep. What are you now, except a man with two companions and a squad of fifty Nubians? Hardly the Prince I once knew."

"And you are telling me this because…" Moses wanted to stand in order to leave but realized that he had drunk too much wine.

"Because I am your friend but more so because I loved your grandfather and would do anything for him."

"Reminding me of what I have lost, hardly sounds like friendship to me," Moses retaliated.

"It is the best kind of friendship," Jethro explained. "For men of power, it is easy to be surrounded by those that call themselves friend but it is those that stick by you after you have lost everything that truly are your friend. Are you aware that there is a bounty on your head?"

"Amenhotep would not dare," Moses stammered. "He knows he'd be in violation of the law as laid out during the tribunal. Though he has tried to kill me once already, I doubt very much he would publicly announce a bounty."

"Who says it is from Amenhotep? Any man can place a bounty on another. The trail of the money can be so convoluted that no one could follow it. The assassin only cares about being paid, not who is actually doing the paying."

"So are you threatening to turn me in or do the deed yourself?"

Jethro slapped his knees and laughed heartedly until tears wet his eyes. "You Egyptians always have the flair to be so melodramatic. Everything is the world ending with you. I want to help you, not turn you in. But to do so we need to trust one another. Is that not so?"

"So what is the cost of that trust," Moses demanded to know.

"We have many laws and customs in this land," Jethro explained.

"So I have heard earlier today," Moses quipped. "Many seem to end with a beheading."

Jethro laughed again, holding his belly which shook as he did so. "Always so melodramatic," he repeated. "Unlike your country, a father will never turn on a son. That is not to say a son won't turn on his father, we've had many instances of that happening but never a father on his son. A father would die before he betrayed his child."

"And by this your inferring that if we were related you would never betray me," Moses put the pieces together quickly.

"Look at my girls Thutmoses…"

"It's Moses now," he corrected Jethro before the chieftain made the mistake again. He looked to his two companions to confirm that he was never to be referred to as Thutmoses again but both of them were passed out on piles of cushions, sleeping off the effects of the wine.

"Moses," Jethro corrected himself. "Each one is a beauty. Each one can fight as the equal of any man. They have beauty, strength and grace but they have no balls, if you follow me. All that I possess will be stripped from them by the other clans as soon as I pass away because I have no son to protect my name and the family heritage. I need a son that will protect my girls and ensure that they all inherit what is rightfully theirs. A son to ensure that all of them enter into marriages with husbands that will safeguard their legacies and not steal it out from under their noses."

"And how do you know I wouldn't take all that you have and leave your daughters with nothing," Moses challenged Jethro.

"Because you are a man of integrity. You fight for justice even though it means sacrificing your own life to do so. You have already proven you will give up everything in order to pursue the proper path. You are the man your grandfather always told me you would be."

"But you seem to forget that I already have two wives," Moses reminded him.

"One I've heard has been stripped from you, your wedding annulled as if it never existed. The other I can never forget. Every week I receive a message, 'Is he there yet? Has he arrived yet? Tell him how empty my days are without him.' The Queen is so obsessed with you that I'm surprised she hasn't erected statues of you throughout her kingdom. I wish my wives were so enamoured with me, but that is my story and we are talking about you."

"So you see, it could never work," Moses waved the idea away with a swish of his hand. "Tharbis would never permit another woman to displace her."

"Who said anything about displace," Jethro questioned where that idea came from. "Of course the daughter of a Chieftain is not going to ever displace the Queen of Saba. A cheetah can never displace a lion as king of the jungle but each is beautiful, special and powerful on its own accord."

"So as your son, you're promising that you won't hand me over for the bounty. That's the price for your cooperation. I must marry your daughter."

"Why do you make that sound like it is such a terrible punishment, Moses? Look at her! Is she not beautiful? Does she not dance with the grace of an angel?"

"Still your loyalty comes with a price," Moses refuted Jethro's argument.

"You have that all wrong," Jethro shook his head. "As my son I will shield and protect you. You can use my encampment as your base of operations. My Midianites will protect you even more than your Nubians can. No one will ever be able to approach you without my men ensuring their motive is genuine. As my son, my men will serve you and do your errands as you plan your revolution."

"Who said anything about a revolution," Moses wanted Jethro to dismiss that foolishness immediately. Such talk was dangerous no matter how secure the surroundings.

"Even a blind man can see what you're up to, Moses. You came here to retrieve your family's magical staff with which I've seen armies stumble and fall before it as if they were suddenly stricken blind. Not to mention, you still have men in Kush, waiting on your beckon call. And I'm not referring to your wife's army. Those are at your disposal as well but I'm referring to the close to thirty thousand Egyptian troops you took into Nubia to begin with and left under the command of two of your own men that are strictly loyal only to you. But as my son-in-law, you will also have all the Midianite warriors under your command as well. We may not be as disciplined as you Egyptians but we certainly know how to kill when we're required to. I might even be able to persuade the Kenites to join with us."

"As soon as the taking of Saba was completed, I released many of those men that had been conscripted to return home to their families and their farms. Others returned to Kemet at the same time that I returned for the tribunal. I would guess that the Kemtu in Kush only number half of what I originally brought south with me."

"Still it remains a formidable force," the Midianite chieftain calculated. "Add them all together and you have an army that can fight against any nation."

"You do make a good argument, Jethro," Moses commended his friend on his list of valuable points. "Protection, a base of operations, safety, even men to do my bidding, what more could I ask for?"

"You can ask for a wife," Jethro added that to the list. "Say yes, and all of that will be yours!"

"You can be very convincing," Moses smiled, warming to the idea.

"Trading is in my blood after all," Jethro responded, "So why not ask for my daughter's hand in marriage? A matter of fact, why not ask for all my daughters? You'd be doing me a big favour all at once."

"Let me think about one for now," Moses cautioned Jethro not to get overly excited.

"Don't take too long," Jethro cautioned him. "You never know when the next Egyptian renegade prince comes sweeping through here and takes all of my daughters with him." Jethro began laughing at his own joke.

"I'm certain the road to you camp must be well travelled by Kemtu princes," Moses concurred. "It is a very tempting offer but I cannot answer this night."

"Sometimes if you want the best then you have to act fast. Zipporah, come closer and dance for our guest. She is beautiful, is she not?"

Moses was falling into those deep dark eyes once again. "Yes, Jethro, she is very beautiful."

CHAPTER NINETEEN

The sun had risen, casting an orange glow across the valley below, which sprung to life in response to the gentle touch of its rays. Looking over the cliff shelf on which they had spent another night, Eleazar appreciated the view of the Promised Land in the distance. Far below he could see the congregation of the Children of Israel, looking like ants filling the valley with their numbers. They would wait there patiently until he descended the mountain and announced that Aaron had died. Then they would both mourn and celebrate the life of the late High Priest for the next thirty days. They would pour out their love for the great man that had stood solidly by Moses' side since they were young, unswerving in their loyalty to one another, and most of all, never wavering in the faith of the Almighty God. Eleazar laughed to himself, knowing that they will never know otherwise because the stories that Aaron was now spewing would be kept safely locked away. The sanctity of Aaron's reputation would be preserved.

Behind him he could hear the old priest stirring from his slumber. "Looks like God has favoured you with another day father. You missed a glorious sunrise."

"Another day to suffer," Aaron did not sound too appreciative. "My lungs are bursting with a searing pain and now every bone and muscle in my body hurts from resting on that straw mat. What is so great about being alive another day?"

"Yahvu obviously believes you should be here today, so clearly he has a purpose for you."

"Perhaps he's hoping that today I will open your eyes to the truth regarding your uncle? Aaron at that point had to stop and drain the fluid from his lungs that accumulated while he slept by coughing up several wads of a red stained viscid mucous.

"I already know the truth about Moses, father and I seriously doubt anything you have to say is going to change that."

"I can always pray that there's a hope you will see through his deceit."

"In the meantime, I want to know more about the communications that were going on between you, Caleb, Machir and Moses. For eight years all of you were in contact so I have to assume you had information that you never shared with the rest of us. Is my assumption correct?"

"Of course we were in contact. How else do you think I would have known Moses was on his way and to meet him at Mount Horeb?" It was my responsibility as well to keep him informed of what was happening in Mitzrayim, and in particular events about Pharaoh and the rest of the family. He especially wanted to know about Amenhotep's health, or should I say his rapid decline in health. From my perspective, it was astonishing to receive reports of his deterioration exactly as Moses described it would take place."

"Surely by that alone you can appreciate that Moses is more than just like any other man."

"Some would argue that the power given to him by Yahvu was essentially a primal and natural ability to bring about events at God's command and nothing more," Aaron argued. "In other words, Moses was nothing more than a conduit by which Yahvu could manifest His miracles. He had now power of his own."

"And you're saying now that this obvious viewpoint is wrong or correct? Which one?" Eleazar tactfully manoeuvred his father into a discussion that he felt was critical when recording it for future generations. "What power does any creature have if it is not gifted by God?"

"Why do you want to know this?" Aaron was curious.

"I will keep a chronicle of your adventures together before the Exodus, father. I think it is important that we still can see the lives of those of you that brought about our liberation in a historical light."

"And what will you call this chronicle of your," Aaron was curious.

"I have thought of the name already," Eleazar was more than happy to talk about his intended manuscript. "The Book of the Yasher."

"The Book of the Upright," Aaron rolled the title over in his mind. "I'm presuming you're referring to the group of us that set everything in motion."

"All of you father," Eleazar replied. "I think it is important to have a record that shows the true nature of all of you. Your good side, your bad side and every shade in between. Years from now, all anyone will talk about is the miracles but it is important that they also have a reminder that those that brought about these miracles were more than just names."

"And I guess you will focus on my bad side," he accused his son in advance of writing this text in a prejudicial manner/

"Believe it or not father, you have done far more good than you have done bad. I pray that you let go of these inner demons that have wrested control of you mind. The things you say now are not the great man that the Children of Israel have come to know and revere."

"You asked about what we communicated over those eight years we were separated," Aaron returned the conversation to the subject matter. "As evil as one Pharaoh Amenhotep proved to be, two on the throne was even worse. The Queen lost any control she may have had over her husband during those years. That's why he defied her in taking his daughters to wife, and then naming them Great Wife to replace Queen Tiye. Her fall from grace meant she had no control over her youngest son either, and Amenhotep was determined to raise this son in his own image. Once the palace of Malkata was completed, there was no relief for the slaves in Goshen. Together the two Pharaohs began to rebuild the old Hyksos capital of Avaris. He had been rebuilding the Temples for a long time but now came a new phase of constructing administrative buildings. But unlike Malkata, these were not buildings made from mudbricks. These were erected from carved stone. And they put the men of Goshen to the tasks of quarrying the stone and then moving these ashlars to Avaris, several miles away. Many men died beneath these huge stones as they rolled towards the northeast of the delta. Even more died beneath the lash of the task-masters that whipped the people mercilessly. The people cried out for their deliverer but Moses still did not come. How ironic that they cried about their suffering when they had to make bricks from mud and straw but now that they had to work the quarries they talked about how much better their lives had been when they were simply gathering straw and casting bricks beneath the scorching sun."

"And you wrote to Moses about what was happening to the people," Eleazar inquired.

"Many times. Because after the construction of the administration buildings came the massive project of erecting the northern palace to house the two Pharaohs. As the projects expanded, so did the suffering and deaths of our people."

"But you knew Moses could not return before the death of his father, otherwise he would be immediately put to death as soon as he set foot in Egypt."

"I knew," Aaron admitted, "But it did not make the tragic loss of life any easier. It did not make the screams of their suffering any quieter. But as Moses had advised, we watched the night skies for signs of the beacons of hope that he mentioned. First came the light in the northwest and even in their suffering, the people sang and danced because they knew Pharaoh Amenhotep had fallen ill. But his physicians gave him medicines and Tushratta King of the Mitanni sent him healing statues of his gods and Pharaoh recovered. And the singing and the dancing stopped and the suffering became worse because Pharaoh knew that the people had been celebrating his illness and he increased their work and reduced their food, so that now many of the people began to starve and their children became ill and died. Once again they begged that I send word to Moses to come and save them, but again he refused, responding that the time was not yet right. Machir continued to feed their hopes and talk of their eventual salvation but I could see the people were rapidly losing hope. Knowing that one must suffer for eight years before they even can see a ray of hope is beyond the tolerance of almost every man or woman."

"But you knew it was only a matter of time and you still adhered to the plans that Moses had set out before you."

"What alternative did I have?" Aaron held out his hands in supplication. "We had no other choice. Whether we believed in Moses' promise to come and rescue us or not, it would not have changed the treatment under the hand of Pharaoh. The people would still be slaves and worked until they dropped from either exhaustion or starvation. So we clung to the hope that he would return."

"You had a choice father. You could have returned to your quiet life at Onu and pretended nothing had changed."

"Not even that was possible," Aaron admitted. "Moses had been correct in his prophecy. As the Temples in Avaris were completed, those of the priests from Onu that were true adherents to Amun were relocated. Those of us that preached the path of Atum-Ra were labelled as blasphemers and accused of leading an insurrection against the two Pharaohs. Had it not been for Moses, none of us would have escaped but I remembered his warning and was able to convince my Lebu brethren and many of the others to flee with me into Goshen before Pharaoh's soldiers came to loot and burn our Temple."

"Aha!" Eleazar shouted gleefully. "Finally you're willing to admit that Moses did something of benefit for you. He saved your life and the lives of practically all the Lebu priests. Admit it father and purge at least one of your demons afflicting your soul."

"I was grateful for him passing on that information to me. But as he said, it was not him but the staff that somehow planted the images in his mind."

"You still can't say it, can you? The staff didn't talk to you, Moses did. The staff didn't tell you what to do for the eight years he was gone, Moses did. What is this bitterness that blinds you so?"

Aaron chose to ignore his son's comments and continued the retelling of those events during the eight years that Moses was gone. "Then we saw the lights in the night sky directly north and we knew this time Pharaoh had fallen ill but he would not recover. Once again the people sang and danced to celebrate his misfortune and impending death. Upon hearing this, Amenhotep assembled a cohort of his men to ride to Goshen so that he could take his revenge on the people personally. But Goshen with its mud and stony tracks is not a place for riding in chariots. The wheel of Pharaoh's chariot became stuck in a rut and turned over, crashing on top of Amenhotep so that not only did he suffer from his illness but also from the agony resulting from the crushing of his bones. His men loaded him into the back of another chariot and rode quickly back to Thebes where they laid him in his bed where he remained for the next two years This time not all the statuettes sent from Mitanni could cure Amenhotep. He died exactly as Moses had described, in great torment as his bowels rotted from the inside, while every bone in his body screamed in pain. The pus from the abscesses in his mouth choked him with every breath but Yahvu would not let him die until he bore this suffering for over two years, just as Moses had predicted. The curse that Moses had placed upon him had not been easily forgotten, for Amenhotep recalled every word that his son had spoken and he feared that Moses would now return to take his vengeance out on the young Amenhotep, his brother. While he lay there dying, the elder Amenhotep, ordered that the people pray to the goddess Sekhmet to stave off the return of Moses. All across the country they erected temples and statues of the goddess and for two years the people of Mitzrayim prayed that Sekhmet would deliver them from the coming doom. But their prayers were in vain."

"And then it was time for Moses to return," Eleazar excitedly added his comment to the retelling of the story.

"Not that quickly," Aaron signalled for his son to calm down.

"But his father was dying. He only had to wait for the day that he passed away."

"Moses was coming but not before the new Pharaoh decided to make the people of Goshen suffer even further for the contempt in which they held the elder Amenhotep."

"How so father?"

"Like his father, he wanted to immortalize himself in stone. To do so he began building his own city on the bones of the old city of Amarna. Now the people had to bear the burden of two massive construction projects but this second one was not close as in the case of rebuilding Avaris. Amarna was two hundred miles to the south along the Nile River. Loading and unloading the barges with these massive stones was exceedingly dangerous. Many of our people were lost to the river. What the Nile takes it does not give back. All the people could cry out was 'Where was Moses, where was Moses?' but Machir and I knew that even when he came, this new Pharaoh would not be bent easily to our will."

1352 BCE

In the distance Moses saw what he thought was a flashing *sasap* beacon on the slopes of Mount Horeb. "Hoshea, Othni, come here quickly."

His two comrades came running as quickly as they could thinking that Moses may have encountered some trouble. "What is the matter?" they both asked in unison.

"Take a look at Mount Horeb and tell me what you see?" Moses pointed to the mountain several miles to the north.

Othni looked towards the mountain and shook his head. "I see nothing."

"What about you," Moses asked his ward.

"I don't see anything either," Hoshea confirmed Othni's comment. "Why, what is it that you think you see?"

"So neither of you can see any *sasap* that is shining like a blazing fire on the southern slopes?" he questioned them both to see if they would change their minds. It was so obvious when he looked into the distance that he found it hard to believe that they couldn't see it as well.

"There is nothing there," Othni did not change his original statement. Hoshea merely shook his head, the look in his eyes suggesting that perhaps Moses was letting his imagination get the better of him.

"I must go now and see for myself what it is, but I'm certain it is the sign that Yuyu wrote to me that I should look for. The same sign that Abraham received to set him upon his mission."

Othni and Hoshea looked at one another confused and not quite appreciating what Moses was talking about.

Moses began relating the contents of the papyrus he and Meri-amun had discovered. "And Abraham turned to his servant Eliezer and his eldest son Ishmael and asked them if they see the light and smoke upon the mountain in the distance, and they replied that they could not see anything. But when he asked Isaac, the boy said that he saw it clearly and he knew that God had approved that only the two of them could continue on with their mission. It is something my grandfather ensured that I read when I found all his papers. Now I realize he was using it to prophesize my future by telling me what I should be looking for."

"Let us come with," Hoshea could not appreciate why Abraham left his servant and eldest son behind. "Now that you explained it to us we can come with you."

"I cannot. Like Ishmael and Eliezer, God has tested you and neither of you can accompany me."

"What? We're not pure enough?" Othni was somewhat offended by the refusal to let them come. "I want you to know that I bathe almost weekly since we crossed the desert. I'm practically a priest I bathe so much."

"I am so happy to know that, I think," Hoshea rolled his eyes upward.

"My father-in-law has informed me that God rests at times upon that particular mountain." Moses pointed towards Mount Horeb to emphasize his point. "To the people of this land he is El-Shaddai, or El-Gibbor and he is beckoning for me to meet with him. But there will be a time that I will need both of you to see his fire as well. Therefore, I must dedicate you both to this jealous god."

"I don't particularly like the sound of that," Hoshea whispered to Othni. "We're not talking dedication as in some form of physical torture, are we?" Hoshea wanted Moses to clarify his last statement before he agreed to any type of dedication.

Moses ignored the question. "Othni, from now only you will be called Othniel and Hoshea you will be called Joshua, in praise of our new god. You will take no other gods into your households. This is the only god you will ever speak of and in time he will show you his holy flame as well. So you must swear this to me."

"I swear," Othni responded.

"Me too, I swear," Hoshea did so eagerly. "Now can we come with?"

"No, I need you both to stay here. Do not worry, God will let me know when it is your time to come meet with Him. Wish me well for I go now to meet our God." With staff in hand, Moses started his trek towards the mountain.

"What are we supposed to do until you come back?" Hoshea called after him.

"Prepare everyone for our return to Kemet," Moses shouted back. "Pharaoh is dead and it is time for us to meet my brother. Send out a messenger to Ahrown and Machir and another to Caleb and Hur. Our wait is finally over."

Turning to Hoshea, Othni felt compelled to ask, "How do you think he knows that his father is dead?"

"Well, Othniel," Hoshea toyed with Othni's new name, "the same way he knows everything else. He just knows."

"I guess you're right, Joshua," Othni taunted his young companion with his new name making Hoshea cringe when he heard it. "We better let everyone know we'll be leaving Midian as soon as Moses returns."

"Things are about to get very interesting," Hoshea thought, while speaking out loud so that Othni knew what was on his mind.

"We'd better let Jethro know. I think after eight years he might be astonished that we're finally leaving," Othni indicated that should be their first task.

"That was pretty dumb of you, saying that you didn't see anything on the mountain," Hoshea pushed his finger into Othni's shoulder to make his point.

"You said the same thing," Othni defended himself. "How was I supposed to know there was something there?"

"I only agreed with you because I didn't want Moses to think you were blind" Hoshea explained his response. "It was a leading question, of course there was something there. I should have known that he wanted a positive response."

"But you didn't see anything and neither did I," Othni retaliated. "You can't blame me by suggesting I put words in your mouth."

"It didn't matter that we didn't see anything," Hoshea continued to argue. "We should have just told him we did."

"What would that have achieved if we lied to him," Othni challenged his young accuser.

"We would have been able to go with him but now we're stuck here why he goes and climbs a mountain. It was dumb. We should have known we were supposed to answer yes. Remind me to never listen to you again."

"Well, actually, I did see it but I thought I would sound crazy if I said I did. Guess I must already be more sanctified than you," Othni taunted his companion.

"That's not true," Hoshea refused to believe him. "You didn't see anything. And you're certainly not holier than I am no matter how many baths you take."

"Of course I saw it. Would I lie to you Joshua?" Othni purposely strung out saying Hoshea's new name as he walked away towards Jethro's tent, laughing under his breath as he did.

The news of Pharaoh Amenhotep-Nimmureya's death spread like wildfire throughout the Midianite encampment. Everyone knew that it meant that Moses would be leaving them but would be calling upon their assistance at some time in the future at when the insurrection would begin. In everyone's mind, they imagined that Moses would reassert himself as rightful ruler of Egypt and depose his younger brother. There were still enough soldiers in the standing Egyptian army that knew of Moses' campaigns in Nubia and Kush, which merited him far more respect than the fourteen year old boy that now ruled the Empire. Combine that with his forces in Nubia which were under the command of two of his officers and the overthrow of the new Pharaoh appeared to be a certainty. Only the fighting spirit of the tribes in Goshen remained an uncertainty but when faced with freedom or continued slavery, it seemed unlikely that they wouldn't flock beneath Moses' banner.

In preparation for Moses' return, his household had already packed their belongings and tied them to the back of several camels. Zipporah with their two sons waited nervously in her father's tent, not knowing what awaited them once they ventured into the land of the Egyptians but she was prepared to face whatever dangers might exist alongside her husband.

Both Othni and Hoshea were readying their horses, while the Nubian Captain encountered a little more difficulty when trying to assemble his men. After eight years, some of the soldiers had taken wives from amongst the Midianites and they were reluctant to be parted from their families, but service to their king always took precedent. One could never doubt the loyalty of the Nubians. The waiting for Moses' return from the mountain weighed heavily on everyone's nerves, knowing that over the next few weeks they would be changing history.

It was only after several hours past that they began to grow concerned for the whereabouts of their leader, realizing that with the dusk settling in, today would not be the day they would begin the long journey back to Goshen. It became even more of a worry when the sun set and Moses had still not returned. A man walking alone through the wilderness at night would be prey for the wide range of predators that inhabited the lands. Zipporah was already suggesting to her father that it was time to send out a search party in case her husband had injured himself on the mountain and was unable to walk. At the precise moment they were about to make the decision to send out several riders to search for Moses, shouts were raised by the sentries.

"Moses is coming, Moses is coming," they sounded their alarm.

Running to the edge of the camp, Zipporah and her father looked out into the twilight, barely catching the glimpse of shadowy figure in the distance. His gait was awkward and at first look, one would have thought perhaps it was one of their own shepherds returning from the fields intoxicated. Closer and closer he ambulated towards the edge of the camp. Those that first witnessed his arrival beneath the light of their torches were shocked by his physical transformation. His eyes were transfixed on some non-existent point of existence, staring far off into space. It was a haunting stare that made one's skin crawl. The stress lines on his forehead and face were now deeply etched into his flesh, making his appearance years older than his actual age. All were in agreement, the Moses that returned was very different from the one that left their camp earlier in the day.

Several of the Midianites quickly ran to his side to support his remaining steps.

His right hand was firmly clenched around the sapphire staff unable to relax its vice-like grip even when they led him towards Jethro's tent to rest. They tried to remove it from his hand, careful not to grip the staff themselves, but his involuntary actions became somewhat violent, so much so that they decided to abandon any further attempts. Laying him down upon a bed of pillows, they thought he may be asleep but his eyes were still wide open in that same haunting stare they first noticed upon his return to the camp. Immediately, the rumours began to circulate amongst the Midianites that the King of Kush was on his deathbed. No one had ever seen a malady like this before and the tribal healers told their Chieftain that there was nothing they could do. Zipporah sat at his side throughout the night and into the next day applying cool compresses to his forehead, praying that her husband would return to her.

On the second morning Moses sprang upright on the bed and looked around somewhat confused until he realized that he was laying in Jethro's tent. He had no recollection of how he had come to be there; for that matter he had no recollection how he even returned to the camp after descending the mountain. Even his time on the mountain was a bit of a blur but after rubbing his eyes, the events of two days ago came clearly into focus. Zipporah was sitting in a chair beside the bed fast asleep. Reaching for her shoulder he gently shook her awake. "I am back," he smiled to her obvious delight as she threw herself upon him, kissing his face and lips repeatedly. "If I knew I'd have this kind of reception, I should have gone up the mountain more often," he joked with her.

She started to hit him playfully about his chest. "Don't you ever do that again to me," she scolded him. "We could not tell if you were more dead than alive," her tears revealing just how happy she was that in this battle, life had won out over the spectre of death.

"How long have I been laying here," he asked, his entire body feeling stiff and sore.

"Two days," she answered.

"I need to tell everyone what was revealed to me," he urged her to call her father and his companions into the central hall of the tent.

As he emerged from the bedroom in which he lay, Jethro ran forward to hug him, jabbering with delight. "My son, my son, you have come back. Happy, happy days.

May El-Shaddai be praised. Sit, sit, have something to eat and drink." Jethro practically forced Moses to sit down at the table and poured him a bowl of goat's milk, while sliding a bowl of figs and dates in front of him, along with a loaf of bread.

"He has a name, Jethro and He told me what it was."

"Who?" Jethro responded, not clear on whom Moses was referring to.

"El Shaddai of course,"

By this time most of the men of the camp had heard that Moses had recovered and were entering the central hall of the tent to see for themselves. Othni and Hoshea pushed their way to the front of the room so that they could wrap their arms around their leader. They were all elated to see that Moses had returned to his senses and even his facial features had practically returned to normal.

"You had us frightened," Hoshea told him. "We thought we had lost you to some other world. I've never seen a man closer to death than you were."

"I am back from that world," Moses announced to everyone around him. "And I have much to tell you. I scaled the mountain to see why there appeared to be a fiery light, only to find a bush there that was in flames but never consumed. I was amazed to behold it but then a voice came from the bush calling out my name!"

Everyone in the hall let out a gasp of awe and wonder as Moses described his experience.

"I approached the bush but then the voice told me to approach no further. It said that the ground I was standing upon was holy and I needed to take off my sandals."

A few of the women gathered in the tent swooned upon hearing that Moses had encountered the Most High God. Others became hysterical from the news, crying uncontrollably.

"I was terrified but I did as instructed and removed my sandals, while I stood frozen before the light. Then the voice that emerged from the flames called out my name again and said, 'Moses, Moses, I am the God of your forefathers. I am the God of Abraham, Isaac and Jacob. My people have cried out to me and I have seen their affliction. You will be my right hand to deliver them out of the land of Mitzrayim, and to bring them out of that land unto a good land flowing with milk and honey.' I wanted to speak but my lips were frozen."

"What does this mean?" Jethro questioned.

"Clearly it is no longer my mission to retake my throne and merely free my people from bondage. Yusef had always known that was not my destiny. God has given me a new mission to lead our people into the land of the Canaanite, and the Hittite, and the Amorite, and the Perizzite, and the Hivite, and the Jebusite. And we will take their lands for our own as the Lord had promised our ancestor Abraham."

"So Egypt is no longer your intention to rule?" Jethro's reaction was one of mixed emotions.

"I don't think it ever was," Moses replied. "You knew my grandfather perhaps better than any other man. He never intended for this staff to remain in Kemet, so he knew that I could never do so. This staff is tied to the original promise he made to Abraham. Now I must see that the promise is carried out."

"So we are to take all the lands of Canaan then. From the sea to Mesopotamia, from the cedars of Lebanon to the sands of the Negev. Correct?" In his mind Jethro was weighing out the value of this alternative pathway.

"Yes," Moses replied.

"Every city, village and fort?" Jethro sought further confirmation.

"All of it," Moses replied.

"The God of the Mountain will help us defeat our enemies!" Jethro shouted to everyone gathered in the hall.

An electrifying cheer went up from those in the tent. War with their traditional enemies had always been part of their way of life but now they had the confidence that El-Shaddai would be fighting on their side.

"And I said to God, give me your name so that I may tell it to our people so that we will fight in the name of God for all eternity." Moses continued to relate the events of two days prior. "And he said to me, 'my name is He that is, He that was, He that shall ever be, He that will be. In your past I was Ehyeh, but in your future I am Yahvu. I am all. Tell you people that Ehyeh who will be Yahvu has sent you. I will bring you out of the land of your affliction with a might hand and all your enemies shall fall before me! I will do all these things for you!"

His statements were accompanied by a further eruption of applause and songs of praise from those in the hall. The Midianites started dancing, taking their celebration outside where they could shout the new name of their God; Yahvu is Great, Yahvu is Almighty, Yahvu is One!"

"I will go before Pharaoh, my brother, and I will demand that he releases our people and when he refuses as Yahvu has already told me he will do, then Yahvu will bring down plagues upon the Kemtu people until he breaks Pharaoh's stubborn spirit. So has Yahvu spoken, so shall it be!"

"So do we march now on Egypt," Jethro wanted to know all the details.

"You will wait by the border frontier of Kemet until I send word for you."

"For how long?" Jethro wanted to know.

"I cannot tell you. Weeks, Months, perhaps even years but you will know when we are coming."

"We can camp outside Ezion Geber," Jethro informed Moses of their future location. "You will find us in the shadow of Mount Seir."

"I will find you. I promise," Moses clasped the fore arm of his father-in-law. "I need to send word to my captains in Kush to camp along the left arm of the Narrow and construct boats to ferry their forces across to Migdol once they receive further word from me. It is time for me to bring Caleb and Hur back home. I will need a separate letter sent to Queen Tharbis to let her know that the time is coming soon to join me but only once we are all safe from the reach of Pharaoh."

"I will send one of our messengers across the narrow sea immediately," Jethro consented.

"And what will be our roles in all this?" Hoshea was curious.

"Yes, what do we do?" Othni added his voice to the discussion.

"It is time for both of you to return to Goshen. I will be busy tending directly with Pharaoh but I need you two to start training the people to be a fighting force."

"Where are we going to find soldiers amongst them?" Othni was not exactly excited by the prospect of success. "They've been starved, beaten and literally dragged through the mud. Those aren't the kind of men you can make soldiers out of."

"If they can swing a pick axe in the quarries, then they can swing a sword. If they can take hammer and chisel to the quarry stones, then they can easily handle war hammers. If I gave you soldiers that could easily fight but chose all their years of oppression not to do so, then what would be the point of saving them? They willingly forfeited their freedom. But if I give you clay to mould, you can make the man into a soldier that believes in fighting for freedom because they prayed for the opportunity to gain their liberty."

Moses talk was inspiring and Othni immediately came around on his thinking, eager to begin their training. Even Hoshea was looking forward to returning to his home, letting the people that once scorned him as a street urchin know that he had returned to rescue them from slavery.

"So how much time do we have to complete the task," Hoshea asked.

"Time is beyond my control," Moses explained. "Only Yahvu can establish the timeframes in which the world unfolds. All that we do is within his hands from now on."

"What else did Yahvu say?" Jethro wanted to know.

"He said that He will stretch out His hand and smite Egypt with various wonders so that eventually Pharaoh shall let all the people of Goshen go. Not only will Pharaoh let us go but the Egyptians will be disposed favourably to us and they will give us their household objects of gold and silver and fine clothing when we leave." Moses repeated the words which he heard upon the mountain.

"He will give us freedom and make us rich," Hoshea shouted Moses words to everyone in the Jethro's tent, who then cheered in response. "Yahvu is definitely my God!"

CHAPTER TWENTY

"I think perhaps it's time I start heading back down the mountain, father. Seriously, you're permitting your own prejudices to begin clouding the telling of your stories. Clearly, Moses had enough faith in you to have you act as his spokesperson from the time he returned to Mitzrayim, which certainly doesn't sound like the man ever betrayed you back then or afterwards as you wish to portray. When he elected and protected you as High Priest he would not permit anyone to object or discredit you. He was loyal to you in every way imaginable."

"No, don't go!" Aaron began to panic at being left alone. "I have been perhaps a little unfair in my appraisal of Moses during those years but there were so many things that were done wrong. Poor Hophni, he did nothing wrong. He died as a result of the decisions we made. So many others that lost their lives because for two years we sat in Goshen while the task-masters whipped them until they could not stand upright. The countless souls buried beneath the stones of every structure we erected. The souls of all those dead cry out and haunt me every day."

"You have that entirely wrong," Eleazar rejected what his father was saying. "Firstly, Hophni died because he killed the General of the Army and a member of the royal family. Seriously, did you think he would simply walk away from that action without consequences? There were laws in place as you heard during the tribunal even if that murder was intentionally planned by the victim. No one could have a hand in the murder of a royal. Hophni knew the consequences of his actions probably more than anyone."

"If we had maintained the story of the General being a traitor, then he'd still be alive. No one would have known he was ever involved."

Eleazar shook his head. "Don't you see, that was a lie? That lie would have trapped you forever under Pharaoh's thumb and none of what we accomplished since then would have ever taken place. Everything that happened was meant to happen. That was Yahvu's doing and it mattered not what you thought or said. Had Moses not been exiled, what would you have done? How is it that you are now filled with such doubt after living a life in which your faith has been so strong?"

"Not everything was Yahvu's doing," Aaron confessed.

"What are you implying," Eleazar demanded an explanation.

"For two years Moses poured through all the historical documents I had rescued from the Temple. What I couldn't explain, Meri-amun was able to clarify. Just as I had told him, our world operates according to a series of interlocking discs. If you can identify the point at which we are on the disc then you can also identify when the exact same point has taken place in time in the past and when it will do so again in the future."

"It is like a map then," Eleazar comprehended what his father was trying to explain.

"Exactly," Aaron agreed, "A code by which the universe functions. Yahvu created laws to govern his creation and it was not meant for mere humans to unlock those secrets."

"But Moses was able to unlock those secrets, didn't he?" Eleazar was driving to the heart of the issue.

"Yes, and no man should have that knowledge," Aaron insisted.

"You make the mistake of thinking Moses is just any man. That is your fatal flaw. That is why Yahvu has forbidden you from entering the land of milk and honey. For all the times you have disagreed with Moses, this is the particular reason why you will die upon this mountain. Because you refuse to accept Moses as being more than just any man!"

"He is not a god!" Aaron screamed, but at the same time he clutched his chest feeling a surging pain rack his body.

Eleazar immediately realized that his father was definitely in trouble this time. Unseen, the angel of death had finally arrived upon the mountain top. Moving on to the slab of rock beside Aaron, Eleazar wrapped his arms around his father to comfort him during his final moments.

"You are right father, he is not a god but he is far more than any man we will ever know. If he was allowed to peer into the secrets of the universe, then it was because Yahvu wanted him to do so."

"Why him, why him," Aaron cried. "We were the holy people from the dawn of time. Why have the Lebu been denied the same favour? My entire life I have pledged to the creator and yet Yahvu has turned his back on me."

"God never turned His back on us father. We Levi are His chosen priests. We have been selected to carry on His word throughout the generations. Yahvu loves us but not in the same way that He loves Moses."

"It's not fair," Aaron moaned as the pain in his chest increased while foam from saliva mixed with blood appeared on his lips.

"We have all suffered father but who are we to say what is fair or not. Let loose your jealousy of Moses and find peace."

"I loved him, I admired him," Aaron struggled to say his final words, "but he lied to me." Clutching the collar of Eleazar's robe, Aaron had the look of desperation in his eyes. "There's a pitcher in my tent. Beside my bed. You must find it. Look for the clay seal and you will see how much I loved him."

The old man suddenly convulsed, his head snapping forward into Eleazar's lap as he began crying bitter tears of death. "I don't want to die," he expressed his greatest fear. "He promised we would live forever. That we were destined for something better than death. Moses spoke of a God that would take us into the heavens on the wings of eagles."

Eleazar had no words of consolation he could offer, stroking his father's long silver hair that was now wet with tears.

"All I am is a decrepit corpse about to perish on the top of a mountain and have my flesh eaten by the birds. I thought there would be more. I believed there would be more. He promised there would be more."

Finally Eleazar understood the issue that had driven a wedge between his father and uncle. It had not been jealousy, it had not been rejection, or any of the other things that Aaron may have pretended it to be in the stories he had been telling. It was simply a fear of being mortal. Perhaps he had deluded himself in believing that if two men had the rare privilege of speaking directly with God then Yahvu should have granted them more than simple mortality. How could he convince his father that he had been gifted with far more than mere mortals could have ever experienced? What could he say that would permit Aaron to face death with a little more courage and dignity than he was now displaying?

"You are wrong father. You will achieve immortality. Your name will never die. People will talk about Moses and Aaron until the end of time. I can promise you that. He didn't lie. He told you the truth. Of any two men that ever lived, once you were like gods and people will always remember!"

"I don't want to die alone," Aaron's pleas were being suffocated from the tears that both father and son wept.

"I will stay father. I will still to the very end. I won't leave you alone. I want to see Yahvu when he comes to this mountain top to carry you away in his arms."

"Do you really think He will come for me…?" Aaron closed his eyes for the last time, the breath escaping from his nostrils in a final burst of life.

"I'm certain of it father. Rest now. I can see Him coming father. I can see Him!"

Epitaph

The pitcher was exactly where Aaron said it would be. The clay seal had already begun to crack after so many years and Eleazar prayed that the contents had not been damaged as a result of any moisture that possibly seeped in. He shook it and could hear the scroll tapping gently against the inside surface. Removing the knife from his belt he tried to cut into the clay but the work was arduous, the clay over time becoming as hard as stone. Not having the patience to chisel away at the cap bit by bit, Eleazar simply dropped the pitcher on the ground and removed the scroll from amongst the broken pieces.

"I, Ahrown, son of Amun-Ramuse have written this transcript of events which took place in the Palace of Avaris beginning in the twelfth year of Pharaoh Amenhotep-Neferkheperure's reign. It had been two years since we first appeared before Pharaoh when we journeyed to Malkata. Malkata was exactly as Moses had described it to me; a pleasure palace built for the glorification of Pharaoh Amenhotep and very unpractical as a legislative building, with its endless corridors and central focus on its manmade pools rather than administrative buildings that were scattered about the periphery. I recall walking through those corridors, escorted by the palace guards, an endlessly long march that seemed to go on forever.

That first meeting of the two brothers was a strange encounter to put it mildly. There were those in the palace that still reacted to Moses as if he was the Crown Prince, bowing respectfully as he passed by them, some even shouting praises much to my surprise. At first I thought it may have been because of his two uncles that accompanied us on this audience, the two sons of Yuyu, Anen and Kephrure there to ensure that the young Pharaoh did not violate the conditions as set down by the Tribunal almost a decade earlier. But the chorus of praise was directed specifically at Moses and I found that most intriguing. Even more so that they completely ignored the marked contrast within our party. Here were the two brothers of Queen Tiye, dressed in their finest embroidered linen tunics, wearing the gold chains of office and their white nemes headdresses, and then there were the two of us, dressed in our colourfully striped Bedouin robes, made from coarse dyed wool that covered us from neck to ankle. Moses walked proudly, sapphire staff in hand, beard down to his chest and still the officers in the palace reacted to him as if he was still wearing the red and gold striped tunic of the Crown Prince, with his red and white nemes upon his head. Perhaps they recognized the gold signet ring that he still wore upon his right hand, the very ring that the Tribunal said he could retain so that anyone that he encountered would know that even though disgraced and fallen from office, he still remained untouchable.

I must admit that I had never been so frightened as when we entered the Hall of Audience within the western sector of the palace. I had no idea what to expect or how we would be received. Moses on the other hand betrayed no sign of any emotion, and I could not tell what he might be thinking at that time. All I saw was the forceful look of determination upon his face that I had seen so many times before when he undertook his missions. At the far end of the chamber sat the young Pharaoh with his mother beside him in a matching throne to the right. I, along with Moses' two uncles advanced according to the normal protocol, bowing and taking a knee when we were within fifteen feet of the throne dais. But from the corner of my eye I could see that Moses remained upright in defiance of the courtesies of the court.

One of the guards stepped forward with the pole of his spear raised to strike Moses on the back of the knee to force him to kneel but it was then that I witnessed the most amazing thing. Moses simply turned towards the guard, withdrawing his right hand from beneath his robe and showing to all that were gathered it had turned as white as cotton and covered in scales. Then he struck the butt end of his staff against the stone tiles of the floor, placed his hand back beneath his robe but this time when he withdrew his hand it had returned to normal. The guard recoiled in terror, withdrawing and shielding his face as if he was about to be struck. None of the guards dared to approach Moses a second time, while we remained on our one knee waiting for Pharaoh to give us permission to rise, Moses stepped forward until he was at the bottom step of the platform. Though I still did not have permission to look up, I could not resist the temptation. I wanted to see this long awaited encounter between the two brothers.

"Do not hurt him, Thutmoses," Tiye pleaded with her eldest son, fearful that somehow Moses would turn his brother into a white scaled statue with but a touch of his hand.

What I witnessed on Pharaoh's face and his mother's was unbridled fear. They were actually terrified of Moses even though they were surrounded by their guards and courtiers. I concluded that it must be the staff confounding their minds in some manner but I could not see anything unusual happening. It did not glow, or emit any vapour that I could detect, yet it was definitely raw fear that I saw seizing control of them both.

"My name is Moses," he corrected Tiye. "You saw to it that there was no longer anyone known as Thutmoses. You successfully managed to kill your son known as Thutmoses but what remained behind is far more dangerous. Nevertheless, have no fear, I will not harm you or my brother. Now please let my companions rise."

Pharaoh gave the command for the rest of the party to rise to their feet.

It was the first time I had been able to gaze directly upon this new Pharaoh and I was shocked by what I saw. The seat of his throne was quite high, much higher than normal to accommodate the abnormal length of his legs. But from his waist to his shoulders, these were completely disproportionate, as if the upper torso of a child had been sewn on to the legs of a full grown man. Never had I seen anything like him. His feet and hands resembled paddles, with toes as long as fingers and fingers like the branches on a tree. Most alarming was the shape of his head. Even beneath the Psechent double crown, I could tell that the top of his head was much wider than the width of his jaw bone. And even that was abnormal, with a chin extending downward until it practically rested upon his sunken chest noticeable by its thick ribs which showed clearly beneath his skin. My thoughts suddenly concentrated on how it was possible for Moses to look so normal whereas his brother was so physically deformed. Whereas a dwarf is subject to having a long torso placed on short bandy legs, it was as if the *Potohikap Neter* decided to create the exact opposite for his own amusement. Suddenly it made sense to me why so many in the palace still paid their respects to Moses. He was to them the epitome of what a Pharaoh should look like but now they were forced to bow before this deformed creature. Their continued respect was an extension of their abhorrence to pay tribute to this most unusual looking ruler.

Both Anen and Kephrure, once they rose, paid the proper salutations to Pharaoh and the Queen Mother as was customary. I said nothing, still not certain why Moses had even asked me to attend. Now that he called me Aaron, I presumed that as his designated High Priest I would be standing by his side on almost every occasion though he never specified the reason why.

"Will you not pay your respects to me brother?" the young Pharaoh asked Moses once he had regained his composure.

"Greetings to my brother, Pharaoh of Kemet, King of the two lands by the grace of the creator, Yahvu." Even by the nature of his addressing Pharaoh, Moses was already making a statement of his brother's diminished authority, having no power other than that which Yahvu has granted him.

Pharaoh did not recognize the name mentioned by Moses, which only confused him further on how he should respond. Turning to his scribes he requested that they identify who this Yahvu was in their pantheon of gods. The scribes quickly looked through their records but could not find the name on their list. "We know of no such *Potohikap Neter* named Yahvu," the young king indicated their lack of knowledge and thereby suggesting Yahvu had no authority within that hall.

"Not yet, but you will soon," Moses warned him, a threat that did not go unnoticed by his mother, though it did not at first register with Pharaoh. "Yahvu has sent me back to Kemet to free His people. But He is a generous and forgiving God that will give you the opportunity to acknowledge the error of you ways. He will give you two years in which to conclude your business with His people and then you must release them. If in two years you have not freed the people then I will come to you in your new palace in Avaris and will provide you with one last opportunity to let my people go."

"Your people, brother? Who are you claiming as your people?" Pharaoh wanted to know.

"The tribes in Goshen are Yahvu's people. They are my people. They were your mother's people as well but she has turned her back on them and now we turn our back on her. We will disenfranchise her in the same manner that she turned her back on her own daughter Sitamun, my wife and let her perish because of the sins committed by this family. Yahvu has had his fill of the debauchery in this land and as his prophet I will take my people and all others that choose to follow me and lead them to a land that is pure and untainted. Any that wish to leave this land are welcome and henceforth shall be considered my people. Does that sufficiently answer your question, brother?"

"Who are these people he speaks of Mother," the young Amenhotep turned to Tiye still not understanding whom Moses was referring to.

"He speaks of the *nehseyt* in the delta Pharaoh. He wishes to be the King of the slaves." Tiye knew better than to mock her oldest son but it was too late, the words had slipped from her lips.

Pharaoh began to laugh at his mother's comment and was immediately joined by all the other courtiers within the hall that were trained to laugh whenever Pharaoh did so. "*Nesew* of the *Nehseyt*. Is that your title now, brother?" Amenhotep ridiculed Moses.

"I am neither king of slaves, nor King of Kush, or even for that matter King of the Midianites. What I am is their voice and the voice of Yahvu, and together we speak as one tongue that says, 'Let my people go.'"

Tiye decided to involve her brothers into the discussion. "Brothers are you supporting this nonsense being spouted by my son? Kemet will never release her slaves. Who will build our cities if we have no *nehseyt*?"

"Sister," Kheper-Kephrure responded for himself and his brother, "Do not dishonour our father. Do not turn your back on your heritage lest it be too late for you to find peace for your *ka*. You know that this was his wish that our people return to Canaan where we belong. You know that it is your people's wish that they leave this land. Do not deny it to them or else you will suffer the wrath of our father's spirit. Even in death he will not let you rest."

"As much as I see the resemblance to my father in my son now that he dresses like one of the bearded Bedouin from which we came, you both, more than anyone should recognize that what our family may have been in the past no longer matters. Surely, neither of you intend to leave Kemet," she giggled. "You both have grown fat off the land. Just like me you know that we are more Kemtu than we ever were Khabru. This is our home. This is our people and those are our *nehseyt*."

"They are Yuyu's people and Moses is now their leader. Let them go sister or I fear you may regret what may follow," Kephrure explained. "Do not underestimate our father's reach from the tomb. That would be a fatal error!"

"And do not forget that we have an agreement brother. One which you arranged to bind all of us. Neither party can harm the other. That is an unbreakable oath to which we have all sworn. Or do you intend to violate that agreement?" Tiye challenged her brother according to the legal arrangement of the Tribunal almost a decade ago.

"This I can swear to you, Moses will not raise his hand against you or Pharaoh Amenhotep Neferkheperure," her brother guaranteed, "That is why we are here. To see that no one violates the agreement. But as for this God of Moses, neither I nor Moses can make such a guarantee for He is beyond the authority of mankind."

"Then there is nothing to discuss," Pharaoh Amenhotep piped in. "No harm can befall me if I refuse, so you may take your threats and leave now."

At that moment Moses interceded into the discussion. "Let me make this clear, brother. I said I would not harm you, brother, and I will not harm your mother either. A mother that cared more about her position of power than she ever did about her children. Sitamun calls out to me to avenge her death. Yuyu calls out to me to punish his daughter, but I can answer neither because I have given my word not to do so. But hear now the word of Yahvu that made no such promise to anyone. Hear His words, 'Since it is only power that you relish then He will strip away that which you hold dearest. He will honour the agreement to which I gave my word but everything else that you care about shall be harmed if you do not let His people leave now. Yahvu did agree that he would not curse your people and crush them beneath the weight of their own suffering. Such will be the fate of the Kemtu if

Pharaoh leaned to his left to consult with his viceroy that stood at his side. After a brief conversation, Amenhotep sat upright and responded. "We do not recognize your god in this land. Therefore, he can do us no harm. So declare the gods themselves."

"I came here only to give you the courtesy of agreeing now to my demand and avoiding all that Yahvu will bring against your nation, brother if you do not let us leave your land immediately. It was not my intention to make your people suffer for the actions committed by your mother and father. But alas, you have refused to listen to the warning from Yahvu and now I'm afraid it will be too late. You have two years in which to rectify your decision, but in the meantime I suggest you lessen the burden upon the slaves in Goshen. You will also give them the right to congregate and pray."

"And if I refuse, brother?" Pharaoh fought back against Moses' warning.

"Take a look at yourself brother. Do you not think Yahvu has already punished you enough? Ask you mother why this has happened to you and see if she bears no shame in what she has done. If she bears no guilt then refuse my two simple requests but I believe she will encourage you to agree lest you wish to see what else Yahvu can do to your family."

"And if he agrees, then you will leave us alone?" Tiye interjected, seeking a way out of this dilemma.

"It is not up to me to forgive. It has never been up to me as you will recognize. Yahvu has heard the cries and seen the tears of His people and he will give you this respite to think about your response for two years."

"And then what?" Tiye wanted to know.

"You know where I will be in two years. Yahvu will send you a message to remind you of our meeting."

"Your god is not even on our list!" Pharaoh exclaimed, still refusing to accept that Moses' god had any authority in Kemet. "I do not recognize this Yahvu. I spit on your god. I fear you not. I will not come to Avaris on your beckon call."

"In two years the earth will shake and your buildings will begin to collapse. That will be Yahvu's message for you to come to Avaris. Until then brother, think hard upon how you can avoid all the suffering that will follow from occurring as a result of your obstinacy."

Not waiting to be dismissed, Moses turned his back on Pharaoh and left the hall. The three of us could not bring ourselves to break protocol. Bowing repeatedly as we walked slowly backwards until we had reached the doors to the hall, then turning to exit alongside Moses.

Never had any man treated a Pharaoh with such disrespect as Moses had done that day. Though I knew that he was protected by the oath they swore at the Tribunal, I still could never have imagined any man could have done what he did. The impact was not lost on those in attendance in the Hall of Audience. The gossip in Thebes regarding the return of the Crown Prince went way beyond expectations. I realize now that was Moses' prime intent of our journey to Malkata. It was not about giving Pharaoh the opportunity to let the slaves leave without challenging Yahvu, because Moses always knew that the offer would be refused. Yahvu had already told him that He intended to harden Pharaoh's heart and would not permit him to consider a peaceful resolution.

Talk of how Pharaoh wilted before the stare of Moses spread across the land. Stories even began to circulate of how Pharaoh and the Queen Mother were forced to kneel before Moses. The spirits in Goshen were raised by the news that Moses not only threatened Pharaoh but lived to talk about it. For the first time I think they all truly believed that Moses was their chosen deliverer. Even when Pharaoh raised the quotas on bricks to be made, it did not destroy the enthusiasm that infected the people. Such was the price to pay for their coming freedom.

Just as Moses had prophesized, there came an earthquake of such magnitude that those checking the nilometer claimed that Nile levels fell by three feet at the height of the quake, only returning to the normal height previously recorded after several hours. It was almost two years to the day that we had journeyed to Malkata and as Moses had predicted, we received word that the royal family and their entourage would be coming to Avaris, but their explanation was that they intended to experience the better winter weather enjoyed in the delta. No one that heard the news of their travels believed it. Everyone knew that Pharaoh was most certainly answering the summons from Moses.

This time I had far more confidence when we journeyed to Avaris to appear before Pharaoh. I knew that we held the upper hand even though we were seen as nothing more than annoying insects in the eyes of Pharaoh. I had no way to explain why we were all filled with such confidence other than some unseen *wasur* that emanated from the staff whenever Moses held it now infused our very being. Everyone's eyes naturally focused on it when he passed by. It drew our attention even when you wanted not to think upon it. It was obvious why Moses' father wanted it but there was truth to the story that it had to be in the hands of those selected by Yahvu. There was an inexplicable relationship as if the staff would respond to Moses' touch and he in turn would change in stature when he felt the staff in his hand.

When we walked through the palace grounds towards the main building, we were confronted by all the new building projects that this young Amenhotep had engaged in. Everywhere we looked we could see the men of Goshen struggling against their burdens, moving, piling and carving stone after stone. The sounds of axes and hammers rang out from every direction, only to be drowned by the crack of whips and screams of agony as the leather straps tore into exposed flesh. But when Moses passed by, they all stopped their work and bowed in respect. Even while the sting of the lash striped their backs, the slaves appeared at that moment to be immune from the pain, practically smiling at Moses, while their task-masters beat them. Such was the power of Moses and I truly was in awe. Both Machir and Joshua accompanied us when we went to the palace in Avaris. Essentially, they were there for protection because two better warriors in close combat you could not find but Moses brought them only for show, not once thinking that their services would be necessary.

The palace at Avaris was very different from the one I had viewed in Malkata. Avaris was built to show the world the power of Pharaoh, whereas Malkata truly was built as a pleasure palace though Moses' father had denied it. Every structure in Avaris was built on a massive scale. Columns were as tall as trees. Tapestries hung from the walls depicting scenes of the Nile. Every table, chair and desk was inlaid with gold and ivory, adorned with beryl and lapis-lazuli. Carvings of ebony and soapstone stood in silence along the hallways and polished granite tiles lined the floors. This was the work of our people, and it was not lost on Moses who recognized that our craftsmen would be essential for our own successful future.

We were ushered ceremoniously into the throne room. It was obvious that the earthquake had impacted significantly on the young Pharaoh's temperament. Where Malkata had merely a Hall of Audience, Avaris's hall resembled a magnificent temple. The royal couple sat on an elevated platform, thirty steps high, so that everyone before them would feel small and insignificant. On every fifth step in ascension, on either side, one of the many court officials stood in their white skirts and leather skull caps, prepared to either inscribe the sacred words of Pharaoh or to tend to his immediate needs. Tiye had not come with him on this journey, rumour having it that the Queen mother had diminished in favour in Pharaoh's eyes after suggesting that he should perhaps acquiesce to some of the demands made by Moses, especially after experiencing the earthquake. On his left sat his Great Wife Nefertiti and she was as beautiful as the talk in the nomes claimed. She wore a turquoise dyed dress that was layered in what resembled fish scales over her torso. Two straps crossed her shoulders, matched by the arm bands that she wore on each bicep. A heavy collar of lapis-lazuli trimmed in gold adorned her long swan-like neck. She wore a braided wig with jewels and beads clasping the end of each braid. A tall *hedjet* crown of dark blue sat atop her head. But it was the paleness of her skin that captivated me most, making me wonder if she had any Lebu heritage that could account for its ivory-like whiteness.

My eyes were then drawn to Pharaoh, no longer a boy but a man of eighteen years. It had been two years since last we met but I was shocked by the rapidity of the changes to his features. His stomach appeared bloated and his hips had widened like those of a woman. The chin as prominent as it had been when I last saw him jutted even further than it did before with lips that protruded even more than those of our Nubian warriors. His fingers, though still long and slender appeared to be crooked similar to what I had seen occurring in very old people. My first thoughts at that time were that Yahvu was continuing to punish this young Pharaoh for crimes that he had perpetrated against our people, exactly as Moses had forewarned. At this rate I feared that in a few more years Amenhotep would be transformed into a monstrosity that no one would be able to look upon without feeling disgust. Unless he acknowledged his sins against Yahvu, he'd be lucky to last another decade.

The viceroy commanded all that stood before Pharaoh to bow and bend the knee but Amenhotep immediately cancelled that order, instead saying that his brother need not be so formal to pay such respect. It was a clever tactic by Pharaoh remembering how Moses' refusal last time to offer proper respect resulted in months of gossip regarding how Pharaoh had to bow before his older brother. It was a calculated risk by Amenhotep that he could avoid such disparaging comments if he let Moses stand solely because of his brotherly love.

The exchange of introductions and titles of proper address were left to the heralds since Pharaoh knew that his brother would never speak the usual words. It wasn't long before Moses was demanding that Pharaoh let our people go once again, knowing full well that Pharaoh's heart was hardened and would not listen to the word of Yahvu.

"Is it your god that has marshalled the Midianites at the frontier of Egypt, waiting there for your signal to invade? Or perhaps your Yahvu sailed the ships that landed your invasion force from Kush at the tip of the Sinai? Did you think I would not know about what you have been doing behind my back brother?"

"No one has invaded your land brother, and no one will unless you raise a hand against my people. Nothing has been done behind your back as you suggest. All has been done in front of your eyes without any attempt to hide our movements."

"I will crush your people wherever they go brother. They will not hide from me in the land of Sin and Canaan. My reach is long."

"Let me caution you know before you do something foolish, brother. You will not touch them brother," Moses warned. "Yahvu will raise his hand and smite your forces should you try. Furthermore, you shall never set foot in Canaan ever again. So says Yahvu!"

"Who is your god to tell me where my army can go and where it cannot," he responded to Moses.

"You do not know His power yet, brother, but soon you will," Moses responded. "Very soon! And after you witness it, you will refuse even your own governors that beg you to send troops beyond the frontiers of Kemet."

"This is my empire to go wherever I please," Amenhotep ranted. "Your god cannot stop me."

Moses ignored the rant, directing Pharaoh's heralds to follow him to the porch that extended from the great hall. Moses walked to the tributary that flowed near the palace gardens. He touched the surface of the water with his staff and then advised those that had followed him to watch the water carefully. As they did so he returned to the hall and stood before Pharaoh. It was not long until several heralds ran back into the hall yelling that the river had turned to blood and carrying cup of water from the river. They poured the contents of the cup on the ground and everyone saw that the water had turned red.

As soon at the courtiers saw what they perceived as blood splashing on the tiles, they began jabbering like a flock of geese at which point Pharaoh called for silence. He turned to his chief magistrate who walked up the steps and spoke into Pharaoh's ear so that no one else could hear. Reacting to his advice, Pharaoh permitted the Chief Magistrate to make an announcement in Pharaoh's name, claiming that it was not the first time nor the last time that the water in the Nile has turned red. In fact each time there has been a major earthquake, it was not unusual to see such an event and it would persist only for a few days. Water will be drawn from wells far from the river and new wells will be dug if they are insufficient. There was no need to panic he advised, ignoring the fact that the water had turned red precisely when Moses wanted it to.

"Your bag of tricks do not frighten us brother," Amenhotep commented. "Is that all you have for us?" In response to Pharaoh's comments the courtiers assembled in the hall all began to laugh and jeer, thinking that he had bested Moses.

"Oh, that was not to frighten you, brother" Moses taunted in response. "That was just to set everything in motion. Everything needs a beginning and that was it. What will frighten you is what is yet to come."

"What do you mean?" Pharaoh demanded to know. "Do not think that you can threaten me and that you will remain untouchable if you violate the agreement.

"Patience brother. We are just beginning the journey to your enlightenment. A single point on a small disc circling around an even larger one." Having said that, Moses turned and gave me an appreciative wink.

"What nonsense is this about discs?" the young Pharaoh had no understanding of what Moses was referring to, instructing his advisors to determine what this talk of discs was all about.

"It will become clear to you soon, brother. I guarantee you will know Yahvu by the time we have finished!" Moses' comment still sounded more like a threat than a caution.

"I do not know your god!" Amenhotep yelled at his brother once y.

"Not yet," Moses smiled while he repeated his refrain, "But soon. Very soon and though you will try to honour him when this is all over, it will be too late. He will not listen to you. Your dynasty will be brought to an end."

"What are you talking about?" the young Pharaoh sounded confused.

"Patience brother," Moses repeated. "We will be back soon again and again over the next few weeks. You will call for me each time and I will respond to your summons but your heart will be hardened and you will dismiss me time after time while your people suffer. Each time you refuse my demands and my God will deliver an even more severe blow against your land. Yet still you will refuse to yield to my demands. Not until your own people will beg you to yield to the God of Moses lest he wipes all the Kemtu from the face of the Earth. Then you will yield!"

"I shall never yield to your demands, never!" Pharaoh shouted.

"True. Only when the hand of the Lord weighs heavily upon your own house, then you will yield. Be prepared brother, we shall meet again very soon!"

"You are not welcome here brother," Amenhotep-Neferkheperure cautioned Moses if he should try to come again to the palace.

"Nevertheless, you will summon me within the week," Moses let his brother know.

"That is ridiculous," the young Pharaoh scoffed. "I never want to see you again."

"Within the week brother," Moses repeated his prediction. "You know where to find me."

It was clear to everyone in the Hall of Audience that Moses had just dismissed Pharaoh, turning his back on the Great King, a second time now, as he prepared to leave without even the courtesy of awaiting a response. Amenhotep-Neferkheperure was at a loss for words, turning to his wife Nefertiti for guidance but from the look on her face he could see that she was as much in a state of confusion as he was.

As we turned to exit from the hall I must admit I have never been so proud of my brother at arms. Never could I imagine there could be a man with the strength of conviction and the determination of character to change the world as I have seen in Moses. He truly is the beloved of Yahvu. I am fortunate to walk beside such a man.

At that point the letter ended and Eleazar rolled it up and tucked it beneath his robes. He smiled silently to himself, satisfied that with this one scroll, his father, Aaron, had redeemed himself. This was the man he had admired all his life, a man he was proud to call father, and this was the memory of the man that he would preserve.

EPILOGUE

John Pearce just sat there in stunned silence.

"What's the matter John, cat got your tongue," I taunted him. "I told you that I was going to turn everything you thought you knew about Moses upside down. Except this time it's right side up."

Holding up a finger I knew that he was about to say something but he just couldn't articulate it yet.

"So let me get this straight Doc. GLEEM incorporates all these memories into you DNA and you've been carrying them about within your family for over three thousand years. So how come none of your other ancestors bothered to tell the story."

"Easy enough. Because it wasn't until my lifetime that all the pieces started to come together and science, archaeology, volcanology, geographical history and Egyptology finally caught up to the point that they could provide the evidence to support my memories. Much of the supporting information about events that I've disclosed in this story wasn't available until the last few decades. For example, the fact that Akhenaton was co-regent with his father for at least eight years only had conclusive evidence in 2014."

"But you've been hinting about this story to me since before the turn of the century. You've had to sit on it for so long waiting for the sciences to catch up."

"Exactly," I agreed with Pearce. "If I had released this story twenty years ago, it just would have ended up in a pile of historical fiction novels. Now it's going to get the analytical rigour it deserves and people are going to realize it is the truth."

"I'm still in shock, Doc. I didn't think you could shake my Catholic roots but I got to admit you did it this time. So what about that warning Moses gave him not to set foot in Canaan or else! Did Akhenaton actually listen to him?"

"That's the amazing thing John," I explained, delighted that for once he actually asked an intelligent question. "There are hundreds of letters from small city kings and mayors begging Akhenaton to send troops into Canaan to rescue them as their cities are under siege. In fact, one of them, Rib-Hadda of Byblos sent so many letters begging for help that Pharaoh Neferkheperure-Akhenaton, recognize he was no longer Amenhotep by this time, actually wrote him back saying 'stop begging already, I'm not coming'. So all of Canaan is in turmoil. Cities like Shechem are mentioned as being under attack, which we already know from the Bible, and their protector is refusing to send his army to their rescue. So yes, he was so terrified of Moses's warning that he wasn't about to challenge his brother. Even though the Hittites recognized this weakness and are beginning to invade Syria and Canaan from the north, he still won't send reinforcements. It's hard to know if part of the deterrent was that he suffered such a significant loss of his troops at the Island of Tiran when the Red Sea parted, so that he just didn't have a strong enough army to send into Canaan or whether he was just simply terrified of challenging Moses."

"Wow. So there are letters that talk about the invasion of Canaan and Pharaoh's refusal to help and nobody has bothered to put this all together to support the Exodus story."

"Hundreds of letters," I informed him. "Sixty alone from Rib-Hadda. So you can understand now, why I couldn't release this story earlier. I had to wait for a point in time when I could say to people, check the evidence for yourself."

"So what about this staff?" John switch gears in the blink of an eye.

"You're sounding like Eleazar now." I cautioned him.

"Did it really have some sort of power?" Pearce was no different from anyone else that saw Moses with his staff three thousand years ago. I guess some things don't change over time.

"Let's look at the legend. It says the staff was a branch from one of the trees in the Garden of Eden. So you have a choice, Tree of Life or Tree of Knowledge. And as scientifically based society, we naturally assume that it could not be either. They could not have existed. And I'm a scientist too John you have to remember. So I would argue in the same manner as everyone else that trees cannot possess special properties. But we're obviously dealing with an artefact that did possess some array of powerful properties. Sadly, we don't have it in our possession to examine, but what if it wasn't a branch from a tree but something completely different?"

"Like what Doc?"

"I'm just supposing. We have too many stories regarding this staff to deny that it actually existed. We have a suggestion that the High Priests of Northern Israel still had that staff in their possession, only to have it destroyed by King Hezekiah of Judaea. So it really did exist but we don't know what it was."

"I didn't know Hezekiah destroyed it."

"Yes, that's something I speculated about in one of my blogs. After the fall of Northern Israel, there is a story of Hezekiah inviting the priesthood to come to Jerusalem."

"I didn't know that either," Pearce admitted, which wasn't much of a surprise to me.

"It's recorded in two places. According to Samaritan legends and what we can glean from 2 Chronicles 30 and 31, following the conquest of the Northern Kingdom by Assyria, the high priests and the Levites from the north travelled to Jerusalem. Chronicles explains this was in response to an invitation from Hezekiah himself in order to unify the people and celebrate the Passover in the rededicated Temple of Jerusalem."

"Have to admit Doc, I haven't really read Chronicles."

"Not too many people do," I let him know that he was not alone in that regard. "So the story goes, Azariah was High Priest in Jerusalem, but when the Northern High Priest came, either Amram or his son Akob, it created quite the dilemma, especially since the northern high priest was carrying the Nehushtan mounted on his staff. So to eliminate a possible confrontation, since possession of this staff would suggest he outranks Azariah, Hezekiah breaks it the staff in two and destroys it."

"So what's that got to do with this sapphire staff of Moses," Pearce asked.

"See this is where we have to realize editors changed the stories because they didn't want us to know the truth. Now granted, the Nehushtan, this snake like statue made out of brass by Moses was in possession of the Northern Kingdom, but it wasn't something transportable. Archaeological evidence in northern Israel of one of the High Places suggests that the Nehushtan was kept on a peak that is carved like a coiled snake. The Nehushtan, being quiet large would have been mounted on a column or a pillar. It was symbolic of God's healing power and people would perform a pilgrimage to this High Place if they had health problems."

"So?"

"So, if the Nehushtan is on a pillar on some mountain top, then what is it that the High Priest of the Northern Kingdom is carrying, that is of such importance as a symbol of Moses' invested authority into this particular line of priests that Hezekiah has to destroy it or else it will cause turmoil in his kingdom?"

"I get it now Doc? But wouldn't the King be afraid to destroy something that was actually that sacred?"

"I would have thought so," I admitted, "But as we know, politics and religion don't mix easily and sometimes one has to make hard decisions to protect the status quo. But it is that same line of thinking that makes people think he couldn't possibly have done it and the staff of Moses must still be out there somewhere."

"But you don't believe that," Pearce read my thought.

"No. It's gone. I do believe Hezekiah destroyed it. The same way I believe that the destruction of the staff led to the series of calamities which has befallen the Jewish people for the last twenty-seven hundred years after it was destroyed. Whatever that staff was, we lost the benefits it would have provided to each succeeding generation."

"But this Nehushtan, Doc, why a snake? I never understood that."

"Now you're thinking John," I verbally patted him on the back. "People should have been asking that a long time ago. It goes hand in hand with the reason the uraeus became part of the crown of the Pharaohs. It was because it was used as a protective symbol since the Egyptians believed the cobra would spit fire at any approaching enemies. So we know from Numbers 21:8 where the Lord said unto Moses: 'Make thee a fiery serpent, and set it upon a pole; and it shall come to pass, that every one that is bitten, when he sees it, shall live,' that this Nehushtan was the same cobra that could spit fire. So as much as Moses is beginning this new life as a prophet leading the Children of Israel, he still has a reliance on his Egyptian roots. The cobra also represented the "fiery eye of Ra", in which two uraei can be seen on either side of a winged solar disk, so in itself it was not a deity but merely a tool through which God would work. So ignoring the obvious connections to pagan Egyptian practices, then this construct of a serpent on a pillar was viewed merely as a medical device, a tool of Yahvu and nothing more. Moses never anticipated that people might actually start praying to it."

"So did it have any supernatural powers?" Pearce was obsessing on the staff.

"I can't believe this," I repudiated his insistence on focusing on the staff. "I tell you this detailed history on the life of Moses and all you want to talk about is the staff. I think you have to get over it, otherwise you are acting exactly like Eleazar. Ask me something about the history. Ask me to prove that what I told you actually happened."

"Okay Doc, I'll give you one. So, how do we know Moses actually fought this war in Ethiopia? Do you have any proof of that?|

"Good! Finally something which we can sink out teeth in to. So let me tell you about the stele that was erected in Amenhotep's name about his conquest of Kush."

"But you said he never led the army in that war," Pearce was quick to challenge me.

"Yes, I did and the stele says the same thing. Listen to what is says on the stele, *'This King of the Kushites did not know this lion before him, this Lord of Ra's Ma'at that clawed his way through Kush until he finally conquered it.'* Now as most people would tell you, in any battle record, the first lines will always talk about Pharaoh, pouring accolade after accolade upon his name until you grow tired of reading how wonderful and great he is. But this stele would suggest that the general was a young unknown, with no reputation that preceded him until he actually conquered all of Kush. And because he was unknown and underestimated he was able to take the country piece by piece, eliminating each chieftain of the Nubians one by one until the finally laid siege to the king's city. Now let's compare this to what is written in Chapter 72 of the **Book of the Yasher**, sentence 24: *'And the king and princes and all the fighting men loved Moses, for he was great and worthy, his stature was like a noble lion, his face was like the sun, and his strength was like that of a lion, and he was counsellor to the king.'* So, it's pretty clear John that it was a common metaphor to refer to Moses as being a noble and young lion, just as it is written on the stele. The collaboration between himself and Kikiani as stated in the **Book of the Yasher** probably accounts for why the stele does not mention the death or imprisonment of the King of Kush.

Check it out for yourself, Pearce, it's all written on that monument but remember this that the scale of the war, to actually conquer all of Nubia and Kush, should have resulted in a huge commemorative city or temple, because of the sheer magnitude of this victory as would have happened at any other time under any other Pharaoh. Compared to the small border skirmishes in which various Pharaohs were lauded and buried beneath mountains of praises and accolades extolling their feats of daring and bravery, this time we're left with a victory that appears hardly worth commemorating. Knowing the political nuances of ancient Egypt, most Egyptologists would tell you that this meant more often than not that someone other than Pharaoh was responsible for the victory. And certainly, from what I've told you in this telling of the story, Pharaoh Amenhotep would not be comfortable in commemorating this victory to any great extent if this general turned out to be the Crown Prince, who also just happened to place the crown of Kush upon his head. Son or not, by doing this he placed himself in direct opposition to Amenhotep III. So it's entirely appropriate that Pharaoh never recorded this war and victory over all of Kush and Nubia in his own royal chronicles, but he would not have been able to eradicate the steles set up independently by his general far to the south near Aswan at Konosso, thereby leaving this connection to the existence of

Thutmoses V. The unknown young lion didn't want to have himself recognized as the conqueror but instead does pay tribute to Amenhotep saying the victory was in his name. Now if that doesn't prove to you that Moses was in charge of the war to take Kush and Saba, I don't know what will."

"I guess that makes sense," Pearce acknowledged as he tried to absorb everything I had to say.

"Okay, one last question John because I'm getting tired. So make it a good one."

Pearce cupped his hands and looked very contemplative as he thought about what he should ask.

"Hello! Not like we have all day here John."

"Okay, okay. Here it goes. How do we know Thutmoses V just didn't die like most of the historians claim and therefore he couldn't possibly be Moses?"

"Not a bad question. Could have done better," I razzed him, "But one that needs to be answered. So follow the dots here, John. Crown Prince Thutmoses disappears from Egyptian records completely between year 27 and year 33 of his father's reign, so as a result, he never becomes Pharaoh, otherwise we would have had a Pharaoh Thutmoses V in the Kings List. Instead we get Akhenaton becoming the next Pharaoh.

Now, if the reign of Amenhotep III from 1390 to 1352 BCE is correct, and I'm suggesting it is, then that means that Thutmoses disappeared between 1363 and 1357 BCE. So he's already a twenty-five year old man or even slightly older. So these other historians attempt to justify his absence by claiming that he probably just died, but that would not explain why his tomb has not been discovered, either with or close to those belonging to the rest of his family nor why his name appears to have been purposely erased from all Egyptian records. Now in regards to his tomb that would have been constructed for his eventual entombment from the time he was named as Crown Prince, so there should have been almost two decades of construction and it has never been found in the cluster area that was reserved for Amenhotep's family.

The attempt to erase his life was a determined effort and the existence of Thutmoses is only attested to by a total of seven pairs of calcite and pottery vases that are currently held in the Louvre. So, trying to make him disappear was highly successful and was a fate one would only expect if you ran afoul of Pharaoh, not if you were a beloved son that died accidentally. You have to remember, we're not dealing with a case of a lack of mentioning a son after the event of his death, in which everything preceding the death would have remained as it was, but instead a deliberate attempt to erase any trace of that son's existence. Clearly there was intent, there was purpose, and there was an act of defiance by Tiye keeping a few items from being destroyed. Those aren't the actions you would expect from a Pharaoh if his beloved son dies.

As for his mother taking his mummified cat, Ta-Miu, into her sarcophagus, sad as that is, we can appreciate had he died, then his cat would have been placed in his tomb and not hers. In fact, his cat would have been buried alive in the tomb with him. As well, there should have been numerous mementos left behind from her son that Tiye would have taken with her into her tomb, but the apparent absence of anything of that nature tells us that they had all been purposely destroyed and nothing was available except those few items I previously mentioned. Her husband obviously had issues with Thutmoses and it was fortunate that Tiye died twelve years after her husband, otherwise I believe Amenhotep would have ensured that there would have been absolutely no evidence remaining from Thutmoses. And that's how we know that what I have been telling you is the truth. Not because I'm telling you so, but because of your own logical deduction. So are we good John?"

"Yeah Doc, we're good."

"Good, I need to sleep, I'm beat."

NOTES FROM THE AUTHOR

1. Ancient Egyptian Glossary of words in this novel:

<u>Egyptian</u>	<u>English</u>	
Amenen	Invisible:	The concept of invisibility was reserved for the gods.
Anu	A scribe	A religious scribe was known as the **seps sep anu**
Ap	Temple	
Artu	Heaven	As in the concept of where the souls would reside
Asert	Sky	
Atef	Crown of Osiris	White crown with ostrich feathers and a golden disc at tip
Dehnet	Mountain	
Deshret	Crown of Lower Egypt	A red bowl shaped crown with a curley-cue on top.
Etaty	Vizier	
Exieti	Fire	
Hedjet	Crown of Upper Egypt	A white bowling pin shaped crown with cobra on front
Hekay	Magician	
Hemneter	Prophet	Most often reserved for a Mater of the Temple
Hem-netjer-tepi	Master of the Temple	
Herey	Master	
Heru	Saviour	
Hetra	Horses	
Iaate	Chieftain	
Ib	The heartlight	Used to judge the value of the man by weighing
Itey	Prince	
Ka	The Life Force	One of the five elements of the human being.
Kefaw	Warrior	
Kemet	The Black Lands	The Theban name for Egypt
Kemtu	People of the Black Lands	The Theban name for Egyptians
Khat	The body	One of the five elements of the human being.
Khu	The soul	One of the five elements of the human being
Neb	Lord	
Nefer	Good or Beautiful	
Nehseyt	Slave	
Nemes	Headress	The gold and blue Nemes was reserved for the dead king.
Nesew	King	
Neter	God(s)	Beings with supernatural powers but not the supreme god
Okai	High:	As in a political position
Pedtay	Foreigner	
Pet	Heaven	
Pharaoh	Great House:	As in Royal House but became used as King
Potohikap	Creator	
Psechent	Double Crown of Egypt	Combination of the Deshret and Hedjet Crowns
Pursofe	Merciful	
Raswet	Dream:	As in a vision or prophecy
Sasap	Light:	As in a physical lamp or illumination
Savov	Royal	Used for a member of the Royal Family

Suten-sa	Crown Prince	
Tept	The First:	As in a first rule or commandment
Tunkeh	Supreme	
Ua-geb-ptah	Egyptian	Those that open the corpse then wrap it
Uraeus	Cobra figure	Seen on the front of the Hedjet crown
Wab-tepi	Priest in charge of archives	
Wasur	Power:	As in an actual force or supernatural ability
Wepwety	Messenger	
Worret	Crown	A variety of headgear worn by the Pharaohs
Wutinpow	Priest	

2. The Ancient Egyptian Calendar:

The Reader is already aware that the calendar used throughout this novel has been based on the one actually used by the ancient Egyptians. In itself, it was quite a marvel, well advanced as compared to other civilizations of the time, which tended to be reliant on lunar calendars.

As a solar calendar, the ancient Egyptians had 365 days to the year, which is comparable to our modern day calendar. They divided the year into three seasons, each consisting of four months. The seasons were known as the Flood Season (Akhet), the Growth Season (Peret), and the Low Water or Dry Season (Shemu). Each season was 120 days long and at the end of the year, an intercalary month of 5 days was inserted to round off the 365 day year.

Each month was thirty days long and like our calendar, these ancient Egyptians had 12 months. The weeks were known as decans, being ten days long, so therefore there were three weeks in each month.

The months of the Flood Season which corresponded to our June through September were called, Thoth, Phaophi, Athyr and Choiak.

The months of the Growth Season which corresponded to our October to January were called Tybi, Mechir, Phamenoth and Pharmuthi.

The months of the Dry Season which corresponded to our February to April were called Pachens, Payni, Epiphi and Mesur.

What is interesting is that having access to such an advanced calendar system, that after the exodus, Moses made the conscious decision to revert to a lunar calendar for the calculation of the Hebrew festivals. There are two possible reasons to justify why he made this decision. The first being that he wished to remove as much of the Egyptian influence as possible from being introduced to the subsequent generations so that they in turn would not share any common background or routine practices with the Egyptian people, or the second possibility is that Goshen even though dominated by Theban rulers after the fall of the Hyksos, for two hundred years, still practiced and adhered to Mesopotamian customs and therefore Moses was unable to introduce the change to a solar calendar because of resistance.

3. The Sons of Joseph:

In this historical novel you were introduced to the sons of Yuyu, who were called Anen and Kephrure. As we know from the Bible, Joseph the Patriarch also had two sons, Manasseh and Ephraim, and as with Yuyu, the second son far outshone the first in recognition and achievements. It is worthwhile to note that even the names provided in the Bible are purely Egyptian in origin.

If we examine the name Ephraim, first presented in Genesis 51:52, then we can clearly say, shame on the rabbinical scholars who have provided us with a false translation being, "Fruitful in the land of my affliction." In their attempt to make the name Hebraic in origin, they seem to have broken every rule of phonetics, using fruitful which is 'poireh' but which doesn't have any similarity in sound with Ephraim. Nor can they claim them meant sexually prolific as in the connotation of being impregnated which is 'hephrayah' which is actually closer in sound to Ephraim but misses the intended concept of being a bountiful harvest. The name used is completely Egyptian as in 'ephrati' which means a royal aristocrat. As an ancient word it was even adopted into the Hebrew, but the Rabbis chose to ignore this translation. The only question is why they did so? The epherates in ancient Egyptian were the districts the land was divided into and under the jurisdiction of the epheru, or magistrate. In this sense, the magistrate was a powerful man like pharaoh but not of the Great House, which was all of Egypt. So what the Bible was really saying was that Joseph's son Ephraim, the equivalent of the Egyptian plural of Epheru, was a governor in the land of their affliction which was a true and accurate statement because we know Yuyu was the Epher of Ahikam, and one of his son's would take over this hereditary position. As master of the horse and vizier, Joseph would have been governor over many of the districts, and though we only know of the single land holding of Yuyu, that is not to say that he could not have been governing over many more. Removing the 'K' from the beginning of Kephrure, we actually have the name of Ephra as Moses referred to his uncle, the name most likely derived from his landholding position in Egypt. The 'K' by itself was a hieroglyph in the shape of a tent, indicating a title such as head of a tribe or a village. Together we have an accurate description of the biblical Ephraim.

The first born, who in the case of both Joseph and Yuyu were minor players and in the shadow of their younger brothers, clearly have a similarity in names. Anen is in fact almost identical to the first part of Manasseh. So the question that needs to be answered is what does the second part of the name Asseh mean. Well that is not difficult to explain at all. His mother, Asenath or more appropriately Asenathiye, translated as being of the Province or Belonging to Isis, has the same name. So in this case, as with Tiye, his sister, he was dedicated to the goddess Isis because of his mother's religious connections. The first part of his name indicates he was also dedicated to the god Amun, which on the part of his father would suggest a strategic political move to appease Pharaoh Amenhotep II whom Joseph became the Vizier of Egypt after interpreting his dreams. I would even go as far as saying that like our modern day traditions of often naming a child after their god-father, Joseph did exactly the same thing for his first born son, thereby gaining the protection of his benefactor and Pharaoh for his first born son. But there is also a play on the ancient Egyptian word 'amenen' which translates as invisible. So though on one hand Joseph may be honouring his benefactor, at the same time he is making it clear that he worships the invisible god Yahvu.

In conclusion, we can see that the biblical story, which so many atheists and non-believing historians have criticized for its lack of sustainable facts or evidence to support actual occurrence in Egyptian history, were mistaken because they merely looked superficially at what was written without making a concerted attempt to actually interpret what was being described, taking into consideration changes to words that would occur as the result of dialect, repetition over time, and editorial prejudices where deliberate attempts over successive centuries would be made to conceal Egyptian origins. Fortunately these editors limited their exercise to do so because of fear of divine punishment for changing the words of Moses and Aaron and original words have been retained, even if they are altered to sound slightly different. But enough of the original linguistics remain to not only determine significant facts regarding the lives of the people involved in the Exodus story, but also to pinpoint the time period in which the events were taking place.

4. The Parting of the Red Sea:

I'm certain by now, many of the readers are asking, 'Where's the parting of the Red Sea,' since that is the most dramatic and memorable moment of the Exodus story. Because of the magnitude of that event, I did not wish to end this story using that particular event as the climax as well as the initiating moment of when a mixed multitude of fleeing refugees and tribal communities cemented their relationship to become the Children of Israel. To do so would diminish the intent of this historical novel, which was to provide you with an accurate retelling of Moses, the man. As a religious scholar, I have no doubt that he had a direct line of communication with Almighty God, but as a scientist, I also have no doubt that the laws of nature and physics are inviolable and therefore not even something as phenomenal as the parting of the sea can defy those principles that God has established in what we see as reality. Hence the true miracle was the ability for Moses to understand and appreciate these cosmic rules, or as Ahrown first said to Thutmoses, "the ability to communicate directly with that central disc at the centre of our universe." By appreciating that Yahvu performed His miracles according to these established laws, and by using the historical documents available, Moses could actually predict the site, location, timing, as well as duration of these miraculous events.

Any good scientist does his research and even someone like myself, who has been criticized by scientific colleagues for my adherence to religious dogma, will perform my own investigations before accepting anything I may be told at face value. Just because my ancestors wrote the story of the Exodus and theocrats later said, 'this is the unalterable word of God' does not necessarily make it so and I can site numerous examples in the Bible where these same theocrats have performed not only edits but complete alterations of the original text. So the scientist in me says, 'Prove it to yourself' and that is what I do in every instance.

Therefore, when asked, 'where's my proof of such an event occurring,' then I respond accordingly based on the research I have performed, which is irrefutable and established fact. Firstly, we can look at a cuneiform text first described by Knudtson in 1915, which was uncovered in Syria and described a huge tsunami that occurred on the Syrian Coast of the Mediterranean as a result of an equally massive earthquake. The dating of this earthquake and subsequent tsunami was 1380 BCE +/- 100 years. As between 1350 to 1347 BCE is the dating of the Red Sea crossing according to the chronology of my story, falls well within this timeframe, then it can obviously be stated that either this initial quake or its aftershocks would have had an effect on the fault line beneath the Red Sea. What kind of effect, well for that, we have an excellent scientific investigation from events that occurred in September of 2005. In brief, satellite images showed that the Arabian tectonic plate and the African tectonic plate physically moved away from each other and as a result the southern end of the Red Sea actually widened. The actual rift occurred along a 37 mile section close to Afar, Ethiopia. Over a period of three weeks, the rift separated by a distance of 26 feet, creating a volume displacement equivalent to over 2000 football stadiums at a depth of six miles below the surface. The majority of this space was filled by magma that had been accumulating in chambers below the crust but had this not been the case, then it would have been filled with sea water from above. The sudden rush of sea water into this void, would have been similar to watching water going down a drain in which it is drawn from the surface in a tidal pool effect. Scientists whom have made it their life's work to study tsunamis have developed mathematical formulas to calculate the wave forms, size and intensity of these tsunamis according to the Maslov Index, which uses as its two primary factors the length of the wave front and the depth of the water at a particular event site.

Based on this formula the most likely site for a tsunami event would be where there is the greatest narrowing of a large body of water as well as the shallowest point so that withdraw of the tidal effect is achieved with the least amount of energy expendable. Identifying the narrowest point of the Red Sea is not difficult. The mouth of the Gulf of Aquaba is approximately ten miles across, and as we now understand that these tectonic plates are constantly separating between Africa and Arabia, it may have even been narrower over three thousand years ago. In addition, the islands at the mouth of the gulf, specifically the Island of Tiran, reduces the wave front even further by about seventy percent. But at the same time, the presence of these islands also demonstrate that this is the shallowest nexus of that particular body of water, dividing the water into three channels measuring 900, 230 and 50 feet respectively in depth. The maximum depth of the gulf is 6,000 feet, therefore a reduction of less than half a percent of the volume of water in the gulf provides the first baring of sea bottom joining the island to Arabia. Reduce the volume by another 2.5% and the Children of Israel can walk safely from the Sinai Peninsula to the Island of Tiran and then onwards to Arabia. Just like a cork in the bottle, when the water withdraws on the southern side of the islands, which is the Red Sea side, then the water to the north is reduced until such point it has diminished by the same depth reducing the Gulf of Aqaba to being nothing more than a large salt water lake so that one could describe it as a wall of water on either side of a path leading through the sea.

So, establishing that scientifically, the crossing of the Red Sea is a physical reality was not the focal point of the miracle. What was truly a miracle was that the combination of events occurred exactly when it was needed the most. Now we know from the biblical account of Exodus that it was not a simple case of arriving at this particular shore, raising his staff, and then crossing as if the sea was responding immediately to Moses' actions. From Exodus Chapter 14 we see that the Israelites had set up camp at Pi-hahiroth on the seashore. They had to be there for some time because reports by Egyptian scouts in the Sinai reported back to Pharaoh that Moses and his people had trapped themselves in this location. This further suggests that the Children of Israel were at the tip of the Sinai Peninsula with very few optional routes of escape. Pharaoh responds by sending out a force of six hundred chariots and an unidentified amount of infantry to pursue the Israelites with instruction to either slaughter them or take them prisoner. Assuming these chariots began their pursuit from Memphis it would have taken them a minimum of ten days to reach the vicinity where the Israelites were camped, but this assumes the horses are galloping and achieving the average of thirty miles a day, which they could not do for a sustained pace over that length of time, nor would any infantry on foot be able to cover that distance on a daily basis. Therefore, it is best to assume that it was closer to three weeks before the Israelites spotted the Egyptian forces. Adding these twenty-one days to the time they had already been encamped at the site before Pharaoh received his reports, we can see that Moses was waiting for the event to occur over a significantly long period of time. Although he knew from all the signs, especially having access to historical reports of similar events, that the tsunami would happen, he could not precisely state when it would happen. Therefore, in my view, the miracle was not that the Red Sea parted but that it happened to do so at a critical moment when Moses needed it the most.

The longest part of the crossing was from the Sinai Peninsula to the Island of Tiran, a distance of about four miles in which thousands of people and animals had to reach a point of safety. So the miracle also involved the need for the waters to retract and not return for several hours if we accept that there were tens of thousands of people making the crossing. From what we are told, the event took place at night and was over by the break of dawn. If we calculate on several hours duration, then it was likely the waters were already returning on the west side of the Island of Tiran, while the last of the Israelites were still able to cross to the Arabian mainland on the eastern side. At a jogging speed of six miles per hour, most people would be able to make the initial crossing to the island in less than an hour. The width of the channel would accommodate a mass of people marching fifty people abreast if it were at least 200 feet wide. If this was the case, then in a time span of two hours, with a spacing of several feet between rows of people, it can be calculated that approximately 15,000 people could make the crossing in that short time frame. We double that number of people with an additional hour or by increasing the width of the channel available for the crossing.

To those that think reducing the miraculous event of crossing of the Red Sea to mere mathematical formulas has in some way robbed us of the 'miracle', I disagree. The miracle as I mentioned was not that it happened but that it did happen when it was needed the most.

5. The Mother of Moses:

It is fortunate that along with the Old Testament, we still have the companion text known as the **Book of the Yasher**, which even though there are a number of bogus claimants to that title, when examining the particular source I use, dated from the sixteenth century, it still has preserved ancient Egyptian names. The wife of Pharaoh is referred to as Alparanith which is an actual Egyptian name as evidenced by the ending of her name of 'nith' or 'neith', which was commonly used in such names as Neithotpe, Herneith, Merneith, etcetera. This would suggest that we are actually looking at a royal name. In fact the Egyptian meaning of Neith was either 'belonging to or dedicated to' as in being the possession of a particular god or goddess, or 'water-weaver', which in their mythology was also was an attribute of the primordial goddess Nut. But specifically, the name of the mother goddess Neith, the personification of both wisdom and a huntress was prominent in the Delta. So Alparanith could have been easily referring to a time when 'nith' was in common use in Egypt as part of royal name structures, of which we know for a certainty of one particular period, that being the latter part of the 18th Dynasty.

If we simply divide the word into Al(r)-Para-Nith, the letter 'l' and 'r' are interchangeable in ancient Egyptian, then simply translating the name we read it as 'The Great House of the Goddess Neith', which could suggest that this queen belonged to or was dedicated to the worship of Neith. Having mentioned that Neith was thought of as being a goddess of wisdom, this could therefore be describing a particular characteristic of this Queen, meaning that she was recognized as being wise, or gifted with wisdom, especially evident if she had a been given a role in making royal judgements in the court. It is said by some Egyptologists that Tiye was the most influential royal queen in Egyptian history, which is quite a statement since Queen Hatshepsut had actually ruled as a Pharaoh all on her own. Tiye, as I have described in this historical novel was the daughter of Yuyu, the King's Lieutenant of Chariots and Master of the Horse, the Superintendent of the Harem and *Hemneter* of Min of Akhmim and the mother of Moses.

Tiye was also the niece of Mutemwiya, a wife to Thutmoses IV making her Amenhotep III's first cousin and sufficiently royal to be his Great Wife. But it is Tiye's parentage which is a subject of much debate and provides us with significant clues to support her relationship with Moses. She was not fully Egyptian. We know from the study of the mummies found in 1904. Her mother had Egyptian features, but her father was clearly Semitic and may have been Khabru, Apiru, Shasu or similar coming from Mesopotamian origins. Tiye bore Pharaoh Amenhotep at least seven children including Thutmoses, Sitamun, Isis, Henat-Taneb, Nebetah, Beketaten, and much later in life,

Amenhotep who is better known to history as Akhenaten. Historians believe that Tiye was the power behind the throne as she acted as her husband's advisor and confidant, playing an active role in foreign relations; so much so that she was the first Egyptian queen to have her name included on official records. Tiye even remained visible during the reign of her son, as Akhenaton's correspondence speaks of Tiye's continued political influence. So the picture of Alparanith and Tiye being one and the same has a high probability based on direct translation of the name.

But we also have a second name recorded, Bitiah or Batiya, being Hebrew in origin and coming to us through the Old Testament in Chronicles 4:18. As explained in the chapters of this historical novel, the name can easily be broken down into Bat Tiya (Tiye) or the House of Tiye or as Tiye explains to her son, meaning she was from the 'house' or 'daughter' of Yahvu as her father preferred to consider. This gives us two interesting points considering Moses' parentage. First, it speaks of his mother being from a 'House' and this connotation of being from a House in Egypt was reserved for aristocracy and the 'Great House' being reserved specifically for Pharaoh. But secondly, probably the most significant statement made by Jewish recorders is that the house name was Tiya (Tiye) providing us with a direct statement that Amenhotep III's wife was Moses' mother if we choose not to break it down into the Hebrew definition.

Do we have anything else that suggests that Tiye was the mother of Moses? For that we look at her daughter, the Princess Nebetah, who was apparently the fourth daughter of Pharaoh Amenhotep III and Queen Tiye. Once again we have the last part of her name being Betah which is very close to the Hebrew name Bitiah or Batiya. Though she is not as well-known as her sisters, her name translated from the ancient Egyptian means 'Lady of the Palace (House)' or 'Great Lady', which would be unusual for a lesser daughter and one that certainly didn't marry her brother as was tradition. So like her mother, it would appear that she was given a name that specifically was designed to honour her mother and highlight the fact that she was called Batiya amongst her own people. But if we look for a completely Hebraic translation of the name, then we know 'neb' is Lord from the Egyptian and 'Bet' is house shared by the Egyptian and Hebrew or 'Bat' specifically Hebrew for daughter, and therefore her name could easily be a reference to someone belong to the House of the Lord or Yahvu or a Daughter of the Lord.

Strangely, it appears as if Nebetah has been intentionally removed from Egyptian history by either her father or brother for some act that she must have committed even though it is clear from her name that she was her mother's favourite at one point. All of her sisters appear frequently on statues and reliefs during the reign of their father and are also represented by smaller objects but Nebetah is purposely absent as if any of these items referencing her had been destroyed just like her elder brother Thutmoses. This absence becomes even stranger when we find in official court documents a reference where she was recorded as having the official title of "King's Daughter Whom He Loves' and then she no longer exists. If, as the Exodus story suggests, Batiya went with her attendants and retinue into the wilderness with Moses, as evidenced in Chronicles 4:18, only to marry Mered later and be fully adopted into the Israelite community, then it would make sense that it was not Tiye, who we know never left Egypt, but her daughter bearing a similar name, that did so. As with Thutmoses, her father or brother Amenhotep IV (Akhenaton) would have eradicated practically every memorial to her existence because of the apparent shame she brought upon the royal family.

As we can see, from the various sources that provide us with clues to the identity of Moses' mother, all of them can be shown to point towards one particular person, whose own DNA would show her to be half Semitic, that being Tiye. Although one may argue the evidence is not conclusive, it certainly is overwhelming.

6. The Queen of Sheba:

Tharbis the Queen of Saba, assumes a major role in every ancient text about the Exodus except in the Old Testament. In fact the only reference we have to her in the Old Testament is a result of a Pharisaic editor failing to make a correction to the original text and leaving behind a single clue to her identity. You might ask why I accuse a Pharisaic editor in this case and not the earlier Priestly editor that has been well documented in numerous scholarly articles examining the developmental changes over time to the Masoretic Text. The answer is simple, we have source material written by Artabanus (3rd Century BCE), Manetho (3rd Century BCE) Lucius Cornelius Alexander Polyhistor (1st Century BCE), and Flavius Josephus (1st Century ACE) that clearly shows they had original text available to them in their time periods that still recorded the presence of Moses as the commander of the army in Ethiopia, where he eventually becomes the King of Kush and in some of the recordings, the husband of the Queen of Saba.

The overlooked sentence that the editor failed to correct can be found in Numbers 12:1. When I first raised the issue with religious scholars, my question quickly devolved into a battle of semantics. The wife being verbally assaulted by both Aaron and Miriam in Numbers 12:1 is described as being a Kushite. Kush, as everyone who has read this historical novel should now be aware, is the Semitic name for Ethiopia. My opponents wanted to argue that a Kushite is actually someone from Cushan. They argued Cushan was another name for the land where the Midianites came from but ignored the fact that nowhere else in the Torah is Jethro and his daughter Zipporah referred to as being from Cushan. To actually find a reference to Cushan, you must read Habakkuk, buried in 3:7 but even there, the sentence reads, '*I see the tents of Cushan in affliction; the curtains of the land of Midian do tremble*' clearly indicating that these Cushanites are not the same as Midianites. But even when I would say to them, wouldn't someone from Cushan be a Cushanite, not a Kushite, I was given the most ludicrous excuse possible being that the scribal editors who were copying the Torah made an error and wrote Kushite by accident and the mistake was carried on afterwards until all original versions were lost through time. I say ludicrous because that would imply that there never was more than one Masoretic Text being read throughout all the land or that there only was ever one scribe responsible for writing all of these Torahs, so that the same error appeared in all of them. We know that was not the case because there were schools of scribes copying the Torah and all of them would have made the same error at practically the same time, which never got picked up by any of the proof-readers throughout an entire country. The resistance to simply admitting that Moses had married the Queen of Saba is quite remarkable and in some ways regrettable that it even exists. It is sad to think that God's clear statement to us that we were a mixed multitude at the time of our origins, indicating that we embraced people from all lands, all places, and all races, could so easily be negated by one group that attained control over our religious documentation.

Religion should embrace the statement from the Queen of Sheba, who came to visit King Solomon when she proclaims in chapter 1 Verse 5, that she is a beautiful black woman. In the next verse she repeats that she is swarthy, tanned darker than the daughters of Jerusalem; as dark as the tents of Kedar. The Kedarites were a tribe descended from Ishmael. The expression to dwell in the Tents of Kedar was often used to imply that one was cut off from serving God, therefore she is admitting that she does not follow the Hebrew faith but in Solomon's eyes she is still beautiful. The arrival of the Queen of Sheba in Jerusalem had far more to do with a continuation of a royal lineage and commerce than it did asking Solomon a few questions to test his wisdom. In fact when she returns to Sheba with her young son Menelik, the offspring of Solomon, she is in fact renewing the bloodlines that her ancestor had established over three hundred years earlier with Moses in Saba.

Blood lines that existed because as I record in this historical novel, Tharbis would not have left her throne vacant to join Moses on his march through the wilderness unless they had a child that was already old enough to sit on the throne and rule her empire. We actually might find a reference to this son in the book of Judges. As we know from this story, Caleb had married Othniel's aunt and even though younger had become Othniel's uncle. As family, the two were referred to as brothers and this is indicated in the first few chapters of Judges. The relationship gets even more complicated when Caleb offers his daughter Achsah in marriage to whomever can take the city of Debir. Othniel with his men do so, and therefore Caleb is now Othniel's father-in-law. I bring this up only to indicate that Othniel is very active in fighting battles in Canaan and therefore the title of the book Judges when referencing the two individuals mentioned would be more appropriately titled, Generals. In Chapter 3 of Judges, we're told, *'Therefore the anger of the Lord was kindled against Israel, and He gave them over into the hand of Cushan-rishathaim king of Aram-neharaim; and the children of Israel served Cushan-rishathaim eight years. And when the children of Israel cried unto the Lord, the Lord raised up a saviour to the children of Israel, who saved them, even Othniel the son of Kenaz, Caleb's younger brother. And the spirit of the Lord came upon him, and he judged Israel; and he went out to war, and the Lord delivered Cushan-rishathaim king of Aram into his hand; and his hand prevailed against Cushan-rishathaim.'* We see the use of Cushan, but not as a place noun as in the case of Habakkuk but as an adjective to describe this King. The place he is said to come from is Aram-neharaim. One usually associates Aram with Syria but in this case, the addition of 'neharaim' implies that it is a high place at the conjunction of rivers, exactly as Saba is described in early Egyptian documents. We also have to examine the name of the king more closely. Breaking it down, we see that it is most probably an Egyptian derivation that equivalates to Ra-Seth-Hiye, or the name that I used in this novel for the son of Moses and Tharbis. That being the case, then the adjective Cushan was there to tell us he was a black man in appearance. Unlike the other kings in Judges who conquer a particular city or a tribal territory, this king is actually ruling over all of Israel for a period of eight years. And whereas all the other kings whom the stories will mention are captured or killed, all we know from this particular story is that Othniel prevailed against this particular king and liberated the Children of Israel from his rule. The story appears to be more of a coup d'état over a regional governor than an actual war of nations. It would not have been surprising for the actual son of Moses to have made an appearance in Canaan to claim what he believed was his legitimate birth right, to rule over Israel. The Kingdom of Saba was still powerful, and well enough connected through trade with the tribes in Arabia to have extended its rule over the fledgling nation. Being the son of Moses and Tharbis would have made many of the people overjoyed to accept his authority initially, without any need to actually conquer Israel through military might. But once established as a colony of Saba, like so many other colonial outposts throughout history, the need to pay taxes, goods and services to a foreign king soon becomes burdensome and the people longed to have their freedom restored.

So from the time of Moses until the reign of Solomon, there was likely a well-established link between Israel and Saba (Sheba), thought as indicated in the story from Judges, it was strained at some times. It all likelihood, it will just be a matter of time before more of their common history is uncovered through archaeological research. As for the 'Song of Solomon' we should accept this song for what it is, a beautiful poem from a black African Queen about her handsome Middle Eastern lover. As soon as we do that, then we recognize the special relationship that must have existed between Moses and Tharbis as it persisted through the ages.

7. The Ten Plagues:

Of course, the Ten Plagues and how they were even possible, has been a subject of discussion for thousands of years. During the Passover Seder in Jewish households, the story is retold from the Haggadah, but the events are never questioned. They are simply accepted upon faith, even though the Old Testament does provide us with specific clues as to the natural occurrence of these plagues. On initial reading the Old Testament, the impression is that Moses is returning every few days to appear before Pharaoh and pronouncing a new plague each time. In reality, if you read it carefully, we are provided with no time frames and it is not until we refer to the **Book of the Yasher** that we get a better appreciation of the delays or down-time between the plagues. In fact, the first encounter with Pharaoh and then the second appearance when Moses delivered the first plague is separated by two years according to the **Book of the Yasher**. So clearly, it was not Moses bringing about each plague, but instead each plague determining when Moses would appear before Pharaoh. Thereby suggesting, that by using the historical records obtained from the temples and reading the signs correctly, Moses could determine with reasonable certainty what would happen in the chain of events and would thus make his pronouncement of the impending plague.

From our own present day knowledge of how death, decay and disease follow one another, we can assume the time span between the initial plague of the water turning to blood to the time the animals were afflicted by disease would have occurred fairly rapidly, but the final plagues of locusts, darkness, fire and brimstone and the human deaths, were probably less predictable and Moses had to wait extended periods of time before appearing before Pharaoh with any confidence to make those pronouncements.

We also know that during this same time period, there were major population migrations and replacements throughout the region, including Cyprus and the Levant all while the Mitanni Empire was collapsing. From what we know, the question focuses on our ability to identify the epi-centre of this earth shattering event. Scientific research tells us that in the century prior to the events presented in this historical novel numerous eruptions and earthquakes were taking place to the Northwest in the area of the Aegean Sea. These events resulted in the end of the Minoan civilization, the great commercial centre of its time. Current day knowledge of the Ring of Fire in this region, has identified a clockwise movement through the ring, thereby indicating events in the northwest will be followed by activity to the northeast over a period of time. From the Old Testament, we know that at the time of the Exodus, if one was situated in Goshen, then there was a pillar of light at night and a pillar of smoke by day that guided Moses initially to the Northeast, towards Yum Suf, or the Sea of Reeds.

To the northeast, across the Mediterranean, we find present day Turkey, the home of the once mighty Hittites. It is highly probable that the source of the plagues was Karapinar, a volcanic field located in central Turkey, consisting of five cinder cones, two lava fields and several explosion craters and maars. The 300 meter-high Meke Dağı, is surrounded by the crater lake known as Meke Golu and it is one of the largest cinder cones in Central Anatolia. It is confirmed that around the time of the Exodus, this field was very active and was not only large enough and powerful enough to destroy many of the civilizations at that time but would have impacted significantly on Egypt, across the great sea.

Examining the first plague, it is hardly a surprise that as a result of major earthquakes in the region, water supplies become contaminated:

And Moses and Aaron did so, as the Lord commanded; and he lifted up the rod, and smote the waters that were in the river, in the sight of Pharaoh, and in the sight of his servants; and all the waters that were in the river were turned to blood. And the fish that were in the river died; and the river became foul, and the Egyptians could not drink water from the river; and the blood was throughout all the land of Egypt.

As awe-inspiring as this first plague may seem to be, rivers turning to blood are not that unusual. We know from events like the eruption of Krakatau, when there is a major disturbance to the bedrock, there is often the release of corrosive toxins such as iron oxide. It is iron oxide which gives Mars the nickname, the Red Planet. As with Krakatau, fish died in the hundreds of thousands and this devastation extended for hundreds of miles.

Since an event of this nature also occurred during the eruption of Mt. Saint Helen's where fish were found floating dead on the surface of the rivers hundreds of miles from the volcano, any drinking of water in the area was forbidden until such time that the impurities could be filtered from the reservoirs. So we see on a much smaller scale, a repetition of biblical events, which as a result of our scientific knowledge we can rationalize.

It is of note that in the **Book of the Yasher**, Pharaoh's advisors were not very impressed by this first plague. In fact they advised Pharaoh to send word throughout the region for people to dig new wells away from the river, informing him that everything would be fine. Clearly, his advisors had prior knowledge of similar events and how to deal with it.

And the Lord said unto Moses: 'Say unto Aaron: Stretch forth thy hand with thy rod over the rivers, over the canals, and over the pools, and cause frogs to come up upon the land of Egypt.' And Aaron stretched out his hand over the waters of Egypt; and the frogs came up, and covered the land of Egypt. And the (hekay) magicians did in like manner with their secret arts, and brought up frogs upon the land of Egypt.

Once again we see that Pharaoh's advisors were unimpressed by this plague as well because they knew that as soon as the river became contaminated by the metal toxins, amphibians have a choice to make. Either stay in the water and die or find another water source in the hope that it would be cleaner. Even the most primitive of neuro-responders have built in fight or flight receptors that tell them when they are facing dire consequences. So the swarming of the frogs over the land would have been a normal sequelae and Pharaoh's advisors knew it.

Once again, in modern times we have witnessed a similar event and I refer to Mount St. Helen's, where it was reported Washington State that the frogs were making a run for it but with nowhere to go following the eruption. People reported that they could not drive down the roads without literally squashing them in the thousands and this became a driving risk as the roads became slick with frog blood. In the local newspapers the stories talked about people finding their lawns covered in frogs, and in their search for water, the amphibians were even invading the houses. Very biblical.

Later in Chapter 8 we read: And they gathered them together in heaps; and the land stank.

The significance of this sentence is paramount to our understanding of events. What we read in sentences 10 are in direct contradiction to what Moses stated he would do in sentence 7. His promise to Pharaoh was to make the frogs depart, essentially return to the river where they would be confined once again. But even as he prayed to God, the resultant solution was not as he had promised but instead was massive deaths of the creatures indicating that Moses did not have complete control nor full understanding of the events occurring. He believed that whatever had caused the water to be toxic would be flushed from the river within a few days permitting the frogs to return to the river, but survival of aquatic frog species out of their natural water habitat is very short unless they can find another means to keep their skin hydrated. As soon as they dehydrate, they stop moving, making their return to the river impossible. Despite Moses' lack of appreciation for the limitations of his authority over scientific principles, the Egyptian's response to the frogs dying proved highly beneficial to Moses in that he had obtained a degree of knowledge on how disease was spread. Rather than burn the dead bodies of the frogs, the Egyptians chose to let them remain in rotting piles until they stank.

And they did so; and Aaron stretched out his hand with his rod, and smote the dust of the earth, and there were gnats upon man, and upon beast; all the dust of the earth became gnats throughout all the land of Egypt.

I prefer this translation of the next plague being that of gnats, and not lice as some versions have been translated. I would suggest that the Egyptians made little distinction between gnats, flies or mosquitoes and this is evidenced by how few words to describe these insects exist in the ancient hieroglyphics. Wherever there are decomposing bodies, such as the piles of dead frogs, you will find massive numbers of flying insects. For an appreciation of the event being properly translated as gnats or flies then we simply have to look at more recent situations such as the volcanic eruptions of Mount Pelee in 1851 and again in 1902. After the eruptions, swarms of flying ants descended upon the villagers and viciously attacked the people. The ants caused the people to flee, consumed their plantations and were reported to have killed babies through their bites and acid stings. Gnats, flies and mosquitoes fly, lice don't. Either way, gnats, flies or mosquitoes, their lives were made miserable. We know, that mosquitoes in Egypt bring other plagues, such as malaria, Viral Encephalitis, and Nile Fever. Tse Tse flies bring the sleeping sickness. Flies and gnats carry a wide range of rickettsial diseases. In essence, Moses could predict with a high degree of certainty that these insects would bring with them one form or another of variety of contagious diseases.

And the Lord did so; and there came grievous swarms of flies into the house of Pharaoh, and into his servants' houses; and in all the land of Egypt the land was ruined by reason of the swarms of flies.

As mentioned previously, the flies should be seen as a natural consequence of the rotting corpses of thousands of frogs, fish, and everything else that may have been affected from the toxic nature of the water. And as any entomologist will inform you, flies go through cycles in which they become active biters, a carnivorous phase when they are seeking out living creatures on which to feed. Some flies will also lay their eggs beneath the skin of mammals, leading to bots erupting from the skin as they eat their way to the surface.

And the Lord did that thing on the morrow, and all the cattle of Egypt died; but of the cattle of the children of Israel died not one.

The loss of all the Egyptian cattle is contradicted in sentences 19 and 20 of the same chapter and therefore we realize that the events of sentence 6 were intended as an exaggeration, emphasizing that the Egyptians suffered more than the Israelites but then it was unlikely the Israelites had as extensive a farming industry as the Egyptians. Therefore they would have experienced any effect of this plague with far less impact. As well, living in Goshen has certain features not ideal for insect growth, such as the ocean breezes and the salination of the river waters. As the rivers empty into the delta's basins of salt water, the brackish pools result in the insect populations being far less than those found inland due to the unsuitable salt content for laying eggs in the water. As for the cattle deaths, these can be attributed to the diseases carried by the biting flies, mosquitoes and gnats as described previously.

And they took soot of the furnace, and stood before Pharaoh; and Moses threw it up heavenward; and it became a boil breaking forth with blains upon man and upon beast.

Because of the volcanic activity, we can assume that a majority of the clouds that were passing overhead weren't rainclouds. In fact the plagues to follow suggest that the Egyptians were looking at a major problem of volcanic ash that far exceeded that which was spewing from the volcano in Iceland that grounded all European air traffic for a week. It may have come in waves, it may have come all at once, but whatever the case, its high acidic content caused severe rashes and burns to all that came in contact with it. This is right in line with reports of hundreds of people following the eruption of Mount St Helen's that had to be taken to the hospital for treatment of acid burns from the fallout. The Old Testament actually suggests that this is exactly what it was, a severe contact dermatitis, because as seen by Moses' command to the farmers of Goshen to take their beasts inside and shelter them, then neither they nor the animals developed any of these sores.

And Moses stretched forth his rod toward heaven; and the Lord sent thunder and hail, and fire ran down unto the earth; and the Lord caused to hail upon the land of Egypt.

Without a doubt we are looking at the fire and ash that one associates with a volcanic eruption. Being from New Zealand, I have witnessed the eruptions of Mount Ruapehu numerous times, with its covering of ash for hundreds of miles in circumference, and its throwing up of stones anywhere from the size of baseballs to refrigerators. It rumbled like cannons and rivers of fire flowed from its summit. Any one that has witnessed a volcanic eruption can comprehend the Egyptians' perception of the rolling thunder resulting from the massive rumblings of a distant volcano or the earth shattering sounds associated with earthquakes.

And the locusts went up over all the land of Egypt, and rested in all the borders of Egypt; very grievous were they; before them there were no such locusts as they, neither after them shall be such.

Chapter 10 of Exodus involves the final obliteration of anything that has not already been destroyed, leaving Egypt with nothing of value. The possibility of locusts swarming after a major devastation of crops from the ash and fires would not be out of the question. North Africa is actually famous for its locust swarms but what is of interest is why this particular plague did not appear to bother the Egyptians to any great degree. Examining the **Book of the Yasher**, it describes this plague as a blessing in disguise to the Egyptians because they ran outside to gather as many locusts as they could as a food source. Therefore the sudden salvation from starvation definitely hardened Pharaoh's heart.

And Moses stretched forth his hand toward heaven; and there was a thick darkness in all the land of Kemet three days.

We know from an earlier plague that there were clouds of acid ash descending upon people and the beasts. Initially it would have looked like snowflakes but as the clouds of volcanic ash and debris increased in their magnitude and extent, they would have eventually formed an ash cloud that blotted out the sun. Three days of darkness gives you an appreciation of just how large this cloud had to be and just as the ancients would panic about an eclipse that lasted for minutes, that fear would be intensified exponentially as each of those days appeared to stretch on without end.

And all the first-born in the land of Egypt shall die, from the first-born of Pharaoh that sitteth upon his throne, even unto the first-born of the maid-servant that is behind the mill; and all the first-born of cattle.

The final plague was intended to be the one which would finally end Pharaoh's resistance. We are made aware in the story of how fresh blood was to be painted on the lintel and door posts of the homes where the Hebrews dwelled. Whereas the emphasis has always been placed on the 'sign' perhaps it should be focused on the blood itself. Having suffered through what may have been days or weeks of catastrophic events, the penultimate plague could be nothing less than death. Epidemiologist will tell you similar stories of how people were able to thwart plagues carried by insect vectors by similar means. Insect vectors will be attracted to the easiest food source available. The path of least resistance so to speak. Moses through the word of God, knew how to avoid this last plague but not necessarily why.

What was unique about this last plague was the enormity of the events which followed, being the actual exodus of the slaves from Goshen. Not only does it imply that Moses had been gifted with an apparent knowledge of exactly how everything would play out, and the predictability of Pharaoh's behaviour, but that he knew this last plague would actually touch Pharaoh's family. 'Firstborn' is a common expression for those of the aristocracy and here it is most likely suggesting that the princes, nobles and wealthy of Egypt were not immune from this final plague. This is further emphasized by mentioning the maid servants, suggesting that it was not restricted to the royal family but to those that worked within the palaces as well. Cattle don't have firstborn so it is clear that the term is being used figuratively to emphasize that the elite of society would be affected, even one's prize cow. We can contrast this event with the earlier plague affecting cattle in which Moses had the farmers move them inside in order to protect them, the point being that this time there would be no escape because there was an insect vector involved.

Historically, what we do know is that by the fourteenth year of his reign, Akhenaton loses four of his daughters and his concubine Kiya to the plague. As he began his reign by being co-regent with his father around 1361 BCE, then we are looking at the deaths in his family taking place around 1347 BCE. Compare this to Moses not returning to Egypt until 1352 BCE and according to the **Book of the Yasher**, having to wait at least another two years before his second audience with Pharaoh at which time the first plague is unleashed. As I stated earlier, we have no known timeframe over which these ten plagues occurred but we do know that around the same time of his daughters' and concubine's death, Amenhotep IV makes the remarkable and unprecedented decision to make Egypt monotheistic by worshipping Aten as the Creator God or *Potohikap Neter*. Can we assume that this decision was influenced by the confrontation with his brother, in which over a period of three to four years, Moses brought the power of Egypt to its knees, defeated the Egyptian forces twice, once by the Bitter Lakes and then by the Red Sea, and on a more personal level brought death directly into the house of Pharaoh? I definitely see this as a likely outcome and I can only hope that this historical novel has been able to answer that same question for you.

8. The Descendants of Aaron:

For those of you that are unfamiliar with the series of books known as the Kahana Chronicles, you may be wondering why this book was referred to as a 'Family' Historical Novel. The answer is actually quite simple, since it is well established that Aaron, the High Priest of Israel, was my direct ancestor. What is most interesting is that the DNA testing of the last decade has only reached this point to actually confirm what was well known throughout the centuries. Since time immemorial, the Kohenim have ingrained into our offspring of each successive generation that they are part of this priestly family and in the case of certain families, such as mine, which were known as Kahana, we knew that we belonged to those four particular families that preceded the common era, known as the Kohen Gadolim, which essentially indicated we served in the Holy of Holies, wearing the robes of Aaron, as members of the Phiabi, Kamithos (Boethus), Anan or See families. In spite of rabbinical arguments that all the genealogical records to prove these familial facts were either destroyed at the time that Titus burned down the Temple or when the Nazis destroyed the mountains of Jewish records in Europe during the 1940's, nothing could be less true. Family oral traditions do not die as long as a single member of a family still survives, and as centralized as the Jerusalem Temple may have been two thousand years ago to Jewish lives, it certainly was not the only repository of records as Jewish communities were widespread across four continents at the time. Similarly, as much as the Ashkenazi (European Jews) may consider themselves the Judaeocentric point of our universe, not all of our families were in Europe to suffer at the malicious hands of the Nazis.

In particular, my family, the Kahana are of the J2a4h haplotype, which immediately sets those of the J1e haplotype on the attack, proclaiming that they are true Kohenim, or priests and that we were nothing but a genetic aberration. A more ridiculous statement I could not imagine, but since most of them are supported by the Temple Faithful Movement, a group dedicated to rebuilding the Temple and under the control of Rabbinical Judaism their resistance does not surprise me. Since 200 BCE, Rabbinical Judaism as the inheritors of Pharisaic philosophy have been in direct opposition to the Sadducees, the progenitors of the Kahana family, and therefore I expect them to make their preposterous statements regarding who should be considered a high priest and who shouldn't be.

Now that my readers have had the opportunity to gain insight into the historical lives of Aaron and Moses, then you will be able to appreciate the factual arguments that will follow, in order to once and all put this argument to rest. The fact that the J1e Cohen Modal haplotypes outnumber those of us having J2a4h haplotype, should indicate to them immediately that their arguments are wrong. As only four families served in the Holy of Holies from the twenty-four that were in existence, then of course the Kohen Gadolim would be in the minority.

Fact One:

To those that can appreciate and comprehend genetic matrices and geometric progression, then the first clue should have been that those having the greatest number are least likely to be from the original source. It was well known that only these four families served in the capacity of High Priests in the Jerusalem Temple, but there were many families serving as Kohenim throughout the countryside. In fact, there were hundreds of other families that served as Kohenim throughout the land and they were only distantly related to these four primary families. So while these hundreds of others married amongst themselves, their genetics drifted and mutated over time to a significant degree from those that served as Kohen Gadol. And as the geometric progression would suggest, even after the persecutions, genocides, etc., they would still be in far greater number by the year 2018 than the descendants of the primary four families.

Fact Two:

The J1e family members point out that their genetic matrix is much younger than the J2a4h, and so it is. Almost 1500 years younger by the best estimates of geneticists. And as a result of that calculation, they are quick to argue that the J2a4h's were in existence long before the Exodus and therefore couldn't possibly be descended from Aaron but must be a subclass of his ancient Levite Ancestors. But here is where they make their chief error. For some reason they assume that Aaron would be of a different haplotype from his own ancestors. Why would that be? Why would he be any different from his father, or his father's father, or from his father's father's father and so on. He wouldn't be. And in that regard, he wouldn't be much different from Abraham his patriarchal ancestor. And since we know that Abraham was a resident of Mesopotamia, then Abraham would be most likely a J2 haplotype which is typical of the people of Mesopotamia, Anatolia and the Levant. As the historical evidence of this novel, supported by Egyptology and the **Book of the Yasher** suggest, the Lebu were the direct ancestors of the Levi, and their phenotypes of fair skin and red hair, definitely suggests an Anatolian origin. In contrast, the J1 haplotype had its origins in the Arabian Peninsula and therefore would have been a later migration into the Fertile Crescent.

But for Aaron to be carrying this established haplotype of his ancestors meant that they were already a closed clan or tribe long before Moses appointed him as High Priest and in this regard the family structures would have had clan restrictions on who they could marry and in that way they preserved a specific genotype. We actually have proof of that in the **Book of the Yasher**, specifically Chapter 65 verse 32 where we find the following is written. *'But the children of Levi were not employed in the work with their brethren of Israel, from the beginning unto the day of their going forth from Egypt.'* Not only does that tell us that the Tribe of Levi was not part of the oppressed people but that they were a distinct people that were already unified and remained separate from the other foreigners. In fact, they were considered an elite population and therefore not subject to manual labour, or treated as inferior to the native Egyptian population from the time of their arrival in Egypt. This is further emphasized in the next sentence 33 in which it is written, *'For all the children of Levi knew that the Egyptians had spoken all these words with deceit to the Israelites, therefore the children of Levi refrained from approaching to the work with their brethren.'* Their access to Egyptian laws and statutes suggest they were an educated and learned class which at the time usually meant a religious class since most scribes and lawmakers came from the existing priesthoods in ancient Egypt. The fact that they neither became embroiled in the issues nor attempted to intercede in any manner to stop the persecution would suggest that they saw themselves as being set apart or different from their Hebrew brethren. The book then makes its most startling of comments in the next verse 34 which reads *'And the Egyptians did not direct their attention to make the children of Levi work afterward, since they had not been with their brethren at the beginning, therefore the Egyptians left them alone.'* What this sentence clearly implies is that the Tribe of Levi was not identical to the Hebrew slaves. It had different origins, different roots and in the eyes of the Egyptians, were not considered Apiru, Shasu, Khabru or similar which made up the Hebrew stock. Later on in Chapter 69 verse 9, the author of Yasher reaffirms his earlier statement thusly, *'But the tribe of Levi did not at that time work with the Israelites their brethren, from the beginning, for the children of Levi knew the cunning of the Egyptians which they exercised at first toward the Israelites.'* This is a most surprising statement because if you read it correctly, not only are the Levites distinct and separate from the Hebrews but in fact, they persecuted the Hebrews no differently than did the other Egyptians. From this we can surmise that that the Levites were actually an Egyptian caste that for reasons provided in **Once A God,** threw their lot in with the Hebrew slaves at the time of the Exodus. We can appreciate that the Lebu support of Moses offended his father Pharaoh Amenhotep, and therefore they lost any status that they once held in Egypt. The Egyptian records describe it as a revolt by the priesthood in Onu, but we can appreciate that any support of the Crown Prince would have been considered treasonous and Pharaoh would have attempted to suppress it.

So, we can determine from all of this that Aaron was not the first priest in the family, but was the first priest of Israel when he left with the other tribes during the Exodus. Therefore, his haplotype was established long before the 13th Century BCE, extending fifteen hundred years earlier to the time of the arrival of the Lebu in Egypt.

We do not have an exact copy of the original text of the **Book of the Yasher** and those wishing to argue against my supporting facts will argue that it is apocrypha and cannot be accepted as fact, but nonetheless, we do have references in Joshua and Samuel that do tell us that the **Book of the Yasher** was a holy book beyond any reasonable doubt and was in existence prior to the Torah being written. Therefore it cannot be dismissed as merely apocrypha and instead we must identify those parts which are sacred history and have been overlooked all these millennia because certain parties have tried to bury the contents because they run contrary to their present teachings.

Fact Three:

For the third argument I'm afraid I must become very scientific in my explanation. We must look at the scientific report of J.E. Ekins et al. in which they wrote: Since the definition of the Cohen Modal Haplotype (CMH) in 1998, the 6 SNP-6 STR genetic motif has been utilized to infer connections of contemporary individuals and communities to the ancient Hebrew population. The elucidation of the YCC SNP Phylogeny has allowed cataloguing of chromosomes compatible with the original CMH definition into several different Y-SNP subclades. Haplogroup membership was determined for 266 samples matching at ≥5 of the CMH STR alleles, defined as the Cohen Modal Haplogroup (CMHg). The bulk of the CMHg chromosomes were observed in J1 (53.0%) and J2 (43.2%), with a small portion falling outside of haplogroup J (3.8%). Members of the CMHg were observed throughout the world, with significant frequencies in various Arab populations: Oman (20.1%), Iraq (15.2%), and Palestine (9.5%). Coalescent simulations were performed for CMH chromosomes within each SNP haplogroup using 24 STR loci. Estimates within J1 [6.5kybp(4K-12K)] and J2 [13kybp(7K-27K)] were substantially deeper than previous figures obtained from a heavily weighted Jewish sampling, indicating a likely origin of the compound haplotype prior to the establishment of the Hebrew population. The significant presence of CMH chromosomes in deeply divergent clades J1 and J2 (>20kybp), indicates the present CMH definition is not sufficient to distinguish lineages that likely arose by parallel IBS mutations. An expanded STR definition is proposed which allows differentiation between CMH-compatible chromosomes in J1 and J2. The inference of Jewish ancestry based on the original CMH definition should be performed with caution as subjects may be falsely categorized into the eponymous CMH lineage when the true origin is in the deeply divergent IBS branch. These observations underscore the importance of using updated SNP classifications when utilizing the CMH to infer ancestry in Jewish populations, or the use of the expanded STR definition.

I'll simply paraphrase a translation of the above for those that may have had difficulty following the argument. The author is saying that their initial statements in 1998 were wrong. They had made several errors in estimation, they didn't have a large enough sample from which conclusions were erroneously drawn, and in fact, they now postulate that the common modal (known as the Cohen Modal Haplotype) could have arisen in divergent genetic lines without any common ancestry and therefore is presently found in totally unrelated populations, specifically Arab populations and some families with absolutely no history of being descended from Jewish priests. In addition, they have stated that the haplotype actually preceded the birth of the Hebrew Nation of around 1300 BCE, thereby supporting what the **Book of the Yasher** claims as a distinct Levite (Lebu) clan or tribe existing with its own rules of marriage and inheritance well before Aaron was confirmed as High Priest for the Children of Israel.

In Conclusion:

So what can we learn from all this. We learn that the claims of the J2a4h haplotype are just as legitimate for being representative of the High Priesthood as the J1e's and based on their being the older derived line probably even more so. We learn that the J2's share more in common with our Mesopotamian ancestors, for if we truly believe the Biblical story of Abraham, we know our Patriarchal father did not come from the Arabian peninsula, the land of J1's, but from Ur of the Chaldees, which was the ancient civilization of Mesopotamia. We also know that the strict laws of inheritance were in place long before Aaron became high priest and that this means as Levites we were a distinct and unified people perhaps forty or fifty generations prior to the establishment of the Children of Israel. As a result, it became clearer that the stories passed down within my family were based on knowledge that is only now being confirmed through scientific research and evidence. The Kahana were and always will be the Kohen Gadolim, of that there is no doubt.

Descendants of Joseph (Yuyu)

The Great House of Amarna

FamilyTree**DNA**

Certificate – **Haplogroup**

Family Tree DNA certifies that a DNA sample from

Dr. Allen Goldenthal

Sample # 182634

was analyzed for Haplogroup determination using the **Single Nucleotide** Polymorphism test. The analysis shows that you are positive for the following SNPs: PF5366, L254, L25, L24, FGC30681; and negative for the following SNPs: M318, M158, M137, L192. According to the current classification, you have been assigned to:

Haplogroup J-FGC30681

Haplogroup J-M172 is found at highest frequencies in the northern Middle East, west of the Zagros Mountains in Iran, to the Mediterrean Sea. It later spread throughout central Asia and south into India. J-M172 is tightly associated with the expansion of agriculture, which began about 10,000 years ago. As with other populations with Mediterranean ancestry, this lineage is found at substantial frequencies within Jewish populations.

June 23, 2018

Concetta A. Bormans

www.ingramcontent.com/pod-product-compliance
Lightning Source LLC
LaVergne TN
LVHW051253080426

835509LV00020B/2944